Eustace Clare Grenville Murray

Turkey, being Sketches from Life

Eustace Clare Grenville Murray

Turkey, being Sketches from Life

ISBN/EAN: 9783743316485

Manufactured in Europe, USA, Canada, Australia, Japa

Cover: Foto ©ninafisch / pixelio.de

Manufactured and distributed by brebook publishing software (www.brebook.com)

Eustace Clare Grenville Murray

Turkey, being Sketches from Life

TURKEY

BEING

SKETCHES FROM LIFE

BY

THE ROVING ENGLISHMAN

E.C.G. Murray

REPRINTED IN PART FROM "HOUSEHOLD WORDS," WITH
NUMEROUS ADDITIONS

LONDON
GEORGE ROUTLEDGE AND SONS
THE BROADWAY, LUDGATE
NEW YORK: 416, BROOME STREET
1877

LONDON:
PRINTED BY WOODFALL AND KINDER,
MILFORD LANE, STRAND, W.C.

PREFACE TO THE FIRST EDITION.

TO MY PUBLIC.

MY AMIABLE AND DISCERNING FRIEND,

I have ventured to intrude upon your leisure to acquaint you with a few loose facts, which I have learned in various ways, respecting our mutual connections, the Turks.

The dominant fraction of a people without a head, torn by discontented and stubborn or frantic nationalities, with a most abominable internal organization ; acting upon principles of government utterly false and absurd, yet rooted in their minds ; harassed and waylaid at every turn by foreign influence, often in the hands of interested and improper people ; bowing a stiff and unwilling neck to that influence, but resenting it in their deep stern hearts ; undoing, therefore, with the right hand that which they have been just forced to accomplish with the left ; seemingly pliable and easy, but really obstinate and austere beyond belief,—such (and something more) are our estimable allies. I am sorry for it ; so, I dare say, are you ; but this, unfortunately, does not alter the fact, or the results which are likely to arise from it, be those results what they may.

I have a high respect for the individual Turk ; I have often felt a warm personal friendship for him ; I have found him brave, simple, charitable, sincere. But, do you know, I am afraid this merely means that there are a great many good people everywhere. I am even very apprehensive that any person who might fairly discuss the general character of the Turkish nation would be likely to come under the charge of using rather strong language in the statement of his views.

I will therefore, if you please, decline the opportunity which you have so obligingly afforded me on the present occasion, of enlarging any further on this topic.

I will merely be so bold as to observe that it appears to my limited understanding as if our wards were likely to become, at no distant period, the subject of a good deal of conversation; I have been also led to believe that an honoured Public will find itself under the necessity of asking several questions about their progress and good behaviour, which the Tutors appointed to superintend their studies and deportment will not be able to answer so clearly and cheerfully as we could all wish, considering the pains we have been taking for their welfare, and the cost of their establishment. I most sincerely apologize for expressing this opinion, should you consider it premature or incorrect, but I really do not think you have altogether full and trustworthy information about their goings-on. I should be disposed to remark, might I take the liberty of so doing, that many portions of Turkey are almost as unknown to you, from credible report, as the interior of China, or the immediate neighbourhood of the North Pole. Some people who are acquainted with several things likely to conduce to your advantage or instruction have their lips sealed according to the tenets of an antiquated statecraft; while those to whom that ingenious system has accorded the faculty of speaking and writing (in the stocks, of course) are not always the individuals who are able or willing to give you the best intelligence on matters which might sometimes bring to light their own backslidings or delinquencies.

I should expect to hear from a few dignified elderly persons who are constrained to pass most of their time in lonely rooms by the seaside—according to the rules of their order— an account of the manner in which those rooms are papered, emotional complaints about dampness and rheumatisms, some energetic remonstrances respecting the inconvenience of the furniture supplied to their official residence by the Government contractors, mingled with lively reminiscences of their youth;—rather than a very accurate account of what is passing in Syria, and Asia Minor on the Lower Danube, or in the Ægean Isles.

Diplomatic gentlemen of the old school who were at least half educated before the foundation of the *Daily News*, do not receive new impressions so readily as could be sometimes desired for the general convenience. Their minds were made up on most points several centuries before they were born, and their creed rigidly enjoins complete abstinence from fresh ideas. You have a great many elderly gentlemen of the ancient philosophy, not to say elderly ladies, among your recognized Oriental correspondents ; you will remember, indeed, that an orthodox belief in the miracles and mysteries of a diplomacy secret, tortuous, and incomprehensible has been hitherto held the primary and indispensable qualification for any one who has aspired to represent you either in the East or elsewhere. It is not therefore surprising that conscientious endeavours to deceive you are considered the first necessities of every political crisis throughout the world.

Nevertheless I would ask permission, my revered Patron, to submit for your consideration, when you are inclined for a brown study, that now and then, there may perhaps occur a new event upon which it might be worth your while to collect precise evidence ; and, unless my information is altogether at fault, the concerns of Turkey have a fair claim on your attention, because they are more or less your own ; they are both affairs of your heart and affairs of your pocket. Indeed, foreigners with unfriendly notions about you are beginning to say that you have married an extravagant shrew whose intemperate rioting disturbs your neighbours, and that you will neither teach her good manners yourself nor allow other folk to do so. Suppose, now, you were to show that this allegation is untrue and libellous?

It might be easily done. As a question of fact you may plainly assert that you are not married to this termagant whose violence is attracting all the police of Europe; and you may declare with perfect reason and good faith that you have no mind to remain on amicable terms with her unless she determines forthwith to behave in a decent and orderly manner; also pray be so good as to remember that domestic scandals cannot be hushed up and healed merely by ordering servants to deny their existence when every one can hear the sound of shrieks and head-cracking.

But I have done. I feel that I have already trespassed too long upon your most valuable time; I only presume, therefore, to add that the information which I have humbly offered to you has been acquired among the scenes and people I have attempted to describe. If it seems here and there to be contradictory or obscure, I would plead with awe-stricken contrition that the most diligent individual does not acquire his knowledge upon any subject all at once; and the news which we shall receive to-morrow may altogether alter the conclusions which we have formed to-day, unless, indeed, we have our reasoning faculties entirely set at rest by that pure and lively faith in official reports to which such a very few mortals ever can attain.

In conclusion, permit me to beg your indulgence where I may be in error; your favourable construction of my intentions and of my wish to please you. If you will allow me to wait on you frequently, at any bookseller's you can think of, either in town or country, perhaps some day I may be able to offer you the riper fruits of a more mature experience.

I have the honour to be, my excellent Friend,
Your faithful, devoted, and affectionate servant
to command,
THE ROVING ENGLISHMAN.

CONSTANTINOPLE, *November*, 1854.

A PRELIMINARY WORD.

THE writings collected under the title of "The Roving Englishman in Turkey" have been before the public nearly a quarter of a century; and therefore the reprint now issued requires no introduction.* Lord Palmerston, who was himself a high authority upon Eastern affairs, by reason of his long experience in dealing with them, used to say that the Roving Englishman papers showed a more intimate knowledge of Turkey than any other publications with which he was acquainted. This opinion was endorsed by Lord Dalling, who was for several years Ambassador at the Porte; and by Sir Charles Alison, formerly Oriental Secretary to the British Embassy at Constantinople, who was acknowledged by competent authorities to be more deeply versed in the practical management of Oriental business than any diplomatist of his time.

It was these writings which first started the shy question of administrative reform in England, and which abolished some powerful abuses. They thus excited much controversy, and have been warmly praised or bitterly blamed, by the opposite parties interested in the public service, ever since their first appearance. No human effort can aspire to more satisfactory results than to have called attention to great national dangers,

* The Roving Englishman Books are five in number, and they were printed in the following order:—1. "The Roving Englishman"; 2. "The Roving Englishman in Turkey"; 3. "Pictures from the Battle-fields"; 4. "Embassies and Foreign Courts"; 5. "The Press and the Public Service." London: 1851-1856.

and to have diminished the evil effect of them. The notice sometimes taken of a new book arises only from specific and temporary causes, which have no connection with merit. But a second life is only granted to those creations of thought on which Fame has stamped a recognized value; and as this life is purely spiritual, it is also commonly immortal. A book which has been tried by the varying tests of public opinion for well nigh a generation without losing any of its popularity, and which is still as hotly attacked and as warmly defended as ever, may assuredly lay claim to the most intelligible sort of reputation known in this age of the world's history. Whether worthily or unworthily, it has passed in our language, and become a classic. The ultimate judgment of a nation, moreover, is generally quite as wise and just as it is generous. For such work is what all written truth has been since the invention of letters; and it is treated as an ensign set up by courageous citizens for honest men to rally round during those venal tumults which are always led by the Barabbas of his day. The rabble howl aloud about it; it is cheered and mocked, upheld and pelted, till its very fashion and colour are obliterated by the mob; and it becomes at last a downtrodden invincible thing all covered with mud and glory.

CONTENTS.

CHAPTER I.
THE SULTAN 1

CHAPTER II.
OUR EMBASSY 16

CHAPTER III.
THE PASHA 40

CHAPTER IV.
MY CAVASS AND I 48

CHAPTER V.
THE CADI 54

CHAPTER VI.
LEVANT CONSULS 58

CHAPTER VII.
LEVANT CONSULATES 68

CHAPTER VIII.
KAIMAK (MANNERS OF THE TURKS) 75

CHAPTER IX.
ON A VISIT 82

CHAPTER X.
THE BIN-BASHEE 88

Contents.

CHAPTER XI.	PAGE
THE SEA CAPTAIN	94
CHAPTER XII.	
DOWN THE DANUBE	99
CHAPTER XIII.	
THE SCHOOLMASTER	105
CHAPTER XIV.	
A TURKISH RAYAH	112
CHAPTER XV.	
THE GREEK EASTER AT CONSTANTINOPLE	118
CHAPTER XVI.	
THE PRINCE OF VENDÔME	122
CHAPTER XVII.	
A TURKISH AUCTIONEER	133
CHAPTER XVIII.	
THE FLEAS IN CONSTANTINOPLE	139
CHAPTER XIX.	
A MESSENGER IN DIFFICULTIES	143
CHAPTER XX.	
A TURKISH HOUSE	147
CHAPTER XXI.	
VILLAGE DIPLOMATISTS	154
CHAPTER XXII.	
THE FEAST OF ST. DEMETRIUS	158
CHAPTER XXIII.	
A GREEK GIRL OF THE ISLANDS	167

CHAPTER XXIV.
Hadji Hassan. 173

CHAPTER XXV.
Greek Fire 179

CHAPTER XXVI.
Greek Waters 185

CHAPTER XXVII.
The Castaway 192

CHAPTER XXVIII.
A Greek Funeral 196

CHAPTER XXIX.
A Travellers' Home in Greece. 203

CHAPTER XXX.
Pleasant Chios 207

CHAPTER XXXI.
A Sketch of Epirus 213

CHAPTER XXXII.
Capitan Jorgeij 217

CHAPTER XXXIII.
Greek Tricks. 223

CHAPTER XXXIV.
The Postman 228

CHAPTER XXXV.
A Greek Carnival 233

CHAPTER XXXVI.
Barataria 239

CHAPTER XXXVII.
A Pasha's Paradise 252

CHAPTER XXXVIII.
A Turkish Bath (Rhodes) 255

CHAPTER XXXIX.
Monks at Home 260

CHAPTER XL.
The Saint and the Sultan 263

CHAPTER XLI.
Macri 267

CHAPTER XLII.
A Pasha at Sea 272

CHAPTER XLIII.
The Man of Cos 278

CHAPTER XLIV.
Cos 283

CHAPTER XLV.
Chios 288

CHAPTER XLVI.
The Monastery 294

CHAPTER XLVII.
The Road 298

CHAPTER XLVIII.
The Road-side Coffee-House 305

CHAPTER XLIX.
Magnesia 309

CHAPTER L.
The Hakeem 313

CHAPTER LI.
"The Saucy Arethusa" 317

CHAPTER LII.
Dolma Bakjah (The Sultan's new Palace) 321

CHAPTER LIII.
The Despot 326

CHAPTER LIV.
Historical Anecdotes of the Greeks and Turks . . 331

CHAPTER LV.
A Son of the Desert 347

CHAPTER LVI.
Consular Freaks 353

CHAPTER LVII.
Army Interpreters 360

CHAPTER LVIII.
Reform in Turkey 365

CHAPTER LIX.
Hints to Travellers going to Turkey 371

THE ROVING ENGLISHMAN IN TURKEY.

CHAPTER I.

THE SULTAN.

THERE is a large crowd assembled on the shores of the Bosphorus to see an Ambassador, who is going to pay his visit of ceremony to the Sultan. Let us suppose him to be the Austrian Internuncio, for the sake of example. He will do as well as any other chief of an important Foreign Mission. The new Envoy and his suite embark in their gilded caique to have their first official audience of his Imperial Majesty. The Ambassador is not only accompanied by his secretaries, attachés, interpreters, and a whole host of minor functionaries, but his following is considerably increased in number, while its splendour is vastly augmented by a number of Austrian Naval officers who have come up from the Dardanelles; and by the magnificent uniforms of several strangers of distinction who have arrived here to see one of the last acts of a most splendid and wonderful historical drama.

Preceded by some half-dozen cavasses, a kind of body-guard allowed to Foreign Missions in Turkey, the glittering crowd marches on, with not a little clanking of spurs and trailing of sabres, all of which, of course, adds considerably to the imposing character of a grand ceremony of State. Meantime, fancy grows busy with anticipations of their reception. The Internuncio and his suite, however gorgeous, will surely not proceed at once into the presence of so mighty a potentate as the Sultan. Most of the Turks in place have been told quite often enough of their weakness and decay to understand the Western world's opinion of them perfectly; and although the mild Prince* who now sits upon the tottering throne of Constantinople is far, very far, from vainglorious, yet the magnificent traditions of the East can hardly be quite forgotten. The bitter humiliation and consciousness of his own impotence, which must have weighed so heavily on the kind heart of Abdul Medjid of late years, do not perhaps prevent him from being surrounded with a certain faded state which will have something impressive in it; I had almost said touching. The incense of his own courtiers, indeed, think some of us, must sound like a most sorrowful and unreal mockery to him, when he is torn away from it so often to hear the stern lecture of first this hard-mouthed Ambassador, and then the other; but his own rare efforts to keep up his dignity may be respected as one should respect the fallen fortunes of any man or thing that has been great, and is sorely humbled.

Let us follow the Ambassador and his suite, however, and we shall judge for ourselves. When they arrive at the palace, they are conducted by some stragglers, who happen to be lounging about the premises, through a little garden, formally laid out in the old French style. It is one of those gardens which have nothing but the name—a garden with little patches of flower-beds cut into triangles and crescents, and having hard, dry, pebbly useless paths between; paths upon which nobody ever does or could walk. The garden may possibly cover a quarter of an acre of ground, not more, and is soon passed. The Ambassador and his train are then led into a low stone passage, which has many mysterious doors on each side of it. This passage is very dark, rather damp, and particularly bare and sordid in appearance.† It has nothing of Oriental pomp about

---

* Abd-ul-Medjid; *now* means 1853.

† The late Sultan has been often reproached with his extravagant mania for building; but had his predecessors built more, perhaps he would not have built so much. Twenty-five years ago there was hardly a royal residence in Turkey.

it. Yet here we are in the precincts of the Imperial Palace, and the Sultan is, I dare say, within hearing of us somewhere nigh. Meantime, half a dozen servants and officers of the household seem as busy as Orientals ever are, in showing us upstairs to the State apartments. There is nothing brilliant about the aspect of these Turkish gentlemen-in-waiting. Except for their red caps with gilt badges of office in the crowns of them, they might be taken for German artisans of the lower order in their Sunday clothes. They are quite as heavy, as awkward, and as consequential, and their things bulge out in the wrong places, precisely as though they had been made by a Teutonic tailor, more intent on philosophy than on thread or scissors. A few guards clad in brown, with sashes of gold lace, and having no arms but sabres, are also posted here and there without order or regularity. The day is bleak and drizzly; nothing can be more commonplace, dreary, and uncomfortable than our position and surroundings. Things change a little for the better as we ascend the stairs, in spite of the gloom which still seems to hang over everything. Upon the first landing is stationed one of the Sultan's body-guards, and he is dressed in clothes which are at least meant for a uniform. The intention of their maker is not very successfully carried out, but it is obvious that it has existed, and we are satisfied, for that is at least a commencement of scenic effects befitting the time and place. We go up some dingy stairs with the Ambassador's splendid escort, and from the dingy stairs into a dingy room, a room dingier, I vow, than a lawyer's office in Gray's Inn. It is ill-furnished, and there are not chairs enough in it for the Ambassador's suite; more are brought from another apartment, but still there are not enough, so that a fresh supply is imported. Then the carpet, which is dingier than anything around except the sofas, does not half cover the floor; but this apparent parsimony is merely Oriental fashion, so we must not be surprised at it. At last the Grand Vizier turns up with a dazed look, as though he had just been disturbed in a nap, and would rather be in another place where there was not too much light. He is followed after a brief interval by the Grand Interpreter, who is a high officer in Turkey; then comes the Minister for

Foreign Affairs. They are all dressed in ill-made European clothes; and their advent is immediately succeeded by pipes and coffee.

The pipes are very handsome, though not so beautiful as those often served in private houses. They have richly jewelled mouthpieces of amber, sometimes black, sometimes of a pale lemon colour, and the cost of them is often as preposterous as that of Dutch tulips, bearing no relation whatever to their value. The coffee is served in little cups of jewelled filagree, of which the best are made at Trebizond. Neither the coffee, nor the tobacco brought with the pipes is very good, and the coffee is drunk unstrained, without sugar, according to the fashion of the East.

There is not much conversation: everybody feels very cold and strange; everybody also is ignorant of the etiquette of the place, and no one likes to commit himself for fear of becoming the butt and laughing-stock of his acquaintance for evermore. There might be, perhaps, plenty to say, for men must be dull indeed who cannot talk to a Minister for Foreign Affairs; but the making of a remark is rather too serious a business to be repeated often. Thus, for instance, the Ambassador observes, for want of anything else to say, that "it is a cold day."

No sooner are the words out of his Excellency's mouth than the Chief Dragoman of the Embassy, a plethoric Levantine, whose breath comes uncommonly short, leaves off snorting over his scalding coffee; and dropping what remains of it on his knees, rises with an expression of haste and confusion. A tear of intense anguish is in one of his eyes, and the tightness of his uniform has forbidden him the solace of a pocket-handkerchief, so that the tear gradually descends and tickles his nose, till he is driven to the verge of madness.

"It is a cold day," repeats the Internuncio, nodding, for he is a pleasant, cheery man, who has been oppressed by the stony silence about him, and wants to break it up.

The Dragoman does not hear or does not catch the words, for he has a pipe in one hand, a coffee-cup in the other, and an incipient cough in his throat, while his mind is wholly absorbed in the dreadful tickling of *that* tear.

"It is a cold day," tell him, says the First Secretary of the Embassy, in a sharp tone.

"Whisper to Nooderl to tell Birbantaki it is a cold day," says one of the Attachés who likes the Interpreter, to another who does not.

"I won't speak to the fellow; tell him yourself," is the answer, in the same undertone.

Grand Vizier (who thinks the Internuncio is impatient to see the Sultan): "All in good time!"

Minister for Foreign Affairs (mortally afraid of a threatened complaint from the Austrian Government about the unsatisfied claims of an inventor for extracting sunbeams from cucumbers): "Let us go."

Grand Interpreter of the Sublime Porte (a phlegmatic old man who thinks slowly): "That's not it."

Internuncio. "What does he say?"

Dragoman (keeping down his cough by a great effort): "His Excellency, the Minister for Foreign Affairs, is anxious to know what your Excellency said."

Internuncio (who supposes that the whole affair of the cold day has been settled long ago): "I? I said nothing! What was said to me?"

The Dragoman is puzzled, and struggles desperately with his cough. While he is doing so the friendly Attaché pulls him by the skirts of his coat, and communicates to him the first observation of the Internuncio.

Dragoman (gasping): "His Excellency the Internuncio takes advantage of this opportunity to remark that it is a cold day."

Minister for Foreign Affairs (who has been whispering piteously to his colleagues) is much relieved, and murmurs, "God is great," amidst general silence.

Internuncio (smiling good-humouredly to thaw the ice around): "Eh? What?"

Dragoman (just remembering that the Stock Exchange at Galata closes in an hour, and that all his family will be waiting in vain for him): "His Excellency the Minister for Foreign Affairs observes to your Excellency that 'God is great.' It is a Turkish——"

"Eh? Yes! of course, I dare say! But when are we going to see the Sultan? My feet are quite chilled."

The Ambassador looks bored, and the pipes having been changed for others still more expensive, the whole party rise. They take their way along a passage and pass through a faded curtain, which is drawn aside for them, till presently they reach a suite of moderately large rooms, dotted sparsely over with dejected-looking chairs, none of which stand quite straightly on their legs. A freshly lit fire of coal burns sulkily in one or two of the grates, and gives forth a dispiriting smoke in splenetic and fractious puffs. The rain rattles spitefully against the palace windows, as though it had a quarrel with them; the noses of the guards ranged in a line along a corridor are quite red with cold, their hands are blue. Let us hurry on.

The last room of these state apartments is smaller than the rest. It would be used as a refreshment-room if Strauss were to give a concert there. A dim and surly fire smoulders sluggishly in the grate, and there is a plain sofa without a back, placed next to the wall at the extreme end of the room. This is the presence-chamber; and as the Ambassador enters with his suite, an individual is seen to rise slowly from the sofa, and he stands mutely up to receive his visitors as though he were an automaton wound up for that purpose. He shows no sign of life or thought.

In person he is a dark, wearied-looking man, apparently about forty years old, though he is in reality ten years younger. He is dressed in a dark blue frock-coat, with a Prussian collar. The sleeves and the collar of it are embroidered with gold and diamonds; both his coat and his trousers are much too large for him; they hang about his frail limbs and puny body in disconsolate folds. Thus he appears bandy-legged and top-heavy, like a child's toy, and there is something uncanny about him, as though he were stuffed and not alive. He wears no ornament but the Nisham, a large gold plate encrusted with diamonds, which is hung round his neck; and a heavy Turkish scymitar, set with jewels also, but dirty and lustreless. On his head is a red cap, and on his feet are a pair of French boots with varnished tips, but so large that it is marvellous how he walks in them without tumbling down. This is Abdul Medjid, the Sultan of Turkey.

As the Ambassador and his following approach it is painful to see the monarch's embarrassment. It amounts evidently to constitutional nervousness, and is manifested in all his movements. His eyes wander here and there like those of a schoolboy called upon to repeat a lesson he does not know. He changes his feet continually, and makes spasmodic movements with his hands. I am sure his beard, a very fine one, is uncomfortable to him, and that he feels as if he had a hair shirt on. I am still more sure that he feels literally Ambassadored to death. One was at him yesterday, just after breakfast; here is another to-day, before he has finished his pilaff—as may be noted by the curious; and to-morrow is not the Ambassador of Ambassadors announced, that terrible Sir Harry Needybore, who is half crazed by contradictory instructions from Lord Partyman and Mr. Jonas Worrit, C.B., the permanent under-secretary of the department which rules over him? Oh for a little rest! Oh for his quiet ride where the sweet waters flow and the melons ripen! Oh for repose ·beside the bright-faced Lesbian girl he left behind him in the harem; who will soothe his aching temples with cooled rosewater, and lull him to sleep with her songs!

The Ambassador stands forward, his suite fall back, and he begins to speak after the manner of a popular preacher who is talking at a weak-kneed member of his congregation, for reasons known to both of them. Meanwhile the cold drops gather visibly on the Sultan's forehead, and his poor thumbs and toes are never still a moment. Excellency Internuncio, however, has not much to say just then; the sterner part of the discipline he has to administer must be done privately. For the present he merely pronounces with a loud voice some of the commonplace civilities which are always offered to royalty, and concludes with a flourishing encomium on the power and glory of his own nation. Nothing more. The Sultan replies. What he says nobody knows: not the best Oriental scholars in the room, though they listen with strained ears, can make anything of it. Certain dislocated sentences are jerked painfully from his Majesty's lips in syllables and fragments—that is all. The Grand Interpreter, however, is by no means at a loss: he at least has got a neat little speech cut and dried; he learned it by heart at mosque yesterday; so he begins to bob and duck with great assiduity. He is a fat little man, whose clothes are too tight for him, and he does not appear to advantage in them, but he delivers himself successfully. The Sultan gazes hopelessly up at the ceiling, then down at his boots, and once—oh, how longingly!—at the door. There is silence; one might hear a pin fall, while every eye is turned upon the changing countenance of the monarch. Then comes a bustle. Strangers must withdraw; and the Ambassador, with his interpreter, the Minister for Foreign Affairs, and the Chief Dragoman of the sublime Porte remain in company unobserved. No wonder the Sultan looked so harassed; he is safely shut up for an hour's lecture against all his most cherished opinions, against his prejudices, his education, his conscience, and religion.

> "The weary thing
> To be a king."

Let us go scuffling out with the rest of the throng, dear Public, turning our backs upon Majesty with rather too little ceremony. We shall return to the room from whence we came, and there await the Ambassador's coming. Our feet are damp, our noses are blue, our uniforms pinch us under the arms, our corns are shooting wildly, for the costume in which usage requires men to present themselves before Princes is the most uncomfortable which can be devised by perverse ingenuity. We rejoice at the second appearance of coffee and pipes; and when they are disposed of we look stiffly at each other from the giddy heights of our embroidered coat-collars, and our backs ache not a little.

A fair hour has elapsed. Many of us have long ceased to feel our noses at all; they have passed from a state of chill and smarting into a comatose condition; and our pipes have been burnt out and carried away before the Ambassador returns. But when he does dawn upon us, yellow as a living pancake, with gold lace before and behind, we perceive that he is quite radiant. He has delivered himself with startling effect; he is a kind, good, sympathetic man in his ordinary intercourse with other people; yet I soon learn that he has said things in his private audience with the poor limp Sultan which would provide him with his passports in twenty-four hours at any Court in Europe—yea, even at the court of Schwartzwürst-Schinkenshausen. Glancing from this self-satisfied Excellency to the Minister for Foreign Affairs (who has been recently appointed because his predecessor did not obey the orders of the Russian Prince Knockoff with sufficient promptitude), I note that he is blushing red with anger and humiliation; that Minister's under lip has fallen, and he seems to be literally wincing corporally under the treatment he has received. If the Ambassador were to speak to him suddenly just now, I should not be surprised to see him stand up with an outstretched hand in the attitude of a schoolboy who is going to receive punishment for having been caught beyond the limits of his playfield. However, as I said before, the Internuncio* is delighted, and his entrance into the room causes quite an agreeable reaction on our spirits. After a few words of course, we all rise, and putting on our clogs in the dark passage before mentioned we wade across the garden, which has now become deep in mire, and then cuddling ourselves up in our cloaks go coughing and sneezing homewards.

Such is the ceremony at the reception of foreign ambassadors in Constantinople during the month of April in the year of grace one thousand eight hundred and fifty-three, while the Crimean war is brewing briskly. The court of the Sultan has neither grace, dignity, nor splendour; I confess I could not help being saddened by the spectacle. I was sorry to see the most gentle and merciful Prince who ever sat upon the blood-stained throne of the Caliphs so shorn of that magnificence which is especially prized by Orientals.

* The words Internuncio and Ambassador are both used in this chapter as though they had the same signification; but, strictly speaking, the Austrian Internuncio at Constantinople ranks between an Envoy Extraordinary and an Ambassador.

No one, indeed, can seriously regret the humbling of the Turkish power in Europe. One is too apt to remember the epitaph on a famous brigand, in which the traveller is advised not to mourn for the robber chief, because had he been living the traveller would have been dead. The decay of Mussulman power is synonymous with the advance of Christianity ; and even the most sceptic philosopher could scarcely lament the gradual passing away of almost universal dominion from a race who never founded but one civilized* empire in the world, and who, from the palsying influence of Mohammedanism, have done nothing for art, science, or literature during the four hundred odd years that they have possessed in wealthy leisure one of the finest countries upon earth. They have done absolutely nothing, and worse, for they have suffered sand to collect over some of the most precious monuments of the past, and let the pride of many beauties crumble unheeded into dust. Where stood the Forum of Constantine, founder of the great city which they took from the Byzantines, with its porticoes of marble and lofty columns of porphyry? Where is the colossal statue of Apollo, supposed to be the work of Phidias, and innumerable other treasures which genius created for immortality? Where is the stately Hippodrome of the sport-loving Greeks of the lower empire, with its statues and obelisks? The public baths, with their threescore images of bronze? The circus? The theatres? The schools? All those wonders of architecture which would have been standing to-day had they fallen into other hands? Alas! every one of them is destroyed, and the traveller may look in vain for anything to remind him of the thousand glories of the past, which were committed to their keeping, and which have been either destroyed by neglect and unthrift, or ignorantly defaced. It is not fair, however, to cast up accounts with Turkey, so as to show too large a balance against her. The Turks who came from the Golden Mountains, and followed the banner of the Blacksmith's Apron to the shores of the Bosphorus, were a far nobler and more vigorous type of men than the effeminate rabble they overcame ; and Providence never seems to have decreed that the

* Granada.

arts and treasures of a degenerate people should be any defence against the armed avengers of their sins. Tyre and Sidon, Babylon and Nineveh, not to speak of Jerusalem, could have doubtless shown finer collections of antiquities, and marvels of human handiwork more wonderful than any which were shattered or dispersed when the captain of a Paynim host rode on horseback into the Church of St. Sophia. Every now and then, in course of ages, the world receives one of those stern lessons which bids nations to put their trust on high, and there only. The Turks have been long recognized by the wisest of statesmen as a political necessity; and it is easy to show the truth of that estimate of their position. The Ottoman Empire is an important barrier against a sullen military despotism of which all thinking persons stand most reasonably in dread. Let us therefore protect Turkey with a good-will, since we shall find our interest in doing so; and perhaps while we are about it we might give our help a little less contemptuously, at all events till we can find an ally as useful and as strong. Moreover, it is altogether a queer and dangerous notion to suppose that if we did not extend our patronage and protection to the Turks they would all appear in Basinghall Street before Mr. Registrar Moneyman, and subsequently dissolve in writs and law costs. On the contrary, they are a most fierce and warlike folk who, with exception of a few officials, would feel much rejoiced to be freed from the infliction of unpalatable advice. The result of a lovers' quarrel between us would probably be a massacre of every Christian throughout the Ottoman dominions, and the foundation of a new Mussulman Empire under a warlike leader, who would gather together the loose tribes of Moslems now scattered about from the Danube to the Oxus, from Syria and Egypt to Turkestan and Cabool, till we had to reckon with him upon our Indian frontier and make it up. Timurlenk and Bayazid, and Orchan, Suleyman and Saladin were all rough customers, and several Mohammedan gentlemen with sidelong looks and uneasy manners at a civic feast, have shown us, even within living memory, how Orientals can fight. Havelock and Outram, Lawrence and Clyde did not get their laurels without a tussle for them, whatever the organist's assistant at Exeter Hall may think about that objectionable business which happened during the sixth decade of the nineteenth century in Hindostan or elsewhere.

I cannot, perhaps, conclude this chapter more conveniently than by contrasting, as a reminder to hectoring ambassadors, the reception which their predecessors in diplomacy received from the Ottoman despot, with that which I have already related. It may be useful to them.

The receptions always took place on grand divan days, immediately after the payment of the troops ; so that Foreign Envoys admitted to the honours of an audience might see the Sultan on parade ; and that the soldiers under arms might give the stranger a fitting idea of the Ottoman might. The Ambassador was usually granted an audience upon a Tuesday ; and as the divan assembled shortly after daybreak, the Ambassador had to get up betimes in order that he might present himself at the Bagdsche Kapussi (garden gate of the palace) before sunrise, for after that there was no admittance. Here he was met by the Tschausch Bashi, an inferior dignitary of the Empire who was charged with his reception. This functionary welcomed the stranger Envoy as his guest, and arranged the order of his further proceedings. The Tschausch Bashi rode before a Minister Plenipotentiary, but gave a kind of surly precedence to an Ambassador, taking place, however, at his right hand, and before all his suite. When the procession reached the "Divan Joli," or grand street of the divan, it halted, and the Ambassador went on foot to visit the Grand Vizier. He was often kept waiting the pleasure of the Grand Vizier for many hours. When the Vizier deigned at last to show himself, his suite took precedence of the Ambassador's, who were directed to march in order behind them at a respectful distance and at a measured pace. A little further on they were commanded to halt again, and the High Chamberlain made his appearance, carrying a silver staff, which he struck haughtily upon the ground as he walked. I cannot help fancying that he must have been a strange sight. Preceded by the important functionary with the silver stick, the Ambassador and his attendants, who must all have been rather tired and hungry by this time, moved slowly on once more. At the divan the Ambassador was obliged to leave the greater part of his suite behind him. The Grand Vizier now caused numerous leather sacks full of money to be brought, and began to pay the soldiers. A more grotesque piece of Oriental make-believe than this can hardly be imagined. Behind the place where the Grand Vizier sat was a little window, from which the Sultan could see all that was going on without being seen himself. When the divan was over, the Ambassador was allowed to dine at the table of the Grand Vizier, and his suite were huddled pell-mell together somewhere else.

A formal demand was then made by the Grand Vizier on the Ambassador's behalf for an audience with the Sultan; and it was the wont of the Sultan to answer: "That if the stranger had been already clothed and fed by his generosity he would graciously consent to receive him." The reception, however, did not take place at once, but the Ambassador and his suite were still kept waiting an hour or two in the open air at the gate of the Sultan's palace. This was the time when the Ambassador presented his gifts, if he had brought any, and it was the almost invariable custom of foreign envoys to do so; at the same time his Excellency and all the members of his Embassy were clothed with costly robes of great magnificence. The Sultan then gave orders that the stranger should be admitted into his presence, but the court etiquette did not allow an Ambassador's whole suite to exceed twelve persons. The chief of the white eunuchs, and the long-haired axe-bearers, with a crowd of white slaves carefully prepared for domestic service in an eastern household, took part in the audience, and occupied prominent places near the Commander of the Faithful. All the white ennuchs were dazzlingly arrayed in cloth of gold. The Ambassador and his suite were borne into the presence of the Sultan by two stout men, who seized each of them under the arms and lifted them in this manner off the ground, in which fashion the bearers carried them as near to the person of his Majesty as they were allowed to approach. When at last they stood before the Sultan, the High Chamberlain took them by their heads and made them bow before his Highness with due reverence. The Ambassador presented his letters of credence upon a velvet cushion embroidered with gold, which was carried by his Secretary. These letters were received by the Grand Interpreter, who handed them to the Grand Vizier, and he laid them humbly at the Sultan's feet. During the whole interview the Sultan never deigned to address a word to the Ambassador. When the latter had said what he had to say, he was again lifted off the ground and carried away without further ceremony. An Ambassador was never permitted to see the Sultan more than twice: on the first occasion to present his letters of credence, and on the last to take leave.

Ambassadors were looked upon with such small esteem by these fierce infidels, that the representative of Sweden at Constantinople was once beaten by a janissary; and was unable to obtain redress. Even an English Ambassador lies unburied in unconsecrated ground, on the little island of Halki, in the sea of Marmora; and the place of his interment was uncertain till Sir Stratford Canning erected a simple monument to his memory. It seems odd that such men as stout old Shirley, who represented so potent a sovereign as Elizabeth of England, the Envoys of the proud Kings of France and Spain, and of the punctilious German Emperors, should have submitted to be treated with such indignity. But the fact is that all of them had at different times measured their strength with the Turks, and got the worst end of the dispute; so that whenever they wanted anything they had to ask for it in the only manner in which it could be obtained. Each and all of them wanted the Turks, the Turks never wanted any of them. The English have always been keen traders, and they had factories and establishments in every part of the Levant, immediately after the crusades; the Spanish navies were almost unmanned by adventurous Algerine cruisers, and their galleons were constantly intercepted and plundered by the corsairs of Tripoli and Tunis. The Italian republics had numerous rich outlying settlers and merchants in the Euxine, and scattered throughout Asia Minor; Hungary and Austria trembled at the Turkish name, and the Crescent had constantly menaced the Cross at Vienna, till John Sobieski settled that business for awhile.

France had likewise many merchants, missionaries, and captive sailors in need of protection. The Turks had hardly a single subject out of the Ottoman dominions; they stood aloof, quite independent of the Christian powers, and were thus able to dictate the terms upon which they would consent to hold a parley. Now, however, the question is altered, and Ambassadors are everything. The present state of things in Turkey may be said to exist only for the embassies. They are above the law and the prophet; they take small account of either. I never see an Ambassador going down the Bosphorus in state, to scold the Sultan, without being filled with a solemn joy at the greatness of Europe and the progress of Christianity; though now and then I may also, perhaps, own to a regret that he is not about to assert our glory before a prince less helpless and brow-beaten than the Sultan of to-day.

CHAPTER II.

OUR EMBASSY.

The Chief—The Attachés—The Secretary—The Dragoman—Reforms—Appointments.

I DO not know that I had anything to do at Constantinople; but I know the name of my appointment, which was a kind of information possessed by few of my colleagues; I was sub-Vice-Consul, and I think the only salaried functionary of that sort to be found in the Queen's service. I was appointed because Sir Hector Stubble, at this time her Majesty's Ambassador to the Sublime Porte, had quarrelled with every one else about him so cantankerously and so often that the business of the Embassy could no longer be carried on without assistance from beyond its walls. I need scarcely add that he also quarrelled with me. His Excellency would not have anything to say to Mr. Faddleton, our secretary, because he lisped; nor to the first attaché, because he did not lisp, nor to the six others for equally cogent reasons, and he led them the life of dogs.

Between the Consulate and the Embassy there was again open war; one pretending to all authority, and the other granting none. A person arriving at Constantinople from any other quarter of the world, and finding himself in an official situation there, might have thought easily enough that he had lost his way and got into a department of the Inquisition.

Sir Hector Stubble had set every living being within his influence by the ears; he had an innate faculty for producing troubles, as some soils naturally grow crops of noxious weeds. It was impossible for any inhabitant of his neighbourhood to walk across a street with a British subject whom he had met by chance, without hearing that British subject immediately fall foul of every other British subject round about those parts, and there were a good many of them—all at loggerheads. Slander and backbiting, complaints and annoyances, jarring and sparring, were going on from morning till night, and vexed the steps of peaceful folk like burrs or brambles. The very cats and dogs in the Embassy learned to look shyly at each other.

It was long before I could explain to myself how it happened that a man so widely respected as Sir Hector could have contrived to make himself so completely disagreeable; yet the solution of the problem was not difficult. He was a person of fair average capacity indeed, hard-working, continent, careful of his own interests, a patriot according to his dim lights, and a gentleman in speech when he was not crossed ; but a more hard, unkind, unjust, unlovable man, never stood within the icy circle of his own pride and ill-temper. He was haughty and petulant beyond anybody I have ever seen. He trampled on other people's feelings as savagely and unflinchingly as if they had been soulless puppets made to work his will. He was essentially a narrow-minded man, for he had favourites, and jealousies, and petty enmities ; he had small passions, and by no means an intellect strong enough even to keep them decently out of sight. But he was a fine specimen of Donnishness, and would have figured well as the governor of a penal settlement, or the master of a reformatory.

He had been at Constantinople nearly all his life, and Constantinople was a very bad school for the rearing of an English public servant. He had also exercised too much irresponsible power over others ; and at last he could speak to no one save in the grating language of harsh command. The most respectful remonstrance or the most courteous explanation opposed to his immediate wishes had the same effect upon him as a red cloth has upon an infuriated bull ; and he could not refrain from asserting his superiority over all who came near him in a manner which made his words like gall and wormwood to the humblest. With the best will in the world, it was impossible to like or to esteem him ; the longer you knew him, the more you tried, the more hopeless became the effort ; he would meet those who had served and obeyed him during long years of cowed and abject submission to his caprices, and he would pass them without a look or a word of recognition ; he would see them sicken and die under the same roof as himself without a thought. He seemed to look on mankind merely as a set of tools ; when he wanted an instrument, he took a fellow-creature, and when he had done with it, he put it aside with its edge taken off for one while. Possibly it was the long habit of dealing with persons placed in an improper position of subordination to him which made him treat every one under his command as a slave, whose best endeavours to please him were not worth thanks ; nature never could have made a man, from the first, so thoroughly unamiable and mischievous.

He did material and visible harm to others, of malice prepense and sheer naughtiness. He strewed his path with ruined hopes and blighted careers; he caused much anguish and many heart-aches. Even when he was not actively vicious in darkening the lives and blasting the prospects of his officers, he made the young men among them despair of winning honourable triumphs in their profession by honourable means ; he forced them to take mean and pettifogging views of their country's needs and of their own duties. Those who bowed the neck to him passed straightway into sneaks and sycophants ; they had no choice indeed. To stand well with Sir Hector Stubble was to be his blind unreasoning tool. He would accept you on no other terms. Those who could not or would not cast away their conscience and free will at his bidding appeared to him as utterly worthless and abandoned ; while they generally looked upon Sir Hector with the same pleasurable feelings as travellers through an awkward defile entertain towards any person who is likely to take a long shot at them from a safe distance whenever he sees an opportunity of doing so. He was an oppressor; he could oppress with impunity, and he stretched his power to its furthest limits. He wanted magnanimity enough to leave any one he disliked alone ; so he raised the hard hand of authority and crushed the defenceless with an unpitying scowl. He had no heart, no feeling, no eyes,

teristic of Sir Hector's mind became, at last, an insane jealousy. He was jealous of every small official who wrote good English, and he would have been jealous of his own body-servant if he had caught him reading a newspaper.

I have sometimes thought that he had a painful consciousness himself of being extremely disliked ; and that this made him shy of people who did not assure him at once of their allegiance. Even a kind man will seldom make advances if he s also a proud one. But the truth is there was no explaining Sir Hector Stubble. Foreigners called him "*Sa Potence;*" his staff nicknamed him "*The British Embarrasser.*"

He was surrounded by a nice set of snobs and toadies. They fetched and carried and told lies to him. They fell down before him, and slandered all the world to exalt him, and they sang his absurd hallelujah from morning to night. The place where he dwelt was so split into factions that it would have been as pleasant to have an abode in a hornet's nest, as in beautiful Stamboul.

Such was Sir Hector Stubble; yet he was one of the recognized celebrities of the world. In Mayfair it was highly dangerous to express a doubt about him, so numerous, rich, and influential were his connections. Moreover, people who had no knowledge of him believed that there must be something in a man who had been so long in receipt of a large salary without having it snatched away by one of the cousinhood, who were for ever clutching at each other's good things, and fighting over them. But in Turkey we had found him out ; and, indeed, there is a great difference between seeing people like Sir Hector near, and seeing them from afar off. What celebrities cease to command our respect when we get close to them and note how they are made? The greatest of men will hardly bear too minute an inspection, and hence is, perhaps, the wisdom of not making one's self too cheap; not appearing too often to be stared at and interrogated. The world is quite ready to admire what it does not know ; with the best intentions possible it can hardly admire anything with which it is familiar. Hear the conversation among the hangers-on of a court when they are alone ; listen to those young aides-de-camp laughing together as they take their afternoon's ride in the Phœnix Park. Hark to the

Archbishop's chaplain at tea with his maiden sister. See the great minister's private secretary so utterly bored and desponding! and such are the daily intimates of those we are accustomed to look upon as the foremost men of our age and country.

Not one of them beholds the object of our veneration with the same eyes as we do, and if we could see our great men as often and as near as they have seen them, and know as much of them, perhaps our admiration would melt away also. There are a vast number of persons as disappointed with reality as the old lady who went to see the king, and who remembered having beheld an individual of much more regal appearance in a booth at a country fair.

It is now nearly a quarter of a century since these lines were first penned, and one of those who wrote them, after pausing long to reflect whether he could upon his honour and conscience answer to God and to man, if he deliberately edited them for republication, can only express his regret that the sombre picture then drawn of Sir Hector Stubble was not painted in colours dark enough to give a just resemblance of him. For when a fair and clear account is rendered of the public and private troubles which were, either in part or altogether, directly or indirectly, caused by the hidebound humours of this official person—the waste of blood and treasure for which he is responsible, the useless miseries of the Greek and of the Crimean wars, the bankruptcy of the Ottoman imperial treasury which arose out of them, the ruin of Turkish bondholders, the desolation of a thousand homes, the grinding taxation of the rayahs which has resulted in the Bulgarian massacres; when all these items are honestly summed up, and many still worse iniquities left out of the fearful total which makes up the balance against a man who was for more than forty years virtually absolute ruler of Turkey—it is not decent to speak of him otherwise than with stern uncompromising censure; and it is not easy to think complacently of the official family party who upheld him in his misdoings, and who encouraged him in his unrelenting ferocity.

Leaving this question at rest after placing on record the mature opinion of Sir Hector and his policy above reprinted let me try to sketch the remainder of our staff; for we had some pleasant fellows among us, as there are everywhere. Some of them were perhaps not likely to do much for the world's improvement, but they were all genial and good-natured. Indeed, the talents which go to make up a great man, and those which form an agreeable one, are far too seldom joined; the one has small time for the graces, the other can think of nothing else. A jolly fellow or a carpet knight can sing a good song; he has a complacent smile for every one and nearly always knows the last fat joke or pungent scandal. His conversation requires no effort to follow it. But who ever saw a young man likely to turn out a sage pass much of his days in making half moons on his finger nails and waxing his moustache to look smart? We must choose our specialty, for it will stick to us.

The specialty chosen by the Attachés at Constantinople here described was more in the agreeable than the intellectual line. They had pianos in their rooms and sang little French songs, that did not respect anything very particularly, to impossible tunes. They rode and dined together, and were grand personages in a small way. They knew the poor players of the Italian opera-house—then but a sorry speculation—and were proud of entertaining them in private life. They were the despair of the Galata bankers' sons, and they snubbed them from the height of their grandeur; while the bankers avenged themselves in charges on their remittances from home. They were fond of patronizing tradesmen and travellers, and behaved themselves as people having authority. I am afraid we were official snobs.

We gave our minds to secrets in the same way as our chiefs: we were mysterious, and fond of saying nothing to each other in an undertone. Two or three of us were never gathered together without many statements of a private and confidential nature being exchanged between us. We took each other aside for occult purposes, and told the same thing privately and confidentially in this way to every one of the party, however large it might be. Many people were so impressed by our behaviour that they went away fully persuaded that some exclusive political intelligence of great importance had been entrusted to them, but that they could not, for the life and soul of them, understand what it meant. We would not for the world have spoken out intelligibly upon any subject, even although it had been town talk for several days and our hotel waiters knew more of it than we did. Our communications both to each other and to outsiders were often untrue, and more often still they would have been perfectly insignificant had they been otherwise ; but mystery was the mainspring of our lives ; our minds fed upon it, and grew all turn, twist, and shuffle in consequence.

The only reason I could ever find for this our deportment, was that we were sometimes ashamed of what we were about, and did not like the public to know how sillily we were acting till we had got our Government over head and ears into difficulties and it was too late to complain. We had, moreover, found out that it was much easier to explain an error committed months ago, when all interest in the subject had generally died away, than to behave in so straightforward a manner that we might fearlessly let all who would, look over our work at any time. I never saw a really gifted man have the dusky tricky sort of mind which we were taught to believe necessary for carrying on the business of the world.

As for our Secretary of Embassy, he was a myth : we never saw him at all. Sir Hector, of course, hated him, as jealous men almost invariably dislike their heirs presumptive, and his appointment was an uncomfortable sort of sinecure, which made him feel ashamed of himself in society. He never saw a despatch and he never sent one, except on the days when he drew his salary and filled up his life certificate. When Sir Hector went away on leave of absence, therefore, he knew as much of the current business of the Embassy and the manner of conducting it as people in general know of the invisible side of the moon. He was supposed to live somewhere with a very private and confidential establishment, to comb his hair with a spoon for fear of entanglements, and to feel constantly in dread of being sent to one of the South American republics as soon as any of the cousins wanted his place ; but further we knew nothing of him, save that he was a pale, frail, nervous man, rather over-dressed and very much afraid of committing himself.

It often occurred to me, that considering Sir Hector almost excluded him from society and would not allow him to know anything that was going on, and that Sir Hector was all-powerful at Constantinople, the Honourable Mr. Faddleton would have been much better employed in travelling leisurely about the country till he was wanted, thus improving his mind and picking up ideas. But the rules of the Service—who was Mr. Worrit, C.B.—put this out of the question; for are they not as the laws of the Medes and Persians?

I had rather an unpopular personal respect for the Honourable Faddleton myself. He was as dull, honest, good-natured a gentleman as ever put on a boot; and there was no harm in him at all. Perhaps many persons might have filled his place better had they been allowed to do so; but the truth is, that nobody could have performed creditable work under Sir Hector; so that perhaps the Honourable Faddleton did as well at Constantinople as any one else could have done. None of us had any fixed duties; we were at the mercy of our Chief's indifference and incapacity to judge of us, and he contrived usually to employ each of us in the business we least understood.

The Honourable Faddleton was fifty and only a Secretary still. He had, indeed, been too long a recognized mediocrity to accomplish a worthy aim or object now, or to care much about anything so long as he kept his place, which was all his living. I know of nothing more likely to improve the quality of a man's intellect than success which is not too tardy afoot; that is, success which is honestly inherited or even boldly won. Too long labouring in vain is apt to create indifference and want of hope and confidence in ourselves; whereas the man who has already achieved something, is careful of his reputation, grows to have a deeper trust in his own abilities, and succeeds better ever afterwards. This is what the French maxim-monger meant when he told us that one honour is security for more. Poor Faddleton neither had any honours, except his hereditary one, which was but small, nor was he likely to win them. The world, which is never quite right in its conclusions, had long ago agreed to consider him a goose, who had neither claws nor golden eggs, and who could be therefore securely shelved and forgotten.

There was another class of persons attached to our Embassy at Constantinople, whose existence I confess I could never contemplate without being filled with a serene joy. They were the Interpreters. In other British Embassies the ignorance of the staff respecting the language of the country in which they are sent to reside, is only tacitly connived at, and the price paid for translations of official documents is put into what is called the "Extraordinary Expense" account. But at Constantinople this ignorance was proudly acknowledged, and a species of interpreter had grown up indigenous to the place. The chief of them was officially rewarded with a salary of £1,000 a year. These gentlemen—I mean the Interpreters—display the beauty of our diplomatic system in a very refreshing and delightful manner; for it must be borne in mind that the very keystone of that system is secrecy.

Now let us, just to pass a few idle moments, examine into the position of diplomatic interpreters, and we shall at once see how well and effectively this system is carried out. In the first place, then, they are Foreigners; they are not English gentlemen. In official rank they are beneath our seventh unpaid Attaché, a raw lad of nineteen. In fact, the members of the Embassy snub them and look down upon them as inferiors. It is needless to say that they are cordially despised in return, and that no social or friendly intercourse is possible between them. Thus there is no general society of which they form part to cry shame on the Interpreters if they do things, now and then, which ought to be left undone; and yet it is through the hands of these gentlemen that pass all those secret and confidential things which we take so much pains to hide. They have brothers and cousins, fathers and uncles in trade; men who make their bread on the Exchange; and they have relations who serve as interpreters to the Embassies of other countries, whose interests clash with ours. They form a class apart, with their own morality and their own feelings. I wonder, therefore, how many or how few of the private and confidential affairs of Embassies, likely to affect the price of funds or other public securities, are communicated by these gentlemen to each other, or whether they have always been proof against the witchery of gold and the attraction of promising speculations without risk. These Interpreters, it must be remembered, are bound to us by no ties of patriotism or nationality, but merely by such private notions of honour as are current in the Levant. I would most scrupulously avoid bringing a charge, or even the least shadow of a definite accusation, against any body of men: I simply point out the system at work.

Once upon a time, indeed, there were four Englishmen who were appointed by Lord Palmerston, during his wise administration of our Foreign Affairs, especially to perform the difficult and delicate duties of Interpreters. They were educated at the Government expense, and became admirably fitted for the discharge of their functions. Why they were not employed is a secret probably only known to few. Perhaps some one or more people of influence had a reason for ignoring them.

The duties of Interpreters to most of the other Embassies at Constantinople are filled with gentlemen of the country to which those Embassies belong—and who are bred to the business. In Austria, they are usually chosen from the most distinguished Oriental Scholars of the University of Vienna; in France, they begin their career as *jeunes de langues*. Foreign Embassies have a decided advantage over ours in this respect. Russia, indeed, employs one or two Levantine interpreters, but then every member of her Embassy speaks Turkish, so that it does not matter.

The fact is, our Interpreters ought to be Englishmen and English gentlemen. Their duties are extremely important and demand intelligence of a high order, to fulfil them becomingly. The whole business of the Embassy with the Turkish authorities passes through the hands and minds of these Interpreters; and it depends much upon their understanding and much upon their integrity whether it is well or ill done. There are, perhaps, no diplomatic duties which require more close attention and trained ability, more tact and judgment, than those of an Interpreter in a political negotiation. He should not only render the words of his Chief, but reproduce the very tone and manner in which they are said. A remark made in one voice and repeated in another may have quite a different meaning; and a sulky, stupid fellow might do a good deal in this way to bring about an international misunderstanding—perhaps a war. Every smile, every intonation of a speaker, therefore, ought to be scrupulously copied. A Dragoman should consider himself merely as the instrument and mouthpiece of the negotiator who is using his services. If he explains where he thinks a meaning obscure, if he puts one word more or less into a phrase transmitted through him, he may spoil the work of the finest diplomatists, for no man can possibly know what train of ideas or what line of argument may be in the mind of another, till he sees every link of the chain complete. The most trifling word added or omitted by a thoughtless Interpreter may express more or less than a negotiator intended, and a conjunction or a preposition may be the very keystone of the building he wishes to raise. The cross-examinations of a barrister would be utterly unintelligible if translated into another language without the strictest accuracy.

No one can discharge such duties as these unless he has considered them gravely and long. I will go further, and say that nobody can construe rightly the ideas of one English gentleman but another English gentleman. By the words "English gentleman" I mean a man who has been educated in the ideas of persons of our national standard of honour, and accustomed to live habitually with them. For we have our own straightforward island way of looking at things. We may be right or we may be wrong in our judgment of them; but for my part I believe that a high-minded and honourable Englishman makes the best and safest of negotiators. He must, however, be clearly understood; for if he is bothered and put out by blunders about his meaning, he grows hot and confused. Now in our negotiations with the Turks, the language of no British ambassador is ever completely understood, for the simple reason that not one of the Interpreters employed has a thorough knowledge of English; and even their reports to the Embassy on the most serious occasions are made in a kind of barbarous French, which the Ambassador, in his turn, generally fails to comprehend ; for the French of the Levant and the French of France are two very different languages. An amazing state of confusion is thus kept up. Bless my heart ! have our schools and universities no youths between the ages of ten and twenty-five who will make themselves thoroughly acquainted with the English and Turkish tongues for the fair chance of an honourable career?

To change the theme, I am not at all surprised that the select Parliamentary Committees which from time to time take o inquiring into the state of our Diplomatic Service invariably fail to effect any satisfactory change in it. They are usually put on the wrong scent, and purposely misled by experienced witnesses who wish to conceal everything which they are not obliged to reveal. The members of such Committees, moreover, seldom know very much of the subjects which they meet to investigate, and they spend their time in putting questions altogether wide of any mark, while permanent persons, who have often sly interests in mystifying them, laugh complacently in their sleeves. Occasionally an ill-informed member who wishes to make a figure in the eyes of his constituents after the session is over, or a penny-wise cypherer, looks for some rank and glaring abuse out of which he can coin political capital—and he finds no such abuse. There is no branch of our public service in which conspicuous and easily provable abuses do exist ; but there are many things which might and which ought to work better than they do, and some which require the investigation of clear-headed and resolute people who know what is wrong, and who really desire to set it right. Such men are very rare, whether in or out of Parliament, and those who are out of Parliament may as well be out of the world for any good they can do in England.

I should like to see our Embassies form more of a council than they do. Many heads are better than one. The wisest Ambassador may sometimes be the better for a little wholesome advice, though he will never be induced to take it unless it is imposed upon him. He grants a voice in an affair of importance to any of his Secretaries as grudgingly as an absolute king grants a constitution. It is human nature for placemen to love power. Perhaps, however, if there had been a few moderate councillors and British Interpreters at Constantinople, we might have been saved a deal of cost and trouble on many occasions. All the large foreign Embassies have councillors; why should not we have them also?

I should like to see the duties of each member of an Embassy plainly defined, as in other branches of the public service; so that he may qualify himself to discharge them in the best manner possible, and that he may not be forced into an employment for which he is unfitted by habit and education at the pleasure of a capricious or malevolent chief.

I should like to see men of more mark and importance attached to our Embassies. Our representatives abroad would thus acquire an immense increase of weight and importance. A young lad in his teens can be of no use upon a foreign mission, except to bring it into disrepute while sowing his wild oats. He is a mere incumbrance, and can learn his business much better at home.

The Attachés to our more important foreign Embassies should be chosen from men who have already distinguished themselves, and who, perhaps, need a little repose; from our rising barristers of acknowledged ability, who might study foreign laws from so advantageous a position, and who, by comparing them with our own, might often introduce valuable ameliorations into our legal system on their return home. Sometimes an eminent physician, longing for a year's mental rest in travel, should be appointed to inquire into the treatment of disease abroad, and his reports should be published for the general benefit of the medical profession; sometimes an engineer, an artist, or a skilful soldier* who has drawn all eyes upon him, and whose plans of campaigns might be of infinite importance in war-time, might be sent to pick up such improvements for our army as escape the flying visits of royal Dukes during autumn manœuvres; or even an author, who is a national honour to us, and

---

* Military attachés were appointed to some of our Embassies in consequence of this suggestion.

whose genius fills the world, might occasionally represent us as Bunsen once represented learned Prussia, before she was seized with the scarlet fever, and Prescott and Motley were sent as envoys from the Great Republic.

I have thought more than once that Britain should be represented abroad in her best colours; not as a nation made up of a small cousinhood, with no other person belonging to it fit for any office of trust and honour. Surely a few foreign Embassies composed of our best home-made material, would advance the progress of civilization all over the world; they would carry the healthy spirit of our land from one hemisphere to the other, and bring us back numberless benefits in return. We might thus, too, invest the salaries of our servants at a high interest instead of throwing them away, which would be something altogether new in our practice and history. What stores of useful information—not only to our Government, but to all mankind—might be gleaned by really able and active-minded men, attached to our foreign Missions, and having leisure for prolonged uninterrupted study; by draughtsmen, surveyors, engineers, physicians, soldiers, lawyers, philosophers, and men of science.

The staffs of our Embassies might be much more numerous than they are. At Paris, Vienna, Constantinople, Berlin, Madrid, Rome, and Washington we could hardly have too many clever, sagacious men; while perhaps some of our smaller missions might be reduced or used as diplomatic training schools, especially for the acquirement of foreign languages and methods of transacting public business.

At present our case stands really thus: not one in twenty of our diplomatists knows anything of our real interests, either in art, science, or trade. Perhaps still fewer are able to estimate the value of foreign inventions and ideas as they come into light. Yet there are scores of original-minded men rising up every day in the capitals of foreign countries, and who conceive of marvellous things which never come to the birth for want of a little encouragement. An inventor generally calls at the British Embassy to ventilate his notion, and as often finds that the Ambassador will not receive him, or cannot comprehend the purport of his visit. Fancy grows irritable when trying to imagine the scene which must have often passed between one of the cousinhood and a man of genius with a great thought which had just ripened in him, such as the first scheme of Telegraphy, which is said to have been actually revealed to Lord Asterisk while he was at Vienna, squabbling about the rent of his Lodgings with a Foreign Office clerk called "Timbertoes." Poor old creatures both of them!

Yet Asterisk is but one example out of several. Little as our Ministers at foreign Courts generally know about our real interests, they care less; and this calm state of mind is not the result of any want of good feeling towards their countrymen, but from inability to see where British interests really lie; they have been taught, perhaps, all their lives to look down on traders, and they consider them as an inferior race. They may be living among societies which despise commercial folk, and they learn that habit of mind also. Useful treaties are seldom made, except by men like Ashburton and Bruck, who were altogether out of the regular line.

Now, right or wrong, we seem determined to be a commercial people, and therefore our Envoys abroad should look diligently after the good of that commerce which they are placed in positions of honour and emolument to protect.

This is precisely where our diplomacy fails. It writes home despatches about the sayings and doings of Serene Princes and their relations to the third and fourth generation; about the opinions of this lord or that upon questions which hardly matter to us a button, and which the lords commonly fail to elucidate. It presents the assurance of its high consideration, and it smiles and it dines and bows with curious felicity. That is about all it does.

I do not mean to laugh at the dining part of the business. Lord Palmerston never said a truer thing than when he assured us that dining is the soul of diplomacy. No good was ever done without being on pleasant terms with the people required to do it, and an invitation to dinner is merely an assurance of friendly intentions. It saves a vast deal of trouble, talk, and loss of time; most persons understand this. They feel expansive and good-natured at dinner-time; they are ready to listen to suggestions adroitly made. After the fish and Madeira little angles and asperities of character begin to wear away; a cause is sustained with more wit, and heard with more patience; things could be said which could not be hazarded in a formal audience; and I have known a matter which had kept all the pens of all the Premiers' Private Secretaries in Europe at work brought to a happy issue in taking up the odd trick at whist; for whist, like dining, is part of the education of a diplomatist.

We need not complain, therefore, that our diplomatists dine and make merry; but that they never brighten up and strike out new lights over their feasts. An official peer, of weakish intellect, indeed startled the diplomatic world by saying, in one of his speeches, that an Ambassador is merely the mouthpiece of the Minister who appointed him, and nothing more. But possibly this was a very confused idea of the true function of an Envoy to a Foreign Court. Instead of being merely the mouthpiece and representative of an individual party man, he should be the representative of his people, and the most trusted because the most competent adviser of his nation upon certain special subjects.

No man at the head of our Foreign Office can attend to the details of all the business which all the countries of the world have to transact with the Government of Great Britain. It is the duty of Envoys to relieve the Minister of work which he cannot do himself, and which yet must be done by his department, and under the guarantee of responsible officers belonging to it, who are credited with a general knowledge of public opinion upon every question at issue. It is the duty of an Ambassador to present projects, already formed and examined, for the Minister's approval or rejection. It is the proper function of an Envoy to a Foreign Court to make himself specially acquainted with everything relating to the country where he resides. If he waits for orders from the Minister who appointed him upon many important subjects, which are sure to demand his attention, his mission is a mere farce. The Secretary of State for Foreign Affairs is too busy preparing his seven hours' speech for the House of Commons; with the Brobdignag question, with his pet bill and pet crotchet, with B.'s attack and D.'s defence—to attend to him. Besides, the minister positively dreads any further accumulation of business, and, unless urged by very strong pressure from without, will hardly create new work for himself. Indeed he has no time to investigate questions which are not of immediate interest to his party, as they ought to be investigated.

Therefore, if our Envoys to Foreign Courts and Republics would make themselves thoroughly masters of the commercial relations between the countries to which they are accredited and their own, they might often suggest some important new arrangements; they might put forth ideas of which the value would be evident at a glance, and mark every change of circumstance from which advantage could be drawn. If our diplomatists were a different class of men, I wonder whether international postal treaties would be such clumsy things as they are. There is not an intelligent merchant in any trading city who could not suggest improvements by the handful on this subject alone. British Envoys should mix more with the commercial classes; and contrive always to have intimate acquaintance and constant intercourse with the foremost traders corresponding with each other in both countries where business is entrusted to their protection. In short, there should be a few more hard-working heads at the tables of Ambassadors, and a few less stars of the order of the Tartar.

Diplomatic agents might do an incalculable amount of good if they could only be taught—or it might be fairer, in some cases, to say *encouraged*—to take a larger view of their missions than they do—if, instead of keeping a scandalous chronicle of foreign courts and notabilities, they made it their business to become acquainted with the wants and produce of the country in which they live, and to see how it could best be brought into more mutually advantageous dealings with their own.

It may be urged that a great deal of the business above mentioned is the proper concern of Consuls, and that the duties of Ambassadors are altogether different. If so the public should be infinitely obliged to any one who would boldly point out the nature and character of Ambassadorial functions. Are

Ambassadors appointed to spy by deputy upon the actions of royal and imperial families, so that they can neither eat, drink, cough, nor sleep without being the objects of impertinent curiosity? If so such functions are degrading to all parties concerned in their performance, and are most completely and perfectly useless.

The truth is, our diplomatic service has been allowed altogether to run riot. . Instead of being a most important part of the machinery of an enlightened and progressive State, alive both to her own interests and to the general advancement of civilization, it has been allowed to become the mere useless lumber of an obsolete statecraft; and it is at once expensive and mischievous. It would be easy to cite many instances in which our Government has been dragged into discreditable scrapes by its Envoys; but this is neither the time nor place for such a discussion.

On the other hand, the Consular service has been remarkably well looked after. Lord Palmerston's numerous regulations for the guidance of Consuls are models of language, style, and proper feeling, and though the circulars of some of his successors have not been always so happily expressed, yet it is often easy to trace through them the same hearty English right-mindedness. The Consuls were chiefly men of humble rank, who could be told what they were required to do. It was impossible to use the same freedom with Lord Manyvotes. But Consuls, however well instructed, have quite enough to do with the details of commerce; they are the working guides and police of trade. It is for Ambassadors to consider first principles, to suggest, and to negotiate; it is for the Consul to carry out instructions, and to report how new things work. It is, above all, his duty to supply those facts and figures which are the materials with which a diplomatist builds up his designs.

In the present stage of the world's history perhaps we could altogether dispense with resident Ambassadors and Ministers, if we want our work done in the most efficient manner. Their pride and pretensions are not only ridiculous, but they are terribly in the way of public business. The diplomatic corps, as a body, is offensive to every government in the world, because of its arrogance. We should have, therefore, no permanent embassies at all. The objects for which they were established have ceased to exist. When news was scarce, and intercourse between nations rare and difficult, it might serve a sound purpose to have the power and majesty of a great nation represented by the quantity of lace on an Ambassador's coat, and the number of tawdry servants in his suite. Now all the nations of the world know each other too well to have any need of such follies. A black coat and a walking-stick are as potent, for all national purposes, as a harlequin's jacket and a marshal's truncheon.

For ordinary current business in a Foreign capital, a Chargé d'Affaires is always sufficient. If on any special occasion an Ambassador is wanted to manage some particular piece of business he should be selected with a view to his fitness for the work in hand. The salary of a Chargé d'Affaires might be fairly fixed at £3,000 a year, exclusive of table money, at Paris, Berlin, Vienna, Rome, St. Petersburg, and Washington; at other places it might conveniently vary between £1,000 and £2,000 a year. Table money, in the larger capitals, should be put at £1,000 a year, and would be money well spent. If, however, it appeared really desirable at any time to choose a special man for a special purpose he should be paid in accordance with the value of his time, and the necessities of his mission; and by all means let him have any title he might fancy, or which would facilitate the business of his Embassy. No people governed by a rational administration should ever be subjected to the expense and humiliation of having two Ambassadors at the same time at the same place. All the higher diplomatic missions should be temporary; and when an Ambassador has done the special business for which he was appointed, he should be recalled. If he has earned his country's gratitude, it will always be easy to employ him in some other way; if not he can retire into private life as unfit for public service, at least in that direction. It is manifest that in all serious international questions this manner of acting would be attended with advantage, and that a negotiator having special knowledge of the business confided to him would be much more likely to bring it to a useful and satisfactory issue than a man who had never given five minutes' attention to the subject in his life. It is therefore a queer sort of blunder to make Diplomacy a close profession.

The fact is, the rank and privileges of an Ambassador are in the way of his duties. It is proper, indeed, to appoint men of a certain recognized position in the world as personal representatives of the Sovereign, because it is absolutely necessary that they should be in constant intercourse with the first men of other countries. But here the necessity ends, and innumerable squabbles and absurdities for which we have to suffer would be done away with by having Chargés d'Affaires instead of men of higher official rank. I speak of *official* rank because any other rank is of course mere moonshine and water; nobody pays attention to it whose opinion is worth having.

Heaven knows how long ago it is since Miss Edgeworth pointed out the evils of Patronage in one of the best novels ever written. Heaven knows how long since it is that Pitt said, with a sigh, "he had never, but on one single occasion in his life, been able to appoint the right man to the right place." Yet the evil of Patronage exists to this day—it flourishes even; it has passed into the catalogue of hoary abuses, and promises to have as prolonged an existence as the Wandering Jew.

The mischief is that a vast deal too many people look to Government for employment. High place is not, as it ought to be, the reward for great services rendered to the State, or the meed of evident abilities. It is merely an inheritance in certain families: and it is considered as a provision for their dependants with as much certainty as any other species of hereditary property. It is shocking to hear, every now and then, of some man of great intellect dying in the utmost distress; of another cutting his throat with the bailiffs on his staircase; of a third slowly breaking his heart—while the very places they seem born to fill and to adorn are seized as of right by a tribe of Tweedledums and Tweedledees, who have no quality of any kind to recommend them except their pedigrees. Heaven and earth! what is a pedigree? Can any one give an explanation of his pedigree, which will hold water? It may be a sort of guarantee for the honesty and decent behaviour of a very young person; but as an indication of capacity it is null. Great men have no successors. They are usually the first and the last of their race.

Among all the ill-considered things which Lord Russell has written and said, perhaps he never emitted a fallacy more unstatesmanlike than when he announced his opinion that Government ought not to provide for eminent literary men.* If Government do not provide for men who are the glory of their age and country, who will provide for them? Are we to have another Otway choked by a crust, another Chatterton die by his own hand in an obscure garret; another Johnson insulted by the offer of a pair of shoes? It is precisely the very highest order of talent which is the most ill-remunerated. There are scholars who would gladly render a chorus of Æschylus into English verse at a penny a line. Political essays will not sell at all unless they are written in the interests of a party for a party newspaper. No book of importance likely to be expensive in the getting up will sell in manuscript; and scientific works go begging by the dozen for a publisher. Masterpieces which will last as long as the English language endures—Milton's "Paradise Lost," and Gibbon's "Rome,"—certainly never paid the expenses incurred while writing them; and one need hardly cite more striking examples.

While all the world are running after Government appointments, one of the most profitable books published of late years points out plainly the means of obtaining them. They are notoriously bartered for political considerations or private friendship. Fitness and interest of the public service have nothing at all to do with the chances of a candidate. Places under Government, to be sure, are anything but highly paid. They are not always agreeable, but they require small abilities, and no experience; the veriest dunce may fill the highest posts, paid by the public taxation. We have men enough in England whose recognized talents, whose writings, or whose speeches show as plainly as possible their aptitude for public employ-

* *See* Russell's "Life of Moore," the Biography of a Poet, by a small politician, who has dropped all the points of it.

ment. But the governing families resolutely ignore their existence. Connection they persist in holding as the first thing necessary for royal honours and rewards, and there is a joke on the subject which has passed into history. When Lord Nortiman was appointed Minister Plenipotentiary at Vienna, one of the Kinskis, who prided himself upon his knowledge of our language, asked lazily of a grey-headed secretary of legation, "What are his antecedents?" "Oh!" replied the disappointed subordinate, "you had better ask who are his relatives."

Are you, expectant reader, a cousin of the great Duke of Drowsylands? Do you belong to the eccentric family of the Stranges? Did you marry into the cousinhood? Are you the son of the confidential steward of Lord Hussle's first wife's half-brother, who is a rich man like to die? Have you got a friend with a borough in his pocket and who does not want anything for himself? If so, nothing in the world is easier than to get a place. If not, go dig.

If any one wishes to see patronage in another point of view, he will not have far to look. Not very long ago, a certain diplomatic post was suppressed at the request of a Foreign Government; and the person to whom it had been given was shelved with a pension of £1,000 a year. He was quite a young man, and, what is rare in the higher ranks of the public service, a remarkably able one; yet there he was, in the prime of life, quartered in idleness upon other men's earnings to the end of his days.

He was fully capable of filling almost any official situation whatever in our public service; but it was easier to give pensions than to find vacancies, and the Government of the day wanted every one which fell in for their own supporters. Patronage is such an excellent thing that the most honourable man hardly blushes to sell his vote and influence for it, if the affair can be managed with any delicacy at all; and it must be confessed that the Ministry of the day was hard pressed. Well, it was not long after the bestowal of this snug pension that the young pensioner's friends returned to power, and they lost no time in providing for him afresh. But he kept his pension, and possibly got another when his friends went out of office again.

Yet it would seem that the remedy for all this nonsense is not hard to find, and that one cure for it would be to submit the list of candidates for public offices every session to Parliament when the supplies are voted. The Ministers of the several departments might have the advantage of recommending this man or that; but his appointment should be in all cases ratified, at least by the tacit consent of Parliament, so that if there should be any well-grounded objection to the appointment of any particular person it might be heard and discussed. A Minister would be ashamed to recommend a Nortiman or a Drone if the business were not carried on quite so snugly in the dark.

The system of requiring the sanction of Parliament to the bestowal of public offices would soon do away with the abuses which cling like barnacles to our administration. But reform is a fearful word, and the mere sound of it nowadays scares every man but a hero. It is so hard to persuade people that everything is not quite right; even if they suspect it to be wrong they would rather not be assured of the fact, and when experienced persons speak of men who hold the terrible engines of power in their hands, they know it is only safe to do so with hats off and bated breath. Moreover, the formation of opinion in most minds is as curious as the obstinacy with which opinions become fixed there. The majority of mankind are like sponges, and imbibe whatever comes in their way; they think this or that because they have heard somebody express these views; somebody, perhaps, who knows as little on the subject to which they refer as themselves. Many persons have also a numerous class of inherited opinions, that were held by their uncles, their guardians—who knows? perhaps by their grandmothers—and all these seem to them as the very essence of superior wisdom; whoever has the misfortune to differ with them, or to hold altogether contrary notions, is tabooed as a dangerous fellow; and this is why reforming the world is such a thankless task.

CHAPTER III.

THE PASHA.

THE Pasha is a pleasant elderly gentleman, and a great friend of mine. He is about forty-two years old, he says, not being very particular on this subject; but he looks a fair fifty. He attributes this circumstance to the cares of wedded life, and to the imprudent act of having married a wife at fifteen. I inwardly believe this a libel on the Turkish ladies, but I could not banter the Pasha on such a subject, for the harem is forbidden ground even for a hint to stand upon. Upon the whole, therefore, I think it is best to acquiesce in the forty-two, and take those years for granted. The Pasha himself believes devoutly in them; so will I.

Picture to yourself, reader, a tall, spare, aristocratic-looking gentleman. Gentleman is the only word which would give you any idea of the Pasha; it is written by Nature's own hand on every feature; seen in every quiet dignified movement; in every subdued smile; in every lofty and winning courtesy belonging to him. The man would break his heart if his ermine were defiled. He was born a knight, after the old romantic idea of such an individual, and he will live and die with a name as unsullied as Bayard or Amadis of Gaul. I believe it would be physically impossible for him to utter an untruth; to forget his honourable pride; or to do one mean, paltry, or unworthy action. I have a high opinion of the Pasha; I would take his plain simply-spoken word in almost any possible circumstances; and I would place any interest which I held dearly, in his keeping as fearlessly as in that of a Christian gentleman. To get him thoroughly before your mind's eye, however, you must give fancy the rein. His dress is a plain single-breasted coat, of the rich plum-colour which the Turks love; it is made of a peculiar cloth, which I understand comes chiefly from Belgium.

The Pasha's trousers are too large for him—I am sorry to say that I cannot deny the fact : they give him the appearance of being bow-legged : they are too long, too wide, too baggy generally. Indeed, it is surprising to me how he keeps them on, as braces appear to be an undiscovered mystery in Turkey. The Pasha wears two pairs of shoes, one pair over the other ; the under-shoes are of exquisitely fine Russian leather, about the consistence of an English kid glove ; his over-shoes, which he puts on when he goes abroad, are the unromantic blucher. The top of the Pasha's head is surmounted by a small fez or red cap, which the late Sultan brought into fashion : it has a tassel of at least half a pound weight of corded blue silk. Beneath it is a finely-worked linen lining detached from the cap and peeping in a snowy ring all round it : this is the sign of a Turkish dandy. His cap is also surmounted by a broad flat circular piece of gold : this is his badge of service as a Turkish officer ; and I wish it was always worn as worthily. It is, of course, needless to add that the Pasha wears his coat buttoned up to his chin, and is far too military a genius to shew anything in the shape of a shirt-collar. He displays no decoration or mark of his rank, but on his right-hand little finger gleams a diamond ring, which once belonged to the Dey of Algiers, and cost £1,000. The expression of the Pasha's face is mild and placid almost to a fault ; his nose is aquiline, his beard spare, his mouth well cut, and his eye lively and well opened ; his voice is as habitually low and soft as those heard in well-regulated English drawing-rooms. When he is at home, he sits generally wrapped up in a dressing-gown lined with furs, and put on over his other clothes (for he tells me the climate even in June is treacherous). With his legs curled up beneath him on the sofa, he gives his calm audiences to suitors, who prostrate themselves before him as soon as they enter his presence. When he wants anything, he touches a little spring bell, which is placed beside him ; it makes one *tink*, and in a minute several of the fifty-six servants he keeps come noiselessly in, and await his commands with their right hands placed above their hearts. When he has spoken, they touch their foreheads in sign of unquestioning and implicit obedience ; then they disappear as silently as they had entered his presence. The "yezzir" of a British hotel waiter would, I believe, cause the Pasha immediately to faint away; for his Excellency has a great opinion of his own importance, and upon the whole inclines rather to the belief that the world was made for that class of its inhabitants to which he belongs. It is not surprising; for most orders of men secretly cherish the same idea, however unwilling they might be to confess it.

Generally speaking, it may be said to be an agreeable thing to be a Turkish Pasha: he is not indeed so potent and despotic a prince as an Ambassador; he cannot utterly destroy the comfort of every one about him; he cannot exile this officer and disgrace that; he is obliged to permit gentlemen holding commissions under the Turkish Government in the same place with him, quietly and peaceably to fulfil the duties for which they were appointed; but he is nevertheless a personage of great power and authority: he is about as absolute a provincial governor as can be conceived. It is therefore pleasant to add, that he is as easy and good-humoured as the majority of his fellow Pashas in other places: indeed, his power of late years has been rather nominal than real: he is fettered a good deal by personal enemies in the *medglis* or mixed tribunal, by the intrigues of the Greeks, and by the growing power of the press. He is obliged, therefore, to be something of a trimmer in his official conduct, and he is mightily afraid of the European consuls, who all watch him like so many policemen in private clothes, and often worry him out of health and spirits with their litigious and troublesome conduct. They interfere in the affairs of his command on the most improper occasions, and they hector him with singular effrontery. Of course, if the Pasha was well acquainted with European politics, and understood the real position of these gentlemen, he would not tolerate their impertinent pretensions upon any terms; but he is not a traveller, he is of the old school, and his education has been neglected. It is a painful thing, however, to see the courteous and highbred old gentleman so often cowed by their vulgar and unauthorized bullying; and I venture to state my opinion publicly, that no part of our own or other services needs more careful and prompt reforms than that of the foreign consuls in Turkey. I have heard, though I do not take it upon myself positively to vouch for the truth of my information, that there was a certain petty consular officer who made a demand for pecuniary compensation to one of his subjects, who had received some wrong at the hands of a Turk. The money not being immediately forthcoming, I have been told that this representative of great and just England presented himself to the Pasha, accompanied by a captain in the navy. I blush to continue, I hope I have been deceived, but it has been positively stated to me that the petty consular officer above mentioned now angrily repeated his demand. "Sir," said the Pasha, "I have not as yet been able to obtain you the compensation you demand; allow me to repeat to you my regret, with the assurance that no effort on my part shall be wanting to see your subject satisfied." "Tell him he is a barbarian," roared the consular functionary, through his dragoman; "and that if the money be not at once paid into my hands, the town shall be laid in ashes in one hour from this time." So the Pasha, trembling, sent for his own private money-box, and paid the indemnity forthwith; and the consular officer received it, and his nautical friend (who should undoubtedly have been cashiered) smiled, and the matter ended. I repeat that I do not and will not vouch for the truth of this anecdote; but the very fact of its being in circulation is enough to make one's flesh crawl with indignation, and it speaks much for the abuses of the consular system in Turkey.

It would be a mistake to suppose that the Pasha profits by his office in a pecuniary point of view: on the contrary, it costs him money. His pay is about £700 a year, and his mere charities, with the necessary or customary expenses of his post, must exceed £1,000. After the fashion of his brethren, he keeps a whole army of retainers; and every now and then he finds it good policy to send a valuable present to Constantinople, otherwise he would lose his place: or at least this event would be highly probable. Upon the whole, perhaps, in round numbers the pashalik costs him £1,500 a year, besides the pay he derives from it: the sum, however, is a mere bagatelle to him, for, though he would not own it for anything, he is really one of the richest gentlemen in Turkey, his father and grandfather having both made very large fortunes in trade. When I say that he is one of the richest gentlemen in Turkey, I mean that he may have £20,000 or £25,000 a year in land,—of course there are many far richer; but this may still be called a first-class fortune in the East. Having said so much, it is proper to add that my Pasha is not a portrait; he is the type of a class, and few persons who have lived familiarly with the higher order of Turks will fail to recognize him in many places.

I have said the Pasha would be sorry to avow that he is a rich man: but in ways of concealment he goes much farther than this. So strong is the force of tradition, and so dangerous was it at one time to be reputed wealthy, that there is no nobility in the world more deeply indebted than the Turkish Pashas; they borrow money at exorbitant interest, not because they want it, but to conceal the true state of their fortune; and a man who has perhaps £100,000 sterling buried somewhere in the ground, will designedly seem to have the utmost difficulty in paying a thousand piastres. The Pashas as a class are kept poor by the number of their useless retainers, the constant drain for presents to the higher authorities, and the general muddle which seems to cling inevitably to all Turkish affairs. Besides, they are bad financiers, and though some of them have acute ideas enough on trading matters, very few can be made to comprehend the advantage of profitable investments. Till very lately there was no national debt in Turkey; there are * still no banks, no railroads, none of those enterprises on a grand scale which present an attractive employment for private fortune; and if there were, the Turk would long look shyly on them.

In concluding this sketch, let me describe a visit to the Pasha, and I think I shall then have exhausted all I have to say about him. It is early morning, and I have something to communicate to my friend, so I shall send to know when he can receive me; the polite answer is soon returned: " His Excellency will receive me at once." I may as well say, that

* 1853. Few Turks of the old school invested much of their hoards in their country's bonds. Possibly they foresaw what might happen.

so great is British influence in Turkey, however, that I believe his Excellency would receive me in the middle of the night if he had just gone to bed with a severe cold. Foreign officers usually pay official visits preceded by a cavass to clear the way, and accompanied by their secretary and interpreter; I, of course, being a shadow, and going to a shadowy Pasha, proceed alone. A quarter of an hour's walk brings me to a large rambling whitewashed house. This is the konaki, or Pasha's residence. A score of armed men are lounging about the court-yard, also some suitors, and some dogs: a rabble rout of slippers of all sizes and denominations encumber the threshold. Having passed over these without stumbling, I am received by the Pasha's chief secretary, who conducts me up a broad flight of wooden stairs, the banisters of which are painted red. Making our way through a bowing crowd of cavasses, hojas, petitioners, and all sorts of people who already throng the anteroom, we soon come before a heavy curtain, which serves for a door to the Pasha's private apartment. This curtain is noiselessly drawn back, the word is passed to the men-at-arms that the Pasha is giving an official audience, and is not to be disturbed. The next moment we are in his presence. He has risen and advanced to meet his shadowy guest—he takes me by the hand and presses it almost affectionately; then he leads me to a place beside him, and we sit down together.

It would be a breach of all etiquette to begin upon business at once, so we look round the room. It is a large apartment, with a bright copper mangal or charcoal-burner placed in the centre of the matted floor; it has a sofa and some chairs for furniture,—nothing more; the ceiling, and the little cupboards (like pigeon-holes) let into the wall, are quaintly painted; the open windows have a grand view of the surrounding country, and a fine Dollond telescope beside my friend testifies to the interest he takes in the prospect. Indeed, looking through this telescope is, I know, one of his most favourite and constant amusements; it is his occupation, his relief and consolation amid the affairs of state. As I am taking mental note of these things, two servants enter, always in the same silent way; they bring two pipes, each of the same size, and each with jewelled amber mouthpieces. These attendants draw themselves up opposite to us like automatons; each puts his right hand on his heart, two other servants place silver pipe-trays for the bowls to rest upon, and the next moment we are inhaling some wonderful tobacco, the first draught of smoke penetrating both our lungs at precisely the same time, though the Pasha had half a second the advantage of me in the presentation of the pipe, to mark his quality of host: he would explain this, if I were to ask him, by saying it is Turkish hospitality first to taste yourself whatever you offer to a guest.

The pipe business being disposed of, there enter two other attendants: one bears a crimson napkin, richly embroidered with gold, over his left shoulder; the other a coffee-tray, with cups of elegant filagree-work. These servants are usually the most favoured of an Oriental household. We are presented, in the same manner, with two small cups of unsweetened and unstrained coffee; and then the attendants retire, and I open my business.

Everything, of course, goes upon wheels. Sir Palaver Tweedledum himself could not make things pleasanter than the Pasha. If I wanted his signet ring (upon which he has just breathed, and used on the spot to sign an official document I have requested of him)—I might have it; if I asked for the best horse in his stable—for the loan of the wonderful fur dressing-gown—or any possible thing under the moon—I might have it for the asking. Never mind; we must try the more earnestly to ask nothing incompatible with the strict principles of justice and good feeling; we must be the more fully aware of the solemn responsibility which rests upon every British public servant in Turkey. Let us turn the conversation; let us tell the Pasha all sorts of stray odds and ends of news from Europe, which he asks after so anxiously; while we listen, in return, to his ideas on things in general, and on politics in particular. They have the true game-flavour about them; a racy smack that is quite refreshing. You and I, and Smith and Thompson, all think the same way: I would not give a button to hear either of you; I might as well talk to myself. But the Pasha has got quiet ideas of his own stowed away in sly corners of his mind, such as might make the hairs of common men to stand upon an end. Well, we shall go chatting away very pleasantly for an hour or two, smoking chibouques and laughing in our sleeves till his Excellency has got quite a colour with the invigorating exercise. Then I shall depart. Again the Pasha will get up and lead me by the hand to the doorway; and then he will draw his gallant figure up to its full height, and take leave of me with the air of a prince and the cordial words of an honest man; and to-morrow or the day after, a gorgeous apparition of arms and gold embroidery will appear at my house, and ask when I will receive the Pasha; and I shall also answer, at once. Then the Pasha will come on horseback, with running footmen and pipe-bearers beside him; and the folding-doors of my little cottage will be thrown wide open to receive him. The neighbourhood will assemble with a mixture of awe and admiration; there will be a clattering of arms in the hall; and the Pasha, with his sword on his thigh, will stride through with the mien of a king. My Greek servant, who has been sent to borrow some coffee-cups next door, and who has a talent for getting things in a pickle, will enter behind him; and as I step forward with a smile and a bow to welcome my grand acquaintance, I shall see Demetri, coffee-cups and all, tripped up by a cavass's sword, and falling with a mighty crash. But the Pasha never turns his head: he knows very well what a European household is in Turkey. There is but one thing more to be noticed; and it is, that whereas I gave but 30s. as the official present to the Pasha's servants, I learn, when he has departed, by the exultation of Demetri and the statelier joy of Hamet, that his Excellency has given mine £2.

CHAPTER IV.

MY CAVASS AND I.

MY Cavass is eminently a fine gentleman. The Greeks say that he walks like a lady in an interesting condition : I should be rather inclined to describe his gait as a tragedy stalk, like that of a tragedian of very great power at a provincial theatre; but this is merely a difference of opinion. A Cavass is a sort of body-guard or man-at-arms off duty, who is the indispensable appendage of an official personage in the great country where I am accredited. I have a Cavass, therefore, because I am an official personage. I am her Britannic Majesty's deputy-assistant sub-vice consular agent at the island of Barataria. My former profession was that of dancing-master at a ladies' school. It was at my school that Lord Luckidown, eldest son of the pauperized Earl of Strawtherby, met his wife, the then Miss Plumbus, eldest daughter of Plumbus, the great tea-man, of the firm of Plumbus, Chops, and Twigging, who died worth one million and a half sterling. This is the reason why I was appointed out of gratitude, and by the interest of his Lordship, when he got into Parliament, as deputy-assistant sub-vice consular agent to the island above mentioned ; and why the Pasha and barbarians of the place are made to tremble at my nod. It is also, probably, why I am not averse to nodding as often as an occasion turns up which admits of my so doing.

It is an instructive and refreshing sight to see me walk abroad with my Cavass. He carries a stout stick, and he uses it with singular diligence and vivacity on the heads of all who come between the wind and my nobility. Being representative of a friendly power, I love to show the importance of my Government, of my mission, and of myself. This is the cause of my being preceded by a Cavass with a stout stick, whenever I appear among the base, common, and popular of Barataria. My Cavass and I are about on a par in our knowledge and fitness for the public service, and we entertain very much the same idea of the duties which have devolved upon us; we cherish a conviction that they may be briefly summed up in a frequent and vigorous use of the stout stick. We are not fond of arguing; we consider truth and discussion as a mere useless disturbance of our opinions on this or on any other subject; and it is but justice to us to add, that our notions are those of the majority of Levant consuls.

I am not a Levant consul, but I am a sort of apology for one; and I live in the halo of that glory which surrounds my august and potent chief. My Cavass and I have really irresponsible power over the liberties and comforts of the whole population of Barataria, and it comprises nearly eighty thousand souls. This power was secured in a very striking and agreeable manner by my predecessor (Lord Fitztoady's steward's favourite sister's son) in a dispute about the right of a Maltese sailor to knock somebody down, and to receive compensation for the damage done to his knuckles on the occasion. The Pasha did not seem to be clear-witted on the subject; for, although he is, as I have just said, a gentle, dignified old person enough, he is rather slow. My predecessor, therefore, whose name was Podger, took advantage of the arrival of a British man-of-war to enlighten his understanding, and to quicken his motions. Podger and the commander condescended to pay a visit to the governor in person. "Tell him," roared Podger to his dragoman, who fortunately could not speak English; "tell him he is a brute, a beast, a lout, a barbarian, a brigand, a cheat, a scoundrel; and that unless he pays for my subject's knuckles, which have been injured by the jaw-bone of the miscreant who is cursed by his rule, we will batter his town about his ears. Tell him this; tell him this!" And then Podger, aware of his interpreter's deficiency, made a sound as if of cannon, and thrust his beard (a remarkably angry beard) within a short space of the Pasha's nose. That reverend old gentleman, comprehending the actions of the deputy-assistant vice-consular Podger better than his words, began to tremble. He had strength enough to gasp out a request, however, that his life might be spared; and an humble asseveration that he would do anything or anybody it might please Podger to have done. By means of the word "para," however (which signifies money), and the frequent use of his beard, and some complicated digital arithmetic, the Pasha was made at last to understand that Podger insisted on receiving compensation in money for "his subject's" knuckles. It is needless to add that the money was paid; and I should like to hear of the quiet, gentle, dignified old Pasha ever bringing anything to a wrangle again with a representative of any future assistant sub-vice-consular agent of her Britannic Majesty at the island of Barataria.

Indeed, what with the consequence consumed by me and my Cavass, as well as by the consuls, and the assistants, and sub-vices, of the other protecting powers, together with that used up by each special and particular Cavass of each and every of these extremely amiable foreign officials, the Pasha of Barataria has mighty little consequence of his own left. He is generally obliged to sing small, to use a mild and familiar expression. He is considered rather in the light of a bell-rope for angry consular agents to pull at, than anything else; and whenever they want anything which ought not to be granted, he is pulled until he tingles sufficiently to cause what is wanted to be brought.

My Cavass and I are perfectly above the jurisdiction of the barbarians among whom we live. We pay neither taxes nor respect to anybody, and treat the world in general from the extreme height of our grandeur with condign indignity. There is nobody who could be found bold enough to make any observation to us; for we are our own parliament, judges, jury, police, and executioners. We cannot hang malcontents, to be sure; but our power only stops short of hanging people; and indeed, if once we were to get seriously out of humour, we might scourge, and cuff, and make things so desperately uncomfortable to the Baratarians in general, as to occasion a wholesale transportation.

My Cavass and I are accustomed to be treated with distinction, in consequence of these powers and attributes. When we deign to go and show off our ill-temper to the local authorities, we insist that horses and proper attendants shall be sent to fetch us. When we are visited by meaner people, we expect that they will acknowledge the happiness of being admitted into our sublime presence by taking off their shoes, and raising the dust from our shoes to their foreheads. We do not, indeed, receive tribute in money; but we take it out in adoration. Upon the whole, perhaps, my Cavass and I are rather more locally absolute than the Emperor of Russia; and woe to the abandoned wretch who declines to koo-too to us. We mark him down in our black books, and he may understand thenceforth that it would be inconvenient to him to have any affair to settle with her Britannic Majesty's deputy-assistant sub-vice-consular agency.

My Cavass has another important prerogative from which I am unhappily debarred. It is that of making British subjects: when any of the natives of Barataria desire to cease the payment of taxes to their own Government, and the disagreeable ceremony of submission to the laws of their land, they are apt to present themselves at the D.A.S.V.C. office, and to express their wish for a passport. I cannot speak Turkish, nor Greek, nor Italian, nor anything else but English and a few words of dog French, which my Cavass understands. I therefore refer to this functionary with the interrogatory, "Anglaise sudjit?" "O Dios!" replies my Cavass, laying his two hands by turn on his heart and his head. I understand this as an affirmative answer. Some papers are then presented to me which I cannot read; one of them I suppose to be a certificate of the applicant's baptism in some British possession. I know there are no means by which such a document can be recognized with certainty, even if genuine; I know that it bears no stamp nor official mark of any kind, as it ought to do. I am, therefore, more or less indifferent; and create by my sign manual the law-breaker a subject of my Queen, exempt from his native taxes, his native bastinado, and maybe from his native bow-string. Thus another sham native of Britain is created, and another national affront is offered to a weary and helpless ally of Britannic Majesty. I believe that British subject-making forms a recognized portion of the revenues of my Cavass.

For the rest, my Cavass and I are by no means bad sort of people. I was an excellent dancing-master, and a very decent member of society, before I was sent to Barataria vice Podger (promoted, in consequence of his father having lent money to young Fitztoady, who was a wild lad before he came into the peerage). More power than is good for them has turned the heads of all official personages in Barataria; it has also turned mine. Perhaps if my head had been a little stronger, it would not have been turned quite so much; but it would probably have been turned more stiffly; so it does not much matter. I am not too inflated or too stupid to see that I am merely a person whose official existence in a responsible post should be impossible; in other respects I am a nonentity. If I had been otherwise, the Lord Cacus, who appoints all the servants on this establishment, would never have thought of me for a moment. That cautious creature desires, like another Atlas, to carry the world entirely upon his own shoulders; and if though a large gentleman, he is not quite strong enough for such a burthen, this fact is more perceptible to others than to himself. One thing is also quite certain, that he would sooner let his load fall and smash it, as he has done before now, than receive any sort of assistance, advice, or counsel, from his nearest blood or party connection. I am not the less a mighty man at Barataria; and I know that so long as I do nothing which ought to be done, I shall preserve the regard and good-will of the big man in Downing Street. I know that by neglecting all serious duties, I have everything to hope from his patronage; while if I were ever to display the smallest intelligence, he would infallibly ruin me.

My Cavass is conscious of these sentiments on my part; and he therefore carefully keeps from me all persons who are likely to break in with troublesome projects or information upon that tranquillity which is essential to the dignity of a deputy-assistant sub-vice consular agent of her Most Gracious Majesty the Queen of the United Kingdom of Great Britain and Ireland. The consequence is, that I know no more of what is going on within ten yards of my house, than I do of the immediate affairs of Bokhara or Samarcand. My chief is fond of making valuable discoveries for himself; and if I were once to break in upon his gainful labours by a truthful communication, I might as well be officially dead. The affairs of the world have been going on, (I hear) also, far too pleasantly of late for correct information to be of use to anybody; and there is nothing I admire more in my august superior than his determined and consistent antipathy to all sorts of facts.

And now, paymaster public, farewell until quarter-day. You have read enough about me and my Cavass to understand that we are an ornament to the good old sleepy service to which we belong. We aim at the highest merit which that service recognizes; the merit—officially speaking—of doing nothing. I can lay my hand on my heart and declare most conscientiously that, in that respect, I do my duty thoroughly. Hence, I am in hourly expectation of having my inutility rewarded with promotion. My Cavass lives in a similar hope. You will therefore pay proper respect to us; and then your business with us ends. We are willing, indeed, to receive your money, but we wish to hear nothing further about you. A word in your ear, also :—If ever you should make a tour in the East, I would very strongly advise you as a prudent fellow to keep out of the way of me and my Cavass.

CHAPTER V.

THE CADI.

THE Cadi is an august apparition, and I sit in a kiosch, or summer-house, which overlooks the sea, conversing with him. We are having one of those dear dreamy conversations that I used to love in old time, when I lived among the quaint and simple scholars of pleasant Germany. But I think that the talk of the Cadi is still more strange and amusing. There is a delightful and childlike gravity about it, which refreshes and improves me as I listen.

Let me describe the Cadi. He is a tall, fair man, beautiful as the hero of an Eastern tale. He wears a snow-white turban on his head, and flowing robes, of a texture at once rich and delicate. I am sorry, upon the whole, that the Cadi wears the British shoe, because I think he would look better in Turkish slippers: I would rather not look at his feet therefore; my eyes repose with much greater pleasure on the chaplet of amber beads which he is playing with, and on his dignified and manly beard. His face wears an expression of habitual good humour, and there is that general sunny openness about it which bespeaks a clear conscience. If I were a prisoner, I should like to be judged by the Cadi, for I am sure that his judgment would be tempered by mercy. I think you might believe in the Cadi's word as implicitly as in that of the best gentlemen in Europe; I feel instinctively that he is incapable of anything tricky or vulgar; there is a something at once frank and grand about the man; he commands immediate friendship and respect from all who know him.

One of the Cadi's attendants has refilled our pipes, and he presents them silently, with his right-hand upon his heart. He presents the Cadi his pipe first, according to the custom of the East; but the Turkish gentleman smiles a mute apology to me as he takes it, and does not place it to his lips until I am served. Then, as we sink back luxuriously in our cushions, and the westerly breezes come trooping in through the open window, the Cadi requests that I will "be at large." This is a Turkish manner of telling me to make myself at home; and I take it in that sense.

I now inform the Cadi that I called on him a few days since, and was so unlucky as not to find him at home. I merely say this by way of commencing the conversation; but the open brow of the Cadi looks quite troubled, and he tells me that when he returned and found that I had been to his house in his absence, the circumstance had the same effect upon him as "a second deluge;" for the Cadi, like all the Turks of the higher class, is as large in his language as in his clothes. I am not quite prepared for this view of the case on the part of my host, and I assure him that the regret should be on my side; but he stoutly adheres to his former opinion, and repeats it several times with the utmost gravity.

So we sit silent for a few minutes, looking out towards the sea, which is spread beneath us; for the Turks do not love idle prattlers. Discourse, with them, is too grave an affair to be entered on lightly. I know this, and inhale my pipe with great dignity; though I am aware that my utmost efforts in this particular are put utterly to shame by my august companion. The silence is not awkward or unpleasant: it is merely Turkish. There is the utmost goodwill and desire to prolong the interview by all polite means on both sides; and the Cadi is merely thinking how he shall make himself most agreeable.

At last we see a little boat tossed rather roughly on the waves out at sea; but it is pulled by a stout fisherman, and makes its way gallantly. This leads to a discourse on Turkish caiques in general; and I ask the Cadi if he does not think them dangerous in rough weather. The Cadi says that they are indeed dangerous; and to support this opinion he tells me one of those sententious stories in which all Orientals more or less delight.

"Once upon a time," says the Cadi, settling himself in his cushions, and laying down his jewelled pipe, " one of our Sultans was crossing that very sea in a bark as frail as yonder one. A storm arose, and his Highness, growing frightened, nearly overturned the boat by the abruptness of his movements. ' Be still !' said the boatman at last, and addressing the Sultan with a stern countenance ; ' seest thou not I have three kings to wrestle with—the winds, the waves, and thee ?—but thou hast ears, and therefore I bid thee to be quiet !'" The Cadi assured me that the Sultan was so delighted with the fearless wit of the boatman, that he immediately made him capitan pasha, or high admiral—and he was beheaded shortly afterwards in due course.

Then we are again at peace until after a fragrant cup of unsweetened coffee, when I ask the Cadi if he has had much professional business lately. He says yes ; and adds that it has been chiefly with the Greeks, who have grown very troublesome. He shakes his head doubtfully when he speaks of that people, and says he fears that there is nothing good to be done with them. "I am like a certain father," says the Cadi, again illustrating his opinion by an anecdote, " who had three sons. My eldest always tells me the truth : he is the Osmanli. My second always tells me falsehoods : he is the Zingari, or the Bulgarian ; and when I have to deal with either of these I know how to act ; but my third son tells me sometimes truth and sometimes falsehood; he is made up of cunning, and deceives me always : he is the Greek, and I never know how to treat him."

I am anxious to know the opinion of an honest Turk about the Tanzimat, and I take the present opportunity of putting the question fairly to the Cadi. I am glad when he answers unhesitatingly that it has done good ; he says that there is nothing new in the Tanzimat ; it merely provides that those laws to which violent men had not attended sufficiently, shall be carried out—nothing more. It only enforces the spirit of the true law of the Prophet, which was that all men should do unto others as they would be done by. I tell the Cadi that his is also briefly the meaning of the Christian law, and then we doze away in the same passive state of goodwill as before, until the Cadi sends for some sherbet, which freshens us up again.

I mention in a cursory manner that we do not appreciate sherbet properly in Britain; and the Cadi smiles as he pronounces the word "Wine?" in an interrogative form. "No," I answer, "beer is, I think, upon the whole, our national drink." The Cadi grows suddenly expansive: he has tasted it—it fizzes, and has a pungent pleasant taste. He would like to have some more, but vulgar people would think it a scandal if he were to send to Smyrna for fermented liquor, though bottled beer was by no means forbidden in the Koran. Perhaps, I think inwardly, because it had not been invented; but I do not communicate this reflection to the Cadi. On the contrary, I resolve privately to give him half my stock of bitter ale that evening. I am not sure that he does not divine this intention, for he turns the conversation on tobacco, and says that he has lately received some of a very fine sort from Constantinople, and he would like my opinion upon its merits. The Cadi, in his smiling way, I see, has been making a bargain; so I shall find a small leather bag waiting for me when I get home, and its fragrance will fill the house. This will be the Cadi's tobacco.

Now I must think about going; and I make a preliminary observation to this effect. The Cadi says that "he hopes to see me with grey moustaches." He means that he wishes me long life. But seeing me look puzzled, he adds—sliding again into one of those dear sententious stories—" This is a Turkish compliment. But there was once a jester, who, seeing a certain Sultan go forth to prayer, cried out, 'May your Highness and I live to see your brother's son a greybeard!' The Sultan inquired what he meant, and the wit replied: 'Your brother has yet to be born. He must be twenty years old before he has a son, and that son must be fifty before he is grey; therefore I am wishing your Highness a reign of seventy years, and that I may live to witness it." The Cadi's story had the good old Eastern conclusion; and he assured me that the Sultan immediately raised his ingenious subject to the highest offices in the state. I wish there were more Turks like the Cadi.

CHAPTER VI.

LEVANT CONSULS.

THERE are one or two important consulates which frequently change hands in the Levant; and as it is a very sensible proverb which tells us that prevention is better than cure, I shall go on to say a few words upon this subject. To understand clearly, however, the duties and precise position of our Consuls in this part of the world, it will be necessary to go back a little.

Let me observe, therefore, that bad as the state of Turkey still is, it was formerly very much worse; the Greeks had given the Turks such an indifferent opinion of the Christian world, that they looked upon our race as a species of game it was lawful to hunt. Unbelievers had neither justice nor mercy to expect from the followers of the Prophet; and if one Frank did wrong, the Cadi not only punished the sinner, but every other Frank who was to be found. Ships were stopped on the high seas in time of peace, and made to deliver up their cargoes and cabin-boys; sometimes the ships also were taken. Turkish officers not only exacted arbitrary taxes and custom dues, but they levied them as often as they pleased. They would not give receipts for money paid to them; and taxgatherers who had nothing to do were calling on the Franks all day long. Merchants were compelled to exchange their money for the debased currency of Turkey, and to take it at its nominal value. There were all sorts of vexatious monopolies; tradesmen were obliged to sell their goods to Turks in preference to better paymasters. Whenever the Sultan wished to reward a favourite, he was apt to him give a charter to annoy the Franks in some way. Even the lowest employments in private houses were disposed of by law. All commercial travellers were Jews; and if one of them was turned away for misconduct or dishonesty, he had a claim for indemnity, and was able to enforce it. Turks pretended to have bills of exchange upon Frankish merchants, and insisted on being paid on their mere assertion to that effect. Franks were often detained in captivity under pretence of making them discharge debts which they did not owe; if they refused to ransom themselves, Turks stormed and plundered their houses. If a Frank had ever had any charge brought against him, the Cadi reopened the case whenever he felt in the humour, till that Frank's life became a weariness, and he was obliged to buy the Cadi off; if a Turk brought a charge against a Frank, the latter was not allowed time to prove his innocence; if he had witnesses on the spot, their testimony was inadmissible by law. One Frank was not unfrequently even put to death for the sins of another. The Turkish tribunals insisted that all the parties to a suit should appear in person; so that a troublesome fellow might take up the whole of a busy man's time by making the absurdest allegations against him. Many persons followed the trade of false accusers, and it was not a bad business in a lucrative point of view. The Cadi decided all questions with a lofty contempt of evidence; and as even the man who gained a process paid the expenses of it, there was no punishment for the most wanton malice. The giving and receiving of presents was also a gigantic evil; they were required upon all occasions; and they were merely an authorized species of robbery.

At last, after centuries of the most extraordinary patience, the Christian powers began to take heart, and to negociate treaties for the prevention of these things. The result was the gradual blossoming into fuller and fuller flower of the Levant Consuls. I shall, however, for the present limit these remarks to our own.

The British Consul in the Levant is entrusted with both civil and criminal jurisdiction. Fortunately he has not the power of awarding capital punishment; but he has almost every other: he may banish, dishonour, imprison, and fine at pleasure; he is banker, notary, arbitrator, judge, priest, registrar, and administrator of dead men's goods; untold property is confided to his care; the many interests of travellers and merchants are almost entirely entrusted to him; finally, he has power to enforce attendance at his office by a fine; he is recommended to prefer summary decisions, and not to give his mind to juries; in a word, he is in the same business as a British Secretary of State, only in a small way, and consumes more consequence than is good for him.

A British Consul has such weight and authority in the Turkish district where he resides, that he may cause almost any amount of mischief unchecked. There is no press to watch his doings; no society to cry shame on him; no means by which an ignorant Maltese or native of Gibraltar can make a grievance known and obtain redress. There is indeed no control of any kind over a British Consul in the Levant; and a very august and singular personage he has become in consequence. If we grant that the Consul is always a high-minded and conscientious man (and I am not doubting it), it must be still borne in mind he has to deal with a numerous class of persons who speak no English, whose depositions he is obliged to receive through interpreters, who are not always honest, and whom he cannot always understand. He has to decide cases also where every effort is made to deceive him; where the evidence is often particularly difficult to sift; and thus, however upright himself, a British Consul is often made the involuntary instrument of cruel wrong. I know that this is not the tenor of the reports sent in some time ago by the Consuls to the Foreign Office; but I have seen the system at work, and, in a word, it wants altering.

"Her Majesty's Government," indeed, "expect" that the British Consul "will exercise great caution in using the large powers confided to him;" but lest this language should seem a little rough, "Her Majesty's Government" courteously adds, that it "will always be disposed to place the best construction" on a Consul's conduct, "and will make all due allowance for the errors into which he may inadvertently fall."

Now all this is very polite and pretty; but I would respectfully suggest that it is not quite right. Persons should not be employed in responsible posts who are at all likely to fall into errors which may be avoided; and they should be therefore punished if they do so. It is not sufficient for "Her Majesty's

Government" to "trust that powers so extensive will be used with prudence and moderation." It is an imperative duty to provide that they shall not be used otherwise, by appointing them to be wielded by proper and efficient persons learned in the laws which they are called upon to administer.*

It is very far from my intention to offer an insult to any body of men; but many of the appointments hitherto made in the consular service have been very indecorous. I can recall several instances of Consuls exercising judicial authority who have been bankrupt traders. I attach no ungenerous shame to the mere fact of a man's having been at some time in his life a bankrupt trader; but I think we have a right to insist that a person who was unable to attend satisfactorily to his own affairs, shall not be entrusted with those of the public. The rest of the Consuls, it is needless to say, in the Levant as well as elsewhere, have received their appointments through patronage; and I cannot at this moment remember a single distinguished name among them. White gloves and pedigrees are not required in the consular service; we have already too many of them elsewhere; we want plain sensible men, who have been brought up to the business, not persons who have taken to it because they have failed in other occupations; and no considerable place should ever be confided to a man who has not given some public and obvious proofs of his capacity. What are commonly called "snug berths" should be rewards for hard work, or premiums to ability; they should not be gratuities to idlers, whose only qualification is that of having toadied or worried some person of influence.

I would be clearly understood, as by no means wishing to lessen the powers confided to Consuls in the present state of Turkey; but we ought to have a better guarantee for their proper use. No official left perfectly uncontrolled should ever have much power in his hands, for all are alike liable to errors or to human weakness. Firstly, then, it seems to me that Consuls should be required to have a thorough knowledge of the laws and language of the country to which they may be sent, as well as of their own. This is not setting up a very high standard of

* The appointment of Judges to the Consular tribunal in Turkey and Egypt was effected by this suggestion.

education for appointments so well paid and comfortable. It should be further ordered that no interpreters should be employed in consulates but such as thoroughly understand English; I would suggest also that they should be officially paid, and that they should be nominated by the Crown.

The interpreter, *cancelier*, or dragoman, for he has all three names, might be made a very valuable officer in a consulate. He might prevent any misconduct of a Consul completely; he is a sort of justice's clerk; he manages all affairs with the local authorities; the whole business of his consulate passes through his hands: he is the guide, philosopher, and friend, the tongue and ears of his Consul.

In French consulates, therefore, the *cancelier* has distinct and important functions; while we, who delight to throw all power, might, majesty, and money into the hands of one man, do not even pay or acknowledge him. The British *cancelier* is usually a gaunt hungry young man, rather out at elbows, who has been at some time or other servant to the Consul or his friend, and whose bread and character usually depend on his pleasing a master who may be, or may not be, little better than a short tempered blockhead.

The French *cancelier*, among other duties, is bound under fine to register and transmit to the Secretary of State any complaint made to him against the Consul; a French Consul may be cited before his *cancelier*, and even judged; a British Consul, can only be compared to the King of the Cannibal Islands, and there is no present remedy against him.

The property and deposits of French subjects are kept in a strong box with two locks to it: the key of one only remains in the possession of the Consul, the other is kept by the *cancelier;* neither can go alone to finger other people's money unperceived. But British consulates are subject to no regulations at all on this matter; and a most disgraceful case lately occurred of one of our officers having dishonoured our flag by the embezzlement of some £600 of poor suitors money. The affair became, indeed, publicly notorious, and he was dismissed; but I am unable to perceive that this makes the existing state of things any better.

I am not setting up the French service as a model, for I think many of their arrangements both intricate and inconvenient; I am simply trying to suggest a few practical hints, and to make some new appointments which are very much needed for the general good.

I am now also going to touch upon a very tender question: it is that of *fees;** and I say unhesitatingly that they ought to be abolished. The proper salaries of Consuls would be much better provided for at home by special taxes, than by allowing such a crying abuse to go on any longer. For what happens? Nine times in ten the Consul himself does not deign to touch his fees, and he hands them over to somebody who very often touches too much; they afford a premium to delays and vexations in civil suits brought before Consuls, and they often occasion serious altercations with sea captains, who are disposed to pay less and to charge their employers more than they should. I know that there is a table of fees hung up in all consular offices; but several of the items specified in it leave very large margins. Consular servants sometimes profit by these, so do sea captains. By permitting fees also, we are lending our authority to the system of passport exactions, which we have not scrupled to condemn elsewhere. The fees in places like Constantinople and St. Petersburgh are an abuse quite startling; they amount to thousands of pounds a year, and I know of one English consulate in America where the salary is £200 a year and the fees £1,600. Now this is merely deceiving taxpayers. If a Consul is worth £1,600 a year, let him have it by all means, but let him have it openly. Do not permit him to figure in the estimates as receiving but one-eighth of his actual pay, for this is an insult to the taxpayer's understanding, and may reasonably surprise him into rough measures. To conclude this branch of my subject, consular fees have been allowed to become a hoary abuse: and they are a disgrace to the service: for it is an uncourteous supposition to assume that English gentlemen would not do their work properly unless paid by the piece.

---

* Consular fees were for the most part abolished in consequence of what is here printed.

Having said thus much on the one side, I have now to make a few serious observations on the other. Consuls are subject to several very offensive regulations: and somebody*at the Foreign Office has drawn up a list of questions for them to answer on the first of every January, which would put to shame a schoolboy of ten years old. It is not proper to tell a body of English gentlemen (as the consular instructions do *thrice*) that they shall not correspond with respectable people in their own country on any subject they may understand sufficiently to make their ideas valuable. A man's ideas are his property; if they are sound and practicable, they cannot be known too widely: if they are otherwise, he will soon grow tired of offering that which nobody will receive.

I see with perfect astonishment that the consular instructions forbid all correspondence on public affairs with so respectable a body as *Lloyd's*, to whom trustworthy news is of the highest importance. I confess that I am completely unable to understand why a Consul should not be free to work in off hours in the trade he understands best, as well as any other man. It will be quite time enough to punish him when he slights his official duties in consequence.

Truths cannot be known too certainly, or guaranteed by authority too respectable. The public ought not to be obliged to feed on falsehood, and then be sneered at for their ignorance, if on the one side there are persons in their pay able and willing to teach them, and, on the other, they are desirous to learn. It is from the idle communications of people who know nothing, that a general and absurd system of mystification is kept up;

---

* As a curious instance of irresponsible Government it may be mentioned that this person was an obscure Maltese, who called himself "James Murray." He and his partner, the notorious John Bidwell, carried on for many years an impudent trade with public money; and nearly four millions sterling of it was traced into their hands. Moreover they actually contrived to pension themselves, out of the national taxation, even after the corrupt abuse in which they were concerned was abolished as "abominable" by act of parliament. Murray was ultimately removed from employment, and retired to a landed estate in Hampshire. See Foreign Office List for 1870, and parliamentary reports on "The Foreign Office Agencies." London. Harrison.

and even Downing Street can have no possible guarantee for the soundness of its information about a country, when it is content to receive it only through the fuddled wits of some silly old gentleman, who may be, and often is, most miserably mistaken.

It would be ungraceful, and I believe sincerely wrong *in fact*, to suppose that Her Majesty's Government ever demand or offer anything to a foreign State, which ought not to be known as widely as possible for the true interests of all parties. One thing is quite certain, that in our days no act of any government can be entirely concealed, and as the case stands, we are always getting on the wrong side of things, and so starting at shadows.

We ought not to be compelled to blunder about in the dark till the meeting of Parliament about public events affecting the prosperity and happiness of thousands; and at last to receive only some explanation sufficiently unsatisfactory from a minister, who may not always have understood rightly the communications made to him.

I am unable also to perceive why we, the public, should be obliged to take the unsupported allegations of a Needybore or a Nortiman about any important event; even if Government has been so unwise as to appoint such persons to serious employments. Let us, at all events, hear what people have to say who are placed in positions equally favourable for judging.

A public servant should not be hopelessly snuffed out because he is in a petty post. We should be always ready to hear everybody who has got anything to say, by which practice we may perhaps be saved from a national imprudence. If petty officers can show proofs of notable abilities, the door of preferment should not be closed to them; and the advantage of their judgment and capacity lost to us, because they *are* petty officers. They should not be soured and rendered useless by seeing noodles of ancient family walking constantly over their heads till they are rendered quite bald by the soles of those noodles' boots. Let us have some means of knowing pretty accurately what all men can do, that we may be able to treat them accordingly. No better gauge of ability than writing to newspapers or public bodies could possibly be found for petty consular and diplomatic officers; and if a government once decide on permitting a free press, there can be no greater danger than that such a press should be ill-informed by persons who have not the means of getting at truth. The influence of the British press is far too serious for it to be allowed to circulate nonsensical conjectures, because it is now and then unable to get at facts. In a word, let us not endeavour to imprison the mind of a clever man because he is a petty officer; and that the public service may thus be made a dreary affair to all but Needybores and Nortimans. Let the race be fair among all public men; and as the press is the people's parliament, where all have a voice, let all be heard who are worth hearing. The only possible advantage of the other system is, that persons like the wise man of Bickerstaffe may be allowed to get into scrapes without being found out in time to save us from the consequences of their folly; and, indeed, some people's surprise is great, that while in England all affairs of importance are honestly submitted to the consideration of both houses of Parliament, abroad we are content to confide them to the puzzled wits of some poor perplexed creature who has wriggled himself and his peerage into a place for which he is notoriously unfit.

In conclusion I will endeavour to answer the arguments of those persons who wish to join the consular and diplomatic services, by stating my idea of the true functions of each. Their business then appears to me as different as that of the Cabinet minister who frames a law, and the magistrate who executes it; the business of the diplomatist is to collect and digest information from many quarters, and to negotiate treaties and conventions, based on various and conflicting data. They must be such men as this. They are thinkers and men of the world.

Now the sphere of the Consul is altogether confined to the affairs of a seaport town; and he is therefore seldom in a position to form quite a sound judgment upon a subject of general interest. His duty is to collect facts, to see ideas in action, to judge of their effects, and to report upon them. He is a *doer*, and a man of business.

The duties of diplomacy, properly understood, will be continually varying: now there will be a commercial treaty which requires one man; now a peace congress which requires another; on one occasion the quarantine regulations will require discussion; upon another, the international copyright question, or a new postal treaty.

To leave one diplomatist, therefore, always at the same place, to attend to all our wants there, is as singular a proceeding as though we should require the functions of cook, boots, and ostler in a large hotel to be performed by the same person. But the functions of Consuls are settled and determined; they are everywhere and always the same, and they require a certain species of knowledge which can only be acquired by practice. This is why I recommend that the consular service should be, and that the diplomatic service should not be, a profession.

CHAPTER VII.

LEVANT CONSULATES.

I WOULD further suggest that some such regulations as the following should be drawn up in the shape of general instructions to Consuls, and that they should be directed,—

To celebrate divine service on Sundays in places where there is no chaplain or British clergyman :

To notify all circumstances which may interfere with the accuracy of the Admiralty charts as soon as possible after the time of their occurrence :

To report on the state of local trade, manufactures, arts, industry, agriculture, and commerce generally : *

To examine into and report upon the value of all useful inventions, or improvements in art or science :

To state the annual produce of the district in which they reside ; whether in wool, cotton, corn, cattle, wine, tobacco, manufactures, &c. ; to observe upon any increase, or decrease of the same ; to state the local consumption of such produce, together with the quantity exported, and where exported ; to state the average current prices of such produce, with the reasons which are apt to influence them :

To report upon the yearly increase or decrease of local population and riches. If such information as the foregoing be only to be obtained with difficulty, such difficulty should be overcome almost at any expense of time and trouble ; for no facts can be more entirely necessary to a safe and progressive commercial policy.

To make the covering despatches of such returns contain

---

* Consular reports were first published in consequence of this suggestion.

something of more importance than the usual truism, that the writer has the honour to be, with the highest respect, the most obedient humble servant of his official chief for the time being ; to endeavour to link causes with facts, and try, at least, to observe sufficiently during twelve months, to be able to communicate a few pregnant facts on the 31st December; to give, indeed, a plain useful account of the state of the consular district, putting forth opinions on things which might be done with advantage, or should be left undone, a suggestive, thoughtful, and business-like report, something better than mere red-tapism ; a report in which the writer shall be allowed to speak out his ideas like an honest man, instead of being shackled like an official.

To give receipts, stamped with the consular stamp of office, for all fees (till their final and necessary abolition), and especially to register the same ; noting on the receipt given, in what book and page among the archives such registration may be found, in case of reasonable demur on the part of ship-owners or others, and to prevent fraud.

If fees are still to be allowed, to subject them to a better system of examination and control, especially in bankruptcy cases, in which they have been known to amount to thirty-five per cent. on the sum total realized by the sales of the bankrupts' property.

To cause all fees to be collected, under proper supervision, and transmitted by bills of exchange to the Treasury, instead of forming part of the consular perquisites.*

To write all despatches on thin strong paper, such as that used for foreign bills of exchange or bankers' correspondence, instead of the thick heavy blue foolscap now employed, and which more than quadruples the necessary expense of postage ; in all ordinary cases to use official wafers instead of sealing-wax,† and to condense all despatches, not referring to topics of immediate interest, into a quarterly or even annual report, under one cover, for the same reason.

I would suggest also :

That plain dealing should abolish the enormous expense of

* This suggestion was adopted. † Adopted.

queen's messengers, as part of a bygone and ridiculous system, seeing that in these days no circumstance could transpire between friendly nations, which could possibly be kept secret, and which ought not to be known as widely as possible.

That a premium should be offered for official envelopes and fastenings to despatches, which would prevent the possibility of their being opened without detection. That they should then be confided to the honour of foreign governments, and sent through the post on all ordinary occasions. As much security would be offered in this case as under the present more costly system ; for it is obvious that a government disposed to incur the consequences of discovery, would have little hesitation in seizing the papers of a messenger, either by fraud or force.

If no means can be found by the ingenious stationers of Britain, through which a safe envelope shall be made for important despatches, perhaps we have already an old plan which would puzzle the cleverest scoundrel who ever lent the aid of his cunning to the worst foreign post-office.

If the envelope be made of thin paper, and closed first with a wafer, and then with sealing-wax, the precaution is complete, for the means used to melt the wax (a thin stream of gas) will harden the wafer, and the means used to soften the wafer will of course have no effect upon the wax. However, if to this precaution you add a thread, passing round the despatch, and fastening under the wafer ; and if, subsequently, the person to whom the despatch is really addressed, *cuts* the said envelope open on the address side, any attempt to tamper with the fastening on the other, will be at once ascertained by the partial burning or division of the thread.

If there should still be persons so mysterious as to be dissatisfied with these means, there is still another method of securing secrecy, which is far beyond all dispute.

Let despatches be inclosed in little leather covers, fastened with patent locks (the famous American lock, or Chubb's, or Mordan's enigma locks, would be all unimpeachable keepers of secrets). If one set of keys were kept at the Foreign Office, and the duplicate keys by officials abroad, and the patent of the lock fixed upon, purchased for Government, we should be gainers of a great many thousands a year. If anybody should consider such a consideration beneath the dignity of a great nation, I beg most respectfully to disagree with him. Whether it may suit patrons and borough-mongers; whether it may be agreeable to opera-girls, to my lord's valet, and my lady's maid, who gets her fashions from Paris by the courier, is altogether another question.

It would be well to adopt a better system in preserving official archives. If despatches were kept flat, in book-form, instead of creased and folded, they might be kept in much less space, and preserved more easily from the effects of time and dust. If they were bound together in yearly books, and properly indexed, reference to any particular despatch would be infinitely easier than now, when it has to be hunted out from a clumsy bundle, tied with red tape, and which takes a quarter of an hour to put together again whenever it is disturbed.

I would recommend :

That Consuls should be subjected to the orders of the Board of Trade rather than the Foreign Office, in control of which department they would seem as misplaced as when formerly under the direction of the Colonial Office. The fact is, no nation ever sorted and divided the public work worse than we do ; the most liberal nation in the world in other respects, we are all for nonsense and despotism in our offices. It would be impossible to give the shadow of a reason for more than half the odd things we witness with such pride and complacency in Downing Street and its dependencies.

Political despatches only should be addressed to the Foreign Office ; and as the world generally is a great deal too busy about politics just now, the less Consuls add to the hubbub on ordinary occasions, the better. A gentleman living in a seaport town is seldom placed very advantageously for giving valuable opinions on politics. I know there are exceptions, but this is the rule.

I would recommend that Consuls be entirely freed from the control of embassies, to avoid disputes and ill-feeling ; though they should be directed to forward all despatches under flying-seal through the embassy, for the information and guidance of the public servants belonging to it.

There are other regulations so necessary and obvious, that I blush to be obliged to call attention to them. They are :—

That no Consuls be ever appointed who are not acquainted with the language of the country to which they are sent. That none but persons who have passed an examination in civil and criminal law, and are of mature age, should ever be appointed to the important consular magistracies of the Levant; and that in all cases a thorough knowledge of the laws and regulations affecting trade shall be deemed indispensable.

That Consuls in the Levant be allowed to charge in their accounts such expenses as they may be conscientiously obliged to incur in the discharge of their magisterial duties,—especially in procuring the attendance of witnesses, and for medical examinations and advice in cases of criminal assault,—lest Consuls should sometimes be found whose straitened circumstances compel them to shrink from taking all possible means to seek truth, and to support the honour and dignity of the British law in those countries where we have been mercifully allowed to establish it.

That an experienced clerk be appointed to all Consulates to fulfil the functions of a foreign *cancelier;* to be joint custodian with the Consul of all deposits and sums received on behalf of British subjects; and to give joint receipts for the same, stamped with the consular stamp.

The post of *cancelier*, or clerk, in French Consulates, is justly considered so important that it is never, under any circumstances, permitted to remain vacant.

If it should be urged that the qualities necessary to make a useful Consul cannot often be found in a good linguist, and that the world is not made up entirely of Admirable Crichtons, let us at least provide that the Consul's clerk shall be a linguist, and specially informed on the nature of the duties required of him.

It might, perhaps, also be well to separate distinctly the career of Consul and clerk, as is done in other services, to prevent rivalry.

. Then I would suggest that a certain number of young men should be educated specially for the consular service, as in France and Germany : that, after they have passed fitting examinations, and attained a reasonable age, they should be eligible for employment as acting Consuls.

No person should ever be allowed to officiate as acting Consul, in the absence of that functionary, unless he have previously passed an examination, or served three years in a Consulate. The boys sometimes sent to mind the great British Consulates in the Levant bring discredit and ridicule on the service; it is at once wrong, also, and absurd to place the serious interests of a whole community under the protection of a lad of nineteen, who can possibly have no one quality for acquitting himself properly of so grave a responsibility.

Such a regulation, also, would prevent the crying abuse of those private arrangements by which a Consul may, and sometimes does, recommend an unfit person to replace him during his absence, upon an understanding that he will refund all or part of the allowance awarded by Government for such service and deducted from the Consul's salary.

The French have a wholesome dread of family embassies and consulates. They have all sorts of regulations to prevent them, as injurious to the public service. We seem to take a different view of the case; and, look where we will, there is a family gathered together where it ought not to be. The consequence is disagreeable in more respects than I would wish to name more particularly.

It is extremely necessary that Consuls should be instructed as to the importance and propriety of having the consular office at their residence.* If this should be inconvenient in large unhealthy seaports, at all events let there be *an* office at the Consul's house, as the want of it often occasions a very inconvenient amount of running about and loss of time to men of business and invalids. Let it also be rendered culpable in Consuls to refuse to execute public business, either personally or by deputy, at any hour between daylight and dark. Some of these gentlemen are only to be found ready to do their duty

* Lord Malmesbury issued an order in accordance with this suggestion.

for one or two hours of the day; and an opinion (which cannot be too sternly and frequently snubbed, and laughed to scorn) prevails among them that bumptiousness and discourtesy add to their importance.

It is a notorious fact that passports according the privileges of British subjects, are much too lightly given to foreigners—especially in the Levant. Let it therefore be provided that no Consul shall be competent to grant passports, except on evidence satisfactory to the local authorities; and that, in the first instance, such passports be countersigned by the said local authorities. Thus a large amount of evil will be prevented; for it now happens that a great many dishonest foreigners continue to escape the legal burthens borne by the rest of their countrymen, and that others have to pay their share.

Finally, I would suggest that there should be no such thing as a political Consul. Let Consuls be gentlemen learned in the law and in commercial affairs. Their duties, properly understood, will then be sufficiently onerous. Politicians should be persons of general information, and of special studies, wholly apart from those required by Consuls. As affairs now stand, however, we have consular diplomatists and diplomatic Consuls, neither of whom know their business.

CHAPTER VIII.

KAIMAK* (MANNERS OF THE TURKS).

THE Turks have four fasts yearly, and they keep them with rare good faith. They pray five times a day, and commence at daybreak. They are constantly washing themselves, from the belief that it purifies their souls. They are bound in conscience to make at least one pilgrimage to Mecca and Medina ; but they frequently perform so troublesome a journey by deputy, and this is understood to answer quite as well, and even to be in rather better taste than the incurring unnecessary fatigue. They abstain from wine, especially in public, or in the presence of talkative people ; and they are very much given to charities, particularly with other persons' money.

The Cadi marries his fellow Turks, and finds it a very good business. The ceremony is brief—only a few words, indeed—but it is necessary they should be pronounced in the presence of credible witnesses. These were often difficult to find, in a country where truth was seldom spoken, and every man's lies were of course notorious enough. Under these circumstances, it occurred to the green-turbaned descendants of Mahomet to set up in trade as witnesses, inasmuch as their respectability was shown to all men, like a judge's wisdom, by the nature ot their headdress. These gentry, however, in process of time, professed to witness so many things which had never occurred, that the profession fell into disrepute, and is now altogether a mere refuge for decayed noblemen—like British diplomacy.

Your genuine Turk was allowed four wives ; but he found the

---

* The word "Kaimak" means "Cream;" and weary readers of the many complications of the Eastern question may take this chapter to be almost the cream of what it is necessary to know about the manners of the Turks.

practice of maintaining them in the highest degree inconvenient. They not only contrived to keep him penniless, but they made use of their nails upon each other's faces with such liveliness and ability, that no one of them was ever fit to be seen ; and their determined and noisy hostility was invariably a scandal to every neighbourhood in which they lived. Such circumstances have usually induced our Mohammedan friends to confine themselves to one. The number of their other ladies, who have had nothing to do with the Cadi, depends entirely on the size of their establishment : for long experience has shown the Turk the only way to prevent them tearing each other's eyes out, is to lock them up in separate apartments. Vacancies, therefore, in a Turkish harem occur on the same principle as in a private lunatic asylum, and depend altogether upon the empty rooms. Your Turkish damsel is an odd sort of body : quaint, fat, painted, bedizened, tattooed, and childish. Her occupation is eating sweetmeats, and tossing about her clothes ; sometimes her occupations are varied by dances and songs, which are, to say the least of them, improper ; and pinching her slaves. In the last mentioned art she is an adept, and is as fond of worrying them as a boarding-school boy is of impaling flies.

The children of each lady are brought up separately, having no communication whatever with the establishment over the way, except for the purpose of making themselves in some way disagreeable. Whenever they meet, there is usually a stand-up fight, in the same way as there would be with their amiable mammas ; but a prudent parent prevents the occurrence of any unpleasantry of this kind, by not making them acquainted with each other. A youth on leaving the harem, therefore, is often astonished at the number of his unknown relatives ; more surprised, indeed, than gratified. A sure title to his favour used to be to dispose effectually of a few of them ; no matter how, so that they were never heard of any more ; but recently this practice seems to have fallen off a good deal.

Fine fat slaves, sound in wind and limb, and good steppers, are on sale daily at the bazaars ; and there is always a large stock on view for ready money, or the bill of an approved party. Ladies *enceinte* are unsalable by law; but all others may be had at reasonable prices, according to the season and demand. If a Jew or a Christian wants a good serviceable machiner, there are always plenty of his own persuasion ready for inspection or purchase. The Mohammedan animals are kept for Mussulmen. A slave-merchant is a highly respectable person in Turkey; indeed, almost on a level with a British horsedealer; a profession so frequently followed by our noblemen as to have become nearly confined to them. In fact, all good judges of flesh hold both trades in the highest esteem. On the whole, however, perhaps the Turk has the best of it: he does not require stables, and the animals in which he trafficks fetch a larger price.

Mr. Urquhart gave a tolerably long list of the things in which we differ from the Turks and the Turks differ from us, but there are still some others. In Turkey the left side, and not the right, is the place of honour. The Turks are so lost to all sense of proper feeling as to bury their dead without any unnecessary fuss or parade; whereas we think it just the proper time to make a disturbance, and fire off the great family guns, so that the delightful vanities of life may not desert a man at least till we have done with him. Their dead are so buried as to be dissolved speedily; ours are preserved, in order that we may be always in a lively state of expectation for the return at least of their diseases; and as they cannot come back to us, that we may join them as soon as possible: a sentiment reflecting great credit upon us as an enlightened nation, to say nothing of the affecting light in which it places our sensibility and tenderness of heart. The Turk loves fine horses and servants, but he is more or less indifferent about his clothes, and keeps but a poor table—*pilaff*, in short, *et præterea nihil!*

As for the fine arts, our excellent acquaintances have not hitherto troubled themselves much about them. They think the acquisition of useful knowledge and the motives which founded the *Penny Magazine* as altogether beneath the dignity of a wise man of the East; crossing your legs and smoking an unmanageable pipe is more rational and easier: such is their opinion. Thus it turns out that the art of writing is a rare accomplishment in Turkey; it is considered a trade, and practised by very few. It is understood to take twenty years' diligent sapping to acquire as much knowledge as may enable an individual to look out a word in Mr. Redhouse's Turkish Dictionary, and then the individual must be Mr. Redhouse himself; indeed, it would be hardly going too far to say that every man makes his own Turkish. It is certain that during a tolerably close and extensive experience in the country I never met even two intimate friends, one of whom would agree that the other understood his mother tongue as it ought to be understood. Printing is terribly in the background; at Constantinple there are but two newspapers, and one is constantly knocking up for want of subscribers. Yet there are * 600,000 or 700,000 resident inhabitants in the city, besides strangers. This little fact will show, as well as most others, how well our acquaintances are likely to be informed on current events; and why they often suppose Great Britain to be an island in the Red Sea, not far from Timbuctoo, and ruled over by a fierce female hospodar, who wears huge whiskers, and is tributary to the Emperor of Austria. Indeed, their wisdom and intelligence in this way is hardly to be surpassed; and the facts which I have related and a few others, seem to hint to me that their language is likely enough to be extinct in a few years. The Greeks positively will not learn it, and the abolition of the Christian disabilities will throw almost all public business into their hands.

Nearly all the notable artisans in Turkey are strangers, down to the men who serve in their docks and arsenals; but it is not easy to see how this should be otherwise, for the Koran expressly forbids the carving of any kind of image, and with a refreshing contempt for practical people, declares the finest efforts of handiwork in the world simply abominable. The only really worthy employment for a rich Turkish gentleman's money appears to be building a mosque; but the triumphs of Turkish architecture of late years have been anything but remarkable. They always lacked the airy and elaborate grace of Arab buildings, and I could point out very few edifices erected by them which are altogether satisfactory.

* 1853.

The political history of Turkey will not exactly be found pleasant reading for a merciful man : it seems little else than a foul story of poisonings, assassinations, massacres, and the moral reflections of Sultan Somebody at every new enormity. But I am not, therefore, of opinion that the Turks are cruel as a nation. Too much power is good for nobody ; the Sultans had too much power, and they misused it. For the rest they were generous, simple, and sincere, when it was not their interest to be otherwise, and when their childish wiles were not called into action by having to deal with a Greek. Such they were ; such they are. I see no valid reason to assert that our acquaintances are much changed since Bertezena chastized the Khan of the Geougen, or Disabul harried the unwarlike subjects of Byzantine Tiberius. Europe is changed, however : the Emperor of Austria is no longer the insignificant person he was when John Sobieski rescued Vienna from the Ottoman hordes ; and France is another guess-sort of country to that which it was when Charles Martel saved Christendom on the plains of Tours. Russia also could hardly be brought to understand a joke as well as when Achmet III. dictated peace to a snubbed Peter the Great upon the banks of the Pruth : 400 years of oppression have even united the Greeks, and nerved their arms a little. Thus, turn which way our acquaintances will, they have no elbow-room. They would be delighted to have a quiet little game of conquest and pillage, or even one which was not so quiet, for the matter of that ; but the fact is, that there is no longer a field for Turkish talents ; and many a stiff-bearded elderly gentleman believes firmly that the world is coming to an end in consequence.

Our new acquaintances (I continue to call them our new acquaintances, for really the present generation of Europeans seem almost to have been ignorant of their existence till lately) have a great dislike to renegades. They explain it from an interesting observation of the Caliph Omar. An Arab chief appeared before him, and desired to renounce the faith of Islam, because it did not allow him to marry two sisters at the same time. The Caliph immediately applied a stout stick with great vivacity to the applicant's head, and as if this were not sufficient argument for such a person, the Commander of the Faithful gave the wretch to understand that an apostate ought to suffer death. Thus, whatever your worthless adventurer, now setting out to swim in the troubled waters of Turkey, may think to the contrary, he will not gain much but contempt by turning Turk. I have seen swarms of deluded miscreants who did so; but they won nothing by it, and shamble about Constantinople haggard, seedy, and despised.

One of the questionable things about a Turk in the eyes of all British gentlemen of honour, must be his inveterate dislike to duelling, which he cannot be brought to understand. He supposes that our duels are fought by command of our Sultan, and constitute merely a means at the disposal of that potentate for getting rid of disagreeable people. They have an extremely convenient custom for quarrelsome folks: at the feast of the Bairam every Turk is bound to make *it* up with his enemy, be that "*it*" what it may. Whether they hate each other more cordially afterwards or not, let us leave the cynics to decide.

They do not appear to object to duelling, or to danger of any kind, from fear of death; their downright pluck upon all occasions is beyond all question or dispute. They decline to go to lonely places on cold mornings for the purpose of murdering a friend who has trodden on their toes, because it is not in accordance with their principles. They do not give people a chance of treading on their toes, by persevering in the excellent old system of crossing their legs and sitting down upon them; while they carry on all intercourse with each other in such a flowery and wonderful strain that cause of offence can hardly occur. If, however, cause of offence does occur, they perhaps still prefer poisoning to any more noisy means of quieting a person who has become obnoxious to them. They have not, however, attained that elegance in the art of silent destruction which has been attributed to the Italians and Russians; nor is, or ever was, the custom of poisoning so common among them. A Turkish difference, especially with a Greek, is often settled by hired servants, whose chief employment is to shake and thump persons who cannot be brought to reason by other means. The Greek gentlemen understand this, and avoid personal encounters, therefore, as frequently as possible.

Our new acquaintances are fatalists; they are not of the opinion of Pope and most modern philosophers; they think that Nature is not only held fast in fate, but the human will also; they believe that everything, from the growth of little apples to the roasting of rayah rebels, was preordained. Thus they are not fond of taking useless steps to avert disaster, and insurance offices are unknown among them. They would consider an insurance office as a temple of Mammon and iniquity. Even quarantine is an institution comparatively new, and by no means pleasing to them. The doctor does not appear to them the potent personage he seems with us: they respect him, indeed, as a soother of pain; but they hold that no man can avert that which is written, or rather that which is *to be;* for many things are written in these days of august diplomacy, which are not to be, or at all likely to be. For this reason, the Turk takes no delight in meddling with the proceedings of fate in the case of a house on fire; and he would shake hands with an individual who had the small-pox with the utmost gallantry and politeness. He is not averse either to wearing the clothes of an acquaintance who may have just died of the plague. Turks reason upon this subject with great truth and wisdom; they assert that the plague is a spirit, who walks the air carrying two lances, one white and the other black. With these he strikes mankind: those struck with the white lance will not die, but nothing can save those struck with the black lance. Other learned doctors maintain, with equal erudition, that the plague is not represented by one spirit, but by many. This dispute has often waxed warm; but up to the present time the Wise men of the East have not come to a decision; indeed, they do not love decision or decisive people.

I do not know that I have anything more to say about the Turks this evening; among them are many strange, weary, old, broken-down, cranky, rickety, crotchety people. One hardly knows exactly whether to laugh at or be angry with their rulers; but this I know, that we are certainly not going the right way to mend them, and we are likely to have a mighty amount of bother in consequence.

CHAPTER IX.

ON A VISIT.

I AM on a visit to a great Turkish lord, and have every reason to be satisfied with that state of affairs. I have a handsome suite of apartments allotted to me entirely, and my host's servants are commanded to pay more immediate attention to my wants than to his own. The establishment is, indeed, given over to me, and my nod is law. If a well-bred public will promise entire discretion and good behaviour, I will take it in with me to dinner.

An armed man has drawn the curtain of my room, and makes a deep salaam. He has come to announce that his master is awaiting me, for it is the hour of festivity. This messenger marshals me the way, through halls and passages, and along gardens and terraces, till we come to a delightful summer-house, where sits the superb Effendi. This summer-house is brilliantly lighted up, and in the centre of its polished marble floor is a fountain at play. Before the Effendi is a small table, spread with various fruits and stimulating things. There are also some little bits of fried mutton, highly salted, and some rakee, with other liqueurs. These provisions are intended to awaken an appetite; but they are omitted when any Mussulman of a sacred character, such as the Cadi, is about to dine with us. I perceive, therefore, that our party of to-day will be composed exclusively of merry-makers.

The Effendi rises as I enter, with a brisk joyous air, and laughs loudly as he tells me a story of something which has happened during the day. Then he pledges me in some rakee, prepared after a peculiar receipt of his own; and the other guests dropping in, our mirth becomes a little boisterous;

indeed, I have often noticed in Turkey, that the half-hour before dinner is the gayest of the twenty-four.

At last we have all drunk enough; some of us rather too much: my host waves his hand; the rakee and sweetmeats disappear. Some very palatable soup begins our dinner. Wine is placed on the table for me, but I know it would be bad taste to touch it; so it is removed. Indeed, after the immense dose of raw spirits we have been drinking, wine would be disagreeable. The soup is succeeded by some five-and-twenty dishes at least. We have small tortoiseshell spoons of exquisite workmanship for the liquids; everything else is discussed with the fingers. Knives and forks are, indeed, placed for me, but it would be ill-mannered to use them. The proper way to eat is to cover the two forefingers of your right hand with a small piece of bread; then to dip them into the part of the dish you have chosen. Do not interfere with anybody else's part of the dish. Each dish remains on the table about two minutes. Our host himself gives the signal of attack on it, saying, "Booyourum," —by your leave. Everything is cut small, and excessively overdone. The dishes, though numerous, have little variety; and mine host tells a story, *à propos* of this subject, of a Persian who once dined with him. The Persian finding there were gourds (a species of vegetable of which the Turks are very fond) in almost everything of which he had partaken, at last cried out in despair, "Bring me at least a glass of water in which there are no gourds!"

Another of the vegetables at table goes by the singular name of Greek horns. A vulgar Turk once twitted a Greek on this subject: "They call them *Greek* horns," replied his quick-witted adversary, "because they are so small; *yours* would be, of course, larger."

The dinner is over: it has concluded with some cold cherry sherbert, eaten with spoons, and some delicious melons. The pipes are brought, and we are soon all seated, cross-legged and shoeless, on the sofa, looking out on the lovely moonlight, as it sleeps on the flowery terraces beneath us; the conversation completely free and unrestrained.

"Yes," says a singularly lively little man, with a head like that of a French artist, "we are allowed to marry four wives and to keep forty slaves. We may divorce the former and change the latter as often as we please: but it won't do; the four wives would fight among themselves unless they had separate establishments, and then it would be costly. You Franks appear to suppose that we have half-a-dozen lawful ladies putting their fingers into our pilaff at the same time, and at the same table. I will tell you a story. There were once upon a time two friends who always frequented the same coffee-house, and one was constantly reproached by the other for coming too late and keeping him waiting. The tardy man excused himself by saying that he could never find his clothes of a morning. 'Why don't you marry a wife?' said his companion.

"'I have one,' replied the other.

"'Then take *two*, as I have done.'"

"So believing that the reason of his friend's orderly habits was the fact of his possessing two wives, who were thus enabled to attend to his wants more readily than one, the tardy man married again, and the next morning he was at the coffee-house early enough.

"'Hail, friend!' said his companion; 'I see that my words were the words of wisdom.'

"'Not so,' replied the other, ruefully; 'I am indeed here early this morning, but it is because the clamour made by my two wives prevented my sleeping at all last night, and this morning they have fairly driven me from the house.'

"Divorces," continued the garrulous little Bey, "are expensive, all things considered; and we look shyly at divorced women. We have, however, no prejudice against widows; but we have a story that they are apt to twit their new husband with the virtues of the defunct. A man who married a widow was once so worried in this way, that he beat his wife severely. She complained to the Cadi, who summoned the pair before him. 'The fact is,' said the husband, 'the whole thing is a mistake; she has been indeed beaten, but she is hardly entitled to accuse me, for we are three in a bed. There is my wife, her late husband, and myself. Perhaps he may have beaten her, *I* did not.'

"'Oh, then,' said the Cadi, who was a wise man (like the Cadi of all Turkish stories), 'if such is the state of the case, madam, get rid of your late husband, and you will sleep quietly enough.'"

"But how do your young scapegraces manage their love-making, your gay young bachelors, and unattached widowers?" asked I, emboldened by the turn which the conversation had taken.

"Why, I am afraid very much as elsewhere," interposed my host; "but they have adventures which often end tragically enough. A Turk who finds a stranger within the precincts of his harem may dispose of him as he pleases. The law will ask no questions."

"And the lady?"

"Is divorced."

"But not sewn up in a sack."

"Oh no!"

"As for other women, not our wives, we really have very few. Our wives, if rich or high-born, keep us in order much as yours do. Turks only can purchase Turkish slaves: their price varies from £10 to £1,000 of your money: some are highly educated, especially the Georgians."

From ladies the conversation changed to horses; and my host said that a leopard-skin saddle-cloth was regarded as fatal to men in place and power; if any one was so imprudent as to use such a thing, he usually found his dismissal from office awaiting him on his return home. The rank of a Turkish rider may be known by his saddle: every different grade in the public service has another saddle appointed for the use of the officers who belong to it. Black horses are devils; white horses are slugs; chestnuts, either very good or very bad. There are two Turkish proverbs: "As slow as a chestnut," and "As fiery as a chestnut."

Horses with white on their tails are unlucky: a white star on the forehead is a good omen. Horses with three white legs are fortunate: one white leg is also good; two or four are bad. Horses for common use should be brown or iron-grey; that is, between the colours of black and white, that they may be neither devils nor slugs. No quality in a horse will make a

Turk buy him, if of an unlucky or bad colour. No wonder, with such ideas as these on the subject, that the breed of horses in the East has degenerated.

A certain pasha was very fond of horses, and very proud of his appearance as a cavalier. Another pasha, however, being of a different opinion as to his friend's perfections, determined to rebuke him.

"Hark ye, friend!" said he; "I can understand that the Sultan should make me a pasha, for he has never seen me; but how it can have chanced that he should have made *thee* a pasha, whom he has seen, and seen on horseback, is, I confess, a mystery to me."

"The splendour of our rich pashas has a great deal fallen off," said my host; "it was a different guess-sort of thing when I was a lad. A certain Halil Pasha once paid a visit to my father. His travelling-trunks alone, all containing precious things, filled a large room. I paid twelve hundred piastres alone to the porters who carried them to our konack. Yet Halil was at that time in disgrace, and thought poor. No matter how many guests he had, he never allowed the same pipes to be served twice. We have no such pashas now.

"There are two stories of your friend the Caliph Haroun al Raschid," said my host, *à propos* to another conversation, the purport of which escapes me.

"In a time of great drought, the people besought the Caliph to intercede with Heaven for rain: he agreed to do so; but walking out in disguise, as he was wont, the same afternoon, he met a gardener working on his lands.

"'See,' said the Caliph, 'your plants are dying for want of moisture, why do you not water them?'

"'Know you not, O indiscreet stranger,' answered the man, that while the sun is high in the heavens water would only kill them more quickly?'

"Then the Caliph, returning to his palace, summoned the unwise people who had asked him to pray for rain, and rebuked them, saying, 'If this poor man knew when to water his plants, shall not God know also?'"

"It is also related among our own traditions, that when a

youth, he once required a favour from a great man. Going to solicit it, he found his patron stretched on a sofa, while slaves fanned away the flies. 'Helas!' cried Haroun; 'if this mighty man with all his power, cannot protect himself against a fly, how shall he help me against a a real danger?'"

The conversation having by this time waxed dreary, the vivacious little man rose to depart. He made a rapid salaam, and ran, rather than walked, out of the room, as all Turks do, lest their entertainer should be kept too long on his legs. The rest of the guests now began to rush off one by one, and at last I rose also, and my host, with lofty courtesy, conducted me to my bedroom door.

"My house is yours," he said, bowing grandly as he bade me good night; "I ask you but one thing : allow yourself to want for nothing which I can either offer or procure."

CHAPTER X.

THE BIN-BASHEE.

THE Bin-Bashee is an officer whose name signifies, in the imaginative language of the Turks, that he is the chief of a thousand warriors. This is, however, an assertion more imposing than correct; in fact, I am informed that our Bin-Bashee has not more than fifty-three men under his orders. I see them very often lounging about, hitching up their trousers, or sitting together in rows upon the ground smoking nargillies or conversing. Their complexion is oily, their hair lank, their eyes small, their noses have no cartilage, their lips are thick, their shoulders round, and they look sulky, as if they would like to punch the heads of mankind generally. If you could fancy soldiers made of a pale species of chocolate, and dressed in clothes much too short for them—a blue jacket and canvas trousers,—you will not have a bad idea of fifty-three men who are commanded by the Bin-Bashee. They seem to be all alike; I could not tell one from the other, if I were paid to do so.

They interest me. I delight in endeavouring to ease their minds; I waylay, and offer them stealthy cups of coffee; they are not used to such civilities, and though upon the whole they are still inclined to the belief that I am a dog of a Frank, they begin to entertain a conviction that even in dogs there may be a difference—that some are rabid and hostile, some are friendly, like poodles. They are learning gradually to consider me with a more good-humoured contempt, as belonging to the latter species.

Having thus prepossessed them in my favour, I am not surprised to observe that the eyes of the martial Bin-Bashee himself are now and then turned disdainfully towards my lattice as he passes that way.

I think, therefore, that I may safely employ Hamed to open negotiations on my behalf; to sing of the goodness of the sherbert we are beginning to manufacture this hot summer weather, the fragrance of my tobacco, and the friendliness of my disposition. The result is, that one of the chocolate men in the short clothes appears one morning at my dwelling; and his business is, to know when I will receive the Bin-Bashee.

Having shown all due honour to the nut-brown messenger, and assured him that I shall be happy to see the Bin-Bashee at any time or in any manner that it may please the Bin-Bashee to be seen, a solemn apparition smothered in a uniform as uncomfortable as possible, descends the little hill beneath the kiosch, and makes towards my abode; he is followed by a pipe-stick in waiting and several of those loose-looking satellites who seem to be an indispensable portion of the train of a Turkish gentleman whensoever he appears abroad.

The loose-looking satellites all wear slate-coloured trousers and straight plum-coloured coats—coats of a melancholy aspect. They are moody and taciturn; they have nothing to say in particular to anybody: they appear born to do the looking-on part in life. Their shoes are too large for them; they appear made for going to sleep in rather than for walking about. Their faces are of a length such is as only seen among that race of men to which they belong. Their hands are nowhere; perhaps they are waiting for yesterday's dinner; at least, this is the idea they give me as they sit bolt upright, and hold the pipes which are handed to them, as if uncertain what to do next.

It appears during a slower conversation than I ever remember to have had with anybody, that the Bin-Bashee has been as desirous to make my acquaintance as I have been to establish an intercourse with him: there the matter ends, however.

The Bin-Bashee is averse to any ribald gaiety of talk. One would almost like to shake him, to see if his words would come out any faster—I mean, to shake him bodily, for as to shaking him up mentally, that could only be done by a miracle. He belongs to the sleepy and desponding class which really forms so large a portion of the Turkish people, and which is said to form a larger. He is used up. Sir Charles Coldstream is vivacity itself compared with him; for the Bin-Bashee gives you an idea that his father, and grandfather and his great-grandfather, had all been used up before him. As I sit preparing fresh questions to draw him out, and thinking on what point I shall tickle him next, I wonder what would be the effect of a cracker or a squib let off under his nose, or of cunningly inserting a bunch of stinging nettles in the immense gulf which appears between his neck and the collar of his coat: I would give a moderate sum to be allowed to prove the experiment without indecorum.

I have tried him upon every convenient subject with which I am acquainted, but I might as well talk to a dignified owl, supposing that owl to be in a uniform which was not made for him: in short, it is impossible to move the Bin-Bashee any way. The conversation comes to a dead lock. I try with all my might to look interrogative and agreeable—I try till the skin of my forehead is almost cracking with the effort—but it positively will not do; and, after a deep silence of some five minutes, there is a movement among my visitors—they have all risen at once, as if moved by some slow piece of mechanism. I perceive that they mean going. I ask the Bin-Bashee to permit me to return his visit at the fort which he commands; he acquiesces with great solemnity; and then Bin-Bashee, satellites, and pipe-sticks in waiting all stalk drearily away, as if their steps were determined by the Dead March in Saul. I really feel that a cigar and a gossip with my neighbour are necessary to recover from the effects of his visit: the man is like a walking nightmare.

However, it is but courteous to return a call; and a day or two after our first interview I make up a party to go and see the fortress and the Bin-Bashee at the same time.

It is a glorious morning, and we walk through fields which literally look like gold and silver, from the profusion of white and yellow flowers which cover them. There are no flowers of any other colour except one, and that is a flower of a bright blue; it is almost hidden by the others, however, and, far away as the eye can see, stretches the same wealth of gold and silver blossoms.

Some Greeks accompany me; they are glad of the chance,

for the Turks would not admit them alone. As we go, they are eloquent as to the utter ruin, weakness, and rottenness of all things Turkish; they are certain that fifty determined youths from the town below might take the fortress, and put the Bin-Bashee and his chocolate soldiery to the sword, without the smallest difficulty; they have a mocking and bitter contempt for the conquering race—a contempt which is quite unpleasant, from its settled and purposelike intensity. I know, however, that any attempt to silence them would be merely an act of useless self-sacrifice on my part; that it would only make them hate and despise me, without softening their feelings a whit towards the Turks. We wind up a grass-grown path to the heights on which the castle stands; we pass beneath a ruined gate, rudely built up again, partly of shattered marble columns bearing ancient inscriptions, partly of unseasoned wood, which gapes in great thirsty cracks from the heat, and partly with rough blocks of the coarsest stone,—a melancholy type of ignorance and unthrift. The Greeks sneer as they point at it; well they may. The rest of the place, however, looks military enough: it has an orderly air; the stones are cleanly swept; the walls are of immense thickness. The guard turns out and salutes in a soldierly way, though their swords are awkward, and the short uniforms do not improve upon acquaintance; I vow the men's jackets seem made of shaved blankets, or dried sponge shrunk to half its size. We are conducted by a soldier (to the full as brown and taciturn as his comrades) towards the quarters of the Bin-Bashee: they are situated in one of a nest of dreary little houses; they look out on a dead wall; blue devils must hover by the score in the gloomy atmosphere, and have quite an established residence in every melancholy chamber thereabouts. Our host receives us politely, and, after a silent nargilly, prepares to accompany us over the rest of the castle.

It is a strong place; large piles of ammunition lie stored away in the magazines, and arms are cunningly arranged against the walls; every rampart bristles with guns, and they appear kept constantly ready for service. The Greeks try in vain to wrestle against the conviction of its strength, and wish to sneer it off; but the attempt is a failure. At last we come to a very grim battery which overlooks the town, and the Bin-Bashee informs us, with sleepy unconcern, that he could lay it in ruins in half an hour if refractory. There is something almost ludicrous in the haste with which the Greeks now urge our departure; a kind of panic seems to have seized them: but there is nothing funny in their dark plotting faces, if caught for a moment in repose: their eyes glare with an unhealthy light upon the Turkish philosopher; and I can see that they are writhing like wild cats in the toils of the fowler. Well, the place has been unquiet lately; the visit will do them good and keep them cool. They evidently were not prepared to find out how utterly powerless they would be in case of a riot. I hear no more of the fifty youths who would have no difficulty in seizing upon the fortress and putting the garrison to the sword; on the contrary, my friends have become all at once the very essence of meekness and compliment; their deference for the Bin-Bashee is notable, and they would play their parts with flattering success, were it not for the dangerous gleam in their eyes, which never softens or changes a moment.

The fortress is perhaps five or six hundred years old; it was built by the Genoese; it has been four hundred years in the hands of the Turks, yet the fetters and uncouth instruments of torture used in the Middle Ages still rust in the very places where, perhaps, they lay when the fortress was surrendered by the last Christian governor to Mahomet the Second. The drugs of some Byzantine physician are festering in ancient bottles; the memorials of a bygone race moulder where they were left when that race passed away from the land; the very corn in the granaries was never touched or cleared out, and its dust, disturbed by our tread, falls showering above us through the chinks of the ceiling.

I can fancy all sorts of hoards of forgotten treasure hidden in obscure parts of the vast rambling building, or buried in the earth upon the ramparts, by men who were struck down suddenly during the siege or hurled from the walls by the Moslem soldiers, and who so died carriyng their secrets with them. I can fancy the inhabitants of the town having brought much of their wealth there, as to a place of safety, and finding, with angry sorrow, that they had only collected it in a more convenient heap for the pitiless victors. I can fancy it was here that despairing patriotism made its last devoted stand, and frantic beauty sprang in horror from the walls. Thus musing upon war and warlike things, I take a dreary farewell of the Bin-Bashee, and so depart.

CHAPTER XI.

THE SEA-CAPTAIN.

THE compliments are over; there have been a good many of them, and the sailor sits curled up beside me on a most uncompromising little sofa. Twisting myself round as nearly as possible, I front him fairly, and we examine each other with much benevolence; so much, indeed, that the forehead of my friend quite shines with it. He is about fifty, a spare man with a slight stoop. He wears a brown surtout coat rather too long for him. He is buttony, too buttony. His trousers are short: if he were to mount on a donkey with them, he would have the sort of appearance which usually occasions enthusiastic delight to a turbulent boyocracy. He wears double shoes and the inevitable fez.

For the rest, he is as unlike the idea which you have cherished of a nautical Turk as can be. He has a hale mottled face, and a cold agreeable blue eye; he is completely shaved; his voice is pleasant, and he has an "eminently practical" way of speaking, which sounds more like Lincoln's Inn then the shores of the Bosphorus. Let us set him on his hobby. Two men who have never seen each other before, and have not, perhaps, two ideas in common upon any conceivable subject, hold but a dull conversation, without one will consent to mount his hobby, and the other is content to look on with a mild and subdued interest.

To do my excellent acquaintance justice, I must admit that I have no difficulty on this subject. He is not one of those stubborn, bristling gentlefolks that require coaxing or shoving up into the saddle, and, may be, prick your fingers for your pains. Quite the contrary, he vaults into it with a refreshing spring, and is off to the uttermost parts of the earth in a less time than it would have taken a slower man to pronounce the cabalistic name of *Jack Robinson*. He will pull up presently, and we shall take breath.

"Yes," says my eminently practical friend, "the ship *is* dirty very dirty; but we have been taking in a cargo of oil for the fleet. She has twenty-four guns; she does not go fast, she is too old for that; besides, we are not good sailors. We have been cruising about, looking for Greek pirates, and keeping watch over the safety of the Turkish islands in the Ægean. I should like to go into the Black Sea; there would be more chance of a prize. The Black Sea swarms with Ionian vessels.* The English Government have warned them not to go there; but they will do so. They say the Ionian Islands are not at war with Russia, and they have nothing to do with your quarrels; the consequence is, they *do* go, and are taken. One of your ships caught an Ionian schooner the other day: she had a cargo worth £8,000 on board. She will be sold, and there will be a fine amount of prize-money; I wish I had some of it, but we have seen nothing. How do we act when we meet a suspected ship in the high seas? Oh, it is all the same, suspected or not suspected! We signal her to hoist her colours and send somebody on board our vessel with her papers. If they are all right, we say 'Good day!' and there is an end of it; but if there is anything odd about them, we send an officer on board, and we can tell then by the language and appearance of the crew what she is, and what she is about. If she has deceived us, we tow her along into the nearest port: she is sold there, if there be a good bid; if not, she is sent to Constantinople; sometimes our Government buys her. We get one half her value, the Sultan gets the other. There is no mistake about that, not in the least. We are never defrauded of a para. The half we get is divided among us; I do not know in what proportion (I never made a captuer, worse luck; I wish I had, I would tell you in a moment. Turks and Britons should tell each other everything); all I do know

---

* Written during the Crimean War.

is, that I should get the largest share if we took a prize, the rest would be divided among the crew by Government. I might have the distribution of it, if it were a small sum, not otherwise; we do not do things in that way, we are very sharply looked after.

"How is our navy recruited? Oh, there is no difficulty about that! The sailors come of themselves, mostly from the islands. If they do not volunteer, they are pressed: the local authorities look to that. I should like to see the man who would not go as a sailor if he were ordered: they like it. I received fifteen volunteers the other day at Chios, and might have had fifty. Their term of service is eight years. If they have been wounded, they get good pensions; about thirty shillings a month, sometimes more. They may live anywhere they please. Thirty shillings a month is a handsome sum for a poor man in Turkey. When they first come on board, they receive only four shillings a month: their pay increases every year. A steady fellow is sure to do well in the navy, and to become an officer in a few years. We do not like the officers, however, who have been before the mast: they cannot read their orders from the admiral, but are obliged to show them to somebody who can. This makes things known which ought to be kept secret. I did not win my commission by merit or service; I was appointed by favour. There used to be some appointments of this kind, not many. Now officers are made at the Naval Schools; they turn out some very good ones. They enter as midshipmen, pass an examination, and then may or may not be promoted lieutenants. Our crew live very well. Should you like to taste their dinner? It is just ready. See! artichokes in a rich brown gravy, and with stewed bits of meat among them; also a thick white soup. Do you like it? So, that's right! Another mouthful, eh? You won't! Haidi, Youssouf! (Be off, Joe!)

"Your officers are quite right; it is impossible to do away with flogging in the navy; the sailors go on shore, and bully quiet people. There would be no keeping them in order without the lash. We do not bowstring; those times are gone by. Capital punishment is only for murder, or treason in war time. If a man deserts, we give him one hundred and twenty thumps with a double rope's end, about as thick round as your wrist; this leaves a wound on his back as big as your hand, and raw enough. Sometimes it mortifies, and he dies; sometimes it does not, and he lives. These, however, are extreme cases. If any of my men were to run away, I should let them go. This is, perhaps, why they stay.

"We are very fond of visiting; we have rules about it, in the same way as you have. The rank of a captain is determined by the number of guns in his vessel; the captain who has the fewest guns pays the first visit. He is saluted; the visit is returned, then there is another salute, after which both vessels salute the flags with twenty-one rounds; that is to say, silly people who like a noise do this. Some of our captains are more sensible, and spare the powder.

"Yes, my uniform is very comfortable; but you are not to suppose that this old brown coat is my full uniform! God forbid! I have one so distressing to wear that I could by no means pass two hours imprisoned in it; I keep it for grand occasions. I used to have the *nishan*, a large golden medal ornamented with diamonds; everybody had the *nishan* in those days. It was a sign of rank, like the epaulette with you. I have not got it now; a year or two ago the Sultan called them all in: it was said to be a measure of economy, but nobody ever yet heard what has become of the *nishans* which were returned. I was much distressed at being obliged to give back mine; it was a pretty ornament, and I had just laid in a large supply of the regulation ribbon; I now use that ribbon, indeed, for my watch; but my friends joke me about it. We sailors, however, are not rich, and cannot afford to throw away anything.

"Mind you do not tumble down the ladder; it is very dark down there; that is where the men sleep. Here are the hooks for hammocks; I do not know anything about ventilation, though I am ready to learn. The arms, as you say, are all old and worn out; yes, useless I am afraid. Our cannons, however, are newer, and very good indeed. That is an officer's cabin: he cannot lie down in it, he must go to sleep sitting. There is no place for the light to come through. We have a

H

surgeon on board. That is *his* room ; he is a properly-qualified man, a Greek. When he is not here, I serve out the medicines myself. When the men first join, they are always asking for medicine ; when they have had a dose or two, they leave off.

"Well, I am sorry you are going, but it is better to put off before sunset, or else we shall not be able to give you a salute. We might forget that it was sunset for a little while ; but the cutter anchored off the shore there is sure to announce it with her guns. We never give salutes after sunset ; I do not know why, or why we give salutes at all, except that they shake the ship a good deal. I am sorry we cannot hoist a flag for you, because we have not got one. Many thanks for your visit ; I hope you have not been disappointed. My ship is not so fine or so clean as Admiral *Slade's;* but then Admiral Slade has done a great deal for our navy in a very quiet and sensible manner; we ought to be very much obliged to him, and we are. There was never an officer more able and popular; but we cannot learn everything at once ; by-and-by there will be a great difference in our navy; there has already been an immense improvement, there will be a greater."

"And so a jolly good night to you, old gentleman ; a more communicative, easy-going fellow never mounted a hobby-horse. Britons and Turks, as you say, should be on good terms ; come and smoke a pipe with me ; we will have some bottled porter, and a yarn of any length you please." I would say more, but the rusty rail of the companion-ladder has given way in my hand ; I am precipitated into the boat with some indecorum and presently a salute nearly blows us out of the water. Our boatmen (there are ten of them) pause upon their oars as the guns are blazing. When they cease, we take off our hats in acknowledgment, and the chatty old boy looks after us as we go upon our way. He is gossiping with one of his officers, and seems highly satisfied with the world in general.

CHAPTER XII.

DOWN THE DANUBE.

THE navigation of the Danube is always difficult; but, when the waters are low, it is dangerous: so we ran aground for the third time in the neighbourhood of a small Austrian military station in the Banat of Temesvar. I landed. It was well to do so, for there is no village in the world so desolate and uninteresting that an observer may not glean something there.

It was a savage little place at the foot of a grand range of hills, but semicircled by meadows and rich lowlands towards the river side. I entered one of the peasants' huts. It was built of clay, and roofed with wood cut in the form of tiles. It was composed of a single room, with a large stone block in the centre. Upon this block burned, smouldering, the half of a tree in one huge log fresh felled. There was no chimney, so that the constant smoke and heat of the fire had completely charred the interior of the hut, and it was quite black. For furniture was a three-legged iron cooking-pot of an uncouth shape, three wooden spoons, a mat of rushes, a sheepskin, and a little tin oil-lamp hung against the wall. At the doorway, for there was no door, a man sat on the uprooted stump of a tree, larding and combing his hair. He was very particular about it, and it was easy to perceive, from the expression of his countenance, that he enjoyed a deep-seated satisfaction in his personal appearance. After some time he rose, shook himself into trim array (his loose clothes required no other arrangement), entered the hut, and taking the three-legged pot off the fire, marched with it in a stiff military way to a barn, where some messmates awaited him. In this barn was piled up a large quantity of Indian corn in sacks ready for market. And the quaint-shaped, three-legged pot contained the dinner of the rustic coxcomb and his friends. It was a stew of pork and a savoury miscellany of vegetables, chiefly onions. The party required neither dishes nor plates, but, seating themselves upon their hams, each man took a knife out of a wooden sheath at his girdle, and fished for the juiciest bits. So they sat on the floor with the pot in the midst of them, silent, but busy. I noticed that every man wore a ring and some other articles of personal ornament, also that they were dandies in their way, though one would not have thought it.

I watched them till they had finished their meal, and then followed the most promising-looking of the party, for the purpose of holding a short conversation with him. He was a pleasant open-faced little fellow when you got close to him, and of the same healthy brown colour as most wild animals. His conversation had a fine game flavour in it, too, which I liked amazingly. For a dress, he appeared simply to have cut off the legs of a sheep, and to have got into its skin. His primitive garment was tied at the throat with thongs of roughly-knotted hide.

"I am fourteen years old," says the wild little man (he was, probably, eight-and-thirty), "and I am, of course, a private in one of the Austro-Wallachian frontier regiments. There are eighty thousand of us altogether employed in this service. We serve on military duty one week in four, and we each receive a florin a month for pay. The rest of our time we devote to our own affairs. I am married. I have eight children, ten pigs, and two cows. I and my friend" (a long man of the same species, who sat smoking on a sack of Indian corn) "have also some sheep between us. We have no money. We do not like soldiering, but we must like it." Here he grins slyly, and I take the opportunity of observing that his legs are bound up with dingy twisted woollen rags, about the size and colour of haybands. Lowering still further the glance of observation, I become aware that his feet are shod with undressed sheepskin—a kind of sandal. While my new acquaintance was reposing smilingly after this brief discourse, a woman came out of a neighbouring hovel and strode with a firm free step towards us. She was a splendid gipsy-faced dame, with bright black eyes, deep set and full of meaning; they glowed with a far-away and mystic fire quite bewildering. Her hair, the glossy blue-black of the raven's-wing, shaded a complexion rich with the warm hues of health and exercise. There was something striking in her beauty, and her carriage was graceful and stately as a stag's. Nature seemed to have created her a huntress queen—fate had made her a peasant girl. The wild little man told me with a familiar nod of intelligence that she was the wife of his long friend on the corn sack; and, emboldened by this introduction, I tried to engage her in conversation, mustering all my Wallachian for the occasion; but she only showed a dazzling set of teeth, and squeezed my hand in a half-shy and remonstrative, half-patronizing way. Then, mounting a little springless waggon, to which two wiry ponies were already harnessed, she struck her husband laughingly over the head with a pig-whip, and called out with a short, good-humoured, but imperious exclamation of command to his partner. Both grinned from ear to ear. My little acquaintance cast a sort of apologetic glance at me, as much as to say, "You see there is no resisting this bewitching vixen;" and I am bound in candour to confess that he was right. So they climbed up into the waggon, and stuck their wooden pipes, about a foot long, to repose in safety, in the bandages round the calves of their legs. The short man seized a pair of rope reins, and away they rattled. The dame kept the pig-whip, and, by a smart use of it, judiciously distributed among the ponies and the swains, the little waggon was soon whirling away at a brisk gallop. It was quite surprising to see how the small horses were tugged and pushed about by it, for every wheel seemed to act like a member of an experimental government, in perfect independence of the rest. I watched it appearing and disappearing among ruts and hillocks, like a boat in a wintry sea, and I was sorry when a turn in the road hid it finally from my view.

Wandering onwards, I soon came to the Austrian corps-de-garde. The officer on duty was an intelligent, gentlemanly young man. He said he was very busy (how, I did not inquire), and that he had neither time nor inclination to go after the game in the neighbourhood, though it abounded with wild boar and waterfowl, and there were even some deer. His dinner, he told me—a simple meal—cost him two shillings a day. It was prepared at the village inn. He might have had a better in London for half the price. So much for cheap living in these countries.

As we were talking, a cart, with a decent, orderly company of country-folk in holiday-clothes, came slowly along. They were a wedding-party—bride, bridegroom, and old folk on both sides. The Austrian officer, who was at liberty to go where he pleased, followed them home, and he was so obliging as to permit me to accompany him.

The bride was a stout square-built country lass, with a short neck, splay feet, and broad hands. Her complexion was pale and sodden. Her eyes were small and dull; moreover, they turned slightly inwards. Her mouth was fat and white; yet the local peculiarities of race were as marked and evident in her, as in the gay, dashing, gipsy termagant who had just flaunted by; only this poor bride was probably reared in some damp, unwholesome, marshy district, and bore the traces of it in every shapeless and passionless feature. For a bridal costume she wore a red handkerchief folded into a narrow band, and encircling her head like a coronet. Her hair (of a rusty brown) had a few flowers stuck awkwardly into it, and they drooped as if ashamed to be there. She had on a short sheepskin jacket, with the wool turned inwards. It was embroidered with a rude device in coloured wool. A girdle of untanned leather was round her waist, and to this was suspended a pouch, which hung down behind, like the sabretash of a hussar. It was bordered with a long parti-coloured woollen fringe. Her petticoat and chemise of undressed linen were profusely studded with little spots of red and blue embroidery, diamond-shaped. On one of her fingers was a silver ring, a necklace of coins and blue beads glittered round her throat, and blue glass earrings adorned her ears.

The bridegroom, a shy, abashed bumpkin, washed for the

occasion, wore a high, black, peakless, sheepskin cap, embroidered woollen leggings, a dirty calico tunic, or petticoat, descending below the knee, and a brown frieze jacket, with rows of little brass buttons, intended for ornament, not for use. His long, straight hair, which had never felt the scissors, descended to his shoulders. His small twinkling eyes were deep set, and had a puzzled expression. Though young, his skin was wrinkled quite in plaits, like the front of a shirt. He was shaven, save for a ragged moustache clipped close to the lip, but descending in long uneven locks at the ends. He was very thin. He talked readily, though he was somewhat confused and flustered with the events of the day. He told me that when I had first seen him, he was returning from the chief station, whither he had been obliged to go with his bride to ask permission to marry of his commanding officer. The compulsory attendance of the lady on these occasions, he added, often caused hot blood among the peasantry. His commanding officer was a captain and a count. He had four subalterns, also young men, serving under him, and twenty-four privates. They were stationed at a small village about a league away.

Leaving the wedding party, after a time, to finish their rustic merrymaking undisturbed by the presence of a stranger, I wandered forwards among the rich pastures of the river-side, and at last lay down a-musing by the troubled restless waters of the mighty Danube. At a little distance from me were a herd of some two hundred swine. They lay chumping their food and fattening in the mild grey air of the November noon. They were strange pigs, with woolly coats, long tails, long heads, and monstrous tusks. Two swineherds tended them. One carried a rude musical instrument, made of a reed, and played on it, from time to time, some plaintive and monotonous airs, not unmusical. The other leaned on a stout staff (it was a peeled sapling newly cut) and listened silently. When the music ceased they spoke together in drowsy murmurs. There was a world of untold poetry in the little group, a poetry of which the dwellers in cities little dream. But I could hear their low voices mingling with the ceaseless flow of the haunted river, and they seemed to me very eloquent.

Of such a race as these poor youths was the last * Prince of Servia—a swineherd, who hewed his brave way through many vanities, galled and sore, through fierce enmities and hostile interests, up to sovereign power. What wild will-o'-the-wisps among the marshes of human affairs are such rare successes, gleaming only to lead astray and lure on young ambition unto scorn !

So I mused on. From a little distance came, at intervals, the listless tinkle of bells round the necks of grazing cows. Some geese walked in grave dignity among the reeds and stubble further a-field. The wind sighed like the voice of human sorrow grown gentle in its solemn depths, and spoke its sad message to the leaves, in a voice low, soothing, and full of pity. The rich tints of wondrous autumn are departing fast. The forest kings upon the opposite hills put off their glorious panoply of state with which they welcomed in the new-born month, and soberly prepare for their winter sleep. A solitary wayfarer goes singing along the road, and smiting the stones with his staff. The echoes of his strokes ring clear and shrill. Their clank startles the partridge in her cover; the wild duck flies with tremulous pinions and a short fearful quack as he draws near; the frog dives, with a gurgling croak, among the marsh weeds; and the deer goes bounding over the thicket on the heights. On the other side, where our ship lies crippled with broken paddles, stretch the tall poplars far away by the dusty road. They stand like the spirits of the departed heroes of some patriot band who have fallen in battle, and whose souls have passed into tall trees, ever more sighing over the ruin of their land, according to the mournful traditions and sweet fancies of the Dacian legends. The willows nod in clusters of twos and threes entwined together by the waters, like sisters at a fountain; and afar off stands a noble oak-tree, majestic and alone. I grew sad and thoughtful when the closing evening gradually drew her veil over a sylvan picture so enchanting as that which brooded over these charmed glades.

* Milosch.

CHAPTER XIII.

THE SCHOOLMASTER.

HE would make a fine study for a painter, as the type of a grand inquisitor : he is a small, spare, delicate-looking creature, and slightly crooked, perhaps from mere weakness, perhaps from a trifling deformity of spine ; but there is a wonderful power of evil about his face ; I never saw a man with an expression so determined and dangerous ; his smile is positively deadly. He is very pale, and his strong dark beard is shaved carefully away from his hollow cheeks ; his black hair is scant and lank ; his forehead *narrow;* his brows sombre, heavy, and terrible ; they project in a singular manner over eyes whose meaning has something strangely secret and sinister. His nose is high and hooked, his mouth wide, his chin pointed ; he makes contortions as he walks, and his step is silent and stealthy as that of a cat. His small white womanly hands are always cold and clammy ; it is not good to shake them.

By profession he is a scholar, and there are few Greek books ancient or modern with which he is not familiar—from Hellanicos the Lesbian, who wrote earlier than Herodotus, down to the feminine prattle of Anna Comnena, and the silliest of the Byzantine historians, he knows them all, as well as the last fiery pamphlet of Soutzo, or the last frantic leaders in the Athenian newspapers. His erudition is quite startling : his industry must have been unwearied ; for he was born a rayah, nearly forty years ago, before the educational movement in Turkey had become so general as it is now ; he was born also in an out-of-the-way place, and is entirely self-taught, yet a very cave of learning. He has come to pay me a visit ; to those who know the Greeks it is almost needless to say why, or why he brought a present in an embroidered pocket-handkerchief, which my servant persuaded him to send home again before he went upstairs. He wants something; I know this of course intuitively, as I clap my hands for coffee, and ask him to take a seat opposite me, where the light falls well on his face. He begins with a series of fidgety and extravagant compliments, which make me very uncomfortable; I even feel for the "*fleck on my nose*" which a Greek proverb says is inevitable on such occasions; but I let him go on, and listen without any visible signs of impatience, except one or two abortive attempts to change the conversation. Then I pass the time in wondering how a man, undoubtedly so gifted and able, should suppose that I, or anybody else, cannot read his designs just as well as if they were written on his forehead in letters an inch long. By-and-by he begins to double, and turn, and twist; he is drawing nearer to his subject; why he does not come to it plainly and at once, I cannot for the life and soul of me conceive; but perhaps he finds it impossible to overcome the terrible taint of trickiness which forms one of the most unfortunate and invariable characteristics of his race. It is astounding to watch how the man does turn, and shuffle, and quirk, and writhe, and lose the time in offering flatteries so far-fetched and unreasonable that they eat quite sour, and I wonder how or where on earth he scented them. He has been with me a fair half-hour, and I have not the slightest idea what he has come about; I must find out soon, however, for it is post-day, and I am busy; so I clap my hands again for *Hamed*, and ask, as a feeler, whether the Dahometan consular agent has called or not.

The Greek writhes: "One moment, Kyrie!" he says, with a twitch that is quite spasmodic. I express the utmost readiness to give him as many moments as he pleases, and, putting on an earnest look, I draw my chair close up to him; so I have him at once in a corner: this is what I wished to do. Egad! he has beat me again! Richelieu or Talleyrand were babies in diplomacy to the simplest of Greeks. Compliments again, compliments again! Well, it is no use interrupting him, so I look full into the terrible eyes as good-humouredly as possible, and await the result with as interrogative an expression as courtesy will permit. Eheu! here we are!

The man wishes me to serve him : I can do so, for he is manifestly in the right. I do not come to this conclusion from what he says to me ; I know that I could not place the slightest reliance on that ; but I happen personally to be acquainted with the whole circumstances of his case, and though he has distorted them in a manner that would amaze anybody whose business it was not resolutely to overcome such a feeling, enough truth remains to show clearly that the man has been wronged. A brief word with the Governor, simply informing him of the circumstance, will soon set all to rights. So I re-assure my visitor, who looks positively diabolical, between fear and hatred, and a thwarted thirst for vengeance. I jot down a few names and dates for my guidance when I shall see our kind-hearted Pasha, and again assure the Greek of my conviction that this functionary is ignorant of the matter of his complaint, and will see him righted at once.

My visitor puts forth one of his small clammy hands, and it trembles on my arm ; I look up from the notes I have been making, and a sickly smile passes over the scholar's face. "Tell the Pasha to punish them," he says : "to make them *afraid of me!*" As he speaks, I notice his free hand nervously opening and shutting, and his teeth are so firmly closed that it is strange they do not split each other in twain.

"You will have justice," I say ; "the Pasha is incapable of countenancing a wrong : I think I can venture almost to pass my word for him."

" But the dogs should be made afraid of me," he gnashes out again : "the barbarians, the tyrants ! there *is* no justice for the Greek. I want them to *fear* me," he adds, with frightful emphasis. "For four hundred years we have been under the hoofs of these oxen—these swine ! When will our day of retribution come? Our sins have brought them on us ! our sins have brought them on us !" he reiterates ; when fortunately there is a step on the stairs, and somebody else coming into the room puts a stop to our conversation. I would have given something for the interruption, though it does condemn me to hear another flourish of compliments. Well, I could not have escaped *them*, and as well now as then ! So the door closes on my stealthy visitor, who perhaps under healthier political institutions might have been an honour to his age and country, instead of the pitiful thing we have seen him. The stuff is there, the genius, patience, energy, a desire for knowledge which amounts to a consuming passion; but it has been spoiled in the making up; and he is one of many, perhaps the very commonest type of his people.

I have studied the Greek character carefully and earnestly; I know its weaknesses and its fearful strength, its deep and indelible shame; but the servitude of four hundred years is a sad school of fraud, and the weak are apt enough to be deceived into the idea that deceit and intrigue are the only possible arms against chartered oppression. Had Tancred or Barbarossa established a permanent Latin empire on the banks of the Bosphorus, there would probably not now be a single Greek to tell the story; they would have mingled with their conquerors; they would have accepted the union of the two churches, which was so anxiously debated by the Popes of the middle ages, and the conquered and the victors would have gradually mingled into the same race. But one of the most singular features of Turkish conquest is, that while it was all-potent against nations, it seemed powerless against individuals; the Turks did not succeed in establishing their faith in a single country of Europe, even at the time when they had settlements from the Po and the Darro to the Elbe and the frontiers of France.

Of all the races over which they ruled, none preserved a character more completely distinct than that which was most hopelessly enslaved. The nationality of the Greeks had a marvellous strength of life and energy about it: they preserved their own customs, dress, religion, and even their own peculiar system of local government, in the very teeth of as iron a despotism as ever palsied hope from out men's hearts; for such was the rule of the Turks till within this last generation. I will not pursue that subject. I am not one of those who desire to see a Greek empire; nor do I draw the same conclusion from these facts as the Athenian newspapers. The one quality which the Greeks have not, and never have had at any period of their history, is an enlightened idea of the manner in which a great state should be governed. Their ideas on this point were as disgraceful as many of their other qualities were respectable. Very shortly after the conquest of Constantinople, nearly all the material part of public business was in the hands of Greek renegades. They were mostly men of undoubted ability: they wanted only the single qualification which was requisite to fit them for their posts; just as their ancestors, since the time of Pericles; and even Pericles himself had wanted it. I could go farther into this argument; and without the smallest doubt, as it seems to me, I could prove that the most vaunted governments of the earlier Greek states were as wrong in theory as they were infamous in practice. But such a task is fitter for a schoolboy's theme than a place here. What I desire for the Greeks is not *Power*, but *Justice*. It is a difficult thing to explain the precise state of the Greek Rayah population in Turkey, and one which requires some nice distinctions. The fact is, the Turks are, upon the whole, rather afraid of them than otherwise. They are afraid of their perseverance, industry in intrigue, and of their acute and unscrupulous natures. They are afraid of them, and have reason to be so. No statesman in Turkey has ever kept his place long who was seriously opposed by the Greek interest. The local pashas are positively tyrannized over by them, and their means of action are extensive and powerful. They have quite a genius for complaints: they make a market of their wrongs, and their ignominy may be called a fortune to them.

Then there is a question whether they *are* wronged, or whether, like most grumblers, they have not excellent reason to be contented. I am afraid this question cannot be answered satisfactorily. Their position is undoubtedly improper; yet perhaps they labour rather under the shadow of wrong, than the substance of it. Men, however, who are in perpetual fear for their fortunes and liberties, may be allowed to complain, though they have no fear for their lives. If you flourish a horsewhip constantly before a man's eyes, he may feel almost as indignant as if struck with it. To be a Rayah in Turkey, is a seeming disgrace: it is not a real misfortune. This, however, is quite enough to call for redress. It is in the highest degree impolitic to allow evils to appear, where none actually exist. The Turks derive no benefit whatever from the nominal servitude of the Greeks : it would be therefore as wise as just to abolish their disabilities.* Twice the sum collected for the Haratch, or poll-tax, would be paid cheerfully under any other name; a fair two-thirds of the Haratch is now evaded altogether, though it fills the prisons and is the staple topic of coffee-house politicians. Then the notorious bad faith of the Greeks has been hitherto the great obstacle to their evidence being received in Turkish courts of law; and there is no reason why it should not be always looked upon with extreme suspicion. But why have they trumpeted the fact abroad by an offensive regulation, which will not work one way or the other? Judges may know that, in dealing with Greek witnesses, the greatest caution and patience are indispensable to get at truth; but nothing could justify the exclusion of a whole community from the rights of self-defence and vindication before the law. I may be privately of opinion that the Turks, as a people, are better than the Greeks as a people; but I am not therefore justified in concluding wholesale, that all Turks are better than all Greeks. I may think that a Turkish gentleman will almost certainly tell me the truth; but I cannot be equally sure that a Greek will tell me a falsehood. Legislation must not be based on extreme or even general cases : it should apply to all.

Now, the case of the Rayah gentleman is pitiable. It has made him what we have seen. He is obliged by law or custom to wear a distinctive dress: he is undeniably exposed to personal insult and contumely: his dignity is never safe: his property is by no means so secure as it ought to be. Most of the honourable careers of life are closed to him. He is a mere dweller in the land; he cannot be a patriot, for he has no share in his country's danger or her glory. Her victories only rivet his chains; her ruin could be nothing worse for him than a change of masters. He has even a premium for

* Most of the Christian disabilities were abolished in consequence of these suggestions: but still there is too much truth in what is here said to warrant its being effaced. The Christian subjects of the Porte have not yet equal rights with the Mohammedans.

hoping the latter rather than the former; for the greatest of all the passions in his restless mind is that of religious enthusiasm.

Now these things call loudly enough for attention : their voice is growing fearfully earnest; and I would sum up this chapter by saying plainly, that unless we insist upon the Porte according immediate emancipation to her Christian subjects, we shall have the majority of them constantly working against us by all possible means ; and there is a great doubt if, in the end, public opinion among us will not get gradually much more in favour of the Rayahs than it has been,—not from any faith or hope in them, but from the natural sympathy of Englishmen with all those who are oppressed.*

* The recent demonstrations throughout England (1876) shew how exactly this opinion was verified.

CHAPTER XIV.

A TURKISH RAYAH.

HE is a fine handsome man, tall and upright, with something of the Greek swagger about him; a proud, vain, dashing fellow, the very type of a flaunting young cavalier. His dress is exquisitely tasteful; it is slashed and embroidered in the very latest fashion of *Jannina:* there is something striking about its *débonnaire* and elaborate grace. Smart love-locks curl crisply round the Rayah's face, the purple beard of which is decently shaved away, save for a pointed moustache standing quite on end with consequence. He is in the midst of his women-kind; of the mother who so dotes on him; of the girl of his heart, and, perhaps, an ancient flame or two. The lesser stars of the village cluster enviously round him: they look at him with all their eyes, and they copy every look and motion of the young dandy, to do killing service second-hand; for they know that the hearts of all the belles for twenty miles round have been aching for him these three years.

But if yonder dirty savage Turk, who is beating his over-burthened mule up that stony little hill, were to force his way into the elegant home of the Greek, and to dash his clenched fist in the gallant's face, to cut off one of the young beau's ears or his nose, none would stop him; if, entering with other fanatic companions, he were to beat and insult every man, or woman present, it is more than probable that none would dare complain of him, or be listened to if they did.

I do not mean to say that Turks are outraging Christians night and day everywhere. I only suppose a frequent case in out-of-the-way places.

Standing erect in the market-place is a baggy-breeched man,

with all the importance of fifty winters about him, in his authoritative voice and decent mien : when he speaks, the little knot of listeners round him hold their breaths. His wisdom and prudence, his honest blameless life, are known for miles around in every town and hamlet. They have gained him the general consideration and some £10,000 of well-earned savings, both very respectable things. He has been several times codgea-bashee, or Greek chief of his district, and not a dispute among his acquaintance has been arranged these fifteen years without his advice and assistance. He is a worthy man, who has fulfilled the duties which have devolved upon him conscientiously and well. He is also aware of this : you can see his self-esteem in his composed bearing, and hear it in his measured discourse ; you might tell it, too, by the general deference paid to him. But here comes the Turkish Cadi ! He is a fat, coarse, vulgar person, who is notoriously understood to be amassing money by the vilest robberies ; by the wrongs of the orphan, the widow, and the helpless ; by bribes, corrupt dealing, iniquities, and rogueries of every conceivable kind : a man whose ignorance is only less astounding than his villany. He comes, rolling majestically along with some half-dozen strutting rascals, armed to the teeth, and carrying his pipe-sticks. The road is not large enough for him ; and the little knot of Greeks are scattered by his appearance like a flock of wild ducks by a shot. One of them, however (and I am sorry to find it is our dignified acquaintance of the foregoing paragraph), is rather lame ; he cannot get out of the way so quickly as is prudent ; and, besides, he is not used to hasten his motions indecorously. So one of the Cadi's bravoes seizes him by the nape of the neck : there is a horselaugh among the rest ; they expect sport, and they are not disappointed. The lame man, impelled by the simple mechanism of a kick, and also pushed forward by his neck, is seen in brisk motion for a minute ; then he falls in the winter mud ; two or three thwacks from a stout stick teach him the respect due to a cadi, and on sweeps the judge and his followers.

    I do not say that all Greeks are worthy of respect, or that

every cadi is ignorant and brutal; I am only relating an occurrence I witnessed yesterday.

There is a bride going to her home in a mountain village. Oh how tenderly her husband watches her! How proudly he marches by her side, and how daintily she sits upon her ambling mule! She is a coquette, too, I am afraid, and exacts a thousand little attentions : now there is something wrong about her pillion ; now she is sure her mule will stumble over those terrible loose stones ; now she would like to stop and give him some of the dancing water which sparkles along their path at the base of a hill. Never was there such a delightful journey, and as every halt ends with a little dispute, and a refreshing smacking of the lips before they go on again, they can never stop too often. So the evening creeps on. They are alone ; there is not a house or a human being near for a league, maybe, and what harm in a little dalliance? If a stranger were likely to pass, then, indeed, the jealous hood would be drawn over her head in a minute. But liberty is sweet after such weary years of seclusion. Why does the girl grow pale, and her lover tremble? Was there a whoop, like the yell of a savage Indian, so near them? Oh, yes, there is no mistaking the wild shouts of the Albanians; and in five minutes afterwards the young husband is bound bowed and bleeding to a tree, and his wife is carried off shrieking. The bride of three days is found next morning by the wayside, having been first outraged, and then beaten to death.

I do not say that all the lawless Albanians are chartered murderers on the highway, or that all Greek ladies who come in their way are insulted and murdered by them. I relate merely what I read in this morning's newspaper.

A tradesman is sitting in his shop; he is smoking the pipe of thoughtfulness, and waiting for customers ; but he will not trust. This is a weakness he has. Perhaps because his profits are too small to risk them, and because he has a large family to bring up. Some of his children are at school, some are at work ; but one, the pride of his heart, is studying medicine at Athens. It has taken all the old man's savings to send and keep him there ; it is of this son that he is thinking now, and of how glad he shall be to see him back again, a naturalized Greek subject in Frank clothes!

The entrance of a Turk disturbs the old man's musings. The new comer is a policeman, and he wants some rice. The trader hastens rather nervously to serve him, for he knows the Turks are angry men in those parts. But the money! Who is that old man writhing in the dust under the blows of a cudgel? It is the trader!

The Pasha rides abroad, and where's the wonder? It is a soft, clear day, in early spring-time. The green grass is sprouting freshly from the rejoicing earth; the trees are bursting forth in glad blossoms, and the birds are singing a welcome to the Summer as she comes from afar. But surely there was a devil at that poor tailor's elbow, when he hearkened to his helpmate, and hired a mule to go and collect some debts in the next village. For he meets the Pasha and his train in a narrow road. He is too anxious to keep his seat on any terms, to see how near he is drawing to the great man's cavalcade. Yet that Pasha and his horses are the last things which the tailor will see in this world, as he is pushed furiously aside by a Turkish horseman, and he rolls over the road's edge to rise again, never!

I am not romancing! Make a tour in Asia Minor, and you may see these things yourself.

And there are dark stealthy men mustering by night in many places, and their talk is treason; the gall and bitterness in their hearts makes the expression of their faces demoniacal: each man is a living type of hate and rage. These men, too, are hiding arms; they are collecting money; they are taking fearful oaths of secrecy and vengeance. There is no visible movement among them yet; but they know that in Epirus * their fellow-sufferers have again raised the red hand, and that there is to be another struggle. They are gathering strength, therefore, and awaiting the signal from their priests and elders, from the schoolmaster, who writes so often to Athens; from the archbishop, whose robes and mitre came from Russia. Some of them remember that such men were the leaders of the last

* This might have been written yesterday—1876.

revolt; and they have already been singled out to lead that which is coming.

There is also a wise and cautious creature in Downing Street. His chief pastime is asserting his own infallibility and causing the world to tremble generally whenever he has a fit of the blues. Possibly he is of opinion that the Greek question must come some day under his august consideration; he has already had the same idea any time these last few years; but he has not yet decided in his mind *when* the eventful moment will turn up. Upon the whole, he thinks the best way to proceed would be to cautiously mislead the world into another battle of Navarino, and another independent Greece.

Now, I am not of his Infallibility's opinion on this head. We had an opportunity of putting this theory in practice no less than half a century ago; but it does not appear that any good has yet come of it. As I write, therefore, in the interests of some millions of most unhappy human beings, I shall take the liberty of speaking plainly.

It seems to me that the allies of the Porte are not justified in temporizing with such an evil as this; they have no right to support Turkey till it is remedied. There was an old fable about the rape of Europa by a mad bull; I am sorry to say I see something very much like it in sober reality, and I think I know the bull. It is astounding to reflect that there exist in our own time some three thousand ignorant barbarians in Europe and Asia, who keep in cruel and wrongful subjection more than five times their number of Christian men; who beat, insult, and outrage them daily, because of their belief in Christ. It is still more astounding to observe that liberal and enlightened England is now supporting those barbarians in such a course of conduct.

I solemnly protest against the criminal and singular war in which we are about to take part (1853!!!).* It must be remembered that it is the state of the Christians in Turkey which has furnished Russia with her ostensible excuses; had this evil been done away with twelve months ago, there would have been no seizure of the Danubian provinces; there

* War brewing again under the auspices of Lord Cacus, the wise man of Bickerstaffe, in 1876.

would have been no *Sinope;** and there would certainly have been no necessity for our armed interference to punish Russia, if she had been still disposed to be troublesome. We are simply about to pay the just penalty in blood and treasure of wilfully and obstinately standing up for what we know to be wrong.

And if any one should pretend to say that after four centuries of patient suffering, the time is not yet come for the Rayahs to be relieved, and that if they rise at last in arms against their oppressors, the allies of Turkey ought to knock them down, I say that such a line of argument is more incomprehensible still. If objections to the immediate emancipation of the Rayahs are offered by European statesmen, such objections are simply monstrous; if by the Turks, they are an insult to the whole Christian world.

Now, there is no middle course to be taken; no way of putting off the question, and making things pleasant. The Rayahs will not, under present circumstances, be pacified by promises; nor would any other body of men in their place. They believe they now see a good opportunity of obtaining the undeniable rights of man, and this after ages of shame and pain. They may be right, or they may be wrong; but such *is* their opinion, and they mean to act upon it. Let it be distinctly understood that we, as well as Turkey, have now to choose between the most enthusiastic support, or the most determined enmity of a race of men unexampled in courage and resources; of men who are among the most determined soldiers and the ablest seamen in the world; of men whose very souls are now in arms. And I say, that unless a Christian charter be granted gracefully and at once, Russia will have an active and resolute agent at every Rayah hearth in Turkey; while we shall have an enemy who is already beginning to look upon the policy of Lord Cacus, the wise man of Bickerstaffe, and those of his way of thinking, with almost frantic abhorrence.

* Bulgarian Atrocities.

CHAPTER XV.

THE GREEK EASTER AT CONSTANTINOPLE.

THE Greek Lent is over, and it is Easter at Constantinople; all night long great guns have been firing afar off, and small-arms are being discharged by excitable persons at every street corner; you might fancy the town was being stormed, instead of holding high festival, so violent is the noise and uproar. During the day the streets are crowded as a fair, and perambulated by itinerant vendors of good things, as boisterous as on a Saturday night at Wapping. Fowls, sweetmeats, rank pastry, various preparations of milk and rakee, seem to be the chief things which furnish a Greek merry-making at Constantinople. Little boys, with eager black eyes and tallowy complexions, are in their glory, and go yelling and whooping about, to the dismay of staider wayfarers.

Here is a Greek, and there is a Greek; with their splendid picturesque figures, and dark matted hair falling about their faces in wild disarray; I know of no people more romantic in appearance. They go swaggering about from street to street in all the bravery of their national costumes, and you may hear their voices a hundred yards off, as they wrangle and glare at each other on the smallest occasion of dispute. The dominant race, the grave and dignified Turks, demean themselves far differently: they sit about cross-legged on the benches of coffee-houses, or before the movable stalls of mohahbé and yaourt. However dirty, poor, and miserable a Turk may be, he always smokes his pipe with the same grand calm air. When two or three Mohammedans are gathered together, they will perhaps tell each other now and then that God is great, but this is evidently the only attempt at conversation which is suited to their sense of self-importance and the heat of the day.

Moving on through a motley crowd which fills the sunlit streets, and taking silent note of these things, I saunter along past the guard-house at the street corner, where the officer on service is smoking a pipe, past the artillery-ground, with its useless guns, past the immense dung-heap which has been collecting for years beside it, and past the legion of dog vermin who howl thereon perpetually, forming quite a distinct colony of their kind; at length I arrive at the "Great Field of the Dead," or the Moslem burial-ground, where a species of revel is being held. It is a strange place to choose, but I have remarked that Eastern nations generally are fond of playing above their dead; perhaps because they usually choose the most beautiful sites for cemeteries. The "Grand Champ des Morts," which is the local name for the place where I now stand, occupies indeed one of the most beautiful positions in the country, commanding a magnificent view of the Golden Horn, of the mosques and minarets of Stamboul, and of Scutari, on the other side of the Bosphorus. They look really enchanting, seen through the clear air and reflected in the waves; I would almost rather take my usual seat at yonder café there, and look my daily fill, than remain with the noisy holiday folk. I turn, indeed, to do so, but there is a party of Greeks, hopelessly drunk and shindy-loving, congregated round my quiet corner; just at this time also meeting with a friend, I find that I am fairly in for what is to follow, and so may as well make up my mind to it.

The paths are far too narrow and ill paved for us to walk arm-in-arm, our toes would be broken a hundred times over if we endeavoured to do so; we separate therefore, and pick our way over flat stones and smooth places, as carefully as possible. Thus moving slowly on we muse upon the reasons which have always made Mussulman rule, at least in modern times, another word for semi-barbarism, national sloth, and indifference to all things. The scene around us now beggars description. Though the afternoon is excessively sultry and threatens rain, every tombstone is crowded with a separate party of disorderly Greeks; and there they are again, swinging themselves from the branches of trees, and riding round on wooden horses, made to turn about a pole. Some of the oppressed Christians occupied in these invigorating exercises are reverend greybeards, with bald heads; I need not say they are all of the same illustrious origin—all Greeks.

Women there are of course none but some dainty dames of Pera. The men dance together their uncouth national dances, to a rude and inharmonious music: it is the same dance that may have been footed by the companions of Leonidas and Miltiades, or in the Olympian games; the dance we see pictured on old vases, and in the silent chambers of Pompeii. Some ten or twelve men, of ages between twenty and fifty-five, take each other by the hand, and form themselves into a semicircle; they then begin to stamp their feet slowly, and to excite themselves till the measured stamp becomes a frantic bound, the song a howl. They are headed by a dancing-master, who twirls a handkerchief, and directs their movements. One by one, as the dancers retire from sheer prostration, their places are filled up by others; and sometimes we saw a sunburnt old fellow look bashful as a maiden when asked to join the party; but he always ended by giving his consent at last, and would come scuffling along, blushing and smirking, till he warmed to the fun, after which he jumped away as lustily as the rest. I could have wished the dancers had not been so dirty and down-at-heel as they were, and I could have dispensed with the presence of a fat old lady in a greatcoat, having her head bound up from the face-ache, who came to inspect the proceedings; but in spite of these drawbacks, the scene was curious and interesting.

Let us leave the dancers and look elsewhere; perhaps we shall find that the amusements of holiday-makers are very much alike all over the world. We have nearly tumbled over a thimble-rig table! Gambling games of all kinds are going on as briskly among the tombs as at Ascot Heath after the winning of the Emperor's Cup. There is popgun-shooting, for lollypops of a dirtier and greasier kind than our own, if possible; there is throwing of sticks at a mark, with an ingenious hole for the catching of the prize, to save the proprietor of the sticks from any disadvantageous consequences of a correct aim; there are shows in canvas tents, inconceivably filthy, and music as discordant as at an Irish wake; everywhere there is the same eager, noisy, picturesque crowd, and life and death are jostling each other indeed. See, there is a breechless urchin seated on the sculptured turban placed perhaps above some Moslem hero; he is stuffing himself with a nasty composition of rice and olives, while he yells to his companions, who are charging at him down a little hill.

Let us go away and join the beauty and fashion of Pera; we shall have some difficulty in making our way through the dust, the men on stilts, the music, the booths, the sellers of yaourt, pancakes, rice kabots (fried nuts, olives, and onions, chopped up together, an unsavoury mess), but we shall find the beauty and fashion quite time enough, I dare say. We shall find them among paper cigars, tents, jugglers, and taletellers; but there they are—God is great! There is the bumptious diplomatist's wife, too proud to speak to the Pera belle; and the young official, nervously reining in a horse rather too much for him, as a wild Perote stock-jobber dashes by, thwacking the sides of his sorry hack till they sound again. Then off he goes, that wild Perote, with floating locks, and heels pressed down—the very *beau idéal*—the "love's young dream" of a snob! Fancy a hair-dresser's apprentice with a red cap, and you have my friend to a hair.

There will be parties too in the evening, made up of the New Cut and the Travellers' Club. They will not mix very well together, and there will be all sorts of silver-fork squabbles in consequence. Already four persons have asked me if my companion is entitled to put the word "honourable" before his name, and evidently look upon him with much less respect after my answer in the negative. Ye Gods! society squabbles at Pera!

CHAPTER XVI.

THE PRINCE OF VENDÔME.

AT the beginning of the Turkish troubles, a very singular personage arrived at the court of the Sultan to take part in them; for there is nothing your true knight-errant loves like troubled waters. He called himself Louis de Valois, Duke of Vendôme, and haughtily asserted that he descended from the last scion of an ancient race of French kings, and that he was in reality heir to the throne of France. He said, indeed, that he and his Sublimity the Successor of the Caliphs were the only two legitimate sovereigns in the world with whom he was acquainted.

His arrival created an immense sensation. Selim Pasha assured Hamed Bey, in a confidential whisper, that he came to entreat the protection of the Successor of the Caliphs against the attacks of the Muscovites and Chinese—a race of barbarian infidels who lived near a place called London, of which he had often heard from a Christian dog of a merchant, who bought the figs and olives in his pashalik. He assured the listening Hamed, with many wise wags of his venerable beard, that his Sublimity the Sultan had been graciously pleased to receive the royal suppliant, who had been presented by the French ambassador on his hands and knees, with many marks of his august favour; that he had deigned to accept the suzerainty of France, which was henceforth and for ever to be held in fief of the Commander of the Faithful, and to pay an annual tribute. Finally, the Pasha, opening the inmost recesses of his gifted and amiable mind to the attentive Hamed, proceeded to show him how he meant to undermine the favour of the subject monarch, in order that he himself might be named the Prince or Waywode of

France at some future date. This would be an easy thing, inasmuch as an infidel might always be safely accused of blaspheming the true religion, or of having stamped on the spot where the Sultan's shadow had rested while going to the mosque, or of being a Sheytan or evil spirit. This virtuous man's aim being thus accomplished, he would lose no time in appointing the wondering Hamed as his kaimacam, or lieutenant.

The news flew from mouth to mouth as fast as breath could carry it. The men of Constantinople began to treat the French subjects in the place with unusual marks of kindness and protection, and all were eager in portioning out to their own profit the goods of the subject land which had just submitted itself so dutifully, and had become annexed to their country. Hey! what fat pashaliks would be forthcoming by-and-by!

Meantime, it soon became known that his Highness the Duke de Vendôme aspired to the command in chief of the armies of Turkey in the war which was then expected with the Russians. This seemed reasonable enough under such circumstances, thought his admirers. He was a man, too, whose air and manners were admirably calculated to support pretensions, however extravagant. He had a plentiful stock of the gravity, assurance, and plausibility which succeed so well with Orientals. In person he was of gigantic stature, and though his face was not of the cast which pleases a physiognomist, he was handsome. His forehead was high, but narrow; his nose and mouth well cut; but the shifting and uncertain expression of his eyes could never have belonged to an honest man. It seemed always to be mutely asking how much you believed of him, or trying to penetrate into your thoughts, and see if you had heard or suspected anything against him. For the rest, he wore his beard, already growing grey, after the fashion of the Orientals, and dressed in a manner rather more imposing than is usual among French gentlemen of real rank and consideration; but perhaps this was part of his tactics, and not an ill-judged device if it were so.

He took up his quarters at the first hotel in Pera, and engaged a numerous suite; for the mysterious stranger, who seemed to have well studied his part, knew that nothing is more respected in the East than a splendid retinue. He had secretaries, aides-de-camp, grooms, and horses, all obtained on credit; and things at first went smoothly enough. Day after day he enacted the character of a courtly host to visiting pashas and beys, who went away full of his praises. His Highness and his Highness's wife—one of those pretty quiet women who always fall in love with a lion—were an honour to the hotel at which they lodged. They promised also to be a considerable profit to it, for they occupied the best rooms at a great expense, just at the very time when the *beau monde*, and travellers who came to Constantinople, were all too glad to run away into the country to escape the fierce heats of summer.

At length came the unlucky quarter of an hour, so pathetically mentioned by immortal Rabelais. One morning the bowing landlord presented his bill. The Prince was all affability: he had not leisure to see his bankers just then, but would send to them to come to him immediately he could spare the time. Unluckily, he had no money but a thousand-pound note by him. If, however, M. Bouffet had change, eh?—and the Prince, in his brocaded dressing-gown (got on credit over the way), rose from his honoured seat upon his august legs, and looked towards a splendid escritoire—which was quite empty—for it had only just been sent home—and his Highness twirled the golden key in his hand with an inquiring glance.

Mine host was all blushes and apologies; he was desolated at having deranged his Royal Highness. Might he be permitted to retire himself?

The Prince consented; and, shortly after, the Princess, his Highness's august consort, sent for Madame Bouffet, and made her the prettiest compliments possible upon the general arrangements and excellence of the hotel. Madame Bouffet received them curtseying to the ground. She was an Englishwoman, and had been " own maid to her Excellency the British ambassadress; but she never expected to have the honour of seeing a crowned 'ed under her 'umble reuf; but ryalty was scarce in these rumbustical " (she meant republican) " days, and so it wuss, yer ryal majesty's 'ighness."

Her " ryal majesty's " 'ighness complimented Madame Bouffet

again on the soundness of her political opinions, and having learned all the scandal of the place, and ascertained that Madame Bouffet had never expected to espouse a Frenchman, "which her father was in the oil and Italian business, but had married her mother-in-law, and sent her out to service, which she never was brought up teu," with much other information of a similar nature; and having given Mrs. Bouffet a dress, worn by her royal self at the coronation (it was black satin), accordingly, the storm was lulled for a time. Mercy on us, what humbugs those demure, gentle women are! what proficients in roguery a roguish husband can make them! what a very right arm of help they are in good or evil—true as steel in the darkest adversity!

The days rolled on, however, and all things must come to an end at last. Inquisitive people began to remark, that his Highness's guests were all men of Constantinople, and that neither his ambassador, nor any other considerable person among the Franks, appeared to be aware of his existence, or called upon him, except the *chargé d'affaires* of Tombuctoo; and his character as a Lothario was so well known, and the Princess was so pretty, that Mrs. Bouffet thought his visits might as well have been dispensed with.

At last one of the French *attachés* came in from the country to lionize a party of his compatriots, who wished to see the wonders of the land, and this young gentleman having nothing better before him when the fatigues of a long sight-seeing day were over, brought his whole party to the hotel to dinner. M. Bouffet, who, like every one else in Constantinople, had formerly had something to do with one of the overgrown embassies, greeted the young official with that mixture of respect and familiarity which belongs peculiarly to the manner of foreign upper servants. When, however, he mildly requested the *attaché* not to light a cigar, because they were then standing immediately under the windows of her Royal Highness the Duchess of Vendôme, it was very natural that the young gentleman should require "*ce bon Bouffet*" to explain himself more at length; which he did. The *attaché* laughed, and opined that he had been preciously taken in.

Bouffet persisted in vowing that his story of the Prince's arrival and pretensions was undeniable, for that he had trusted him to the amount of many thousands of francs. " But," resumed the puzzled Bouffet, " Monsieur the Count would have an opportunity of seeing the Prince in person at the *table d'hôte*, where his Highness was graciously pleased to dine."

Poor Bouffet said " Highness," and " graciously pleased " still, though terribly chapfallen. It is hard to give up an agreeable error, and little people are quite as fond of "booing" as great ones are of being "booed" to. Poor Bouffet, he had been bragging of his customer till the rival hotel (kept by two Englishwomen, who quarrelled with everybody) felt quite snubbed ; and now, instead of seeing his doors thronged with a gaping crowd waiting for the Prince to go out, he would become the ridicule of the whole Christian quarter of Constantinople, and be bitterly reproached by all who had trusted his unknown inmate upon his braggadocio representations.

The imposing presence and suite of the Duke, however, at first even staggered the *attaché*. He thought Bouffet might be mistaken, and that he really saw before him a man of royal rank. But, alas! on the left hand of his Highness sat his secretary; and the moment that the eye of the *attaché* fell upon him, doubt was at an end, for he recognized him as a rogue who had been convicted of all sorts of dishonesty, and to whom he had often given a few francs in contemptuous pity. Looking also more fearlessly now at the Princess, a smile broke over his face at the recognition of an old acquaintance. Her Royal Highness turned pale as she met the arch look of this young gentleman; the Prince bit his lips, and the bubble burst.

It was with a very different face that M. Bouffet rendered himself on the following day in the apartments of his lodger. He came with a lengthy bill in hand, with his wife conversing in audible whispers at the door; with the listening servants behind him on the stairs;—but who has not seen the admirable picture of " Waiting for a Remittance ?"

The Duke de Vendôme was not staggered : he did not quail even before the enraged eye of his enemy. The conversation was long between them ; but Madame Bouffet at last stole into

the room; the whispering waiters on the stairs were hushed;
mine host's angry voice died away into a respectful murmur.
The Prince would go to his banker's and pay the bill within an
hour or two.

So he went out into the street with towering crest and courteous
bow; mine host thought that Monsieur the Count (the *attaché*)
had "mocked himself with him," and that the things he had
heard to the disadvantage of their Highnesses were a *mauvaise
plaisanterie*.

It was a wet day; for there are wet days in Constantinople
as well as in London. The unpaved streets were like a quagmire—all mud and slosh; but the erect and stately form of the
adventurer strode on to the quarter where the merchants lived;
there he went at once to the principal French bankers, and offered
them a draft on Aldgate Pump for a considerable sum. He
knew he could make no such mistake as to ask for a small one.

" Had his Highness a letter of credit on their house?"

" No. It had not yet reached him. The war might have
retarded the post."

The banker looked grave.

" Had he a letter from the ambassador?"

The Prince smiled. " What French nobleman would know
M. de ——, the ambassador of the Republic?" said the Prince,
in his grand way.

The banker, like most men who have made fortunes from
very small beginnings, was a legitimist, and also, like many of
the Europeans in Constantinople, was at war with his ambassador. So he acknowledged internally that this excuse was a
valid one. He was just on the point of desiring his cashier to
pay the value of the draft, and then retiring into his gloomy
little sanctum behind the counting-house with one of those
respectful bows to fallen greatness a Frenchman knows so well
how to make, when the adventurer broke silence again and
overreached himself.

One of the great secrets of successful negotiation is to know
how to keep silence—never to speak one superfluous word. This
impostor, however, like all his tribe, was impulsive; and his
way of life had given him an opinion of mankind which is the

most perfectly wrong of all. He thought everybody on the lookout to commit a robbery where they could do so with impunity.

It very often happens that a man looks most stern when he is really most disposed to yield. This was the case with the banker, and while the order to his cashier was just trembling on his lips, the adventurer thought he saw refusal there.

"I only want the money for a short time," he said incautiously, "and if you will advance me twenty thousand piastres, I will give the bill for thirty."

The game was lost; the player had been too eager to win. "I never lend money upon such terms," said the banker, frozen straightway into ice.

The rest of the day was spent in sickening anxiety, in the hopeless attempt of a suspected stranger to talk people, whom he had never seen before, out of that which they valued most on earth—their money. Everybody to whom the splendid gentleman applied on that rainy, sloppy day, referred him at once to the great banker, and he went with wet boots from one sneering trader to another, mortified and humiliated. In vain he tried to stiffen his tell-tale under-lip, and to look his man in the face with those shifty dishonest eyes. He might indeed correct the huskiness of his voice from the contents of a little flask he carried about with him, and put on some of the usual charm of his manner; but more was too much for him, and the day closed with his utter defeat.

Wet through, in spite of his umbrella, bedraggled, dispirited, feeling as if every hair of his head were made of wire which grew an inch a minute, he returned to his hotel. But he was no common Jerry Sneak. There was the same handsome winning smile for Madame Bouffet, who stood waiting for his return; the same pleasant good day for her husband; the same firm stride and gallant bearing, as if he had a few loose thousands for present expenses in the little empty casket upstairs. To the inquiring looks of mine host, he said that his bankers were to send to him on the following day.

But his plans were deranged; he must hasten his movements during the brief time of consideration yet left him. Instead of carrying on a tardy negotiation with the Pashas, to whom he was daily making presents bought on credit, he resolved to go in person to the Grand Vizier and offer his services in the cause of Turkey.

That worthy received the French Prince with much distinction, and offered him pipes and coffee; the pipe-sticks were made of the rarest and lightest wood, and their mouth-pieces were of jewelled amber. The coffee was served in dainty cups of gold filagree, richly jewelled ; for all the luxury of the East has taken refuge in pipe-sticks and coffee-cups. As the adventurer looked round the marble hall, with its long vistas opening on the costliest flowers, the silver tables, the mosaic pavement, and the smiling Vizier, his heart swelled within him.

But here he failed. He failed, because, like all his class, he took too radical and summary views of political matters. It happened that in the famous quarrel between Constantinople and St. Petersburg, the Governments of Great Britain and France had promised to assist the former power in the unequal struggle. It was, however, for a long time extremely doubtful of what this promised assistance was really to consist. Whether it was to be moral aid, or physical aid, or money, or advice, or reproaches, and mere meddling. The Grand Vizier perhaps knew as much about the matter as most people, but his visitor knew nothing at all. He had, therefore, blindly adopted the popular opinion, which was, that the English and French fleets were merely waiting in the neighbourhood to seize on Constantinople during the tumult of the war, and divide the spoil between them; just as a brace of lawyers take advantage of the disputes of individual litigants, to fill their own pouches at the expense of both.

Big with this idea, the adventurer proposed to the Grand Vizier a notable plan for burning the two fleets as they lay at anchor, and thus getting rid of these troublesome and uncertain friends at once. The Vizier never moved a muscle while the soldier of fortune detailed his plan, though the French ambassador had just left him with the most cordial assurances of friendship and support, in which he fully believed.

All Orientals are fond of intrigue. The Vizier continued to listen to his visitor with the utmost politeness, and when he had concluded, begged him to put his proposal into writing, that it might be laid before his Sublimity the Sultan. He saw an excellent means of thus recommending himself to the French and English Ambassadors, and took leave of his guest with many warm expressions of thanks.

The Prince had no need to hang his beard now. He would soon be made a field-marshal at least, and the field-marshals of the Ottoman Empire were paid a thousand pounds a month. He had succeeded beyond his utmost hopes: he had no fear of creditors or hotel-keepers. "After all," he said to the Princess, as he finished and sealed his proposal in the evening, "there is nothing like energy; and if a man has only the courage to pursue fortune boldly, he is sure to win her."

So the duns were put off from day to day, by the most stately and wonderful excuses, and Bouffet and his wife retained in the same awe-stricken respect. At the end of a week, the Prince called again upon the Grand Vizier.

His Excellency received his guest with the same pleasant smile as before, but there were no pipes and coffee. Perhaps the Grand Vizier had no time to attend to such trifles, and was going to despatch him at once on his errand of glory. The Vizier presented to him a paper. It was his own proposal, and his Excellency in returning it said, "That it was a most ingenious idea, but that, unluckily, it had not met with the approval of the French Ambassador, to whom he, the Grand Vizier, had submitted it immediately it had reached him."

The hotel was crowded with duns when he returned to it. In his utter disappointment, he had not given them a thought, till suddenly brought to bay in the midst of them; and there was something touching after all in seeing the lion thus surrounded and yelped at with his claws tied. So thought at least Monsieur and Madame Bouffet, who rescued him, and angrily cleared the house.

And here the secretary, who had first brought evil upon him, proved a valuable ally. That individual had made himself acquainted with every possible and impossible means of obtaining money in Constantinople; and having been first rescued by stratagem from the close custody in which he had been for some time kept by his landlord, he set himself heartily to work, and at last, by judicious puffing of his employer, persuaded one of the wise men of the East to advance sufficient money to the Prince to pay his hotel bill, for so many thousands per cent. that the wise man must surely have thought he was dealing with an alchemist, who did not happen for the moment to have his crucibles with him.

But while the harassed adventurer was rejoicing in the prospect of recovered consideration at his hotel (for we may be sure he did not say how he got the money), he received a peremptory notice to quit. Once paid, Monsieur and Madame Bouffet determined to have nothing more to do with him. People began to flock in from the country, who considered his presence a scandal to the house, and his Royal Highness was therefore turned out.

It was a bitter thing enough for the unmasked pretender to front the clamorous horde of tradespeople who now waited in ambush for him, and dogged his heels wherever he went. The irate Frenchwoman, who kept the nick-nack shop, asked if he thought she called upon him for change of air; the savage horse-dealer, a drunken Hungarian, menaced him, riding-whip in hand. A miserable sort of palsy seized upon his limbs in the midst of his creditors, and his lips grew white, and his heart stopped. Yet, to tell with what inexhaustible resource of trick and evasion he cajoled them again and again—with what wit and ingenuity he battled in the wrong cause, would fill a volume. Driven from one hotel to another, chased hither and thither—hunted, badgered, jeered at, he at last took to his bed as the only temporary means of peace, and how he contrived to keep body and soul together there was a mystery.

I never could ascertain the real history of the man who came to Constantinople, and called himself the Duke of Vendôme. It remained a secret to the end; but he was probably the illegitimate descendant of some branch of the royal family of France. There is no smoke without fire; nor do the most unblushing men often assert a lie which has not some foundation, however shadowy and unsubstantial. Thus much also was certain: he was a brave and able soldier, but most thoroughly unprincipled; a man tutored in a bad school, who believed everything in life might be won by address and trick—who entertained from conviction the mistaken idea that the world is to be juggled out of its respect and consideration, or anything which is worth having. He must have been also ignorant, or he must have known that steam, and "that kind of thing," puts all the world now in such free and constant communication, that there is no place in the world in which his pretensions could possibly have escaped being unmasked by return of post. But many much wiser men than this adventurer know very little of Constantinople. It is the fashion to consider its inhabitants a race of sleepy barbarians; while, heart alive! they are quite as wide awake, and far more wily, than the wiliest in the West. However, after suffering every species of degradation and contumely, the knight-errant sank into a *valet de place*, under the protection of the same *bon Bouffet* who had once bowed to him so lowly; and the beautiful Princess opened a milliner's shop not unsuccessfully.

There may be a doubt, however, whether society is quite right in these cases; and, when the claims of the pretender had dwindled down to a modest request for a subaltern's commission, whether it was wise to place him beyond the pale of hope and an honourable life. The man might have done valiantly enough, sword in hand, and the empire of Turkey have been altogether the better for his aid. If society would give such men a place, they would often fill it worthily. If we would recognize their talents, their genius for invention, their inexhaustible resources, their valour, perseverance, and contempt of obstacles, we might often make them do us good service; and it would be kinder and wiser to look upon even adventurers generally with more discriminating and merciful eyes than we do. Let us, indeed, sedulously keep their hands out of our pockets, and close our hearts against their wheedling; but let us try if we cannot, among the many places and conditions in the world, find some that will suit them. Let us cease to attach suspicion to the name of adventurer, openly worn, and we shall hear no more of dukes of Vendôme perambulating the world.

CHAPTER XVII.

A TURKISH AUCTIONEER.

IT was the sale of a bankrupt's effects, and they were huddled together in disorderly confusion, under a little crazy shed, just outside the town. I was attracted thither by the shouts of a Turk, with a stentorian voice, who was running about in a state of great excitement, and stopping persons in the streets to insist on their examining the articles which he carried in his hand; he was the auctioneer of the place, and as a student of manners, I followed him into his place of business. There was a considerable crowd of the greasy, dingy persons who seem to have an abstract love of second-hand goods, and who have often appeared to me to be evoked by the auctioneers of all countries, like familiar spirits. I think I could number the cleanly faces I have seen at sales; and the priests of a "great sacrifice" in Turkey are very much of the same genus one may meet any foggy London day on the premises of Messrs. Debenham and Storr, which are, or I think were, in one of those naughty little streets in the neighbourhood of Covent Garden.

The proceedings of all parties, however, differ greatly, and the resemblance I have pointed out must be looked upon as merely personal: it is confined to the length and sharpness of nose among the buyers, an air of unpleasant sleekiness about them, with a strong smell of bad tobacco, and a prevailing odour of the damp and fustiness of blind alleys which hangs over the assembly: there the likeness ends. In Britain a sale by auction is a plain, commercial, twice-two-are-four sort of affair; in Turkey it is a source of pleasurable excitement for a whole city; it furnishes the inhabitants of the town with a conversational topic of more than usual liveliness and interest;

it also gives them a delightful excuse for lying or lounging about in the sun, doing nothing, which is a never-ending entertainment to an Oriental.

It is proper to mention that the Turkish auctioneer is by no means so august and dignified a person as his British namesake; he is not the sovereign lord and autocrat of the saleroom; he is the servant of a popular and rumbustical assembly. Before I have well had time to settle myself upon a stone, and light a cigar, I observe that he has returned three times from a sally to sell the same cracked pipkin, and three times he has been thrust back by the scruff of the neck, because he has not obtained a reasonable offer for it. Somebody in the shed bids for it at last, and the delighted auctioneer, with a most villanous wink at me, is preparing to hand over his unsaleable pipkin to the somebody in question, when the same remorseless knuckles as usual are thrust between the collar of his shirt and the back of his head. The auctioneer thus goaded makes another excited bolt out of the shed, and the next moment is heard shouting about the cracked pipkin again, in the same furious manner as that which first attracted my attention. The somebody who was disposed to become a purchaser looks rather disconcerted, I suspect he is not thoroughly broken in at auctions, but nobody else pays any further attention to the proceedings for the present; in fact, the public seems to be rather glad than otherwise to have got rid of the auctioneer, probably in the hope that the festive occasion may be prolonged till a later hour. So they sit down, and light a great number of paper cigars, as a necessary preliminary to the discussion of the news of the day. Their conversation is composed merely of coffee-house politics and their neighbours' business: woe to the Costaki or Nikolaki who does not happen to be present; the character of that Costaki or Nikolaki is handled with a ferocity which quite makes one's ears tingle; and I listen attentively for one pleasant thought or kindly expression—for one plain, sensible idea, or healthy view of anything talked about—in vain.

Presently the auctioneer returns; while the majority of his customers are wrangling, he has slyly disposed of the pipkin to the somebody who first bid for it; and I think another roguish wink to the purchaser signified that he should expect a con-si-de-ra-ti-on for himself at a convenient season. After this sale of the pipkin, the only thing disposed of since my arrival, the auctioneer desires a little repose, and squatting cross-legged on the bankrupt's counter, he sends for a nargilly, and joins in the general discourse. The whole company then present a picture of Oriental manners sufficiently striking and characteristic; they have entirely forgotten why they assembled together, and are idling away their time in that slothfulness which is surely at the very root of all evil, and from which springs as certainly nine-tenths of their national disasters. Lazy louts of boys begin to sneak in and out mysteriously, and to pull about the things of the ruined man; I feel very much disposed to trip up one baggy young gent, whose pockets are fuller than they should be, with the crook of my walking-stick; but I am by no means sure that he is not the son or brother of somebody present, or in league with the auctioneer, the bankrupt, or the principal creditor, or one of the primates of the place; and I *am sure* than any such action on my part would only create a violent row, and that no possible good would come of it, so I abstain.

For the rest, I begin to understand also that the auctioneer is not likely to resume his labours for the present: the talk will go on till dinner-time; then the talkers will disperse. To-morrow it is the Greek feast of the Forty Martyrs; on the following day it is the festival of Saint Nonentity; the next day it is the Turkish Sabbath (our Friday); the next it is Saturday, the Jewish Sabbath; then comes Sunday; nobody likes to do anything, particularly on Monday, while Tuesday and Wednesday are both saints' days; on Thursday everybody will stay at home sobering, and then again follow the three Sundays! By this time I know very well that everybody will have forgotten all about the sale, just as much as if it had been an affair of the last century: should they remember it, I am not quite clear that the matter will be mended. The bankrupt's goods are in a wooden hut; they will not be locked up, they will be nailed up. To-morrow morning, or the morning afterwards, the hut will be found open; something will be said about a robbery; this will supply a great deal of energetic talk, and afford an excellent opportunity of abusing the Turkish authorities.

Those who know a great deal more about the robbery than they would care to own, will be loudest in this abuse, and there the matter will end; so let it be! Everything is settled this way in the East; why should the sale of a bankrupt's effects be an exception to the general rule? Delay hangs like a universal mist over everything and everybody; nothing ever terminates, from the bumptious negotiations of diplomacy downwards. If I were requested to describe the general state of affairs in the East in one word, the word I should use would be "muddle," and I think it would be tolerably expressive to any one who has lived there.

I asked of a person I met in my afternoon's canter, what might have been the circumstances of the bankrupt whose property I had seen so wantonly damaged and pilfered; and the substance of the answer I received is worth recording, as illustrative of another phase of manners in Turkey. The bankrupt had been a prosperous tradesman till he married a widow of considerable landed property. This had been his ruin; and a very snug and comfortable ruin it was; but still a ruin. He had fancied the property of his wife would be improved by laying out some money upon it. The idea was natural; it was also correct. For this purpose, therefore, he borrowed a small amount, and had little difficulty in finding it, for he offered the security of his next year's growth of olives. "Stay," said the money-lender; "as you have olives, I will not lend you money; I will buy your olives. It will make the transaction simpler." It did *not* make the transaction simpler, however. On the contrary, it was merely the beginning of a "*muddle.*" When the time came for the olives to be delivered to the buyer, they did not happen to be grown. A winter of severe cold had destroyed the olive-trees in hundreds, and the olive-trees of the debtor had not put forth a leaf. He offered, however, to repay the borrowed money. "Pray, don't trouble yourself about me," said the obliging money-lender; "it is not money you owe me, it is *olives*. To be sure I bought your fruit rather cheaply; but if I had it, I should make an immense sum in the present scarcity. I want the olives, therefore, not the money."—"Impossible."—"Well, then, suppose *we fancy* I have the olives, and you want to buy them: they will cost you —— piastres at the current price. To be sure it is nearly five times what I lent you; but you need not hurry yourself about payment; we shall merely have to add the usual interest, and you can give me a bond for the whole."

So the affair is settled; and the discomfited debtor finds himself in the position of hundreds of others. He has been borrowing at an interest of about 600 per cent.; and his mercantile destiny sealed. He knows this; but he is a Greek, and has all the trickery and cunning of that people born with him. He will be ruined indeed, but he will contrive even to turn his ruin to account. He will improve and beautify his wife's property till it becomes the wonder of the neighbourhood. He will buy everything that is to be sold and dispose of it again at any price, to obtain the money he requires. What money he does not want, he will hide or bury. He will carry on a wholesale system of swindling for the next year; and the Frank merchants will suffer most. One fine morning he will declare himself a bankrupt, rub his hands, chuckle a little, and leave his creditors to fight out their differences between them. He will have no books, no accounts, no nothing. He will answer no questions, and there is no law to make him. He will acknowledge, indeed, that it is a bad business for somebody, but as far as he is concerned, he knows nothing at all about it, and washes his hands of the whole transaction. His property belongs to his wife, and though he has improved it with other people's money, nobody can touch it. By-and-by, in some dodgy, round-about way, the Greek money-lender will of course contrive to be paid; but everybody else enjoys an opportunity of whistling for their cash, such as is seldom offered. In a few years, or perhaps sooner, this ingenious bankrupt will set up in the same line of business again, and live in the odour of sanctity till he gets into a second scrape, and then he will assuredly wriggle out of it in some other manner equally felicitous.

The fact is, there is no law, particularly in Turkey, which may not be evaded by an unscrupulous man. Some trumpery present will always secure the suffrage of anybody whose suffrage is worth securing ; for, generally speaking, the Aga and Cadi, with all their coadjutors and train, live entirely by little jobs of this kind : without them, they would not be able to live at all. There is no Gazette, no List of Bankrupts, no Report of Law Proceedings, no way of any kind, as far as I know, for keeping backsliders in the ranks. So, notwithstanding the great caution of our prudent friend of Bickerstaffe, I cannot help thinking that, now and then, the Frank merchants fare poorly. I wonder whether things would be altered if we could persuade some sensible statesman like Lord Granville or Lord Malmesbury to take back the seals of the Foreign Office and Lord Kimberley to go one of these days as our ambassador to Turkey. At this present writing it appears that the wise man of Bickerstaffe's negotiations have been lately taking the same turn as Lord Dudley and Ward's in 1827 ; and here we are soaring away from all practical reforms and improvements into the sublime regions of War and Famine. By-and-by, perhaps, we shall be able to refresh our memories about what sort of a thing "the Plague" is. So really I have to apologize for my concluding observations ; and I do so.

CHAPTER XVIII.

THE FLEAS IN CONSTANTINOPLE.

ONE of the peculiarities which strike me most among the inhabitants of Turkey, is their love of fleas! I am obliged to use the word "inhabitants," because all are not Turks who live in Turkey, and all are alike in this respect, whether Osmanli, Armenian, Bulgarian, Wallack, Moldavian, Greek, or Jew. They pounce upon a flea with a cry of delight, wherever they find him, and fondle before putting him to death. They show as much art and address in the flea's capture, as a keen sportsman may evince in trying to get a shot at a flock of wild ducks. The fleas are not ungrateful for being thus held in honour, and have effected a very considerable settlement in the country. They are, in point of fact, one of the nationalities of Turkey —the only one which has nothing to ask of the Government; which has no wrongs to redress, or injured interests to bluster about. Most of the houses being of wood, fleas find warm and commodious quarters in them—quarters which are utterly inaccessible to the broom of the houseman. I use the word "houseman," because there is no such thing as a housemaid in the East. They all disappear from view at Southampton or Marseilles.

The fleas at Constantinople are so prompt and ferocious in their assaults, and have, moreover, such a keen appreciation of the delicacy of any fresh arrival from a distant country, that they keep a stranger in a perpetual state of liveliness and motion which is doubtless extremely beneficial to his health, especially if he be slothful and averse to exercise.

No idea of dirt or disgrace seems to attach to a Turkish house full of fleas; the pugnacious creatures being looked upon as recognized proprietors in the country, and as having as much right there as any one else. Any attempt, therefore, to exterminate them from a bed or a sofa would be utterly laughed to scorn. A Perote lady (and she is the very essence of fine ladyism) will often stop several times in the course of a flirtation, languidly, to catch a flea upon her dress, feebly smiling while she twiddles him in her fingers, and then, passively dropping him on the floor, she will go on with her discourse. Two grave Galata merchants will stop in the midst of a bargain sportively to catch a flea on the shirt-front of an acquaintance, and cracking out his crisp life on the counter, will proceed to draw a bill on London, or discuss the exchange, the depreciation of Kaimés, and the rise of gold, without a remark.

No individual throughout the Ottoman Empire seems to be able to resist the fascination of hunting a flea wherever he sees him. What trapping was to the Red Indians, what the fox-chase was to the squire of our childhood, is flea-hunting to the Oriental. It is a passion—a delight. Immediately the lively little game breaks cover, no matter where or when, the eyes of a Perote light up with an unwonted fire, a keen sporting expression passes over his face; he raises his hand stealthily by a sort of instinct: the certainty of his aim might pass into a proverb; and the next moment the hand has descended, the Perote is twitching his finger and thumb with tranquil satisfaction, and has resumed his occupation, be it what it may. He would stop to catch a flea on his way to be hanged—or to be married. He must have missed appointments—lost fortunes, by the habit; but it is engrafted in his nature, and is unconquerable.

I have gone into rooms where fleas lay thick as dust upon the floor, and each of my steps must have killed hundreds of them; but if I ever ventured to express the smallest distaste upon the occasion, I became as incomprehensible to the men of Pera as if I had told a Chinese I disliked stewed dog.

They (those wild Perotes!) will even argue the point with you, if you press them closely, and maintain that the flea is like the elder Mirabeau—the friend of man: that fleas keep up an irritation on the skin which is highly beneficial in a hot country, and prevents the accumulation of morbid humours. On my remonstrating, also, with an hotel waiter about finding them constantly in the bread (some baked and some alive), that individual, who spoke all the languages of the world in bad French, assured me that the baker had a superstition about them, and thought them lucky! Pumping him also with a light hand, I found that he was not quite free from the same species of idolatry himself, and that it obtains generally throughout the country.

He (the waiter) said, that to allay the irritation they occasioned was at all times a pleasing occupation; that it was to be remarked no flea ever bit a man in a dangerous place, or injured his eye or his ear, or opened an artery; therefore, fleas were the friends of man. He did not know (nor do I) what many of the Perote gentlemen would do if it were not for the unfailing entertainment afforded by fleas. He believed they kept people who had nothing to do out of mischief. He said that the courteous catching of a flea upon the person of another offered a frequent and pleasant opportunity of commencing a conversation, or beginning an acquaintance with an illustrious stranger: that acquaintances so formed had often ripened into warm and lasting friendships. He had even known more than one instance of Perote marriages brought about by a cheerful and inoffensive gallantry of this kind. He was much surprised at the unjustifiable anger of an English lady, upon whose shoulder he had succeeded in catching a flea by an adroit movement of his left hand, while his right was occupied presenting her a dish of kid stuffed with chestnuts at dinner. She had screamed; and her gentleman had threatened to horsewhip him. He confessed his feelings were hurt and his reason confounded by this behaviour on the part of my country-people: no Perote lady would have raised her eyes from her plate during such an occurrence.

I endeavoured to soothe him by saying we were an excitable race, who lived in an inclement climate, and to whom, therefore, the utility of the flea was comparatively unknown: but he would not credit it: he could not bring his mind to bear all at once on a fact which appeared to him so remarkable. I was like the Christian knight who told an African king that he could ride his horse, dry-footed, over some of our rivers in winter; and who was bowstrung as an inventor of tarrydiddles.

I remember a personage of no mean rank once calling my attention specially to see him hunt and kill two fleas, which were reposing together on the linen cover of a sofa. He began by rousing them into flight with the golden point of his pencil, and then pursued them in a state of the liveliest excitement for some minutes. (He had a long white beard, and was a man of such an august presence, that I confess the sight seemed a strange one.) At length he ran down his game, and taking them in the usual way between his finger and thumb, finally slew them upon the pipe-stick of a brother sportsman, who offered it spontaneously for the purpose.

In the mosques, in the market-place, in the palace, and in the coffee-houses, by the sweet cool seaside, and in the hot and sultry town, it is just the same; wherever there is a Perote, there is a flea also; and his greatest delight is to capture it.

CHAPTER XIX.

A MESSENGER IN DIFFICULTIES.

I AM a Queen's messenger, or rather, I was; for, of course, I am a ghost, or I should not dare to write these lines. Well, then, I was a Queen's messenger, and it was while hurrying home from Dahomey with the account of an ambassadorial squabble, that I met with a little adventure in the neighbouring state of Tombuctoo, which retarded my journey. It also caused me for some time to be in bad odour with the clerks of the Foreign Office; and as all my happiness while in this world of course depended on the opinion of those gentlemen, I am anxious, though but a shade, to clear my defunct reputation in their eyes.

About the time to which I refer many people were meeting with similar mishaps; for it was subsequent to the appointment of Lord Drone as British representative at that court, and the Government of Tombuctoo were happy in the conviction that they might take any liberty they liked with such an agreeable elderly gentleman. This, however, was not my fault, it was merely my misfortune.

My mishap occurred in a railway, and in consequence of the suspicious appearance of a commercial traveller who sat on the opposite seat. He had a book of patterns with him—a neat book—an English book, with a morocco cover, and a little patent lock. It might have been a dispatch-box, or it might have been used, indeed, for carrying pamphlets and revolutionary manifestoes; though, I confess, this idea did not occur to me at the time.

Being anxious to do as much business as possible, no matter what was the subject started by his travelling companions, he contrived to turn it, soon or late, to printed cottons, and took advantage of the occasion to open his book of patterns. He was a pushing, bustling, money-making Briton, with spare whiskers, and a smug, clean face.

Between Dahomey and Tombuctoo he had opened his book of patterns twenty times, to different persons, who he supposed might be likely to trade with him; and a close acquaintance had sprung up between us. Indeed, I was never tired of admiring the smart little man and his bits of cotton : his determined earnestness in trying to take fortune by the forelock, and to bear her away from all competitors, had a kind of fascination for me.

We were drawing near to the famous capital of Tombuctoo,* and travelling quite alone in a large carriage. Every now and then the guard thrust his head in to look at us, and see if we were all safe; once or twice he called us by our names, and referred to an ominous-looking paper which he carried in his hand. Various other persons came also to inspect us, and on the appearance of every new examiner, something almost like the ceremony of an introduction seemed to pass between us.

My acquaintance, whose name was Gossop, grew alarmed; and even to me there seemed something suspicious at the close attention paid to us. At length, on our arrival at Tombuctoo, the book of patterns disapppeared for ever. Perhaps the authorities at Tombuctoo were ashamed to return it, after having arrested two peaceable individuals on the strength of its contents. Perhaps they thought it might furnish a clue to some new species of cipher. At all events, we passed just sixteen hours in a most dreary gaol, till the matter was cleared up in some incomprehensible manner; and then we were let out without the smallest explanation.

We had the honour of an interview with Lord Drone's porter, upon the subject, on the following day. My lord was taking a music lesson, and could not be seen. After some delay, we were shown into a room in which were a considerable staff of well-dressed young gentlemen warming themselves in every variety of position; and to these young gentlemen we were

* Vienna? Vienna in 1853, during the quarrel between Austria and Hungary.

introduced by a grave functionary, who could not speak English. The young gentlemen seemed to think we had met with a pleasant adventure, and rallied us agreeably about it.

"But," said Mr. Gossop dolefully, addressing one whose attention appeared to be chiefly absorbed in coaxing a strange wild crop of hair, "I have lost my pattern-book, and without my patterns, I am nobody—nothing—the object of my journey is lost!"

"Oh, you can easily get others," said the young gentleman; "it is not worth while making a row about *that*. But do tell us something about the place where they shut you up." The lively young official assumed an air of awakened interest and delight at the prospect which had thus unexpectedly occurred of our supplying him with amusing information upon a subject with which he was unacquainted.

Mr. Gossop was abashed at this treatment; he grew also irate, and his story became confused. Wrathful, touzled, hungry, red-eyed, fresh from prison, that true-bred Briton was quite a different person from the brisk, clear-headed, well-trimmed little man who vaunted his wares with such a keen eye to the main chance only forty-eight hours before.

I tried to explain for him. Being myself of a rather resigned and phlegmatic temperament, and being, moreover, accustomed, by frequent journeys through despotically governed countries, to take things coolly, I was not so much affected by the indifferent board and lodging which had been supplied to us on the previous night by the Government of Tombuctoo. I think the account I gave of what had happened was plain and intelligible.

"You know *you* can have nothing to say in the business," observed the lively young gentleman with the wild hair; "it is Mr. Toffy who makes the complaint."

"Gossop," said my companion.

"Well, Gollop, then," said the lively young gentleman. "Upon my word, Mr. Gottop, I think you had better forget all about it, and leave Tombuctoo as soon as you can, for fear they should lay hold of you again. You see you were clearly in the wrong——"

"But you forget," I said, "that *I* was stopped also; and, as

L

I am a Government servant carrying dispatches, the consequence of such an arrest might have been serious."

"Oh! If," said the young representative of Britain, gaily, "if my aunt had whiskers, she would be my uncle."

"Stuff!" broke in another young gentleman, who had been trying to fix a remarkably obstinate eye-glass into his left eye. "Stuff, Captain Bolt; Mr. Tiffin, the sub-vice-consul at Dahomey, was stopped the other day. I am afraid Huffey at the Foreign Office will be very angry with you about this."

I had never heard of Huffey, and asked meekly who he was.

"Don't you know Huffey, the chief clerk of the Dahomey and Tombuctoo departments? You had better go to him directly you get to London, and explain the affair privately."

"Explain what?" said I, rather disconcerted.

"Why, about your getting into a mess with the police, and giving all this trouble."

"Oh, indeed," said I.

This was all that came of our complaint. What befell my companion subsequently I don't know; for it was plain that I had better not keep company with such a dangerous character at Tombuctoo, during the glorious mission of Lord Drone.

CHAPTER XX.

A TURKISH HOUSE.

I AM living in a Turkish country house; it was built by a Turkish sea captain, who had made money in more ways than one, and wished to spend it as fast as possible. He did so, and the house passed into the hands of the Pasha for one of his bad debts. The Pasha has lent it to me in the grand way in which people do things in Turkey.

It is a large rambling building, by the sweet shores of the Ægean; it is a place for making merry in; even the swallows seem to understand this; they fly in and out revelling all day long, and build their nests among the cornices. Its first owner was an epicure. There are traditions of big-bellied bottles still said to be hidden in unsuspected places. It has a luxurious bath, always supplied with hot and cold water; the bather sits on a marble slab, turns on the water, and ladles it over himself; the room soon fills with steam, and this is called taking a bath in Turkey. Sometimes several persons bathe together—sometimes the solitary bather is only accompanied by a servant.

The rooms are full of cupboards of quaint shape, and of hiding-places; but there are no separate apartments for the harem, Turkish families really living among themselves much as we do. The furniture is of plain deal, painted green, with white stripes; the wainscots and ceilings are painted blue, striped with yellow; the walls are whitewashed. The divans are covered with chintz, and stuffed with hay; one, however, is stuffed with dried rose-leaves. The beds are arranged at night on benches, built up beside the walls: they are only wide enough for one person. In the hall is a raised platform for the guards and men-at-arms; they command the staircase, and prevent all stranger ingress. In one room is a small European fireplace for keeping coffee always near and ready; but below are the capacious ovens for the mighty cooking of a Turkish gentleman's household. The views from the airy sitting-rooms are positively enchanting. When you recline, *chibouque* in hand, upon the luxurious sofas, you feel in dreamland; with the scented breezes playing round you, and the misty mountains of Asia—another world, a world of marvel and romance!—so near. In a word, the Pasha's house is a strange charming place, and I am fairly in love with it.

It is surrounded by one of those delightful gardens which are the pride of the Turks; a jealous wall closes it on all sides: it is far from prying neighbours. This garden has fountains which fall sparkling in the broken shadow of vines and trellises. The sound lulls me to sleep during the fierce heats of noon. It has trees, and their varied blossoms seem to soften the air which passes over them; deep cool wells, and moss-grown reservoirs, full of fat gold-fish; roomy stables, where the beautiful Arabian horses, sent as presents to the Pasha, look round and neigh pleasantly as you pay them a visit, suggesting far-away gallops in the soft meadows, or rambles in shady lanes, where the wild olive and the fig-tree grow entwined together.

The place is full of silent servants, who glide about mysteriously, and have been sent to do me honour. Some are men-at-arms, always keeping watch and ward for mountain thieves, who prowl about by night; some are sleek coffee and pipe-bearers; some are Greek women, who belong to the household of the Pasha's gardener. I will describe the three whom I know best, and the reader will at once be admitted into the mysteries of a Turkish house.

The Albanian cavass is a soldier; he is the only modern representative of the free lance; he spends his life in wandering about from land to land; he is a rover by nature; confinement would be as intolerable to him as any kind of trade or settled employment. His arms are his fortune, his pride, his friends. They are indeed to be bought, but they never fail the purchaser. He is upright, honourable, and gentle, according to his lights; he would not tell a lie, or harm a worm; yet in his native mountains he was a highwayman of great cunning, and he has killed more men than he can remember. Only a week ago he paid five thousand piastres (£45) blood-money to the brother of a man he slew three years before: he was then living somewhere in Asia Minor. When the murder had been committed, the *Aga*, or Turkish magistrate, advised him to run away till he had compromised the affair; now he may return there unquestioned—he is completely absolved by the blood-money. Punishment for murder is even rare in Turkey, and a cadi once told me that he contrived the damages for killing people should come to very little, when they *were to be paid by a poor man*. All Orientals set a low value on human life.

Hamed quitted his last place in consequence of having slain a trespasser on his employer's garden; but as there appears to have been an unusual degree of conversation on the subject, the Albanian left him with a very high character, and came here. At my bidding he would slay anybody unhesitatingly; while he eats my bread, my will is his law. He would defend my life or my property with his own; he is trustworthy to a proverb. Fidelity is a passion, a point of honour with him; he would not wrong me of a para; yet if he were unemployed, he would immediately return to his old trade of highwayman till something else turned up. He is silent, grave, strutting, dignified in public; in private he treats me as an equal; he is confiding, affectionate, watchful, convenient, and indefatigable; he is popular even with the Greeks, and always contented. Despite his pride in grand appearances, he is a marvellous master of a household, a wonder of carefulness, saving, and economy; for he is profoundly impressed with the value of money. He carries always about with him a supply of the smallest possible coin, and gives one of them with such a flourish, that complaint or objection is quite overwhelmed and awe-stricken. Matters entrusted to him always go well; he is somehow or other always ready and in the right; he never makes a difficulty. He will do any work, no matter what, *unseen;* but abroad his employment must be dignified. He receives £2 a month, and earns it well.

In personal appearance he is small, active, upright, and hardy; his clean well-set limbs might be a model for a statuary: they are all nerve and muscle. There never was anything more rugged and colourless than his face; yet it is not without a wild beauty. His features are well cut, his eyes, though small, are bright and resolute; he has the short, straight forehead I have often remarked in fearless men. His temples, cheeks, and the top of his head are shaved, but a long tangled lock of rusty hair streams down his back. He is scrupulously neat, clean, and orderly; he is vainer than a woman, and trims his moustaches into shape with the agonizing tweezers; yet he will live unmated and die a bachelor.

His dress betrays at once the love of show and glitter, which is a striking characteristic of the whole Albanian race. It is one mass of braid and gold embroidery; his very garters are of scarlet and gold; his arms are of solid silver; everything about him shines, except the snowy and graceful fustanelle. Round his neck is a stout silver chain, to which is attached a watch, made some fifty years since by George Prior, a famous name among the Turks. This watch is his glory; whenever he has any money, it is sure to appear with some surprising alterations. It has already three cases; an inner one of tortoiseshell, and two outer ones of silver. It cost a fabulous sum, and is of great size and weight; it is needless therefore to add that Hamed consults it with much pride whenever any one passes by. He wears a large silver ring on his little finger, and an amulet of strange device round his neck. The latter was given him by a Hoja. Hamed believes devoutly in Hojas, as well as in magic, dreams, and omens.

If any one had told me when I was a little child that I should one day be cast far from my country and friends, in an uncivilized land, and with a murderer for my constant companion, the prediction would have sounded like a curse! Yet the thing has happened, and I am none the worse for it; while the murderer is as pleasant and harmless a Moslem as ever shaved his head. Let this teach us the difference between the realities of the world and the creation of our own silly fears; and let it be another proof that life has really very little bitterness for him "who keepeth his heart whole." It seems, nevertheless, as if I were living in dreamland.

Dimitri is a short, snug, fat, silent, baggy-breeched man, with a marked aversion to soap and shaving. He has few words; he thinks that nothing comes of nothing, and nothing remains. In early life he belonged to the establishment of a Turk of the old school, who taught the doctrine of passive obedience with a private bastinado. Dimitri learned it thoroughly; he is one of those poor humble fellows who have been told so often they were made for the uses of the rich, that they believe it in all sincerity and lowliness of heart; he would take any amount of kicks and beatings, not exactly cheerfully and thankfully, but with perfect content, and a clear understanding that the proper order of things was not to be disturbed for his benefit; that if a master was in an ill-temper it was fitting and natural that he should feel savage, and kick his servant, who was there, in point of fact, *to be kicked*.

It cannot be said that Dimitri is a genius; he has a propensity to leave things undone generally; he will obey faithfully and silently, but he is not an originator. It would never occur to him to light your fire on a chilly morning, or to prepare your supper after a hard day's shooting; he would do either, indeed, with the utmost affability, when told; but even then he would omit the details. The firing would be damp, and go contrary; there would not be enough of it; and when Dimitri brought your supper, it would consist of a piece of fat and grizzle, served wrong side upwards, and looking like a cheerless island, in a dreary sea of broken dish. The bread would be forgotten, the salt nowhere; while Dimitri would recollect that he had broken your last bottle of wine the evening before. He would even hold up the cork (very aggravating this!) in proof of the thirsty fact.

Dimitri has a way of putting things in the wrong place, and applying them to unusual purposes, which is very Turkish; no fancy, however robust and serviceable, can conceive of his doings in this way. He will think nothing of bringing in a half-fried fish on the silver top of your shaving-dish, or informing you, with a peaceful mind, that it has been for some time doing duty as a kitchen saucer—indeed, ever since your toothbrush-tray was broken. He appears entirely ignorant of the uses of clean water, or towels; and though when bidden he has no distinct objection to wipe a plate or a glass with the white trousers you wore yesterday, yet he obviously thinks you whimsical in taking exception to good wholesome dirt; he, Dimitri, has thriven and grown fat upon it; he has an abstract love for it. He is not a man to enter upon discussion with you, but he looks as if he would have a great deal to say on this subject if he had been born in a different position.

His chief joy is food; he ruminates it like a cow; his mouth is never empty, or free from a sort of oiliness, which must be inexpressibly tantalizing to hungry Turks, for it is now the great fast of the Ramazan. Things placed in his mouth seem to melt there; the toughest and most unsavoury morsels become quite luscious, and their goodness is reflected in the intense animal gratification of his small rolling eyes, while his snout of a nose quite quivers with it. He waddles in his walk, his clothes are awry, his cap one-sided; it looks drunk, but it is not. He has a wife somewhere; she is a great, strong deaf woman, who bullies him. Dimitri deprecates her anger, and prudently keeps out of her way. I should say that he knew a thing or two, and in his youth had seen strange sights, but he will never communicate them to anybody; he will die unconfessed, the same useful beast of burden that he is now; the butt of practical jokes, the very catspaw of petty tyrants and dull wits, but getting on really very little the worse for them. He is not only my man-of-all-work, but he is servant to everybody on the premises. In this way he obtains small quantities of the money which he loves, and he has thus amassed a considerable sum, which he has lent to a friend, who will never pay it. Running after this money will be the chief employment of his latter days—but laws are lax in Turkey and creditors cunning—poor Dimitri!

My next sketch is meant to represent the Lesbian woman-servant at full length: let us beg pardon of neat-handed Phillis, far away, while we do so.

It is a fat, loose, rolling, tumbling thing, with its pockets full of odds and ends: the halves of apples, and bits of broken looking-glass; some blue glass beads, a thimble (very dirty) some rice, coffee, and what not! It makes darts and rushes at out-of-the-way parts of its legs to scratch them; it twists itself into uncouth positions for the same purpose; it cries bitterly, and laughs at the same time—(I have proposed in vain to Dimitri to divide this employment with her). It is full of jokes and good living; it talks always; it is loud, and sighs with a mighty sound; it loves money, but spends it on tawdry things with great readiness. It has a short fat mouth and nose, white teeth, and large round black eyes; its complexion is fresh and healthy; its dark hair is never parted properly, and is chiefly remarkable for its tight plaits and strong pomatum. It speaks thickly, and in jerks; it wears a handkerchief, always dirty, round its head, and an amulet (dirtier) tied about its neck; its hands are dumpy and covered with pewter rings; it has large gilt earrings, and stout men's shoes, of which it is proud; its gown is red or yellow, and gapes in many places. It "cleans" itself at unseasonable times; and arches its eyebrows with its fat thumb and a dinner-knife; it makes strange grimaces while doing so.

It has no mind, and despises the pursuits of literature; it is bashful, yet has at times an extraordinary effrontery, and an odd stolid wit; it is fond of horse-play and romping; it thumps its husband, and is thumped by him, and I see its children always roaring, with a lump of food in their hands; it is jealous, and sitteth on the ground wailing readily; then as suddenly commenceth a cheerful and diverting dance. It will stand in the same position for hours, looking straight forward at a flaring oil-lamp, and singing: its songs seem all set to the same droning nasal air, but they are sometimes wildly pathetic, and always characteristic. She was born in a mountain village; she was an island maid. She *is* a wonder of fat, tears, dirt, slovenliness, and good-humour. She is the gardener's wife, and my washerwoman.

CHAPTER XXI.

VILLAGE DIPLOMATISTS.

THE year eighteen hundred and fifty was a terrible year for many of the Ægean islands. The keen piercing cold of the winter lasted long beyond the usual time; it entirely destroyed their olives, and appears to have sown the first seeds of disease among their grapes. All May, and part of June, the bleak winds tore up trees, and carried about the tiles of houses in such a volatile manner, that it became dangerous to walk in the streets of towns there. When the hurricanes ceased at last, and the July sun blazed out in all its deadly heat, the olive-trees, instead of presenting their usual dark luxuriant foliage and ripening crops, looked as if they had been burnt, and were naked of both leaves and fruit. They had indeed withered away: all the life and sap had been blighted out of them, and, except in a few sheltered places, the whole agricultural wealth of the island of which we speak was fit for nothing but firewood.

This misfortune struck utter dismay into the hearts of everybody; till one person, who must have been the same sort of genius as Caleb Balderstone (who made such an excellent business of the Ravenswood fire), suggested that the evil which had befallen the islanders might perhaps still be turned to a good account. Being pressed to explain this notion, while every other gentleman present tucked his legs under him on the sofa, and composed himself to listen, the inventive genius proposed that a deputation of the primates should set out for Constantinople, and magnify their grievances (bad as they were already), until they should not only be exempted from certain arrears of taxation which had been long due from the island to the Turkish Government, but should obtain a reduction in the amount of their taxes generally. The idea was too alluring to be rejected.

A deputation, therefore, was soon chosen, composed of the most hungry and woebegone-looking portion of the primates,— each of whom was probably worth five or ten thousand pounds at least. Arrived at the end of their journey, they bribed Somebody Effendi to introduce them to another effendi; and having then bribed the second effendi to put them in the way of bribing a third effendi, according to the manner in which public business has been conducted from time immemorial in the East, they were at length received by an effendi who really had some power. Having bribed him also, they set forth their troubles, and were graciously heard.

Rejoicing in such a brilliant result, they returned to their island in excellent spirits; and knowing the Turks to be trustworthy persons whenever a promise could be got out of them, they tranquilly awaited the good time coming.

But the Turks have their own way of doing business, and though it is not a very good one, it is by no means always devoid of a certain shrewdness. Admitting the Greek story to be true, the island was certainly entitled to relief, and should have it; but they could not believe any allegations made by Greeks to be true, without strict inquiry; for, judging from the past, they had always found that to act on Greek statements was to be deceived. It occurred to the Wise Men of the East, to whom was entrusted the conduct of the affair, therefore, to send a commissioner to inquire into the real state of affairs in the island, before the amount of relief to be accorded was definitely resolved upon. At all events, it would be a nice fat lazy little employment for somebody; and as Anybody Effendi had recently been suffering from an indigestion of pipes and pilaff, the best thing possible would be to send him to recruit, during a pleasant autumn, in the Ægean. Not that Anybody Effendi probably knew much about the business in hand, but because he had formerly been the favourite coffee-boy of Muffti Vizier, and the old gentleman did not like to see him ailing.

Somehow or other, it sometimes seems that the ability to fill a place is given with the good fortune which obtains it; so, after Anybody Effendi had smoked a sufficient number of pipes, he began to inquire what was the real amount of the taxes of which the Greeks complained. Also, acting upon a hint received from his patron Muffti Vizier (himself the grandson of a Greek sailor), he politely requested to know what the Greek communities were spending in educational projects, in church-building, in gifts to their archbishops, in bringing up young men for the liberal professions in Europe, and for public purposes generally. The Greeks were in ecstasies, for they thought the larger the sum set down as spent in such virtuous objects, the smaller would be the amount of taxes hereafter imposed upon them. Besides, no Greek can resist the temptation of opportunity, when any piece of deception is to be practised; and consequently it is not surprising that the accounts furnished by the village primates respecting their local expenses were quite astounding. With these documents, Anybody Effendi returned to Constantinople; and, by the very next boat, a fulminating order from the Porte was sent down to the local governors, who were instructed to inquire how the Greeks dared to spend such incredible sums on their own affairs, while their taxes were still unpaid.

The village diplomatists were in despair, and the genius who had suggested the visit to Constantinople was now bitterly blamed for the result. Another deputation immediately set out for Constantinople, to explain that the village diplomatists had been telling barefaced untruths to the effendi who had been sent to question them; a natural result, they added, of the effendi not having stated the object which he had been sent to attain; for, had they known it, they assured the Turkish authorities that the accounts rendered of their local expenses would have appeared as small as they now seemed large. In short, they cried out so lustily at the result of their own intrigues and falsehoods, they bribed, and cringed, and flattered, and sued with such pertinacity, that the Porte sent down another of its wise men to unravel the tangled business.

You may be sure the Greeks were ready for the new commissioner. They told him a tale of poverty and wretchedness in wonderful contradiction with the plumpness of their aspect. Again, however, Muffti Vizier, that traitor from their camp, hit upon a means of catching them. He desired that every inhabitant of the island should be made to furnish an account of his live stock. Again the village diplomatists were at fault. Pigs, and fowls, and turkeys, horses, mules, and oxen, could not be concealed; and though they showed the utmost anxiety to deceive, and did deceive as much as they could, yet for once they were obliged to tell what was very nearly the real state of the case. With the new account in his possession, the new commissioner also went upon his way.

The wise men of the East took counsel at Constantinople, and I have a strong opinion that they must have taken also the advice of some sharp hand at figures there. They valued the live stock of the grumbling island, they calculated its probable increase annually, and they found that the whole taxation of the place did not amount to more than twelve per cent. upon its revenue.

The breasts of the wise men were filled with wrath, and a mighty letter went forth to the local governor. He was commanded not only to collect the whole arrears of taxes due to the Porte, but to increase them considerably in future. He carried these orders into effect with such vigour and efficacy, that the people over whom he ruled have not even yet done wincing whenever his name is mentioned. The members of the several deputations were all banished from their homes for various periods; and when they asked whether such were the rights which had been promised to them by the Tanzimat, the governor frowned in such a terrible manner that they thought it prudent to decamp without further parley; and so ended the crooked negotiation of the village diplomatists.

I wonder whether some other diplomatists we know of practically attain results much more brilliant? Whether it is really possible in our days to deceive anybody by diplomacy without being found out and punished? Whether anything whatever is to be gained by lies, and crookedness, and hocus-pocus, secrecy, bribery, and trickery? If not, I wonder why they are kept up. Why all sorts and conditions of pompous elderly gentlemen are allowed to lead the world such a singular dance as they do; and lastly, whether a little plain common sense, openness, fair dealing, and an earnest wish to do right in the eyes of God and man, would not answer infinitely better.

CHAPTER XXII.

THE FEAST OF ST. DEMETRIUS.

I AM in Mitylene, on storied ground; for Mitylene is the ancient Lesbos, and one of the largest and most beautiful islands of the Ægean Sea. It is situated on the coast of Asia, between Tenedos on the north, and Chios on the south. Its first inhabitants were the Pelasgi. It then became an Æolian colony, and attained great prosperity, numbering as many as nine considerable towns. It was subjugated by the Athenians, but revolted during the Peloponnesian war (431—404, A.C.), and again during the Social war (359—356, A.C.). The ancient Lesbos was celebrated for its wines, and its inhabitants were renowned for their beauty and musical talents; but they were very corrupt. Mitylene was the birthplace of Arion, Terpander, Sappho, Erinna, Alcæus, Pittacus, and the philosopher Theophrastus, whom I cannot help considering as one of the most remarkable men of antiquity. St. Paul also "sailed thither from Assos." Among its more modern celebrities, it numbers the famous brothers Barbarossa, who, together with Doria, shared the reputation of being the greatest navigators of their age, and who seized upon Algiers, and for a long time braved the power of the emperor Charles the Fifth with impunity. The younger of them, surnamed Hariadim, finally acknowledged the suzerainty of the Sultan, and added the rich possessions of Algiers, Tunis, and Biserte to the dominions of the Porte.

So much for the antecedents of Mitylene, which I have given that the reader may have some interest in it, and contrast the past with the present, as he will have an opportunity of doing from the following sketch of

THE FEAST OF ST. DEMETRIUS.

It is the 7th of November, the Feast of St. Demetrius. It is, therefore, with a feeling of very considerable satisfaction that I open my eyes in the morning upon a cloudless sky, and a most coquettish streak of sunshine just rising above the sea, which lies glittering so beautifully beneath my open windows. I propose to pass an idle day, and the weather is of consequence to me : I am going for a ramble, and I do not like wet boots, or wind, or clouds, or anything but sunshine. I love to see the shadows lie still upon the valleys, and the tops of the hills stand out clear against the sky of blue and gold, to which I am growing accustomed.

The difference between a fine day and a dull one is often that between light spirits and a heavy heart. If we are busily employed, we can overcome the influence of the weather; but directly we are idle we feel it.

There is a breakfast of new bread, and of goats' milk, of fragrant honey from Mount Hymettus, and of kid chops, fresh mullet and anchovies, awaiting me in the next room. I hear the cheerful clatter of the plates as I am shaving, and the stealthy step of the Greek, who is to be my companion, as he comes creeping up the stairs. I hear, too, the loud neighing of our horses as they come down our mysterious street, with its lattices all closed and barred by jealous trellis-work. In five minutes I shall be doing my duty as a trencherman, and then up and away for the pretty village of *Moria*, which lies yonder on the brow of a hill. In that village, and there only, is the festival of St. Demetrius to be celebrated; for the festivals of the Greek church are so numerous, that the countries where it is supreme would be constantly in a ferment were it not for this arrangement, and that one feast is seldom celebrated in more than one place at a time. To be sure, these feasts put a complete stop to business everywhere; but with that question we have nothing to do just now.

Breakfast is over, and while we are lighting our cigars the girths are tightening and the servants shouting below. It is impossible to start in the East without a large allowance of shouting, and the Greeks have the strongest lungs I ever heard exercised. Then there is one horse short,—a dogged mule supplies his place; we shall have a discussion on this subject which will last an hour. I do not love discussions; I will cut it short, and take the dogged mule myself: perchance I may have learned from Dr. Keith, in my youth, that there is a remedy for doggedness. So, Abdallah Cavass, reach me a stout stick, and away.

The road is narrow, and I give place to my companion: I am not sorry to get him fairly under my eye. Let us examine him together, courteous reader; perchance we may have caught a character worth sketching. He is a small, thin, angular man, with undecided eyes, and an anxious unpleasant smile always upon his face. He is stealthy and cat-like in his movements: he seems to walk with muffled feet. In dress he is something like a *farce* idea of an elderly Frenchman of the old school, save that he wears the red cap, or fez, which is worn by all Turkish subjects as a mark of their nationality. He has a long straight frock-coat of an undecided colour, impossible trousers, and delicate grey jean boots, with varnished tips: he has, also, a superfluity of watch chain. Upon the whole, he is a very frequent specimen of the modern Greek. He is not of the race of Polychronopolis, who scudded before travellers on his wiry horse over the plains of Corinth—he is not the Greek of the loud voice and ready hand—of the brave apparel and the twirled moustache, neither is he like the simple marvel-loving schoolmaster we knew at Prinkipos.* He is, unhappily, of another school far more common: he is of the race which assassinated Capo D'Istrias, who would have broken Byron's heart if he had lived; who had no sympathy with the learning and honesty of Wyse, or gratitude for the services of the brave and gentle Church. He is of the Greeks who are so proud of the ancient glories of the land they are bringing daily and hourly to shame; he is of that plausible and clever race, who have, by turns, won every statesman in Europe to what is called

* See "Doine." London: Smith & Elder.

the Greek cause, only that he might add another to those who have abandoned it with such a deep disgust; of the race whose lives are one festering infamy from beginning to end, and who would rather live despised on a pittance obtained by intrigue and roguery, than make one single effort for honourable independence. They are the sons of men who were oppressed for many generations; of Turkish Rayahs, of slaves; what need is there to say more, or wonder why they are so fallen?

On I ride with my uncongenial companion, while these thoughts are passing through my mind. On, over the unequal paving of ancient roads, which may have been trodden by St. Paul; on, through shady lanes, where the wild flowers cluster, and where the brier-tree and vine grow entwined together in dark luxuriance; on, through whole forests of olive-trees, some in all the vigour of their foliage, others withered to dry stumps by the terrible winter of 1850, which destroyed half the wealth of the island. We passed by merry parties of pleasure-hunters, too, bound to the same place as ourselves. The peasantry were dressed in their own picturesque national costume, and sung gaily on the way; but those who aspired to a higher rank of course deformed themselves with Smyrna coats, which did not fit them; and all who were under the protection of any foreign Consulate asserted their superiority to the law by a European hat, and made themselves ridiculous accordingly.

At length a sound of fiddling came briskly through the pleasant noonday air; and the frequent appearance of little white houses told us we were near the village. After scrambling up one ravine and down another, and crossing a dangerous gutter, which had once been part of an ancient theatre, we found ourselves among a group of men seated on the ground, and smoking nargillies. We were at *Moria*.

Leaving our horses to the care of our guides, who speedily left them to their own, I put myself under the protection of my acquaintance, and began to partake of the pleasures of the day.

Now a Greek feast, I would have the reader know, is a feast indeed. It is the only festival that I know of which is really worthy of the name: a Yorkshire Christmas, or New Year in

Norway, is nothing to it. A Greek feast is one continual round of eating and drinking delicacies, from the beginning to the end of it. From eight o'clock in the morning, when the holiday-makers are ready dressed for business, till twelve o'clock at night, when their palates must be fairly wearied out, they never rest their digestions five minutes. They go from house to house, from café to café, and strut, and swagger, and talk, (heaven and earth, how they do talk!) and eat, and drink, and sing, and dance together, till human nature can hold out no longer. As the night deepens, many an old score is paid off with the ready knife which the revellers carry in their girdles.

The first house *we* entered was that of mine host of the solitary Locanda at Mitylene. He and his family, comprising a good stout serviceable set of children, with wife and mother-in-law complete, were passing a few days at Moria, during the gathering of the olives on their estate, and they received us very kindly. We found a large party of men seated in a circle round the room, and three musicians very busy in one corner of it. All rose as we entered, for there is no nation in the world so naturally polite as the Greeks. We took our places among the rest, after some ceremony. The paper cigarettes of the smokers were restored to the mouths from which they had been withdrawn; a chibouque was handed to each of us, and the musicians again struck up the airs which our coming had interrupted. Their instruments were a lute of very antique shape, a fiddle, and a flageolet. Every now and then the players stopped to sing a few bars of an air, and then went on with their playing: sometimes they played and sang together.

I am bound, however, to acknowledge that the music was detestable; there was nothing even interesting or original in it to a musical student. The best of the airs were filched from second-rate Italian operas, and spoiled by the most abominable variations. In one I plainly and undeniably detected the "Last Rose of Summer"—faded and gone indeed! Even the words of the songs, which I took great pains to catch accurately, were worth nothing, either as poetry or traits of manners; they had nothing national about them. The groan of the patriot and the sigh of the lover were alike but an echo; the songs were only translations, and very bad ones too. In fact, modern Greeks are all mere imitators, and, as far as I know, they have not original talent of any kind: they are alike in all things; in all arrant plagiarists and pretenders.

It is due to the company assembled at mine host's to say that they seemed to have a poor opinion of the musical part of the entertainment themselves; and on a loud clock in the next room striking twelve, the whole party gravely marched off to dinner without a word; leaving their musicians in the midst of as unmusical a howl as ever was called by courtesy a song.

We were going to follow, when we were stopped by the hostess bearing in the glyco, or preserved-fruit jelly, and water, which it is customary always to present to guests in a Greek house. We knew it would be considered discourteous to refuse it, and so stayed. After this came sugar-plums, a delicate sweetmeat, in the confection of which isinglass must play a notable part; a saucerful of the small white fruit of the bread-tree, and some ornamental glasses of a very strong pure spirit called rakee. Having disposed of this second course also, it was followed by a third, of coffee made very strong, and unstrained. We were then suffered to depart.

And so we went visiting, according to the custom of the country, from house to house, feasting at each. The Greeks are very hospitable, though they do not ask strangers to dinner; and I found on my return home, by an aching head, that I had partaken during the day of no less than twenty-one cups of coffee, the same number of small glasses of rakee, with sweetmeats and so on to match. Indeed, the thing at last grew rather beyond a joke, for at one house they brought me in an immense English pint pot, counting on my drinking coffee, as they said, after the fashion of my compatriots. I could only escape it by a compliment to their national manners, which I need not say I paid very readily. People even stopped us in the street to insist on our drinking with them.

Let me smile over my indigestion as I will, however, I confess that there was something positively enchanting in being seated on the spotless sofas of those summery houses, with their open windows, through which might be seen the cloudless sky and the distant olive-woods, while the west wind came in laden with freshness and the happy hum of the holiday-makers below. It was poetical and touching, too, to see the beautiful Lesbian women, with their large downcast eyes and faultless features, bringing in trays of sweetmeats and offering wine. When we put down these romantic refreshments, they always said, "Your health, Lord" (εἰς ὑγίαν σὰς), in voices which were music indeed.

The Greek is naturally clean in his dress, his person, and his house. We never went anywhere but that plain good healthy soap and water had preceded us; the straw matting of the floors was quite dazzling from its cleanliness, and not a spot marred the snowy whiteness of the walls. Everywhere, too, we were received with the same graceful and innate courtesy; our pipes were lit by the master of the house, in the Oriental fashion, carrying first the amber mouth-piece to his own lips, and these pipes were always replaced, before they were half smoked, by fresh ones. Everywhere the mistress of the house herself presented the glyco, and the pure bright water, which glittered like dissolved diamonds. I never tasted water so sweet and delicious.

The houses in general here, and throughout the East, are small and confined, mere little wooden boxes whitewashed; but those we entered did not lack some rude attempt at internal ornament: in most of them there were poor but gaudy prints on national subjects, and the ceilings were generally adorned with gaily-painted flowers. In one house I noticed a picture of Anastathius, the hero of Thessaly, who was cooked over a slow fire by the Turks during the Greek war of independence. He was represented struggling with three gigantic Mohammedans; and as I marked the strained and glowing eyes which even children fixed upon this picture, I thought how well calculated it was to perpetuate animosity between the two races. The tables and window-sills were usually strewed with fragrant herbs, and sometimes a house looked like a fairy bower, from the tasteful adornment of the mirrors on the walls.

One thing struck me especially: none of the women took

any part in the pleasures of the day. The Greek, like the Jew, to whom I often fancy he bears a marked resemblance, is fond of decking his womankind with jewellery, and often sinks half his fortune in this portable form ; but he adorns them for his own eyes only, and they stay in state at home. They are beautiful dolls, without mind or heart indeed, but still beautiful as pictures are, or statues of stone. Greek women have nearly all the same dark stag-like eyes and brilliant complexions, the same delicate hands and feet, and the luxuriant raven hair. In figure, however, they are the same size all the way down, with no more symmetry than sacks of wheat.

In staying at home, and showing themselves rarely in public, the modern Greek women appear to have imitated the manners of the Turks ; and indeed, let them hate each other ever so cordially, a conquered people will always adopt something from the manners of the conquerors ; and women are all aristocrats, from the Dardanelles to the Bay of Dublin. Another thing also struck me as remarkable, namely, the total abstinence from any rough or manly sports. The men danced together the same bacchanalian dances which their forefathers footed 3,000 years ago, if there be truth in ancient urns and vases ; but there was no throwing the quoit, no wrestling, no foot-race, and perhaps not half a dozen men present had backed a horse three times in his life.

As for the dances, I regret to be obliged to assure the antiquary that they are very awkward clumsy hops when actually performed. Let him fancy half a dozen heavy louts, aged between twenty-five and fifty-eight, hopping about and bumping against each other with senseless gestures, while the last man endeavours to win some burly bystander (aged forty-two) to make a goose of himself in the same way. I say let him fancy this, and the burly bystander blushing and sniggering like a schoolboy caught by his sister's playfellows, and then judge for himself.

But the evening is drawing on, already the sun sheds a mellowed light over the sea and woodlands, and the distant horizon grows golden. We have had enough of the feast; our guide has disappeared, drunk, as most guides do disappear when wanted ;

but I have tightened my own girths, and bitted a ragged pony or two before to-day : I can do so again ; and then, lighting our cigars, we go gossiping homewards.

I do not know, dear reader, whether such little sketches of far-away life and manners as I paint so poorly may please you ; but at any rate they are fresh from nature, and I hope no word ever creeps into them to make any man the worse. If, therefore, in passing an idle half-hour with the Roving Englishman, you should now and then acquire a better knowledge of other nations than you had before, it will not be time misspent, for I honestly believe that most of the wars and ill-feeling between nations arise from not knowing each other better.

CHAPTER XXIII.

A GREEK GIRL OF THE ISLANDS.

SHE is a baggy maiden, with a quaint, sly face; and her principal occupation is that of a maid-of-all-work; but she is dressed to-day; it is St. Somebody's feast, and everybody is idling away his time in consequence. It was St. What's-his-name's Day the day before yesterday, and it will be St. Who-is-it's Day the day after to-morrow. Though our young acquaintance is idling, however, it is with a busy idleness; for she has been occupied ever since eight o'clock this morning in carrying about fruit-jellies and sweetmeats, with strong raw spirits, in gilded glasses, and little cups of unstrained coffee. A very singular and amusing picture she looks, as she stands bolt upright, and tray in hand, before her father's guests. She is pretty. Yes, there is no doubt of that; but she has done almost everything possible to disfigure herself. Though certainly not seventeen, and with the rich clear complexion of the Greeks, she is rouged up to the very eyes. Where she is not rouged she is artificially whitened. Her eyebrows are painted, and she has even found the means of introducing some black abomination under her eyelids, to make the eyes look larger. Her hair would be almost a marvel if left to itself; but she has twisted and plaited it, and woven gold coins into it, and tied it up with dirty handkerchiefs, and gummed and honeyed it, till every tress has grown distorted and angry. Her ears are in themselves as sly and coquettish a pair of ears as need be; and they gleam out, beneath her tortured locks, as if they would rather like to have a game at bo-peep than otherwise; but they are literally torn half an inch longer than they should be by an enormous pair of mosaic earrings, bought of a pedlar. Her hands might have been nice once, for they are still small, but they are as hard as horn, and as red as chilblains can make them, with sheer hard work, scrubbing and washing about the house. All Greek women, I think, have been mere housewives since the time of Andromache. Her figure is, if possible, more generally baggy than her trousers; it bulges out in the most extraordinary bumps; and she has a corporation which would do honour to a lord mayor. A short jacket, as much too small for her as the brigand attire of Mr. Tupman, does not make this general plumpness less remarkable; and she has a superfluity of clothes, which reminds one of Mr. Weller's idea of full dress. Numerous, however, as are the articles of wearing apparel she has put on, they all terminate with the breeches, which are looped up just below the knee. The rest of the legs and feet are bare, and hard, and plump, and purple, and chapped, almost beyond belief, even in the fine piercing cold of a Greek February.

Her mind is a mere blank: her idea of life is love-making, cleaning the house, serving coffee, and rouging herself on festival days. She cannot read or write, or play the piano; but she can sing and dance, after a manner. She can talk, too, though never before company. No diplomatist can touch her in intrigue or invention; not even a permanent clerk in charge of secret service money could tell a falsehood with more composure. She does not know what it is to speak the truth, and, to use a Greek saying, she is literally kneaded up with tricks.

I have said she can talk; but she can only talk of her next-door neighbours; and she spends her evenings chiefly in sitting singing in the doorway, and watching them. This she does herself; but she has a little girl (a chit of a thing, about seven years old, and looking forty, that you meet in the houses of most islanders), who is on the look-out all day. No one ever enters a Greek house but the neighbourhood knows it: all down the street, and in the next, and everywhere, those little girls are watching, and flitting about on cunning errands, as stealthy and swift as cats.

The Greek girl has no heart—no affections; she is a mere lump of flesh and calculation. Her marriage is quite an affair of buying and selling; it is arranged by her friends. They offer to give a house (that is indispensable) and so much, to whoever will take her off their hands. By-and-by somebody comes to do so; the priests are called; there is a quaint, strange ceremony, and he is bound, by fine, to perform his promise. This fine is usually ten per cent. on the fortune which was offered him with the lady.

Her father and mother will tell you that her first cousins never saw her alone, or spoke a dozen consecutive words to her; but I rather fancy she has some acquaintance of her own, and she is generally on terms of rather startling friendship with the young man-servant, who forms almost part of the family in a Greek house. On summer nights, too, when good people should be asleep, you will see closely-hooded figures flitting about noiselessly, like black ghosts—they are Greek girls. What they are about nobody knows; perhaps looking for the moon, which will not rise for some hours. At every dark corner of a wall, also, you will find young gentlemen, sitting in the deep shadow, with wonderful perseverance. If you go very near, and they do not see you, you may hear them singing songs, but low as the humming of a bee; so low that they do not disturb even the timid owl, who sits cooing amid the ruins of the last fire over the way.

The Greek girl knows an amazing quantity of songs, and all of the same kind. They are about equal in point of composition to the worst of our street ballads; full of the same coarse wit and low trickery. They are sung to dreary monotonous airs, and always through the nose. Never had the national songs of a people so little charm, or distinctive character; you seek the strong sweet language of the heart in vain among them; they have neither grace nor fancy.

With all this, the Greek girl is pious. She would not break any of the severe fasts of her church even for money, though they condemn her to dry bread and olives for six weeks at a time; nor would she neglect going to church upon certain days upon any account. She has a faith in the ceremonies of her church, and in charms, relics, and saints, almost pathetic; but there her belief ends. She would not trust the word of her own father, or the archbishop: she cannot suppose it possible that any one would speak the truth unless he was obliged; and she judges correctly, according to her own experience. She herself would promise, and take an unmixed delight in deceiving her own mother on a question about a pin's head; but she would scrupulously avoid doing anything which she had promised; and the only way even to prevent her accepting a husband, would be to make her say she would have him beforehand. From that moment her fertile wits would toil night and day till she found means of escape; and find them she would, to change her mind the day after she was free.

She has one hope dearer than all the rest. It is, that she may one day see the Greeks at Constantinople, and wear Frank clothes. This is no exaggeration; the wrongs of the Rayah have eaten into all classes of society in Turkey, till even women lisp and children prattle vengeance. Their hatred is so strong that it has made the Greeks detest one of the prettiest remaining costumes in the world, because they consider it as a symbol of their most bitter and cruel servitude.

By-and-by the Greek girl will grow old; from a household servant she will then sink into a drudge, and her head will be always bound up, as if she had a chronic toothache. You will see her carrying water on washing days, or groaning and squabbling upon others, as she cleans the herbs for dinner. She will have become so old, even at thirty, that it is impossible to recognize her. Rouge and whitening will have so corroded her face, that it will look like a sleepy apple, or a medlar. Her eyes will have shrivelled into nothing; her teeth will have been eaten away long ago by rough wine and noxious tooth-powder; she will be bald, when she does not wear a towering wig, which will only come out on St. Everybody's days. The plump figure, and all its bumps, will have shrunk into a mere heap of aching old bones; and her only pleasures in this life will be scandal and curiosity.

You will find her croaking about, watching her neighbours at the most unseasonable times. She has wonderful perseverance in ferreting out a secret. She will thus know many more things than are true, and tell them with singular readiness and vivacity. She will be the terror of her neighbourbood; and there is no conciliating her. Kindness, good humour, even money—which she prizes all her life long as much as when a girl, and grasps at it as eagerly—will have no effect on her. She must speak evil and hatch troubles, or she would die. The instinct of self-preservation is strong : so she will go upon her old course, come what may. She will be a terror even to her own daughter.

She has been reduced to this state by the abject slavery of her whole race. She has been a thing of bargain and sale so long, that she has learned to consider money as the chief good. She has been subject to insult, to be beaten (sold even, not very long ago), to be carried away into the harem of a man she has never seen, and whose whole kind she despises; she has been subject, I say, to these things, and to many others, so long, that she has lost all natural feeling. All grace, tenderness, and affection, have been burnt out of her as with a brand. She has been looked upon as a mere tame animal, till she has become little better. She has been doubted, till deception has become her glory. She has been imprisoned and secluded, till trickery has become her master-passion. She has been kept from healthy knowledge and graceful accomplishments, from all softening influences and ennobling thoughts, till her mind has festered. When she is young, she is shut up till she becomes uncomfortable from fat ; when she is old, she is worked till she dwindles into a skeleton. None have any respect or pure love for her, nor would she be now worthy of it if they had.

There must be something very wrong about a state of things which makes the most perfect of God's works so unlovely as this ; which would seem to poison the infant at its mother's breast. It is not sufficient for us to cry out against it, and think our part is done when we have expressed a few strong opinions. We have no right to say this is evil, and then preach a sermon about the wisdom of not interfering. Turkey is still in a state of semi-barbarism. She should be taught. It is not enough to wheedle an inefficient law out of the Porte once in fifteen years, by a mere inefficient diplomacy, if we do not see it executed. Bad even as the Tanzimat is, its provisions are seldom observed; if we obtain another Tanzimat, the result will be the same; and nobody will or can believe in it, without we take some better measures to guarantee its observance than we have hitherto done. But I drop the pen in weariness of counsel, only saying that if a Greek girl be such as I have described her, what must be a " Greek boy!"

CHAPTER XXIV.

HADJI HASSAN.

HADJI HASSAN is an old gentleman who is the delight of my neighbourhood. He keeps a small coffee-house beneath the Pasha's kiosch, on the brow of a hill overlooking the sea. He is the familiar of the mighty in the land,—a fellow of infinite jest and humour, whose ill-temper is merely chartered license; whose smile is a condescension; whose sarcasm is more damaging than dishonour. He patronizes the world; and the world, seeing nothing to envy in him, receives his dictatorship with a sort of contemptuous submission: but it is submission, notwithstanding. Hadji Hassan belongs to that class of hosts who lord it over their guests, and would punish anything in the shape of rebellion with the most cutting severity. He accords his protection to the Pasha and the British Consul; he condescends to nod to those functionaries in a confidential manner, when he meets them in private life; but he declines their intimacy; for he remembers a Pasha mightier than this one, and a British Consul who was the friend of his youth. Besides he is Pasha, and British Consul, and everything else in his own coffee-house. He is not fond of the society of people to whom he thinks it as well to nod in a confidential manner! He likes very well to see them sitting above in the kiosch, because, upon the whole, they are respectable people and pay their way; but he shakes his head when he speaks of them among his cronies, as if he dissented from things in general. Upon the whole, I would rather not offend Hadji Hassan: he is one of those who form public opinion in our little world; and I have noticed that those upon whom he looks unfavourably do not thrive. Whether this arises from his discernment in only looking unfavourably on thriftless people, or otherwise, it would be hard to say. The fact is there; let us leave the consideration of it to others. I am writing a report, not a leading article; and the public love facts rather than opinions.

Let me describe Hadji Hassan. He is about sixty years of age. He wears a turban; for he has far too independent a spirit to conform to the undignified modern fashion of the red cap. The turban was the head-dress of Hadji Hassan's grandfather, who was his guide, philosopher, and friend. If fashion has changed since the days of Hadji Hassan's grandfather, fashion is in the wrong. He would not deign to argue the point further with anybody: he has made up his mind on this subject as on most others. Hadji Hassan's mind is a hard, knotty, stubbly sort of mind: it required a great deal of making up; and he probably spent the first twenty years of his life entirely in the process of its formation. It would be impossible, therefore, to unmake Hadji Hassan's mind. His opinions may now and then be modified on public events by a stray remark of his protégé the Pasha; but in all private affairs Hadji Hassan believes himself to be infallible. Hadji Hassan's turban is not the only part of his dress that belongs to a by-gone time. His general appearance is that of an Algerine pirate of the eighteenth century. He has the same short baggy under-garments; the same close-fitting embroidered leggings (rather dirty, it must be owned); the same spare jacket and bare bull neck. In his girdle he wears a most murderous-looking knife, unsheathed. In build, he is as powerful a man as you would find in the prize ring in England. He is a fine specimen of the common Turk. His pride, decision, stiffneckedness, solemnity, and affected wisdom, all belong to his class, and are inseparable from it. He may be ignorant, but he is never vulgar; determined and prompt in action if roused, but never loud or hectoring.

It is highly probable that any Greek who disagreed with Hadji Hassan would receive a sound beating, to teach him a more prudent respect for his conquerors in future; but there would be no previous wrangling,—no hot words. Hadji Hassan would cuff him lustily with the first thing that came handy, and merely uttering a contemptuous *Kalk Giaour* (Be off, dog!) would resume his nargilly with a dignity as unruffled as if he had merely thrown a brickbat at a cat whose mewing had annoyed him.

Hadji Hassan is aware that he is a privileged person; and he turns this circumstance to excellent practical account. It is doubtful whether he has the least knowledge of any portion of the Multiplication Table. It was not a fashionable accomplishment in his time, and his immense double-jointed hands have had too much to do with the musket to handle the slate-pencil or the Hoja's reed. But he has a marvellously keen eye for his own interest, and insists upon being paid altogether an unreasonable price for his coffee, under pain of his supreme displeasure.

"Hark ye," said Hadji Hassan to me, the day after my first invasion of his territory, "*Bachsheesh.*" I mildly remonstrated. "Ah," said Hadji Hassan, shaking his venerable beard, while an expression of utter disgust with the world stole over his rugged features, "I see no good will come of *you.*" I was abashed at this view of the case, and tried to make my peace with a liberal donation and words of homage; but it was long before the coffee-house potentate would have anything to say to me. It was not, indeed, till my abject submission and deferential acquiescence in his counsels upon all occasions had attracted public attention, that he permitted me to enter the circle of his courtiers and enjoy the benefit of his half-reluctant patronage. I still find it prudent to pay him tribute, which he receives on all occasions without the smallest acknowledgment, as a sort of right which he has obtained from mankind generally, at the edge of the sword.

Hadji Hassan, however, is not content with mere tribute, he requires personal homage, and is as angry with all who do not pay it gracefully, as was Mahomet the Second with Gatelusio, Prince of Mitylene, for neglecting to go and kiss his hand, after the conquest of Constantinople. One day, the weather being rather windy, I did not make my appearance as usual; the next, as I was proceeding contritely to the coffee-house, the despot met me half-way, and appeared disposed to contest my further progress.

"Has he been ill?" said the Hadji to my pipe-bearer, indicating me with a contemptuous jerk of his thumb.

The pipe-bearer shook his head mournfully; he has a belief in Hadji Hassan, and dreaded the consequences of his admission.

"Why did not he come, then, yesterday?" resumed the Hadji, and then diving into his coffee-house, ignored my presence for the rest of the afternoon, leaving me a living monument of his wrath till I had been sufficiently punished. Hamed tried in vain to soothe him; he would hold no intercourse with either of us, and when the bold Albanian strutted off to his little den to fetch a chair for me, Hadji Hassan immediately closed the door, and preferred for a time to dwell in utter darkness with his coffee-cups and nargilly bottles, rather than permit me to sit down in his presence. After a time he carefully peeped out to see if my servant was gone, and finding no signs of him in the neighbourhood, came forth in the daylight again, carefully shutting the door after him, and locking it when called away to serve any of his more honoured customers. For three days my public disgrace continued in the sight of all men; in vain the Pasha opened negotiations on my behalf with his brother potentate; in vain I offered to surrender at discretion: Hadji Hassan would have nothing whatever to do with me. At last it was suggested to me by a mutual friend, who must have been born a diplomatist, that I might, perhaps, make my peace by offering a persevering course of civilities to an ill-conditioned little dog, who lived with the coffee-house despot in a state of great intimacy, and was the general terror and aversion of his customers. I acted on this advice, and as I paid court to Hadji Hassan's friend, his heart seemed to soften towards me. On the third day, about half an hour before sunset, Hadji Hassan approached me with his head turned the other way, and a three-legged stool in his hand; suddenly he stopped, and appearing to perceive me by accident, dabbed down the stool, and immediately went off with a sort of grunt, which might mean many things. Shortly afterwards he beckoned Hamed to him, and having sent me a peculiarly bitter cup of coffee, which I drank in thankfulness of heart, I was permitted to receive the congratulations of my friends on my restoration to favour.

What Dick's and Button's coffee-houses were to the wits of Queen Anne, is Hadji Hassan's to the quidnuncs of Mitylene. It is the general assembly-house of the magnates of our little world. It is here we discuss the affairs of the earth, and pass judgment on the mighty thereof; it is here that we tell our best stories, and prepare the business which may not be handled too abruptly; it is here that the Pasha, and the Cadi, with other grave and reverend seigniors, condescend to lay aside the cares of state, and mingle with common men; it is here that I learned the Cadi is a bachelor, and that the Pasha considers flannel good for the chest; it is here that the veil which covers men in public is withdrawn, where they take off the mask and unclose the shutters, letting one into something of the mystery of their inner lives; it is here that I first began to appreciate the Turkish gentleman at home, and to love him; to admire his sweet temper and quiet dignity of manner; to revel in the fresh simplicity of his quaint and harmless conversation; to penetrate his childlike belief in the marvellous, and to reconcile it with his innate and chivalrous love of truth, and all things grand and noble; to find out how ingenuous he is, how naturally humane, how large in his charities, how unenvious in his friendship, how invariably courteous, and how actively kind; to understand the complete loyalty of his character, and his almost nervous anxiety to act as he believes is right: to admire his devoted respect for the faith of his fathers, his tolerance of all others; with the entire absence of bombast and pretension, which I think belongs to him essentially. It was on these delightful summer evenings that I have been wont to mark his mercy to animals, his friendship for his horse, his knightly love of his arms, and the pathos, half-ludicrous, half-touching, with which he regrets the times when the followers of Bajazid and Orchan, at the utmost speed of their chargers, subdued the regions of the East and West.

I have lingered for hours enchanted by his grave and

reverend discourse, by his salt aphorisms and wondrous fancies about far-away things; and I think I have grown wiser by listening to him, more indifferent about frivolous things, more unselfish, and more philosophical. I have learned to estimate at a truer value many of the things after which men often pine in vain, and with aching hearts; I have learned almost to smile at what is called the *battle* of life, with its petty objects, and its small renown: a deeper love of nature has been engrafted in my heart, and a more honest contempt for glittering vanities.

The Turk of our days is as different to the traditional idea of him as can be. I am painting but my daily companions, and if they do not stand out from the canvas as clearly as I could wish, I may at least offer the word of an Englishman that the colours are true to nature, and the outline, if sketched by a 'prentice hand, is at least unexaggerated. So saying, let us drop the curtain on Hadji Hassan and his mimic court.

CHAPTER XXV.

GREEK FIRE.

MY first excursion on this lovely island—Mitylene, the Lesbos of the Greeks—was to one of those convents for women which have been called the reproach and scandal of the Greek Church. I am not going to enter into this question. All I can say is, that we drank fourteen glasses of rakee there, with coffee and sweetmeats to match, and that all were of such excellent quality that we felt none the worse for it. The sisters also seemed to have a happy knack of lighting pipes. We had some hesitation about smoking at first, in spite of the custom of the country; but our scruples were soon overcome. Indeed, the pious ladies smoked themselves, and produced some chibouques from a sly recess to offer us. The sisters had even a clever way of cutting tobacco, and kept a plentiful store of it—an excellent thing in woman.

There were seventy inmates; but as those in our room were rather elderly, we asked to see more of the sisterhood, and several younger sisters came. We bought some gloves and stockings of them—the convent having a thriving trade in those articles—and then went upon our way.

The scenery round the convent, like that in the neighbourhood of most religious establishments, was surpassingly beautiful; and, after all, I thought, as we rode through the olive-trees, why should not ladies have the power of entertaining their friends handsomely as well as gentlemen? For the rest, perhaps the best thing to say about it is, " Honi soit qui mal y pense."

From the convent we went to a monastery, lying within half an hour's ride, or say a pleasant afternoon's walk. It was situated in a delightfully secluded nook, at the foot of a hill; and as the view of it gradually broke upon the eye, embowered in trees, it was positively enchanting.

Alighting at the gate, we were received with a degree of courtesy which carried us in imagination at once two hundred years back. Servitors in quaint religious habits came forward to hold our stirrups as we dismounted, and to marshal us into the presence of the superior, a grave and reverend man, of plump but devout aspect. The convent church was very fine— much handsomer than that belonging to the gay sisterhood within hail. There was a beautiful carved altar-piece, and great profusion of gilding and silver lamps. I was shocked, however, to see the Deity represented with a triangular glory over his head, which might easily be mistaken for a cocked hat.

There was an air of repose about the place, which had its effect upon the spirits; and it was with muffled foot-fall that I followed the superior up the spotless stairs and along the noiseless galleries till we reached his study—a handsome room, richly carpeted. There was a broad ray of sunshine, in which the motes were playing, falling right across it. The human voice sounded strange and unaccustomed there. I might have been in a dream, everything seemed so quaint and unworldly. Through the open window came a plaintive sound of falling waters.

The servants brought us some sweetmeats of delicate flavour and perfume, with rakee having fragrant flowers in it, after the fashion of our burridge-cup. Then they brought us a delicious melon. I noticed that the reverend fathers were the only persons I had yet seen in Turkey who appeared to know how much powdered sugar improves the flavour of fruit. We had a plentiful supply of it; then cakes, coffee, and pipes filled with aromatic tobacco.

The superior pressed us to take up our quarters there, telling us that the convent was open to all strangers, and that the monks were obliged by its foundation to entertain them. We refused; but promised to return. After a time we rose, and the superior showed us over the convent garden, famous far and wide for its fruit. There was a small space set apart to grow wheat for the consecrated bread; and we noticed a well-stocked reservoir of fat fish. The holy man gave us so much fruit and flowers, that, when we came out, we must have looked like so many market-gardeners.

We spent the afternoon shooting over a famous country, and killed four brace of partridges, with two wild pigeons. They were welcome enough at a scrambling dinner we got at a lonely house on the hills, wherein I gave our host some hints about his trade of wine-making, which I picked up long ago in Spain. After dinner, some Greeks, who had assembled to keep us company, abused the Turks with the same bitter and rancorous hate as usual; but I could not get beyond the fact that the Aga had called some of them names. Faith, they returned the compliment. Trying hard, however, to probe deeper, I questioned one of them whom I at last got into a *tête-à-tête*. "You are surprised," said he, "that we so hate the Turks; yet it is natural enough. I, for instance, was made an orphan at three years old by them. My father was shot dead in sport, by some Turks who had crossed over to our island from Anatolia, for a frolic. Nothing was done to the murderers." So do the consequences of good or evil deeds live after them, and even as we sow the seed shall we reap the harvest. This was in the old time. Such crimes could not be perpetrated now; the reforms of the present Sultan* having left the Greeks very little to complain of.

After a light sleep, I rose and rambled out in the grey of the morning, falling into my former walk up the dried bed of the forgotten river. I noticed a very beautiful species of goat, of a bright golden colour, relieved by spots of fleecy white. The gradual waking up of the village was very pretty, and presented some exquisite subjects for a landscape painter. I never saw anything more beautiful in the way of scenery than the lights and shadows on the distant valleys—the morning seemed to rouse itself so cheerfully. I could hear the partridges call from their cover, and the herds low presently as they went forth to pasture; while a thousand cocks trumpeted to the world their joy at the return of daylight. Gradually

* Abd-ul-Medjid, 1853.

there appeared in doorways children, with chubby faces, rubbing their eyes; and mild, patient women, looking very overwrought, stood gazing out beside them. And there were little dogs who made irregular sallies at us, with frantic yelps.

Returning to the village of Kallone, I met the train of a certain Mustapha Aga, coming to collect the *ushur*, or tithe on the olives; whereat was great consternation among the Greeks. I was not surprised, therefore, to find my host away from home. He and the notables of the village were twiddling their beads and hatching intrigues to deceive the authorities, as they had been since daybreak. We spent the rest of the day shooting; but with small success: we killed only one pigeon, and started a hare, but too far off to get a shot. I strongly recommend any one, however, who may henceforth visit Mitylene, to make his shooting-quarters at Kallonè. I hardly know a more interesting sojourn; and the country abounds with game. There is a fellow, also, named Glygor, who is a very fair shot, and understands his business pretty well for a Greek. The ground you have to shoot over is stocked with a quantity of game rare in these countries. There are stones and mountains to be sure, and sharp work it is to get over them; but your footing is all on short, soft grass during the shooting season, and the large smooth rocks offer an excellent cover for birds. They lie in holes among them, and generally get up straight before you. When they drop, however, you want a smart dog to find them, for if they can run a foot, they find a hiding-place, and you lose them. It is hard to hit a hare for the same reason: he need not scamper a yard without getting behind a stone; so that you must either blow him to pieces, or give him up, as we did.

The clock of the Greek church had just struck five—that is to say, at this season of the year, at about eleven with us—I had closed my eyes, and was trying to think of nothing and to doze away, when there was suddenly a great roar of cannon, and up struck the bells a loud and startling peal. At the same time an outcry which arose in the streets too soon told me that one of those fires had occurred which are so fatal to the Greek villages. I sprang out of bed, anxious to visit a scene so fearfully interesting, and the very first person I met was the Greek archbishop, with his robe tucked up above his heels, hurrying like myself to the place of terror. It was pitch-dark, but fortunately it rained a little, and there was no wind. It was a striking scene ; the lurid glare of torches falling on the marked features and gay-coloured costumes of the Greeks ; the shouting of brave men, as they hewed down the wooden houses on each side to prevent the fire spreading ; the wail of women far and near ; the church bells still ringing out that fearful alarum, and distress-guns booming at irregular intervals.

Once, through the smoke and glare, I saw a fine, dauntless fellow descending a scaling-ladder with a half-suffocated woman in his arms. I never before knew how natural is the wild huzza which bursts from men who witness gallant deeds, and which greeted the saver as he stood again amongst us. The Greek despot bustled about bravely, and was so very laudably active and encouraging, that I felt quite an admiration for him. At last the fire was got under ; but the affrighted villagers mostly passed the night at their doors, watching lest any unsubdued spark should break out again.

The alarm caused by the fire was, indeed, so terrible, that one healthy young man was attacked by epilepsy in consequence. I went with the village doctor to see him. We found him foaming at the mouth, and struggling violently with some people who held him down, half-scared and half-amused, I am afraid, by his contortions. He was in a miserably dark little room. His relations were so numerous, and they stood so obstinately near to see what was going on, that the whole apartment was one living mass of curiosity. The grief of the sick man's mother seemed to be most passionate, that of his wife most subdued and practical. It appeared to me as if the one thought she ought to be distressed, and the other thought she ought to be useful.

It was dreadful and degrading to observe the sick man, too, screaming and writhing; for his screams were the screams of the dastard. He called aloud on the Aga to spare him. He was the pitiful thing which centuries of misrule has made the Greek Rayah, and had no more awful fancy than that of undergoing corporal punishment when reason had left him.

I was glad to turn over this painful leaf of Greek life to open a brighter page. I was afterwards present at the anniversary of the Greek schools, one of which flourishes vigorously in Mitylene. The festival was presided over by an *attaché* of the British Embassy, who made a speech in modern Greek. The Euphora, masters, and all the pupils, were present, and appeared to be as greatly pleased as I was.

CHAPTER XXVI.

GREEK WATERS.

PERHAPS our invalid sailors and soldiers would hardly be able to find a getting-well place more convenient and delightful than the island of Mitylene. Steamers from Smyrna and Constantinople touch there four or five times a week, and it is within pleasant hail of both those places. Provisions are usually singularly cheap and abundant; the inhabitants are hospitable, goodnatured, and fond of foreigners. Within a day's journey of Castro (the chief town of the island) are all sorts of interesting places, and really it is almost worth while being moderately ill to have an excuse for a holiday visit to them. When I add that there is excellent fishing, and pretty good shooting, in the neighbourhood, I think I have a right to consider my argument in favour of the sanitary aspects of Mitylene as fairly established.

But if I may expect, as I certainly do, to have a few antiquaries among my readers, I do not know what I have not got to say about Mitylene. With the single exception of Attica, not one of the states of ancient Greece was so famous as Lesbos. Indeed, I am able to pick and choose from an overwhelming amount of riches, and I shall therefore confine myself merely to the business in hand, and look upon the place which gave birth to Pittacus, Theophrastus, and Sappho, where Aristotle taught and Arion sang, where Cæsar won his first public honour, and where Marcellus and the widow of the last Christian prince of Trebizond fled as fugitives, simply as a getting-well place.

Lesbos was so renowned for its wine that even cold Virgil mentions it with approbation; and Ovid, who was a much better judge, is said to have asked for it when dying. The island was so famous for its wheat, that Mercury was sent especially from Olympus to fetch it; and it was used by the bakers of the gods. If this assertion, however, resting as it does merely on poetical authority, should be too much even for the faith of an antiquary, I have still something to say about the Lesbian bread, and support my information by an appeal to the excellent judgment of Archistratos. Archistratos was a lover of delicacies, who flourished about two thousand two hundred years ago; he was the Brillat Savarin, the Soyer, of the ancient world; he knew where everything worth eating was to be found as well as was possible. When, therefore, he especially praises the bread of Lesbos, we are bound to believe that it was good.

Then Lesbos was so remarkable for the delicacy of its oysters that they are spoken of, with a watery mouth and a luscious chuckle, both by Strabo and Pliny; while the beauty of the Lesbian ladies was long a proverb, and might be so still. Now, I fearlessly ask any conscientious getting-well person whatever, " Can there be anything of pleasanter digestion than an oyster, with lemon-juice (yes, I will grant the lemon-juice) squeezed over it?" Mitylene cannot be said in our days to have a very plentiful supply of fresh butter, but it has abundance of excellent brown bread; so that we must look upon the want of fresh butter at Mitylene rather as a misfortune than a fault, and eat our oysters without it. I had nearly forgotten the ladies: for the fact is, I am an old gentleman, in a dressing-gown and slippers, so I cannot judge of these things; but the next time our friends in Australia want a few ship-loads of wives, I think they might do many less sensible things than send to Mitylene. I may be wrong, but this is my opinion.

Physicians are agreed that the climate of Mitylene is decidedly the healthiest even of the healthy islands of the Ægean. It is almost invariably cool in summer, from the sea breezes, and remarkably mild in winter. Frost or snow is unknown to the oldest inhabitant; and there is no day throughout the year upon which the sun does not shine cheerily for a few hours. The ancient writers are unanimous in its praise, and Pompey the Great is one of the many gentlemen who sent his wife here for change of air. Count Razinsky, the most modern traveller of repute, hardly knows how to express his admiration of the climate and scenery of Lesbos; and M. Olivier (a Frenchman) becomes almost incomprehensible from the same cause. Then, every inch of the land is storied. It was from the neighbourhood of the famous ancient town of Methymna that Achilles bore off the beautiful Eriphile, whose supposed fate has furnished the subject of one of the finest of Racine's tragedies. Mitylene was the residence of the diligent antiquary Pocock (the Greeks call him ποκόκιος, which looks odd), during some of the most interesting of his valuable researches: a pensive invalid might go delightfully, book in hand, over the same ground; and lastly, skipping many things, Mitylene was the theatre on which first rose the curtain of the last terrible Greek war of independence. The fighting began by the destruction of a Turkish man-of-war off Erisso; and most of the memorable naval engagements which followed, where Kanaris and Miaoulis gathered their bloody and useless laurels, took place in the same neighbourhood.

Let us now talk about the medicinal waters of Lesbos. They were among the most famous of the ancient world—and the ancient world was bathing mad. If they have now fallen off it is probably because they are unknown, as many things are unknown about Turkey which we should do extremely well to learn.

The baths of Vassilica, perhaps the most important in the island, were certainly of high repute in former times. Careful observation may still trace ruins of considerable extent in their neighbourhood. The waters of the springs at Vassilica were analyzed by Pocock, and found to contain iron and sulphur, with a small quantity of copper; their taste is salt. The water flows in great quantities from a rock, and is caught in a large basin, now used as a bath for men; its heat is about thirty degrees Reaumur. It is of known efficacy in derangements of the spleen and liver, scrofulous tumours, gout, and rheumatism: the last-mentioned disease is unhappily one to which Europeans are particularly liable in these countries. Finally, the waters of Vassilica are said to have *a specific action in the cicatriza-*

tion of wounds; and were employed with success for this purpose by no less a person than a late minister of Sardinia at Constantinople, who had been wounded often in the wars. I have it from credible authority, that this gentleman was lifted out of the steamer on his arrival, and went shooting partridges on the hills three weeks afterwards.

The waters of Vassilica are hot enough to boil an egg; but lest their efficacy in this respect should be proved too often, the country people have a prudent proverb, which says, that the egg "will not boil if it is stolen." For the rest, Vassilica is now a mere collection of huts, situated between Kalloin and Jera. It derived its name from having been the residence of the exiled Erinna, wife of the Emperor Leo III., and mother of Constantine Porphyrogenitus; she died there in 902. Vassilica is mentioned as having been the refuge of the Emperor Stephanos, son of Romanos, in 845. Here also fled Ducas, the historian, after the capture of Lesbos (1462), by Mohammed II. Ducas was the contemporary of Phranza, and far excelled the latter in clearness and elegance of style. It is remarkable that the great abilities of Ducas and Phranza were, in those remote times, no obstacle to their employment in diplomacy; now, of course, the services of men of letters in an office which chiefly requires the facility of communicating the result of acute observation are rejected! Musicians and old soldiers are the proper persons to enlighten us about foreign countries. It is at least singular, therefore, that Ducas and Phranza were undoubtedly the ablest statesmen of their time; both did their country most notable service, and their names are quoted among the very few who gave a dignity almost pathetic to the ruin of the most worthless line of princes who ever disgraced a throne. Both these men were faithful to their country in times of extraordinary temptation, and when political honour was almost unknown; both averted the fall of a tottering throne as long as human prudence and genius could save it.

Let us return to our baths. Olivier has described some other springs near Port Jera. They chiefly contain nitre, and are said to have been beautified by Hussein, a Capitan Pasha of much more celebrity than he deserves.

M. X. Landerer (Professor of Chemistry at the University of Athens) has a great deal to say about the medicinal springs of Lesbos ; I shall therefore chiefly follow his lights in the remainder of the present paper ; for M. X. Landerer was a German, and exhausted his subject with the national patience and honesty of his countrymen. He is not unreasonably surprised that such valuable waters have not attracted more serious attention in modern times. He attributes their origin to volcanic influence, and quotes Strabo (who was not necessary) to prove that the whole island must have been detached from the main land of Asia Minor from the same cause.

Galinos records, that about forty stadia from Mitylene there existed in his time certain hot salt-water springs, which acted as a diuretic. They were highly astringent, and said (like the waters of Carlsbad) to be particularly efficacious in reducing immoderate fat. They were also a remedy for dropsy, and sluggish watery tumours.

One of the mosti mportant springs mentioned by Galinos is situated at a place now called Korpho, and is known as the Pasha's bath. It is within about half an hour's walk of the capital of the island, and its waters are serviceable from the month of April to September. They act as a slight purgative, and are valuable in obstructions of the stomach and liver ; taken internally, they prevent determination of blood to the head ; they are also resolute enemies of hemorrhoids. Hassan Pasha, one of the heroes of Hope's "Anastatius" (still the best book we have about Turkey), beautified these baths. Hassan had the amiable weakness of desiring to leave some trace of his passage wherever he went, so that Lesbos owes all sorts of public works to him. There is a local tradition here, (quite true, by the way) that he went about with a lion ; luckily the lion bit him one day, so that it soon ceased to be the terror of the neighbourhood.

Another of the hot baths of Mitylene is situated at a charming village called Thermi. The springs here are of two distinct kinds, the one sulphureous, the other salt. The latter are merely purgative, but the former are of more consequence ; they act usefully in all diseases of the skin, and eruptions ; they are a sovereign remedy against *the Turkish rash*, as frequent as obstinate during the hot months ; they are also reputed to be an antidote to metallic poisons, and especially to the effects of mercury ; finally, they are employed in rheumatism, with which our army doctors will assuredly have more than enough to do.

Then, near the pretty village of Tellonia (abounding with game) are some purgative waters called the springs of Liota. They gush out from a curiously shaped rock, and are usually visited in August ; on the 24th of that month, there is an interesting local festival held here. Near the springs of Liota is also found a hot sand, in which rheumatic patients are buried for half an hour daily till cured.

Close by the-sea-shore, and near the site of the ancient town of Methymna, which of old time checked the pride of the Athenian admirals, and humbled the daring captains of Mahomet II., is found the last of the Lesbian springs I shall now notice. Its waters are declared to be efficacious in chronic rheumatism, which is one of the most inveterate plagues of imprudent livers in Eastern countries.

God forbid that I should play the part of Mr. Croaker in a comedy, and suppose that all sorts of possible and impossible diseases will follow our soldiers to the East : let us the rather hope that care and prudence will keep them in good health ; still we are not infallible, and if people will now and then do unwise things, it is quite as well to know how and where to get relief from their consequences ; therefore I have prepared this paper with great pains ; it is the result of careful personal examination, some research, and some expense. What the reader may skim over in half an hour has cost me the close attention of six months ; and I hope sincerely that the few observations experience and research has enabled me to offer, may direct the inquiries of abler men in the same direction.

I believe that a moderate amount of common sense, employed in the use of baths and exercise, early hours, one meal of meat a day, a due respect for the sun, the instant change of damp clothes on returning home, an attention to keeping one's feet warm, a wise fear of cold at the stomach, reasonable temperance, and a stout heart, may laugh at medical men or medical waters, in the East or anywhere else. But I am now* writing of soldiers on campaign, not a chapter for a traveller's guide-book.

* 1853.

CHAPTER XXVII.

THE CASTAWAY.

I THINK I have just seen one of the most melancholy sights in the world. I have been to *Lovochori* (Mitylene), or the Village of Lepers; a fearful and terrible place. The village is composed of a few miserable huts, placed at the brow of a breezy mountain. As we drew near to it, I could hardly persuade myself that it was the intended object of our morning ride. I had heard fearful accounts of the bodily and mental infirmities of the lepers; and I was now to witness how true they were. Three fine strong men, however, who were the first persons we met, seemed to have little unenviable about them, till, looking closer at them, we perceived that they had no eyebrows. The few straggling hairs on their heads had a limp strange look, as if they were dead. The features of the men also had a singular indistinctness of outline. The right hand of one was contracted and the first joint of a forefinger destroyed. We asked how his hand had been so maimed. He answered cheerfully that it had been accidentally burnt away one day while he was sleeping too near the fire: a striking lesson enough on the uses of pain, showing how God chastises even in mercy. The lepers are almost devoid of any sense of bodily suffering, and the result was before us.

The next person we met was a fine upright lad of nineteen. He had, as yet, lost only his eyebrows; but the village doctor of Plumari, who kindly accompanied me, said casually that the very worst cases began merely in this way. The young man had been already five years cut off from the world, and in all human probability he would never be suffered to return to it. *Never!*

Then came a girl with a huge swelled ankle, one of the most distressing forms of elephantiasis so common in Algiers and the Barbary States. She had nothing else apparently the matter with her; but the taint of leprosy was known to be in her constitution. She also had been lost to the world five years,—in the first budding of womanhood, in the pride and the springtime of life. It was like a thorn at one's heart to see her, and to know how hopelessly she was smitten.

Going further into the village, the doctor and I stepped thoughtfully on, in spite of the shuddering remonstrances of our companions. We soon came upon a fearful group talking in the sunshine. They were nearly unintelligible from the imperfection in their organs of speech which belongs to the worst forms of the malady in its advanced stages. The group before us was a ghastly sight. The poor creatures who composed it looked each like an obscene bundle of rags; and some were blind, and some were deaf and dumb, and others were stricken with impotence of limb. But the most fearful form of the disease is that of "*the lion-face.*" The palate gives way, the bridge of the nose is consumed inwardly, the lips stretch and swell, and the livid cheeks hang down in flaps. God have mercy on those he has afflicted thus! and let us bow down in reverent awe to the inscrutable wisdom of the Most High, doubting nothing, hoping all.

The lepers are said to be remarkable for their merriment and high spirits. Their love of pleasure degenerates into licentiousness. They seem to be mercifully endowed with an obtuseness of intellect which prevents the sense of their fearful isolation from pressing on them too heavily. Yet they are quite sane. The disease is supposed to be sometimes hereditary, sometimes otherwise. There is no escape for those born *leprous;* yet the children of leprous people are sometimes born healthy. When this is the case, they are immediately separated from their parents and subjected to such treatment as experience seems to warrant. Science and medical research have done nothing for Leprosy. They have slept at their post, they have forgotten their mission, and been deaf to the call of this stupendous evil.

A fish diet, the long fasts of the Greek Church, squalid and long-continued poverty, too much oil or salt in the food, and living in damp places, are alleged to be some of the primitive causes of leprosy. A licentious life is undoubtedly another; but its effects are generally visible in this way only in the second generation. As I have said, however, science is dumb, or only speaks in hesitating whispers on this momentous question. I was told I was the first stranger who had ever been known to visit *Lovochori*.

The lepers do not want for anything. The charity of friends and relatives provides amply for these poor aliens from the great family of mankind; and when the community is joined by any new member, be he rich or needy (for the terrible mandate of exile strikes both classes unsparingly), the castaway need never again know toil or eat of the bread which is won by the sweat of the brow. Among the lepers (they number fortynine) lives a brave priest, a man whose hand a king might be honoured to clasp. Humble and self-denying, the living martyr has taken up his dreadful post, never again to leave it till he hears the approving call of angels for "the good and faithful servant." In outward loneliness and poverty, in desolation such as a healthy mind grows sick to fancy, the Christian hero lives his life away. But there must be surely God's spirit ever with him, and he must see visions and dream dreams to which the glory of this world is as nothing. Surely, too, he is one of "the last who shall be first."

There is a legend among the country people which says that earnest men of God who comfort the leprous bear charmed lives. Certain it is that when one dies in the valiant and steady performance of his dreadful duties, another supplies his place as calmly as though bidden to a feast. None are ever smitten with the disease. It is therefore probable that the idea of its being infectious is merely a vulgar error. Would to Heaven that these lines may rouse inquiry among thoughtful and kind-hearted men in Turkey! Would to God that the prayer of these poor lost people may be fulfilled!—the despairing prayer which they addressed to us, as we went upon our way, that we would soon come back with a remedy for their most awful affliction. As we mounted the hill again to join our companions, and ride back to the neighbouring village of Plumari, our attention was attracted to a little group of people, mostly with baskets in their hands. They were the relatives of the lepers ; and many of them had walked miles and miles, over rough and dangerous roads, to bring tokens of their love to their miserable kindred. Some were manifestly poor persons, who had pinched from hard earnings, and who now gave the time they could ill spare from their tasks to fulfil this errand of mercy—to give from that of which they had but little, and without hope of return—to do a good deed, unchronicled and unknown ; overcoming even their simple terrors in the strength of their affections for those who were scarcely sensible of it. Let such acts as these, passing every hour before our eyes, confound the dull doctrines of the cynic, and show us that whatever the institutions of states and kingdoms may seem to effect, nature has at least bound us together in bonds of sympathy which shall not be broken.

CHAPTER XXVIII.

A GREEK FUNERAL.

HE was the brother of a saint, and his friends were rich; so they dressed him in his best, and they put a turban on his head (for he was of the old school), and they bore him to the tomb upon a bier, and coffinless, after the custom of the East. I joined the procession as it swept chanting along the narrow street; and we all entered the illuminated church together.

The archbishop strode solemnly up the aisle preceded by a priest, swinging censers before him; and with the odour of sanctity exhaling from his splendid robes. On went the procession, making its way through a stand-up fight, which was taking place in the church; on through weeping relatives and sobered friends, till, at last, the archbishop was seated on his throne, and the dead man lay before him stiff and stark. Then the same unctuous individual whom I fancy I have observed taking a part in religious ceremonies all over the world, being yet neither priest nor deacon, bustles up, and he places some savoury herbs on the breast of the corpse, chanting lustily as he does so to save time.

The archbishop takes two waxen tapers in each hand; they are crossed and set in a silver hand-candlestick. He extends them towards the crowd, and seems to bless it mutely, for he does not speak. There is silence; only disturbed by a short sob which has broken from the overburdened heart of the dead man's son. Hush! It is the archbishop giving out a psalm: and now it rises lowly, solemnly, mournfully at first. The lusty lungs of the burly priests are dolefully chanting a dirge. All at once they are joined by the glad voices of children, oh! so clear and so pure, sounding sweet and far, rejoicing for the bliss of the departed soul.

They cease; and there comes a priest dressed in black robes; he prostrates himself before the throne of the archbishop, and carries the dust of the prelate's feet to his forehead. Then he kisses the archbishop's hand, and mounts the pulpit to deliver a funeral oration. I am sorry for him; he is evidently a beginner, and twice he breaks down and gasps hopelessly at the congregation; but the archbishop prompts him, and gets him out of this difficulty. A rascally young Greek at my elbow nudges me to laugh, but I pay no attention to him.

Presently the priests begin to swing their censers again, and their deep voices mingle chanting, with the fresh song of the children; and again the archbishop blesses the crowd. Then the relatives of the dead man approach him one by one, crossing themselves devoutly: they take the nosegay of savoury herbs from his breast, and they press it to their lips; they kiss the dead man's forehead. When the son approaches he sobs convulsively, and has afterwards to be removed by gentle force from the body.

So the relatives continue kissing the body, fearless of contagion; and the chant of the priests and choristers swells through the church, and there lies the dead man with the sickly glare of the lamps struggling with the daylight, and falling with a ghastly gleam upon his upturned face. Twice I thought he moved, but it was only fancy.

The archbishop has left the church, and the relatives of the dead man are bearing him to his last home without further ceremony. It is a narrow vault just outside the church, and the Greeks courteously make way for me—a stranger. A man jumps briskly into the grave, it is scarcely three feet deep; he arranges a pillow for the head of the corpse, then he springs out again, laughing at his own agility. The crowd laugh too. Joy and grief elbow each other everywhere in life, why not also at the brink of the tomb?

Then two stout men seize the corpse in their stalwart arms, and they lift it from the bier. They are lowering it now, quite dressed but coffinless, into the vault. They brush me as they do so, and the daylight falls full on the face of the dead. It is very peaceful and composed, but looking so tired, so weary of the world, so relieved that the journey is over.

Stay! for here comes a priest walking slowly from the church with his mass book and censer. He says a few more prayers over the body, and one of the kindred of the dead drops a stone into the grave. While the priest prays he pours some consecrated oil upon the body, and some more upon a spadeful of earth which is brought to him. This also is thrown into the grave. It is not filled up, a stone is merely fastened with clay, roughly, over the aperture, and at night there will be a lamp placed there, which will be replenished every night for a year. At the end of that time the body will be disinterred. If the bones have not been thoroughly rotted away from the flesh and separated, the archbishop will be called again to pray over the body. For there is a superstition among the Greeks, that a man whose body does not dissolve within a year is accursed. When the bones have come apart they will be collected and tied up in a linen bag, which will hang on a nail against the church wall: by-and-by this will decay, and the bones which have been swinging about in the wind and rain will be shaken out one by one to make daylight ghastly where they lie. Years hence they may be swept into the charnel-house, or they may not, as chance directs.

It is but proper to forbear from making indecent comment on such solemn things as the funereal rites of our neighbours: let us therefore, dear reader, hear and see what we lawfully may; but say nothing which might give pain or offence to any one.

I have said that he was the brother of a saint; it is well, therefore, that I should also say something of the saint himself. The Saint was St. Theodore, one of the most recent martyrs of the Greek Church. I will now give his history, which is a curious comment on the times in which he lived.

St. Theodore, was born about fifty years ago, and of very humble parents, who lived at the village of *Neo Chori*, near Constantinople. He was brought up to the trade of a house-painter, an art of some pretension in Turkey, where it is often carried to very great perfection. The lad was clever, and soon attained such excellence in his craft that he was employed at the palace of the Sultan. The splendour of the palace, and of the gorgeous dresses of some of the Sultan's servants, seems to have fired his imagination. He desired to remain among them; so he changed his faith to that of Islam, and was immediately appointed to some petty post about the palace.

Three years after his apostasy and circumcision a great plague broke out at Constantinople, and swept away the Sultan's subjects by hundreds, with short warning. The future saint grew alarmed; a species of religious mania seized upon him. He tried to escape from the palace, but was brought back again. At last, however, he got away in the disguise of a water-carrier, and fled to the island of Scio.

Here he made the acquaintance of a Greek priest, to whom he confessed the enormous crime of which he had been guilty, and stated his intention of becoming a martyr. The priest is said warmly to have commended this view of his case, for the fact was martyrs had lately been growing scarce. Instead of conveying the young man, therefore, to a lunatic asylum, he took him to the neighbouring island of Mitylene: seeing, doubtless, sufficient reasons why the martyrdom should not take place at Scio, where he might have been exposed to awkward remonstrances from his friends for countenancing such a horror.

So the priest, as we have said, declining to lose sight of his young convert, accompanied him to Mitylene, where the first act of the tragedy commenced, by the martyr presenting himself before the Cadi, or Turkish judge. It is melancholy to think of the poor demented youth thus being urged on step by step to a cruel death. Before the Cadi he began to curse the Mussulman faith, he threw his turban at that magistrate's head, and taking from his bosom a green handkerchief with which he had been provided, he trampled it under foot; and green is a sacred colour with the Turks. The Cadi was desirous of getting rid of him quietly, considering him mad, as doubtless he was. But he continued cursing the Turks so bitterly, that at last an angry mob of fanatics bore him away to the Pasha. This functionary, a quiet, amiable man, if ever there was one, tried also to get out of so disagreeable an affair;

but the young man raved so violently that the Turks around began to beat him, and he was put into a sort of stocks to keep him quiet. Nobody seems to have meant him any harm at first. But the poor lad was evidently a lunatic, and at last the Turks lost patience with him, and his martyrdom began in earnest. He was subjected (say the Greek chronicles from which this history is taken) to the cruel torture of having hot earthen plates bound to his temples, and his neck was then twisted by excited bigots till his eyes started from their sockets; they also drew several of his teeth. He now said that he had returned to the Greek faith in consequence of the advice of an *Englishman*, which so appeased the Turks that they offered him a pipe, and wanted to dismiss him. But he soon broke out again and asked for the Sacrament. He also asked for some soup; both were given to him, the Turks offering no opposition to the administering of the former. When, however, he once more began to curse and revile the Prophet, some fanatic proposed that he should be shortened by having an inch cut from his body every time he blasphemed, beginning at his feet. The Cadi shuddered and interposed, saying that such a proceeding would be contrary to the law, which provided that a renegade should be at once put to death, that the faith of Islam might not be insulted. So the mob got a cord to hang him. Like many other things in Turkey, this cord does not seem to have been fit for the purpose to which it was applied; and the struggles of the maniac were so furious that it broke, and he dropped, cutting his knees severely in the fall.

But they *did* hang him at last; thus completing the titles to martyrdom with which he has come down to us. For three days his hanging body offended the daylight; and the simple country-folk cut off bits of his clothes for relics. After a while, he was carried away and buried with a great fuss, the Turks having too profound a contempt for the Greeks to interfere with their doings in any way. His claims to sanctity being thus perfected, application was made to the Patriarch of Constantinople to canonize the mad house-painter, and canonized he was, to the surprise of many. His body was disinterred and mummified with great care; it was wrapped up in cotton, and the head was enclosed in a silver case; both are shown to the devout on the anniversary of his martyrdom. The cotton sells well; it is said to have worked many miracles, and to be especially beneficial in cases of epilepsy: perhaps it may be. The anniversary of the martyrdom of St. Theodore occurred on the same day as his brother's funeral. I asked if the reputation of the saint had anything to do with the honours which had been paid to his brother. Yes, was the answer, the relatives of the saint are naturally anxious to keep up his reputation, which is like a patent of nobility to them; and none dare to offer them injury or wrong, for fear of the martyr's anger.

For the rest, the festival of St. Theodore was as interesting a sight as I would wish to see.

His body was enshrined in a pretty temple of green leaves, and was placed in the centre of the church. Pilgrims arrived at dead of night to pray there, and there was something solemn and strange to see them coming in, dressed in their holiday clothes. They were mostly women, and seemed earnest enough in what they were about. I did not like to see them, however, buying those little bits of cotton which lay mouldering round the mummy, and putting them into their bosoms.

The church was well lighted, for Mitylene is an oil country. Innumerable lamps hung suspended from the roof everywhere, and some were decorated with very pretty transparencies. If you shut your eyes for a minute, they seemed to open on fairy-land rather than reality. The hushed scene, the stillness of which was only broken by the pattering feet of some pilgrim maiden approaching the martyr's shrine, shawled and mysterious even here, had something very quaint and fanciful in it. I could have stopped there all night watching the pilgrims as they passed dropping buttons (substitute for small coin given in churches) into the salver of a dingy priest who sat in the aisle, with tablets in hand, to receive orders for masses to be said for the sick or the dead. I liked to note the business manner in which he raised his reverend hand to get the light well upon his tablets, and adjusted his spectacles as he inscribed each new order from the pilgrims. At last, however, he gathered up his buttons and money, tying them in a bag, and then glancing round once more in vain for customers, he went his way into the sacristy. I followed his waddling figure with my eyes, till the last lock of his long hair, which caught in the brocaded curtain, had been disentangled, and he disappeared. Then, as the active individual in rusty black, whom I have mentioned as so busy in the ceremony of the morning, seemed desirous of having a few minutes' conversation with me, I indulged him. It was not difficult to perceive from the tenor of his discourse that he was desirous of receiving some token of my esteem in small change; it cost little to gratify him, and then, as the church was quite deserted, we marched off together. I found my brave Albanian waiting for me at the door, lantern in hand; he had come alarmed to look for me, and the clerical genius of course looked upon him with too much disfavour to accompany me farther; so cautioning us to mind the broken steps at the church door, he took his departure, practising an unctuous hallelujah.

CHAPTER XXIX.

A TRAVELLERS' HOME IN GREECE.

THE religious establishments of foreign countries have one very notable point in which they stand in honourable contrast to our own. It is, that important institutions of great public utility are very often founded and supplied by their revenues. Many of the high dignitaries of the church abroad have incomes beside which that of the Bishop of London would appear to a disadvantage; but nearly all have far other claims on them than our prelates—claims to which they are also compelled by law or usage to attend very strictly. I could give a dozen instances in point very easily, but one will serve my purpose just now, and we will therefore confine ourselves to it, premising merely that it is one of many.

Let us not be too proud to learn. We have so often stood in the honourable relation of teachers to other nations, that we can with a better grace afford now and then to turn pupils. If in the present instance the lesson comes from a long way off, and from a place whence we are not generally in the habit of receiving lessons of practical benefit, this is no reason at all why we should receive it less kindly, or be especially surprised; for Minerva's self might, I dare say, have learned something new in the poorest Spartan village.

Having now introduced my subject respectfully, I proceed to say, that there is in the town of Castro, at the distant island of Mitylene, in the Ægean Sea, a small establishment which I am sure no one could be sorry to see imitated in London upon a larger scale. It is a *travellers' home*, built and supported solely by the revenues of the Greek Archbishopric: I very much doubt also if any part of them are better employed.

It is a plain, very plain house, and it is divided into a vast number of small rooms, without furniture of any kind ; each has a fireplace, several commodious cupboards, a strong door with a strong padlock to fasten it; and there is a common fire for all the inmates of these rooms, presided over by the solitary single gentleman who has charge of the building.

The object for which this place was first erected was as a temporary resting-place for the more humble travellers who flock to the capital of the island to take part in the solemn festivals of the Greek Church ; but its advantages have since been extended to all travellers who have no home elsewhere. The only title to admittance is decent apparel, and the right to remain any reasonable time is acquired by quiet orderly conduct, and an understanding, strictly enforced, that each traveller shall keep the room allotted to him perfectly clean while he occupies it, and so leave it at his departure.

There is no charge made for this entertainment : the traveller may give something if he pleases, but nothing is required of him. The numerous respectable people who avail themselves of the establishment generally pay a trifle towards a fund, which is understood to go in part to the maintenance of the building in good repair ; but their contributions are very small, and by far the greater part of the visitors pay nothing at all.

It is impossible to think without satisfaction of the many people whose necessities while travelling are thus provided for. Whether they bring an air mattress and comfortable coverings with them, or whether they sleep on the hard floor ; whether they purchase a comfortable dinner of the smug elderly gentleman, or whether they conceal a crust of dry bread in their pocket, nobody knows. Neither is it evident to any man whether his neighbour pays or does not pay. There is no apparent difference between the moneyed guest and the poor one ; each has his own room and his own lock and key. His privacy is therefore respected whenever he chooses to make it so. It is the only place of public entertainment I think I ever saw where poverty is allowed to be quiet and decent in its own way.

It was on the still afternoon of a grey day late in autumn

when I first visited this place. I had sent away my horses, for the breeze blew chilly, and, lighting a cigar, I had walked musingly among the mysterious streets of the little town of Castro, till chance led my steps thither. Finding myself before a house of such size, I inquired what it was, and having received an answer, I passed unquestioned through the open gate. The wind sighed heavily along the narrow street, and I remember that an involuntary awe came over me, as I seemed to be led by some other power than curiosity up the spotless stairs of freshly-planed wood, and along the silent corridor, till I stopped before a door where there sat a woman wailing. There is something so august in real sorrow, that I should have passed on respectfully, but that her outstretched hand detained me.

"O Frankish Lord!" cried the woman in accents of unutterable despair, "save him, for he is dying." She pressed my hand to her quivering lips as she spoke, after the fashion of the East, and I knew that her simple heart was full of the popular belief that the Franks or Europeans have all the knowledge of the science of the physician.

"Alas, mother!" I answered in the simple idiom of the country, "*I* have no power to save him."

But she detained me in the strong spasm of her grasp, and the next minute I stood within the chamber of death, and was abashed before the nameless majesty of the dark-winged angel.

I knelt beside the bed very gently and humbly, and took the hand of the sick lad: I dared not meet again the mother's imploring look, for there was no mistaking the prophecy of that languid fluttering pulse, or the foam gathering on the lips, and the glassy eye. Even as I knelt there, a strange light seemed to pass over the boy's face, changing its expression, wholly; when it was gone, his head fell back gently, and I knew that all was over, for that light was the ray which comes through the gates of heaven when they open to receive a soul. A low continued moan broke the stillness as I rose. Oh! deal with her gently, the bereaved mother; for her last child is lying cold beside her; and though her darling is gone to the fields where the night cometh not, neither is there shadow of darkness, yet she cannot follow him! Deal then with her gently, for the hand of the Chastener is heavy upon her. As I turned to go from the last home of that lowly traveller, a something that had before lain heavy on my heart was rebuked, and I felt how the little ills of life sink into nothing beside such a grief as this.

CHAPTER XXX.

PLEASANT CHIOS.

SHE is my next-door neighbour,—a farmer's wife; and she told me she had been a slave among the Turks. It was in the dusk of evening when she spoke with me. I was sitting on the low threshold of her cottage, and watching her as she tended her silkworms. The birds had sung their last goodnight to the flowers, and here and there a bat already winged his uncertain flight through the misty air. A beautiful star, which I have watched rising for many evenings, and which is my friend, shone silently above us (it seemed to me like true love, growing brighter as all else darkened), and the soft waves of the haunted Ægean whispered a soothing chorus to the old lady's words. I felt, as she told her tale, as if that scene would never wholly leave my memory; and, in truth, it had a character which was worth preserving. The aged story-teller, pleased to find a new listener, and enjoying so thoroughly the flavour of her own words; the humble work-a-day cottage, with its long trays of silkworms and mulberry-leaves; the herb-pot simmering beneath a stunted fig-tree in the courtyard; a dog watching me with a look of some surprise; and the bright lonely star looking down upon us with such a solemn affection.

We are at Chios, some thirty years ago. In the thronged streets, and by the sea-shore; and again in the lovers' paths which lead up to the pretty villas on the hill-side, may be seen demure and well-to-do Greeks. They walk about with a flaunting importance it is refreshing to behold. They snuff the air and bridle up as they go. They are conscious of being men of property. They have houses ornamented even to the knocker of the street-door. They have fruitful vineyards and fat lands. Their orange and citron groves scent the breeze; and the fruit would break down the branches of the trees, if they were not propped up by stout staves, thrust into the ground, with broad forked tops for them to lean on. They have already in their pockets the money for next year's olives, paid by merchants greedy to secure the fine produce of the island ; and boats are coming swiftly over many seas for the countless heaps of almonds, tied up in bulky sacks and awaiting them. There is feasting and singing in the pleasant houses; and groups of holiday makers are gathering in little parties to rejoice together. The island is overflowing with wealth; for Chios is well known to be the dower of the good Sultana, and is one of the most favoured spots beneath the rule of the Turk.

The *rule*, did we say? Surely there must be some mistake in this. Mark yonder bowed and humble Moslem, greeting that proud Greek horseman on his pampered steed. You would hardly guess that the former is a conquerer ; that the latter would tell you he is a slave. You may know very well the many phases of the vexed question between the Turk and the Greek. You understand that it may not be—nay, *is* not a good thing, to be a Christian in the villages of Asia Minor and many other places ; but you can see at a glance how matters go here. In plain truth, the victors are afraid of the vanquished. Most of the Turks have been shut up for years in the fortress ; and they often feel an uncomfortable foreboding that they will not be allowed to smoke their pipes much longer in pleasant Chios. The rest are glad of the crumbs which fall from the rich Greeks' tables, and resignedly seem to wait the utter extermination which they believe is overtaking them.

The Greeks are also of the same opinion. The primates have had lately a good deal of mysterious correspondence ; a local schoolmaster had suddenly become a Russian archbishop, and writes frequent inquiries after his old friends from St. Petersburg. He sends them presents of large gold coins, to hang round the necks of their womankind ; he sends decorations for their churches and houses ; he sends books, and even money. He sings the praises of the "orthodox emperor," as if he were moonstricken.

Slight daring little barks, manned with stranger crews, have been seen, too, by night, stealing into out-of-the-way creeks and bays; the primates have been there to meet the sailors as they landed stealthily. Those boats have not come for figs or olives, nor have the men rowed on shore with muffled oars merely to take in almonds. They have brought arms and fiery proclamations from that hysteric braggart the Russian Colonel Ipsilanti, who has unfurled the standard of a contemptible revolt in Wallachia, and from those secret societies which have lately grown so numerous among the Greeks everywhere.

The primates read with straining eyeballs, of fearful outrages committed on unresisting people; of violated women, and children struck dead by hands still red with the blood of their fathers. Some of these things are mere tricky exaggerations; some are too true. They learn also, with ears palsied by horror, how their patriarch has been murdered at Constantinople, and that their Church has blessed the cause of the insurgents: that Solomon, Archbishop of Patras, has raised the white flag under the protection of the Cross (there is his picture: he is a fine tall man with a banner in his hand; a crowd is kneeling round him; he looks as one inspired!)—joined their ranks, and helped to form an experimental government. The stealthy boatmen have brought one of his proclamations. Bleeding Greece may yet be free—is free; for are not the forbidden arms at last glittering beside them, and the might of the Moslem but a gigantic shadow? So the fiery papers tell them; so, for a wonder, they *believe;* and the poison has done its work.

The scene is changed. It is a grey, solemn sort of day, and some heavy ships with the red flag at the masthead come lumbering on through the distance towards devoted Chios. Yet a few months, and these ships will be cinders; their crews will have been blown up by gunpowder, or slain by falling masts, or drowned like dogs, by the men sailing in those few poor fishing-boats which are hovering like mere specks in the water, far away astern. Be this as it may, however, the Turkish ships are grim and terrible enough now; and the Capitan Pasha, with his fleet, has anchored in the offing, and opened a deadly fire on the doomed city.

P

There are pale faces now among the primates, as they hurry to and fro, for the despised Turks in the fortress are charging down upon them with loud cries. They are defenceless; the arms to which they trusted in their boastings are but as reeds in their unaccustomed hands, and a wild panic seizes on them as they see boat after boat lowered down from the sides of the vessels, and rowed away through dense clouds of smoke, filled with the fierce men of blood who have come to punish them. There is no safety but in flight, and the next sun shines upon them lurking among the mountains, hungry houseless wanderers, looking mournfully down on the smoking and rifled ruins of their homes.

Among these wretched and repentant fugitives were my neighbour, her husband, and her three children: one was a baby at the breast, another three years old, the third a brave boy of seven. All that day and all the next she heard the sharp crack of Turkish guns, and the shrill screams of prisoners taken among the hills. The same fearful sounds continued daily and nightly at intervals for a whole month, during which time she lay concealed, appalled and trembling in her hiding-place. There was no hope of further flight, for the dark ships still lay anchored in the waters, and the incessant glare of burning houses and the firing of guns told too truly that the angry Turks were on the land. How she lived she knows not; sometime on raw roots and berries. Sometimes she dug a little hole in the ground and roasted them, carefully smothering the smoke, that it might not ascend to betray her whereabouts.

At last the Turks found my neighbour's hiding-place, however, being guided by the cries of the baby, who was ill. Her husband fled and escaped. There was no hope of mercy for *him* if taken; and "why," says my neighbour, feeling kindly towards him even now, "should the poor fellow have remained for a certain and cruel death—perhaps to be roasted, perhaps to be beaten out of life by hammers?" Then the incensed Turks tore the woman's child from her breast and cast it down to perish of hunger, or perhaps, says my neighbour (now wonderfully lost to all feeling on the subject), to be eaten by insects. Her second child was left to share the same fate; but the eldest, the boy of seven years old, was carried away screaming, whither she knows not.

She was driven down into the sacked town with many other prisoners; she walked over dead bodies, festering unburied because of their number. The ground was dark with human gore. She was sold, she does not know for how much money, but she thinks for about eight pounds English currency, there being of course a glut of Greek slaves in the market just then. She saw wild doings enough around her, but she fell into kind hands. She was bought by a wealthy kaimacam (or lieutenant-governor of a district), in Asia Minor; and she still relates with all the pride of trust how the keys of good things were confided to her; how she was promoted to all honour by a fat sleepy Turkish lady, wife of the kaimacam: how she became housekeeper, so that her will was law—a slave in name, mistress in fact.

It is a bitter thing, however, to be a slave even in name, and she pined constantly till she found means to communicate with her brother, who was in the service of the kind-hearted Pasha of Mitylene.

Negotiations were opened for her ransom, but neither her master nor mistress could be brought to part with her. She was an active vivacious little woman; in spite of her troubles she appears to have put really a brave heart on the matter, and to have made herself generally useful. At length, one day, as she was in the garden, she heard that low peculiar hiss with which the Greeks are accustomed to attract attention, and looking up she saw her brother with "*another man*" whom she did not know, peeping over the high wall which as usual screened the dwelling of the kaimacam. They now spoke to her, and said they had come to fetch her away. She climbed over the wall with their aid, and mounting on a pillion behind her brother, was soon in full flight from those whose gentle kindness and unbounded confidence could have no softening influence on a slave. For a long time she sought news of her son, but never heard any tidings of him. Some fugitives, however, told her that her husband had died of starvation in the mountains. So her brother married her to the "*other man*" whom she had seen peeping over the wall with him. The generous Pasha gave her a little farm, and she had other children. Her heart healed, and she has mellowed into a lively old gossip, an excellent cook!

I do not believe that such things as I have related would occur now; some of them *could* not. Still let us have an eye on the proceedings of our new acquaintances, for they are again very angry with the Rayahs; and it is our solemn duty to be careful that in shielding them from violence and aggression on the one hand, we do not on the other uphold them in the wrong.

CHAPTER XXXI.

A SKETCH OF EPIRUS.

I WILL try to give the reader a sketch of a place I once visited, and which has recently acquired a terrible interest in the eyes of all who concern themselves in the momentous questions which are now coming rapidly to a most terrible issue in the East.

Epirus, then, or Lower Albania, is bounded on the north by the river Aous or Voioussa, and a chain of the Pindus, which was known in ancient times by the name of Lyngon; on the east it is shut in also by the Pindus, which separates it from Macedonia and Thessaly; on the south it is bordered by the Ambracic Gulf, and on the west by the beautiful Ionian Sea. Of its inhabitants, a sixth only are said to profess the faith of Islam; and Christians of the Greek Church are believed to form more than two-thirds of the entire population.

Epirus has nearly always been in a state bordering on insurrection or in open revolt; it has been for at least a century the very hot-bed of Greek schemes and intrigues, and it has suffered in consequence horrors more fearful perhaps than any which have been enacted in other parts of Turkey. Under the warlike George Castriot, better known by his Turkish name of Scanderbeg, Epirus became an independent principality; and that famous chief not only humbled the arms of Amurath the Second, but was even able to check the pride of his successor, Mahomet, the conqueror of Constantinople. After his death Epirus was indeed subdued; but it has always been one of the most restless and troublesome countries under Ottoman rule, and was very nearly being erected again into an independent state, under Aly Pasha of Janina, one of the most wily and bloodthirsty tyrants of modern times.

Previous to the war of independence in 1821, Janina was, perhaps, the richest city in the Ottoman empire, after Smyrna and Constantinople. It was especially remarkable for the number of distinguished Greeks who taught in its schools; the scholars Mélétius, Côme Balanos, Psalidas, Villaras, and N. Doucas, are too well known to need further illustration here; and Epirus gave the heroic names of Botzaris and Karaiskaki to the late war. The Greeks of Epirus at this period entertained commercial relations of notable importance with many of the states of Europe, and especially with Russia, Austria, and Venice. Most of the Greeks who have taken advantage of the privileges accorded to their countrymen in Russia since the time of Catherine II., have been natives of Epirus. It used also to be a notorious fact, that they hoarded up their money for revolutionary purposes with extraordinary perseverance and self-denial; an immense sum deposited by Greek merchants at the Zecca, in Venice, disappeared in the fall of that republic before the victorious arms of the French, and it was immediately after this loss that the seven brothers Zossima became so deservedly celebrated for the sacrifice of their whole time and fortune to the advancement of Greek learning. They were also natives of Epirus, established at Moscow, and by their private fortunes and industry almost repaired the loss of the funds, which had been gradually collected for educational objects, and which had shared the same fate as the other moneys which had been deposited in the Zecca.

The remarkable enthusiasm among the Rayahs for learning (which it is proper to say Epirus only shared with the rest of the Greek states) could not be quenched by the fearful cruelties of Aly Pasha, or even by the still greater horrors which followed his fall, and the almost total destruction of Janina in 1821. To this day there is neither town, village, nor Christian community of any kind in Epirus, which does not possess a flourishing school, supported by the voluntary contributions either of Greeks, Albanians, or Wallachs.

The consequence of these long-continued endeavours has been singular enough. The Turks of Epirus can seldom speak their own language, and, with very few exceptions, understand no tongue but the Greek. Nearly all the Albanian Beys, even in Upper Albania as far as Scodra, carry on their official correspondence in Greek, and employ the Greek grammaticos or secretary, instead of the Turkish Kiatib or Hoja. M. Ami Boué tells us that the Pashas of Albania are obliged also to write their watchwords in Greek, that the sentinels on their posts may be able to understand them. This can hardly be surprising, indeed, when we learn in a very able article in the *Eastern Spectator*, that the present population of Epirus comprises only 61,265 Mahommedans to 311,370 Greek Christians, and when all the wit, energy, and wiles of the one race are contrasted with the utter indolence and indifference of the other.

The chief features of the country in Epirus are rugged and mountainous, though there are some laughing valleys and fertile plains, perhaps more delightful from their rarity. The inhabitants, however, are rather a race of merchants and mechanics than agriculturists; in almost every part of Turkey, as well as in the kingdom of Greece and the principalities of the Danube, may be found emigrants from various parts of Epirus, laboriously following useful trades, and hoarding money up for the old dark and sinister purpose. The places which seem especially to send forth these earnest exiles are the districts of Metsovo, Delvino, and Conitza. Wealthy Epirote merchants may also be found in almost every considerable town in Europe, especially at St. Petersburg, and the cities on the coasts of Russia, Austria, Italy, and Egypt. Comparatively few go to France or England, and the leaning which the Greeks seem always to have had towards the despotic governments is one of the most extraordinary facts in their history. The Epirote merchants established abroad are said (though I will not vouch for it) to be remarkable for good faith and simplicity of manners, or their wonderful economy and self-denial, and for a feeling of patriotism, which absolutely amounts to a passion.

Epirus was the very stronghold of the bands of organized robbers who were known as the Kleftai; it poured forth horde upon horde of them during the late war, and perhaps there was no considerable deed of arms of the period in which they did not take a fierce and determined part. They were unmoved by the martyrdom of their heroes, and the Suliote women not only girded on the swords of their lovers for the battle, but fought themselves with a vigour and success which have become matters of history. The Epirotes were the most valiant defenders of Missolonghi, and their name became a terror to the contents of every turban in Turkey; they also comprised the most formidable portion of the venomous little army of King Otho, and many others of the same race have distinguished themselves in the civil service, and in the chambers of Greece. I abstain naturally from calling attention to living persons, but it may be remarked that the most energetic of Greek politicians and agitators in the present day are of the restless, determined, and self-denying race of Epirus.

CHAPTER XXXII.

CAPITAN JORGEIJ.

HONOUR to worth! There is one Greek at least whom I have known, and whom I would except from the contempt which too often attaches to his countrymen. He is a sea-captain, a rough weather-beaten man, with the heart of a child. So valiant and gentle, so true and staunch, that the grasp of his honest hardworking hand does a man good. It makes one better to see him among weaklings and little children, he seems so conscious of his uncouth strength, that he appears afraid of breaking them; though his healthy, merciful heart would not let him harm a worm.

Capitan Jorgeij was once rich; but he had no thought for himself, and was so good and so simple that bad men took advantage of him; and now he is only wealthy in the love and esteem of all who know him, in the affection of boys and girls, who greet him with a shriek of joy, and turn gladly from their path coming home from school, when they meet him; in the gratitude of the widow and orphan, who thank him with moistened eyes for many benefits, and put him to the blush with their praises; and in the kind thoughts of everybody. Capitan Jorgeij was ruined long ago by a hard vile rogue, who now (lest all should cry shame upon him) gives his victim an asylum in his house, and protects, insults, and makes him useful. But Capitan Jorgeij does not seem conscious of this, and it is very touching to see his loyal gratitude and affection for one who has wrought him such cruel injuries. He thinks he can never do enough to show his thankfulness for the rude bed and scanty board which is doled out to him. He has become as a bondsman to his taskmaster. I wish I had such a servant as Capitan Jorgeij; I would try and treat him better. Upon the whole, I think I would rather have him for a brother or a very near friend. He is never absent from the house, except when sent upon some errand. He does all sorts of odd jobs; he minds the children and makes them toys; he stables the horse, drives bargains, and is sent to wrangle about tradesmen's bills. He must overlook the servants,—a hard task this, and tell of their shortcomings; he must give the benefit of zeal, experience, and honesty, all for mere bread and board. Yet I am afraid I could never gain the friendship of Capitan Jorgeij, for he cannot believe it possible that any one should think ill of his spoiler, or suppose him to be unfairly used.

The man to whom Capitan Jorgeij owes his ruin is no ogre for all that, he is merely a very frequent specimen of the modern Greek. Still young, he has acquired a very considerable fortune. In reality superficial, empty, and ignorant; acquainted with no one art or science, and hardly able to read and write correctly, he has yet a natural acuteness that would puzzle the wisest. He is indeed one of the most successful sharpers of the cornmarket, and that is saying a great deal. He has the most pleasant, frank, plausible manner possible; yet he only speaks truth by accident; he seems to divine other men's thoughts and intentions by a sort of instinct, and no one comes in contact with him without somehow or other getting the wrong end of an argument. He will commit the most impudent robberies with a cool air of assurance that is positively astounding. He is grasping, unjust, oppressive, cunning, false, tricky, selfish, all with the air of an injured man. He has his temper under the most extraordinary command, and would never by any chance let slip an expression of a disagreeable nature towards anybody from whom he might ever by any possibility have the chance of winning sixpence or its worth. To dependants he is of course as heartless a tyrant as ever insulted worth or embittered misfortune. No man has ever shown him to appear in the wrong; his labours are only known by their fruits. Somehow or other, everybody who makes his acquaintance and gets mixed up with him in business grows poorer, and yet cannot convict him of dishonesty; the fact is there, the reason a mystery. His very victims are constrained to speak well of him, for they can prove no evil. His acquaintances seem all under obligations to him. Persons formerly thriving and well to do in the world appear to pass beneath his yoke, and into difficulties in a manner that is almost magical. When they fail and sink into utter ruin, he has always contrived to get paid. He has foreseen what was going to happen, and has disposed of their acceptances—sold them perhaps to some friend who desired a safe investment, and who had asked his advice: in short, he is out of the scrape, let who will be in it. To be sure, there are one or two people who look shyly at him. It is possible to be sharper than some men, but not to be sharper than every man. Strange whispers go about respecting him; his mother is said to have died in extreme poverty, and one of his brothers to have fallen into trouble and never issued from it. But he does not mind such reports as these, for he has one of his poor relations living with him, and can point triumphantly to her. To be sure, she cooks and superintends the washing; but he cannot be expected to entertain her for nothing, though she is said to be a perfect wonder of economy, and to live altogether on boiled salads. There is a grand gold chain which her important relative wears rather ostentatiously, and which is said to have belonged to her deceased husband, as well as the watch which is attached to it; but that is neither here nor there. What is more natural than that dependants should show some substantial marks of gratitude to their protectors, if they have any? It does not seem, on the whole, astonishing that the friendship of such a genius as this should have been disastrous to Capitan Jorgeij. Shortly after its commencement, the sea-captain's affairs got into a maze, and they never got out of it. He had then an olive-garden and a little vessel of his own, with which he went about to the ports in the neighbourhood, and sometimes sailed as far as Malta, driving a thriving trade. But directly he began to carry cargoes for Kyrios Oglou and to leave the management of his affairs at home in the hands of his employer, everything went wrong. His olive-trees produced no fruit, his house was burnt down; and though everything was destroyed in the fire, he has since seen some property about the premises of his patron so like his own as to be quite surprising. But this does not shake his simple good faith, and he seems to me so respectable and happy in it, that I sometimes wonder if after all he is not really the wiser man of the two. My opinion is not at all disturbed by the fixed smile that is always on the lips of Kyrios Oglou, for I cannot help fancying that he must feel often uncomfortable, especially in the long windy winter's nights, when I suspect that this smile masks a black heart and its many shameful secrets.

Capitan Jorgeij's olive-garden and his pleasant house by the seaside have all passed into the hands of his grand patron. It makes one quite uneasy to hear him talk about them and brag of their produce with such complacency. It is painful to see Capitan Jorgeij on the summer afternoon toiling home with a large basket of fruit, proud that the land which once was his at least produces something. Kyrios Oglou, however, only receives them with a grunt of disapprobation (it is not worth his while to flatter Capitan Jorgeij now), and an ungraceful observation about the expense of gardening, so that the modest sailor really is puzzled to find that the property which was a little fortune once to him, should only be a burthen now to his patron. He feels quite disgraced by it, and ashamed that he should have allowed his generous friend to have accepted it for such a large debt as was due to him. Capitan Jorgeij knew it was a large debt, though he did not exactly know how much; for there had never been an account between them, and he was not a good hand at figures, if there had been one. Then it was not only a large debt, but one which showed the generosity of Kyrios Oglou, and the concern he had always taken for Capitan Jorgeij's affairs, in a very brilliant light. So Capitan Jorgeij thought that if his patron was a little sharp with him now sometimes, he must remember how much he had lost by him, all owing to an act of kindness too. It would not indeed bear thinking of, and Capitan Jorgeij hung down his head, and immediately set about some hard work whenever it was mentioned, to ease his honest mind.

The fact was, that when Capitan Jorgeij's olive-trees would obstinately persist in bearing no fruit in the most favourable seasons; when his grapes seemed all gathered before they had grown; and when his figs did not consent to grow at all; when he returned home and found his house burnt down and ruin staring him in the face, Kyrios Oglou proposed to him a very notable scheme for redeeming his fortunes: this was to lend money at a high rate of interest to a trader in the town, who had not hitherto borne a very good reputation for strict honesty in his accounts. Capitan Jorgeij indeed ventured to make an observation to this effect at the time; but his kind friend only smiled in a peculiar way he had, and told Capitan Jorgeij that he did not understand those kinds of affairs, which indeed was true. So the worthy sailor left everything to his friend and went on another voyage; not, however, till he had given a mortgage on his property for a considerable sum of money which had been placed out at such famous interest in his name, and which had been lent by Kyrios Oglou with the most disinterested generosity. But fresh troubles awaited him; he seemed born to ill-luck. When he returned, the trader had left the country and taken Capitan Jorgeij's money with him. The stout seaman, however, was not half so much distressed at this, as at the loss sustained by his kind friend, after all the efforts on his behalf, which were detailed to him with such scrupulous minuteness. After this, there was of course but one thing to do, viz., to give up the olive-garden; and though it now began to bear all sorts of produce in a very remarkable manner, considering its recent sterility when in possession of Capitan Jorgeij, yet he was quite surprised that his patron should have been good enough to accept it for such a considerable portion of the debt due to him. To be sure, he held Capitan Jorgeij's bond for the rest; but what was the use of that; he could put him in prison at any time; but he was far too good to do it, which was another reason for gratitude on his part, and another reason (so thought the simple-minded sailor) why he should try by every means in his power to repay the immense debt of generosity and forbearance which he owed his benefactor. I am almost of opinion that Capitan Jorgeij would have thought it nothing but his duty to die or go into slavery, uncomplaining, for that most cold-blooded and heartless scoundrel.

It was a touching and cruel thing to see them together; the humble respect and gratitude of the brave sailor, in his worn clothes so carefully brushed, and the perspiration pouring down his furrowed cheeks from unremunerated toil: his anxious glance to catch the eye of his patron, as that individual, with his tawdry ill-gotten gold chain, sat in state upon an easy-chair in his country house. It moved one's very heart to see the sailor so willing and earnest, so untiring and contented under a rod of iron.

Ah, Capitan Jorgeij, good, honest-hearted sailor! Little didst thou dream how infinitely better and greater thou wert, in the eyes of Him who sees all things, than the bedizened rogue who had robbed thee. How the hands of honest men would have been stretched out to grasp those shy, awkward fists of yours, who would not have deigned to touch the white and jewelled fingers of that amazing scamp for a fortune! What bright, kind eyes of noble women would have smiled on you, which would have been turned with infinite disgust from him! How the world even, which placed no faith in him, honoured and trusted you! and how even angels hovering in the air let the shadows of their wings fall on him, their radiance upon you, while they chronicle your deeds with a loving smile, so that you may one day be rewarded!

This is a true story! Let it ingraft in our hearts a deeper contempt for ill-gotten riches, and a warmer respect for faith and honesty. I do not envy the man who, if he had to choose, would not rather be the *dupe* than the duper, who would not despise the miserable craft of the wealthy thief and honour Capitan Jorgeij.

CHAPTER XXXIII.

GREEK TRICKS.

"THE Greeks indeed try to deceive you, but, after all, they only succeed in making you angry. A village bumpkin will measure his cunning, I know, unhesitatingly against the wisdom and experience of a grey-haired magistrate, who has thought and wrought, and travelled, and studied mankind for fifty years; who can read that bumpkin's thoughts as if they were written on paper and in round text; who *does* read them, and there is an end of it. I am by no means sure that one man, be he who he may, can deceive another, if the other is fairly on his guard. I should be the rather apt to say the former will doubt *too much;* and Heaven knows we are all of us sufficiently on our guard when we have to do with the Greek, for the very name of their nation is used among us as synonymous with that of sharper."

I might have said more, in defiance of Dean Swift's capital precept never to talk more than half a minute at a time; but a something about the expression of my guest's face deterred me. He was a British consul in the neighbourhood, and had seen and known something of the Greeks, so I waited for his reply.

"I think you underrate the capacity of our friends," said he musingly. "I am as well aware of them as most people, yet they have no difficulty in deceiving me. I will tell you some instances. A man rushed breathless into my office the other day. 'Oh, sir,' he cried, 'pray lend me 100 piastres. The steamer is just starting for Constantinople, I want to pay my sister's fare; she is going to join her husband. All your servants know me; everybody knows me for a respectable man: but my wife has gone out, and taken the key of our money-box with her. Pray make haste, sir.' 'Why, who on earth are you?' said I; 'I never saw you in my life.' The Greek crossed himself devoutly at my having made such an assertion. I knew him intimately, to be sure I did; and he referred to my servants, who were within call, for the truth of his statement. Well,' said I, 'if you are a rogue, you are the coolest fellow I ever saw. I will trust you, however: here is the money, return it to me to-morrow.' 'Oh, no, not to-morrow, sir; in an hour, in half an hour, directly I have seen my sister off.'

"Yet this man was a mere village cheat; and, as you hinted, I am a man who has seen something of the world. The fellow lied, I vow to you, with such address, that his very breathing was a lie; and the whole scene one of the most masterly pieces of acting I ever saw.

"Then, again, I have a neighbour. My neighbour has a daughter. This daughter is a girl of uncertain age: she may be thirty, she may be less; she is unmarried; we must make allowances. She came to me the other day, wringing her hands and weeping: she was deadly pale. 'What is the matter now, Katinka?' said I. She answered that she and her mother were to be thrown into prison by a French merchant, and for a debt which they did not owe.

"Now I know very well there is a little clique of Europeans at Barataria who do pretty much what they like, and who 'set themselves above the law and the prophet. I therefore inquired into the business, and I subsequently called on the French merchant.

"Between French and English there is of course a feud at Barataria; such feuds linger in remote places, long after they have passed away from more important ones. I endeavoured, therefore, to allay the feud; and I succeeded. The Frenchman became chatty. 'To say the truth,' he observed, 'the money is not due to *me*, it is due to my clerk; the man's family have suddenly fallen into great distress, and he wants it.'

"'Well, but,' I pleaded, ' he has neither witnesses, security, nor writing of any kind. His simple word cannot be taken in law.'

"This was my opinion, and I held it stoutly. The next day the young woman was summoned before the mixed tribunal of Turks and Christians, who judge of such cases. As the French merchant was a mighty man, and several of the Greeks on the bench had dealings with him, they at once decided the case in his favour. They did not even allow the defendant to speak. -

"This did not suit me at all. I asked the Pasha to see into the affair. It appeared as plain to him as it did to me: the plaintiff had no case. The judgment was therefore reversed.

"The Frenchman grew angry; an insult was offered to his consideration. He could not do as he pleased at Barataria! Decidedly the English were a pestilent race. He went to the Greek archbishop: his holiness immediately excommunicated the woman who owed the clerk money. So I went again to the archbishop, and the excommunication fell as harmless as the judgment. I got a good deal of ill-will in the business; but I was determined that if justice could be had in the country, two helpless women should have it. They did have it, as I thought: but mark the end,—it is worthy of notice. I studied medicine when I was a young man, and now and then am able to do civil things to people in consequence: I am a sort of gratis doctor for small aches in my neighbourhood. I was one day sent for to my neighbour. She had got the rheumatism; and though a well-to-do old lady, had no idea of employing the regular doctor, for the Greeks are economical to a marvel. While I was talking to the old woman, her daughter came in: she wanted something out of the strong box. It was just beside me, and I could not help seeing what was in it. There was a pile of gold, French gold: it was the gold she had borrowed from the Frenchman's clerk! It is needless to say I subsequently paid the money from my own pocket. I never felt a more keen sense of regret—and I may almost say, disgrace—for the conduct into which I had been entrapped to secure 'justice for the Greek.'

"A Greek wrote to me on one occasion a strange wild secret letter, apparently composed under the immediate fear of assassination. He said that a Turkish officer had beaten him brutally, and had then thrown him into prison. He implored me to have the Turk punished, if there was mercy in the land for an outraged people. Very well, I set about it forthwith; I spent a week inquiring into the circumstances. In the end I found that the complainant had been robbing his own nephews. The Turk was a witness against him, and therefore he wanted to get the Turk out of the way. Yet the man's complaint had a circumstantiality as marvellous, as convincing, and as false as Defoe threw into his ghost story. He named place, time, and witnesses; he adduced collateral evidence without end; and he had instructed his witnesses till they were as perfect in the lie as himself.

"Another Greek gentleman called upon me to say he had been wounded by a Turk: he had his arm in a sling. He seemed faint from the loss of blood: he could (or rather would) hardly speak: he wept silently. Again I interfered. I accompanied him personally to the local authority. The local authority offered every satisfaction: in half an hour I should have brought imprisonment and bastinado on an innocent man. Pity, or my good angel, however, induced me to call on the doctor with him as we were walking home. The doctor is a gentleman, and a man of science; I have faith in him; I thought also that so dangerous a wound might be inflamed by walking about and subsequent unskilful handling. My companion overflowed with gratitude till the doctor asked to look at his wound; then there was quite a discussion. A something about the man's manner made me insist. When the blood-stained bandages were removed, it is unnecessary to add that the arm was as sound as mine.

"I hold my house by contract or lease from a Greek. We drew up the lease in Greek together; then we each took home our draft to make a clean copy, and sign the next day. We were each to keep a facsimile of the document in the hands of the other. Now I can speak Greek fluently enough, but I have some difficulty in writing it correctly. My landlord had observed this; he also knew that my interpreter was ill. He begged me, therefore, in a friendly way, when I met him in the afternoon, to let him write out both copies. I consented. 'They are quite the same as the terms we agreed to yesterday,' said he, when I called on him to sign the next day. 'Of course,' I answered, 'but we may just read them over; it will not take long.' 'No necessity in the world,' said the Greek, laughing good-humouredly; 'but if you wish it,'—and he did read them over. So did I afterwards; and I found that he had added just one-fifth more to the rent. I remonstrated. 'Oh,' said he, 'if you Englishmen are so troublesome as that, I will not let you my house at all.' 'Very well,' said I, and went upon my way, though it was the only house then to be had in the place. A few weeks afterwards the Greek, not being able to find another tenant as he had expected, denied the circumstance altogether, said the contract was ready, the other had been merely a mistake, it referred to another house and another person, about whom he wished to ask my advice. 'Oh, indeed!' 'I swear by the cross, and my eyes, and my children!' said the Greek."

I wonder how officials who can speak nothing but English get on with these worthies.

CHAPTER XXXIV.

THE POSTMAN.

IT is doubtful, after all, if Cadmus was really the inventor of letters. A great scholar, by whose friendship I am honoured, was telling me the other day that Cadmus was a mere typical name, derived, if I understood him rightly, from a Persian word. As I am not deeply versed in the Persian language, however, I cannot completely verify in my own mind a mere careless fragment of a lazy conversation we held together while watching the moon rise that pleasant summer evening from the haunted horses of the Ægean. Thus much we know, that letters came from the East; but we know this only from the dim light of a beautiful tradition. It is said that Cadmus, son of Agenor, a petty king of Phœnicia, was sent by his father in search of Europa, who had been carried away by Jupiter. Not having been able to find her, and not daring, under those circumstances, to return to his country, he fixed himself in Bœotia, 1,580 years before the birth of Christ, when he founded the city of Thebes, and brought the lore of the Phœnicians into Greece. It seems to me, in recalling this legend from the musty recesses of memories which have been rarely disturbed since I left school, as if there were a whole painful history in the story of Cadmus; a history of exiled genius bowed down by wrong and petty tyranny, yet blessing and fertilizing by its mere presence whithersoever it went. I cannot remember at this moment that we know anything further of the wonderful discovery which changed the destiny of mankind so completely, and which is identified with all that is noble and elevating in the world. Speculation is idle upon such a subject; for let us look back into history with eyes as farseeing as we may, there will still appear, at the most remote period, to have been nations as polite and learned as ourselves, to whom the wisdom of still more ancient times was familiar; who possessed many useful arts, which afterwards died away in dark ages, and were lost to us. So we get into the mists of fable-land, and are lost also, straying far from the guiding lights of certain record.

I am not, however, particularly interested in Cadmus and ancient inscriptions at this moment. The fact is, I have been *waiting for the boat;* waiting with feverish and sickening anxiety, with a parched mind, for news of home in a distant land. Hour after hour has passed by, and my ears have thirsted in vain for the first sound of paddle-wheels striking the calm water; for the air is so still, the scene so quiet, and the windings of the coast so many, that we can hear the steps of the *Water Queen* long before she appears to our aching eyes. I think, indeed, that I have listened so often on this very spot, that I know the sound of the paddle-wheels of each particular vessel employed on the Postal service; but this must surely be fancy overwrought.

One by one within the last hour I have seen the petty traders of the place thronging towards the little port. By their mustering in this direction, I know that the steamer has been signalled. I shall keep my place, however, by the open window; for I shall be thus able to see her at least half an hour before she is visible from the port. Let me pass the time in reflecting how entirely we are all alike! How one man is not inferior to another, or the other superior; and how beneath the very dirtiest jerkin in yon wrangling crowd is perhaps beating a heart as anxious, and a lip trembling above it as feverish, as mine.

I know not, reader, if you have ever been in exile. If you have, I am sure you will testify with me that there is something positively life-wearing in that *waiting for the boat,* the blank dismay with which we learn that we have waited in vain; the carelessness of some dull clerk or agent, perhaps, to whose care the precious packet may have been addressed, having deprived us of a pleasure which we have hoped for and dreamed about for weeks. Let us think this; let us hope there is at least *some mistake;* for it were anguish, indeed, to fancy that those for whom our hearts are yearning, have forgotten us ; that the bettering affection we cherish for them, the enduring love we feel —the love to which time and absence are as nothing—has been all in vain ; but those to whom our very souls seem to be calling always, of whom we dream by day, and of whom we lay awake thinking by night, would not give us one poor half-hour to bid us hope on ; to recall us one moment from the night of absence into the garden of Eden, which blooms for us around them ; or to spare us the torture of believing that we are too worthless even for reproof.

Did you ever know what it was to lead a life so imprisoned and cut off from all communion with your kind, that your letters positively made you drunk? That they had an effect upon you which was painfully exciting, and caused you to dash yourself against the bars of your prison, and to fret and chafe till you sank groaning down for very weariness of heart, and then buried your face in your hands, or turned it to the wall, and wept with a terrible and convulsive passion. Did you ever feel that this was the time when the Devil was busy with you —when the iron was entering your heart,—when you were conscious, maybe, of a rebellious and bitter sense of wrong that would not be comforted, and the consolations of the Christian philosopher whispered their gentle and sustaining truths for long days, in vain ? Did you ever feel at such times, that you were changing and hardening into stone, beneath the petrifying influence of the mighty grief which had fallen upon you, and did you catch yourself often looking into vacancy with fixed eyes, while your jaws were closed with a clasp of iron ? Did you feel the grey hair growing, and the wrinkle deepening, on your forehead daily? and did you at last, when some angel-thought, some softening memory of happier days, came stealing over you, did you fall on your bended knees and humbly pray to God to drive away your evil thoughts?—pray till the sweat gathered on your brow while wrestling with the Demon who persecuted you?

If so, you have known what it is to dwell in exile ; you can enter into the feelings of those statesmen and sages who have been banished from many lands, and now are passing their joyless days solitary and unknown in the midst of you. You can understand a part, and a part only, of the stupendous wrong which may be wrought by persons being intrusted with power who are unfit to wield it. You will endeavour to shackle and restrain such power by every prudent and lawful means at the disposal of earnest and thoughtful men.

It is to the exile and the hapless—to "despairful widows, pensive prisoners, and deposed kings," that letters have their real value. There is a parable of Pythagoras which says wisely "*Cor ne edito.*" Lord Bacon explains this to mean, "Let us not be secret in our griefs." It is a great lesson, which I remember is echoed also in one of those grand dreamy letters of Göthe.

The principal fruit of friendship, says a very wise man, is the "discharge of the fullness and swellings of the heart, and to be able to impart whatever liveth there to oppress it, in a kind of civil shrift or confession, for diseases of stoppings and suffocations are as dangerous to the mind as to the body."

Now there is but one way of purging our mind in solitude and banishment; and this is by letters to dear ones far away.

Therefore, it seems to me, that a cup so bitter should be offered to the lips of no man, as the wrong which places him beyond the reach of their delightful influence. At this present writing,* there is a vacant chair in many a kindly English home; and he who was wont to fill it stands, sword in hand, amid the ranks of battle, or keeping dull watch or sentinel at his post.

Let us remember often those absent friends, and think the time well spent which is passed in communion with them. Let us picture them hoping, longing, sickening with impatience for news from home, and allow not lighter things to come between us and our sacred duty towards those brave men who have girt on the sword and gone forth to fight for us.

Hark! there is a sound like the hoarse murmur of a distant waterfall! Was it fancy? No; the sound is drawing nearer and nearer. The French steamer will touch at the island without

---

* 1853.

doubt to-night. No envious wind, no gloomy fog gathering over the waters, will rob us of our joy this time. Hark to the plashing of the boats as they row out to meet the mail! How gallantly yon rowers go dashing along over the summer sea! They have stripped to their shirt-sleeves, and look in earnest about their work; every shoulder, every muscle is straining and bent to it.

My Turkish servant, who has been, I know, watching me, goes silently out, and I mark him as he struts along the path beneath my window, on his eager errand, the last rays of the setting sun falling on his shining arms. He will, I know, be first among the crowd waiting for our letters when they are brought ashore. But still an hour must elapse before the boats can return, and the quarantine regulations being fulfilled, I shall hear the martial stride of brave Hamed coming back again. I shall spend it, pipe in hand, leaning over the rails of my balcony and watching for him. The murmur of the sea as it seems chidingly to kiss the shore, will be very soothing the while; and I shall note silently the broad track of light cast on the tranquil waters by one of the larger planets which has just shone out. So I fall into a sort of reverie; I half wish that the boat was yet to come, dreading so much the near approach of disappointment. I am roused by the step of Hamed crushing the pebbles on the road, as he comes back from his mission. But I know, before I have seen his rugged face and sympathizing shake of the head, that he might as well have stopped at home. I can tell it by his footfall. It is not the quick smart tramp with which he brings me news from the Home Land! Bold Hamed is looking on the ground and walking slowly; he has still the utmost dignity of mien, but he appears sobered, knowing himself to be the messenger of evil tidings.

Well! there will be another boat the 11th of next month, and we are one day nearer to it than we were yesterday;—and, Hamed, fill my pipe again, and send up the tea!

CHAPTER XXXV.

A GREEK CARNIVAL.

"WELL, Demetraki, what do you want?"

Demetraki is a paunchy man, and the Carnival appears to have had a rubifying effect upon his nose. He is a shuffler, as all the Greeks, I think, are. He could not say twice two are four in a plain manner; but, at last, as I am turning to my newspaper again in despair of being able to get anything out of him, he hitches up his clothes, and tells me that there are great doings going on upon the other side of the mountain. To-day the Greeks must make the most of their time, he thinks; for to-morrow begins a fifty days' fast, and a fast among the Greeks is a serious business. It is their idea, indeed, of fulfilling the duties of religion in an exemplary manner; and all who never eat meat in Lent, believe that they have gained a passport for heaven.

It is a fine breezy morning. I clamber over the rocks in front of my house, and follow Demetraki, as he waddles toilsomely up the hill; at last, after a moderate number of falls, and one or two dashing leaps, we get into the tide of the holiday-makers. It is pleasant to see them go trooping along hand in hand, and singing in chorus. It is pleasant to notice their homely, decent dresses, and the joy which God has given them, reflected even on the faces of rayahs and slaves. After a little time they begin to form into close companies of six or seven each; and they huddle together anywhere, to be at once in the shade and out of the wind, which is still blowing freshly. Yet five minutes more, and the enormous black bottles which are circulating so freely, will begin to do their work. First, there is a loud, solitary laugh, which goes off from the midst of one of the farthest groups like a shot. It is soon answered, and one of the parties, who have been drinking stoutly for the last ten minutes, open the festivity of the day with some rude music. The palicaria* begin now to rise in all directions; the dancing, singing, and laughing have become general; and, as far as the eye can reach, the uncouth revel is going on, while the same large black bottle is being handed about everywhere.

About this time, if you look away yonder, towards the brow of the hill, you may begin to see bands of gaily-dressed women and children, watching the scene below. By-and-by they come nearer, always timidly, however; and they never join in the games or dances of the men.

I am standing at this moment on one of the most magnificent sites in the world. Beneath, lies the Gulf of Adramiti, to the right I can see almost to the plains of Troy, and to the left, nearly to Cape Baba. Before me there is neither tree nor shrub visible; nothing but one grand amphitheatre formed of sea and mountains; but behind lie the rich woods and emerald meads, the gentle hills and picturesque valleys of beautiful Lesbos. Along the winding shore stretch the pretty houses of the rich citizens; a lofty Turkish mosque from whence the hoja is calling, and two light-houses; the harbour is crowded with vessels waiting for corn to take to England. As my eyes fall musingly on the ground, I see a little oblong piece of metal; and stooping to examine it, I find that it is a coin at least two thousand years old.

But there is no time for musing. About, around, touching me, pushing me, the Greek palicaria hold on their revel; and magnificent as the scene is, I am bound to confess that the quaint pictures which everywhere meet my eye, of another life than ours, are no mean additions to it. Presently we find a band of Greeks sufficiently busy. They take a block of wood, and they dress it in some old clothes which they tie on with cords. It has neither head, nor hands, nor feet; but one can see that it is meant for a very fat man. No wonder, indeed,

---

* Palikaria (παλικάρια) is a Greek word signifying young men, like the "braves" of the Illyrian legends.

that he is fat, for I find on inquiry that he is intended to represent the Greek carnival : a glutton, if ever there was one. The active group I have described now take two stout poles, and fastening them together with some cross sticks, they make a sort of bier. On this they place the Carnival, who is just dead : and some six or eight palicaria supporting the bier, set off to bear him to the tomb. They are preceded by a company of others who dance in line, hand in hand. There may be some ten abreast of them. They are soon joined by all the other revellers, and away they go dancing and singing ribald songs in the same manner as the priests chaunt the " De Profundis."

I watch them as they wind over hill and valley towards the town ; and almost fancy I am witnessing some pagan saturnalia ; for it is wonderful how old games have been always kept up by popular traditions. On they go, performing all sorts of uncouth buffooneries ; but they are not the less picturesque and interesting : at last they disappear in the dirty, narrow little streets of the distant town, and I know that they are going about from house to house begging ; as I cannot very well follow them in such an expedition, I am afraid I shall lose the burial of the Carnival, and I am sorry to add that my fears have been verified.

I enter the town by a street distant from my own house, and pick my way daintily amid foul gutters, where fever always sits brooding, and over slippery stones, rendered dirty and dangerous by all sorts of garbage thrown into the street. I am lightly shod and I do not make much noise, nor am I a very fearful apparition ; for I have too much to do to take care of myself to meditate harm to others ; but I have no sooner entered the street than a change comes over it. When I first turned the corner, young women were gossiping and laughing together in the doorways, and from the windows : now I hear the click of many doors closing stealthily ; and the lattices are shut everywhere. A Frank is a rare sight in this obscure quarter, and the women are wild as young fawns. They are watching me from all sorts of places ; but if I stayed there for hours, not one would come out till I was gone. I know why the Greek girls are as shy as young fawns, and it pains me to think of it: a thousand tales are fresh in my memory of harmless young women who, by chance, caught the eye of some terrible Turk, and soon after disappeared mysteriously, or were torn shrieking from their homes by armed men, and were never heard of afterwards. I hope such times are gone by now, but I am not quite sure of it; and, therefore, I have no right to wonder that Greek maidens should tremble at the step of a stranger.

Gradually I emerge into a more frequented quarter, and everywhere the sound of nasal singing, the clapping of hands, and the jingling of glasses, comes from open doors and lattices; while here and there a Turk smokes his nargilly, sitting cross-legged upon a stone, apart and disdainfully. A long string of mules, tied together, are lading with oil-skins for a journey; they are standing in a perfect quagmire of filth, for we have had heavy rains of late, and I can almost see the noxious exhalations steaming out of it in the noonday sun. I hasten my pace, and light a cigar, for such a neighbourhood is dangerous; and the best antidote for this kind of poison I know of is tobacco. Farther along the street comes a troop of broad-backed hamals (porters); each carries a slain lamb upon his shoulders, to be sent off by the Austrian boat to Constantinople this evening. Other people are also carrying pretty baskets, full of the white sheep's milk cheeses, made in the Levant. They are eaten with honey, and form, perhaps the most exquisite delicacy in the world.

But here come a band of mummers, with masks and music. They are begging, and they will stop me, for I am not supposed to know them. There is one cub drunk with unaccustomed eating, whom I should know from his stifled guffaw in a minute, and from a thousand. I know also that he would follow me about all day if I did not buy him off. I take a handful of small coin, therefore, from a pocket where it has been reposing gingerly for many days, and as I pass on the palicaria are all rolling and squabbling in the mud about it.

The afternoon has stolen on while I have been wandering about, yet I cannot make up my mind to go home; and I halt once more before some young men at play. I think they are all among the most powerful lads I ever saw, and I watch them with the natural pleasure one has in seeing health, and strength, and beauty. They are playing at a species of leap-frog, but the "back" is made by three youths instead of one; they form a triangle as they stoop down, and they do not "tuck in their twopennies" by any means in sporting style. However, the runners charge them gallantly; they bump their heads with great force into the back of the first boy, whose hind quarters are turned towards them, and they turn a complete summerset over the other two. The first who falls makes a "back," and relieves one of the others. It is rough sport and dangerous, but it is the first time in my life that I have ever seen Greeks in violent exercise; and I notice now, that the players are the lowest of the low. Whenever there is any dispute, I observe that they toss a slipper to decide it, and "sole" or "upper-leather" wins the day, as the case may be. It is needless to add, that they are all playing barefoot.

By-and-by, they grow tired of leap-frog; and the game by which it is succeeded is as severe a trial of strength as I ever witnessed. One of the young giants takes another in his arms. The man carried has his head downwards and his legs grappling the other tightly about the neck. Two young men now go down on all fours, and place themselves close together, while the two other players, twined together as I have said, turn a summerset backwards over them, and the man whose head was downwards before is now upwards, and the other has of course taken his position. So they go backwards and forwards, and if they come apart or fall, they have to kneel down and make a "back" for others to tumble over in the same way. I remarked two young men clinging together in this manner who turned a summerset twenty-three times in succession. At last they fell from a feint of one of the "backs," who began to grow tired of the sport. They went on playing till evening gradually crept over us, and the sun was quite lost behind the snow-capped mountains; then, as the dews fell heavily, and the chill air grew keener, they tied up their trousers; and, shuffling on their slippers, returned to our little town, bawling rude monotonous choruses, and dancing as they went—if hopping would not be a better term for their uncouth manœuvres.

I have returned home. A wood fire burns cheerfully in the hearth, and a lamp sheds a pretty tempered light on the desk I am to use presently. The books and maps, the dumpy pens, and the well-worn penknife, the cigar-case, the broken teacups on a side-table, and the milk in a glass, all made ready by kind hands, seem to smile a silent welcome to me, like old friends. Five minutes at the window, a few cups of tea, a short game with pen and ink, and then to bed.

FAREWELL.

Adieu, sweet Isle ! for evermore
   Shall memory linger round thee ;
Though speed my bark from that sweet shore,
   Where lone and still I found thee.

Like things of fair and peaceful dreams,
   Our waking lives still flying,
Sleep'st thou amid the golden beams,
   For ever o'er thee lying.

Like Beauty pale, who fades away
   Too fast, and leaves us weeping ;
Or noble Hope, whose cheering ray
   Was far too bright for keeping.

Or word half spoke, or smile that died,
   On lips too proud to own them ;
And thus to darkened hearts denied
   The light they just had shown them.

Adieu, sweet Isle ! for ne'er again
   These eyes may now behold thee;
And swift my bark speeds o'er the main,
   Whose loving waves enfold thee.

CHAPTER XXXVI.

BARATARIA.

IT must have been a pretty sight for those on board the good ship *Italia*, to see us standing out from that beautiful island shore, and bear away towards them, with the white sails of our little boats courting the breeze, and the farewell songs of the Greeks mingling with their wild and simple music. Now the minstrels pulled smartly ahead of us ; now they lay on their oars, and dropped astern ; and now the song rose clear and high, and they pulled round and round us. The Albanians discharged their pistols in volleys at every pause, as we crept lazily on farther and farther out to sea, where the steamer lay straining at her anchor.

The little community of Barataria were determined to do us honour, and had assembled in their holiday clothes with pipe and tabor to bid us farewell. The flags were flying from the consular houses, and our cloud of little boats must have looked like a mimic squadron. The view of the island was enchanting, and quite won the heart of a gallant elderly French colonel, who was looking over the vessel's side, and wondering what sort of festival folk we might be coming from our lovely shores with music and pistol-firing. It was a pretty poetical incident in any man's life, and I felt saddened as I watched the rustic minstrels steer towards the shore with hushed song and laughter, waving their hands silently. I was going back again into the world, and I had been absent from it some time ; for months I had not heard the sound of my own language, or seen anything to remind me of civilized life. A week ago I had pined at this living burial, now I begun already to look upon the time I had passed among the Baratarians as a pleasant dream, too soon ended. They were kindly folk, and they had loved me. Why should I be ashamed to say that my eyes grew dim, and that I turned away my head, as Barataria lessened to my view? Why should I have narrowed my eyes and lips to look hard and cynical, when I did not feel so? It was better and honester to give way to the feeling fairly : there can be little which puts us really to the blush in nature's promptings. So I strain my gaze lovingly towards the land, and sigh over those thousand and one things which go to make up regret for the past. Another page in life's book has been turned over, and is now closed for ever; another pleasant journey has been travelled through; the thoughts and fancies of eight months have passed all at once into the things that were,—the real into the unreal, the events of daily life into shadowy memories. Life seems such a bustle of change and circumstance, yet we ourselves so still! We bear nothing about with us, save here and there a wrinkle or a grey hair to mark the noisy progress of old Time; and as I pace the deck this clear delightful afternoon, it seems as if I had but slumbered since I took leave of England a year ago. I have nothing tangible to tell of the flight of so many days, nothing but a beard, which would have looked odd in May Fair. Yet here we are, my public, wiser, wearier, and wickeder than we were then—and stay, yonder is Hamed bringing my pipe, so that there is something to lay hold of after all. In Europe we smoked cigars; when we count our winnings from the last year, therefore, let us not forget the pipe. I vow and declare it was worth while going to Turkey to fetch it.

I cannot, upon the whole, undertake to say that everything connected with my departure from Barataria had been so satisfactory as the fiddles and firing. I had been succeeded in my place as deputy-assistant sub-vice-consular agent by Lord Fitztoady's favourite sister's steward's son. This individual having spent many years, chiefly at Clapham, in teaching the art of dancing to young ladies, was considered just the sort of person to become a British magistrate, judge, jury, banker, registrar, and autocrat at Barataria.

I was sent back to Dahomey, because I had completed my studies at Heidelberg; I should have been shelved altogether, as cautious Lord Cacus (our Secretary for Foreign Affairs) was mortally afraid of Fitztoady, and was creating places in all directions for his own creatures, but one of my Christian names is Gray, I have the prudence to spell it *Grey;* and not even Lord Cacus, who, during his cautious tenure of office, contrived to rake up a row everywhere, could venture to dispossess an individual who bore the name of that wonderful family of hereditary placemen.

Well, from the moment of Mr. Podgers' arrival, most of the estimable inhabitants of Barataria declined to see me. Twelve hours before, I had been as absolute a king as any other British deputy-assistant sub in Turkey, as potent, irresponsible, and dreaded; my subjects were therefore ready to treat me as people treat other autocrats, and tear me to pieces the moment they had no longer anything to fear or to hope from me. Men who the day before had prostrated themselves in my presence and passed bare-footed through my cottage door ; who had put me to the blush with the amazing baseness of their cringing and adulation ; who had sung my absurd hallelujah till my own wife would not have had assurance enough to join in it ; yes, the very same men would not answer when I spoke to them, and sedulously turned their backs when we met in the streets.

They were so mean and dark-hearted, so wily and reasoning in their cunning, that they offered me open impertinence, lest any civility shown to me might offend Podgers. They looked on me as a disgraced Pasha, whose good word could no longer be of use to them, and they kept very zealously at a distance. Had Podgers been a bad fellow, I dare say they would have burned me in effigy at the least hint that such a course of conduct would have pleased that newly-arrived potentate. But when they saw us laughing together at their pleasant antics and on the best possible terms, they grew civil again. Though I was no longer in power among them, it appeared that I might have influence with the man who was. The day after Podgers and I had been seen in company smoking a pipe of peace in the balcony, one or two of the primates nodded to me shily again ; one even spoke to me and asked me to put in a good word for his brother ; another sent a petition as humiliating to receive as to write, and finally, as Podgers kept constantly with me, some of the bolder of my former slaves actually came to visit me, and spluttered out entreaties for recommendations to King Podgers, between their pretended sobs at my departure.

But while the Greeks were the very cream of baseness, the Turks never changed. The Pasha treated me if possible with more high-bred and polished politeness after the arrival of King Podgers, than at the time an intemperate complaint from me would have cost him his place ; and it was at his command that my brave friend the Toosoonaga brought the music and his Albanians to see me on board with all honour.

And so I am going to doctor the bruises from many a rough fall, and to while away many a heartache, if I can, among the brisk north winds of the Ægean. Meantime, all busier life, all my part in trying to solve those notable riddles which men call politics, is over for a time. The wheels of my machine are come to a dead lock ; or, if you like the simile better, the curtain has fallen on another act of my little play. Why fret and writhe at it ? Why try to force the engine to go creaking along when we know there is a screw loose ? We shall not arrive at our journey's end a second the sooner. Besides, it is far pleasanter to take things coolly ; and I confess I am beginning to doubt much more than I once did, the advantage of pressing onwards. To jump in sacks for nothing better than a smock frock is no such ennobling pastime after all ; our stopping will not even injure the demand for smock frocks, since more than enough jumpers will join the race without us. Then as for the mere reputation of jumping better than other people, why, not even Ptolemy, who jumped into the mysterious throne of the Pharaohs, has come down to history as a great man ; if he had, his fate would not probably have been a bit the more enviable. Let us receive by all means the good things an obliging public is willing to offer us, but it is useless to take very much trouble about attaining them; for Fortune's emblem is a wheel, and we are much more likely to get our share by standing still and holding out our hats, than by running a bootless chivy round and round. We are also much less likely to get giddy ; and after all, what will be will be, whether we jump or run or whistle for it.

Away then with the sick hope and the diseased ambition, which makes a humble lot distasteful to us. Let us try to be single-hearted, simple, sincere, good-natured with the world if we can. That is, let us rather laugh at and with than sneer at it, and a fig for the rest. For the rest, what is it? You have toiled and schemed all your life till you have not'a friend or a human feeling left. So rise Sir Joseph Surface, or behold Sir Hector Stubble becomes lord of the blue rock, wherever that rock may be, and knight of the most noble order of the yellow rhinoceros. He may take his seat on the bench of hereditary dunces, and provide an agreeable subject of contemplation for his son and a patient public. But enough of such rambling philosophy! We are going to Smyrna, where they would not listen to a word of it, or anything else but the price of figs and the feuilleton of the Smyrna Independent.

It is odd that while everything almost is to be bought in Turkey, while a great man's conscience, a judge's justice or injustice, are so cheap that they are scarcely worth bidding for, there are yet certain things of very general sale elsewhere, which cannot be purchased. You can by no means buy the truth of any man; no money will entitle you to fair dealing, rational amusements, decent servants, or a good dinner. The steam-boat dinner, therefore, cooked by an Italian—and Italians are not a cooking race—seemed to me such a luxurious and delicate repast, that I thought I should never have had enough of it.

Nothing occurred worth remark on our way to Smyrna, except that I noticed the Turks, who were carefully partitioned off from us, and had one side of the deck all to themselves, were very much disposed to be familiar. One who was learning French out of a most incomprehensible-looking grammar, insisted on practising upon me every time I passed the place where he lay in wait with his nose and beard thrust through the bars for the purpose. When I stopped to talk to him, however, another of the passengers invariably bore down upon us, and spoilt the quaint amusing dialogue of the Turk. The new comer was a thin, long, sharp-nosed, contemptible young man, who loved to spend money in an unsatisfactory manner; he was an emancipated Armenian going to Paris, and I fairly wished him and the bad cigars he was continually offering me at Halifax. Most snobs are of wearisome conversation enough, but I think your youthful Armenian snob is the most offensive young bore I ever met.

I was glad to take refuge with the French colonel, who was going down to Syria to buy horses for the war. He told me the French and English troops were getting on famously together, and that there was a good understanding between the generals, a wish on all sides to pull pleasantly. He owned that his countrymen, however, did not like the dismissal of Baraguay D'Hilliers, and thought that if there was a dispute Lord Stratford should have been withdrawn also. From the ambassadors the conversation turned to Marshal St. Arnaud, of whom my companion spoke quite affectionately, as I have remarked that most French soldiers do.

"Yes," said I, yawning at the end of a glowing eulogium on this officer, "on dit qu'il a une bonne tête."

"Oui! oui!" answered the colonel rapidly; "il a joué sa tête avec beaucoup de hardiesse plusieurs fois; tenez dans l'affaire, &c."

I could not translate into English the French colonel's idea of a clear head, if my life depended on it.

This brought us to Smyrna, the Paris of the Levant. The white town looked very lovely as the moonbeams fell upon it, and we anchored shortly after midnight in the tranquil bay. Smyrna is pretty, busy, bustling, and hospitable; but, oh, those Parisian Levantines, what a race they are! The young men have the manners of the London University and the Quartier Latin. The ladies, God bless them! are, I think, the most affected misses I ever met with in this mortal world. Everything and every person seemed to me an out-of-the-way and exaggerated copy of a bad original.

The Smyrniotes, if I understood them rightly, passed their time chiefly in scandal and talk about fine folk. Everybody knew the last lord who passed through the place, and made, of course, a mistake about his name. They talked with strange familiarity concerning out-of-the-way things and people; they knew everything which had not happened at the embassy at Constantinople, and told interesting anecdotes, which were not true, about the attachés. They had a smart story about Consul Wilkins, whom nobody but the Foreign Office had ever heard of, and another about the son of sub-vice-Consul Brown. They believed these stories the cream of fashionable discourse, and they not only brought them out for the delectation of visitors, but positively told them for entertainment at little gatherings among themselves. About politics they were fairly mad, and talked more nonsense than ever I heard in the same place at the same time. The youngest and prettiest of the women had learned whole pages of newspaper off by heart, and repeated them, long words and all, to whomsoever would listen.

The fact is, the heads of all the Europeans in Smyrna are quite turned; each individual fancies himself a monarch, and a monarch he is : they ride roughshod over the laws, customs, and people of the country; they are too mighty and numerous even for their own consuls. Those functionaries, terrible as they are to the Turks, know that they must bow before the great mercantile interests; and the Smyrna merchant has become a wonderful mixture of pride, arrogance, and huffiness in consequence. For the rest, the people seemed thriving and prosperous. I was glad to hear of some large sums of money having been lately subscribed by them to the Turkish government. It is but fair that those who have gained princely fortunes among the Turks should help them out of a scrape if they can; all of which means to say, that the Smyrniotes would be probably very excellent folk if the local laws were strong enough to keep them in a little better order. As it is, they are merely Levantines of the first water; it isn't very clean.

They have got monopolies, government loans, privileges, everything which they ought not to have. They have lent money to powerful pashas, and to ministers of state; and the Christian merchants in Smyrna, I am very much afraid, with their brethren in other parts of Turkey, go a very long way to clog the wheels of the state. The whole machine must come to a dead stop some day. I saw a great many pale-faced, disconsolate looking men in the streets here and there. They seemed so listless and unemployed, that I asked who they were. The reply let a flood of light on recent doings in Turkey; for I learned that they were Russian merchants, mostly poor harmless people, who had been expelled the country,[*] and were going none knew whither.

"But," said I, "Diddleoff and Screwemoff, with a whole host of others, have not been expelled; why should these poor devils be sent away? There are halt, lame, and blind among them."

"Why the fact is," said my informant, "any man who is rich, or an intriguer, who has lent money to a pasha, or bribed him, or who could influence somebody who had done these things, was at liberty to stop: honest or poor men have been, of course, expelled in ship-loads. The expulsion of the Russian subjects has been a fine harvest to the pashas and foreign consuls. I know one man who paid a hundred pounds down for a French protection the day before he was to have been sent away. If the local pasha could not be bribed, and was determined to do his duty, your rich Greek or Russian subject was sure to find some powerful personage with an itching palm at Constantinople, and then woe betide the honest pasha. An intrigue would be got up against him, and he would, ten chances to one, be snubbed or dismissed for his good conduct. The truth is, there is a premium for corruption in these countries, and it is only dangerous to be just. A rogue in authority will certainly thrive here. He may do anything he pleases with perfect impunity; a good man must inevitably get into scrapes and disgrace."

"It is a strange state of things," said I.

"Why, yes," answered my companion, "but there are stranger still. Let us go and see Yanni Catirgi."

My new acquaintance led the way through dark streets, like those of all hot climates, so narrow that opposite neighbours might almost shake hands out of their bedroom windows. The plan is ingenious, for it secures constant shade, but the pent-up and confined air must be unhealthy. On we went, over dead

[*] 1853.

dogs and cats, over rats which lay festering in the summer sun, passing donkeys confined tightly between long planks of wood or bars of iron, at once supported by and made to drag them. The little beasts went staggering from wall to wall, and wrenching their joints almost apart at every yard, the merciful invention of wheels and waggons being unknown. Passing camels sailing in from the interior with their vast burthens and warning bells; men carrying immense blocks of stone or marble slung by a rope between two poles, and shouting to the foot-passengers to get out of the way, as they ran panting along with straining and quivering muscles; on again by smug shopkeepers sitting cross-legged on their counters and fanning off the flies; by shrill water-carriers and pipe-lighters going about with a piece of burning charcoal in a pair of tongs; in a word, passing through all the swarming life of an Eastern city, we reached a large rambling house, with armed men loitering about the gates, and horses exercising in the court-yard. It was the Pasha's palace.

Now it is all very well for a paternal public to come with that virtuous face which becomes our kind mentor so well, and advise me to be modest and unpresuming; but the fact is, the game won't pay for the candles. If I take the lowest place at table, the St. Quentins are apt to leave me there; I shall get nothing but the drumsticks of the chicken and the bottoms of the decanters. The world has no eye for bashful merit; if you doubt this fact, pay a visit to your new acquaintance the Strummers, they are cousins to the eleventh Earl of Fiddlededee, whose insolvent father had the good luck to effect the abduction of a rich tradesman's daughter, and so they are very great people. Strummer thinks you rich or powerful in some way, or else he would not have invited you; he is overwhelmed with the honour of your arrival; the man makes you feel uncomfortable with his civilities, and his wife (a Fitztoady) is all eyes and smiles when you speak to her, so long as you are very lofty and patronizing with them. But set these excellent people at their ease with you, praise their dinners instead of turning up your nose at them, be good natured, be modest, and you shall see the difference. If you yawn in their faces, they will put themselves on the rack to entertain you; they will brag of you, and invite half the country to come and pay you homage; but smile only once, and you are lost. You must give up the best bedroom to Mr. Wormwood, who will tell them that he has only just called on his way to the Earl of Pauperdown's. Therefore I say unto you, oh my public, do not be too censorious when you see a wise man blowing his own trumpet. Modesty is a very pretty card, but it does not count in the game. A few cynic philosophers may pretend to sneer at this, but nine chances to one you will some day find them bowing away among the crowd as energetically as anybody else.

You think we are wandering very wide of the pasha's house, my public, while discussing these subjects, and you show your usual nice discernment and good temper by entertaining this opinion; that is, you are wrong, and a great deal too impatient to be huffed. The observations which I have here placed on paper for your instruction all flashed on me naturally enough as I passed through the palace gates, and oh! if they are true in Belgravia and Cumberland, they are so true in Turkey, that that there is not a bankrupt Christian tinker but has taken them to heart.

We entered a small room on the right, it was evidently a court of justice; I therefore reverently took off my hat, and bowed to the magistrate, who sat cross-legged on the sofa, smoking a pipe. He did not deign to acknowledge my salute, but letting his eyes fall on me for a moment with sufficient contempt, immediately resumed the contemplation of his pipe with great dignity, and left me standing, hat in hand, a comical and abashed figure enough, before him.

My cicerone, a small trader (about on a level with a European laquais de place), had been detained at the door, or this could not have happened, for he soon showed me how to act. Brushing past me with a haughty stride, and his hat upon his head, he seated himself at once beside the Turkish magistrate, who respectfully rose to make way for him. He bade me take a place on the other side; I did so, and again the Moslem gentleman rose, and now making us an agreeable salaam, he at once sent for pipes and coffee

"I wish to see Yanni Catirgi," said my companion, after the customary coffee.

"You must pay two pounds, then," said a person at the other end of the room.

"To whom?" asked my acquaintance, laughing.

"To Yanni Catirgi himself."

And it was the notorious bandit who, with a mere handful of outlaws, had long kept a city of 150,000 inhabitants almost in a state of siege. I think he was one of the finest men I have ever seen. Though loaded with chains, and undergoing an examination upon which his life depended, his bearing was perfectly bold and unembarrassed,—it was even scornful. His face was at once handsome and intelligent: his figure a perfect model of immense strength and activity; in age, he might be seven or eight-and-twenty. He had been ten months in prison, and fettered with irons; yet, but for a certain paleness of skin produced by confinement, his health and energy were perfectly unimpaired. He had need of both, too, just now; for several of his comrades had been taken, and were being examined as to their robberies. The slowness and formality of the Turk generally, gave him an opportunity of putting the first question as each of these worthies was brought in. He turned the opportunity to excellent account: the quick-witted Greeks seized his meaning almost before it was uttered: they had their cue, and took it zealously. It was almost touching to see the affectionate looks they cast at their old chief, and the royal condescension with which he acknowledged their homage; in fact, he kept the ball almost entirely in his own hands, and contrived to amuse the Turks with wonderful wit and ability. One after the other of the robber band were dismissed with smothered smiles, which boded them little harm, and the examination-room soon began to wear the air of a pleasant place of entertainment and popular resort; it filled with wonder-mongers, who were every now and then ignominiously turned out. I am sorry to add, that more mean, brutal-looking rogues than some of the authorities, I never beheld; and I heard that their appearance only corresponded with their very well known characters.

Yanni Catirgi has for some time been one of the notabilities of Smyrna. His history (as I heard it) shows a very refreshing state of things in these countries, and is worth some attention even this hot weather. Yanni Catirgi was a muleteer; his employment was chiefly that of carrying large sums of money for merchants into the interior; he became known for his honesty and good faith. At last, some act of violence or oppression sunk deep into his untaught mind: he fled to the mountains, and turned robber. He soon became chief of a small but resolute gang. No act of blood was ever brought home to him; but it is certain that many deeds of great atrocity were committed by his companions. Their tactics, however, were not those of violence: they caught some of the wealthiest merchants of Smyrna, and held them till ransomed; they received £700 from one, £1,200 from another, and upwards of £2,000 from a third: these are facts. They might have grown rich, but the number of their friends in the town, with bribes to the authorities, swallowed up even these large sums as fast as received. The inhabitants of Smyrna seemed to be absolutely in league with the men who made them tremble. At the time of his most considerable robberies, Yanni himself walked the streets of Smyrna known and unharmed! Persons of unquestionable respectability received him into their houses, and concealed his confederates, when the police were, or pretended to be, in pursuit of them. There is no divining how far the connection of these robbers extended.

At last, however, Yanni seems to have been touched with remorse, and yearned for an honest life again. He proposed to surrender, after all efforts to take him had been fruitless, and to break up his band on condition that he should be employed in the police force and his companions pardoned. This request was formally granted. He did surrender, and was immediately thrown into prison,* where he has remained in irons ever since, worried now and then with the mockery of a trial: nothing more. It is said that he will be shortly liberated, as all great criminals are in Turkey; and really one hardly knows whether to feel most angry with the robber or the fearful state of laws

* July 4th, 1853.

and society which made him what he was, and abetted him so long in his singular career!

For the rest: once upon a time, the British Admiralty sent out some ships to sail round the world, and to each of the captains they gave one of their wonderful papers of questions upon subjects as to which they desired information. Those who are familiar with our public offices, will have seen many of these ingenious documents, I dare say, and admired them as very curious contrivances to make dunces do the work of wise men—an art which British Governments love so well to study.

One of these questions related to "manners and customs," and requested the sea-captains to give an account of all they saw remarkable. "I say," said little Jack Tozer, commander of the Slowcoach, to Tom Childers of the Topheavy, as those ships lay before Otaheite, "what the doose shall we put down here?" "Why, say customs damned bad, and manners none at all!" quoth the practical Childers.

The same may be said of Smyrna,—or, I suppose, might have been said; for, of course, matters have changed there since my time. Then the place was a marvel of pretension, vulgarity, loud amusements, and over-feeding. The cast-off affectations of great capitals are silly and ridiculous enough; but what do you say to the cast-off fashions of Marseilles, Trieste, and the Italian seaports? It was at Smyrna, that is, when I was there, that the enraptured traveller could still see the mighty old nabob, Mr. Capsicum of the farce, and hear conversation as refined as that of Miss Wilhelmina Angelica Heyday. I was glad when I sprung into a trim little boat and pulled out of earshot. The East soon spoils one for cast-off fashions; and after one has lived there for some time, a very amiable contempt for pretension of all kinds gets a pretty fast hold upon you, unless you become a Parisian Levantine!

CHAPTER XXXVII.

A PASHA'S PARADISE.

WE started early in the morning, from wise fear of the sun, and we rode our beautiful Arabian horses at a prancing walk, with our grooms and pipe-bearers walking beside us and hemming us round. There was a good deal of gold lace about our housings, and rather more silence and dignity than I could have wished; but we got on very well.

We rode through the beautiful streets, of which each house seems to have a separate legend. We passed by two Hojas, walking together, and discussing a passage of Persian poetry; by a donkey alone, going wearily he knew not whither, and painfully out of conceit with himself; by some beautiful Cyprus mules going to water; by some laughing Turkish girls worrying an elderly shopkeeper, probably the father of one of them; by a cat sleeping nervously among some figs and almonds; by negro water-carriers with their mocking cries (negroes who were the same good-humoured mountebanks with yellow handkerchiefs that I have found them everywhere); by a Jewish woman whose beauty was a wonder, though I am sorry to say she was cheapening some very unpromising fish with rather too much vivacity. But who can wonder at the degradation of Oriental women? In the East there is no life of the heart; and she herself is, was, or will be, quite as much a matter of bargain and sale as the fish.

On again by men playing chess in coffee-houses;—their earnestness, good temper, and courtesy form a charming picture; by young dandies dressed in green, or in some colour which looks like it at a distance, as some crests I wot of look like coronets; by a boy on a steed which is too mighty for him;

and by long lines of pack-horses laden with fruit and vegetables for the Rhodian market.

So we come nigh to the end of our journey.

It is a Pasha's Paradise; and really, barring that a little dulness might sometimes creep into it, and worry an individual who had few resources within himself, I know not of many places more delightful. It is as completely shut out from the world as a hermitage: it is surrounded by high walls, which seem jealous of everything but the breezes; the gardens, with their luxuriant vegetation, are alive with fountains and rivulets, gadding about hither and thither, sounding merrily. The place is beautifully clean; the floors in the little tower or kiosch are of polished mosaic, of so mazy a pattern that it is impossible to look at them and remain awake. The long mysterious paths about the grounds are trellised with vines tossed about by the romping winds, and overlooked by palm-trees nodding stately. Canaries, suspended in cages from the painted ceilings, sing joyfully; fountains spring up from the floors, and throw their waters sportively about into cool marble basins. Everything gives some evidence of the sedentary and elegant taste of the Turks, also of their indolence.

In the centre of the garden stands a majestic fig-tree. Here and there rusts a cuirass or a helmet of some ancient knight; and shattered columns of a still elder time, standing lovely and beautiful, give food enough for thought.

We had a delightful feast, I remember. Some cool watermelons; some Turkish bride-cake and sweetmeats; rakee (of course), and some small peaches of rich bloom; some sweet hard pears and stony bitter grapes, the best to be got as yet; and there were some great swollen sulky-looking figs, bursting with pride and fatness. There was fiddling and dancing as usual; and two young men of seventeen or eighteen, dressed up like dancing-girls with spangles and girdles, performed some dances for our entertainment, which I would rather not have seen. All this, however, and much more, failed to call up an expression of anything like vivacity on the faces of the Turkish gentlemen present. They sat smoking their pipes, the very picture of folk thoroughly and utterly used up to all intents and purposes, perfectly content, perfectly satisfied ; and as we sat thus gravely revelling, the Rhodian wind became quite a hurricane. It dashed the waters of the fountains about in dazzling spray, and the leaves of the trees whirled jollily in frantic circles. The scene was almost enough to have spurred Sir Charles Coldstream himself into a sort of delirium of high spirits : the house, however, was dilapidated, as most Turkish houses are ; the plaster had fallen off the walls and ceilings in many places ; there was a scarcity of paint ; and, if you looked for it, even here was still the same air of desolation which I think clings to all things Eastern. The gardens were ill trimmed, the furniture was mean ; the servants, numerous and costly as they were, seemed rather down at heel. The details of this Eden were bad ; and the Pasha's Paradise, pleasant as it was for a day, would have been hardly an agreeable place to live in much longer.

CHAPTER XXXVIII.

A TURKISH BATH (RHODES).

PASSING through a pleasant paved court, ornamented with flowers enough, and with a merry little talkative fountain in the centre, I was soon inducted into the bath toilet, which consisted merely of a party-coloured garment, rather rough, bound round my loins, and a towel tied, turban form, about my head. Thus equipped, I was mounted upon a most rickety pair of wooden clogs, and led gingerly into the first or outward chamber of the bath. It had once been a noble apartment, with a lofty roof and fretted marble walls and cornices; it now shared the fate of all things Turkish, and had tumbled into a dreary state of ruin and decay. A large fat black rat dashed gamesomely by us as the door opened, and he sprinkled some water over my leg with his frolicsome tail: I had not thought a rat was such a playful thing.

A strong smell of boiled Turk now made itself so audible that a pipe became a necessity, and while engaged in its discussion, I found myself introduced into a Mahommedan company, rather more numerous than I had anticipated, or indeed than appeared convenient for the purposes of ablution. I soon perceived that the bath is a regular house of call for scandal and gossiping; and I witnessed the pulling to pieces of many persons in authority,—an operation which I am bound to say was performed with the same liveliness and spirit, the same racy appetite for forbidden things, which I have so often observed among the Western nations.

Turks of various shapes and sizes, and in various stages of their interminable washing, stalked about from chamber to chamber, or stood together conversing in groups, while the bathmen shaved the hair from their armpits; but persons of overwhelming dignity shut themselves and their pipes up in little private dens, and kept the vulgar off by means of towels spread carefully over the door-ways. The bathmen, I noticed, seemed to be all characters, licensed jesters, like the one-eyed boots of sporting inns; they seemed to know everybody's secrets and sly places: it was refreshing to observe the use they made of these acquisitions.

It was my belief that a lordly old Effendi went to that bath to obtain treasonable matter for the ensuing week's coffee-house conversation. For the rest, the general and distinctive character of the Turks was here completely lost, as far as their appearance goes to outward eyes; many a man who half an hour before seemed to be possessed of muscular power enough to rouse the envy of a British grenadier, peeled but poorly. I do not ever remember seeing such a remarkable collection of arms and legs; very gnarled and knotty broomsticks will by no means convey to the mind's eye at all an adequate idea of their very singular leanness and crookedness.

From what may be called the talk and perspiration-room, I was now led hobbling into another much hotter. It had a dome-like roof, with little round windows to let in the light: they would have looked like holes, but for the dense steam which collected on them. I remember that a condensed drop fell upon my nose; I did not like it; I could not divest my imagination of an idea that there was a greasiness about the water;—in fact, an impression began to make itself generally felt about me, that one would want rather more good wholesome washing after a Turkish bath than before it.

I smiled feebly as my attendant led me skating awkwardly along over the marble floor, till we came to a little brass cock and a marble basin. Here he bade me sit down, and I did so: I was unwilling to hurt his feelings by expressing my opinion that the whole affair, as far as cleanliness might be concerned, was a delusion and a snare; besides, resistance was impossible. I closed my eyes, therefore, upon the filthy puddles round about, and meekly resigned myself to my fate, whatever it might be.

Now, if anybody were to interrupt an English, and still more an Irish gentleman, taking a bath according to the custom of his country, the bather might, could, should, or would in all probability, knock the intruder down ; but in the East such an achievement would be fairly impossible. I began, therefore, for the first time, to understand how attacking a tyrant in his bath has always been such a very favourite and convenient way of getting rid of him. An Eastern bather six feet by four is as helpless as a child ; he hobbles or skates as the case may be, in wooden clogs three inches high, attached to the instep by a single narrow strap : he is laid down on a block, which looks like a sarcophagus turned topsy-turvy ; he is swathed up like a mummy, and a pipe being put between his lips, he is left till he feels drowsy : then there looms through the mist a gigantic man with a wonderful serious face, who affords himself a very curious entertainment at the expense of his prostrate victim ; his open hands press, and punch, and poke the bather in all possible and impossible places. A fanciful individual suffering thus might suppose himself to be the old original Prometheus, and his tormentor the vulture about to dine upon him. Having been punched, and poked, and pulled, and pressed sufficiently, the victim is lifted up by the hand as helpless as an heir apparent, and then being reseated, he shares passively in a wild orgie, which we will call lathering. The demon of the bath takes a long stringy thing in his hand ; it looks like a mop without a handle, and he scrubs the miserable body confided to him with stern animation ; something comes off it in flakes ; the advocates of the bath maintain these flakes to be composed of the various impurities of the skin ; but I am much disposed to question the accuracy of this opinion ; and having suffered the most acute pain from the subsequent contact of my clothes, I have reason to believe that I was very nearly flayed during this process, though, from having been previously nearly boiled, and the atmosphere being generally warm and greasy, the operation did not cause me so much agony at the time, as it would do under ordinary circumstances. Having been lathered more than sufficiently, with eyes, nose, ears, mouth, and every crick and cranny in his body utterly stopped up and glutinous with soap, the wretched searcher after cleanliness under difficulties is at last perfectly soused with a deluge of scalding water, and being swaddled up anew and led into the outer apartment, the air of

S

which strikes upon him as that of an ice-house, he sinks exhausted beside the consoling pipe and coffee, which have been prepared for him. Never is sleep more grateful than that which follows, though I am bound to confess, for my own part, that I could not help dreaming fitfully of the vulture who had been clawing me, and at last I woke in imminent apprehension of him, and found—the barber.

The Eastern barber is a distinguished personage; he has been so under all rabid despotisms. It was found inconvenient not to treat with considerable deference an individual who also enjoyed a sort of absolute despotism; who, in point of fact, was a rival potentate in his way, and might doom you to execution, if ever the idea should occur to him as being agreeable or advantageous. It is not surprising that barbers invested with so much dignity should have a lively consciousness of their exalted station in society. It is, indeed, a natural sentiment, and common to all magnates alike. I notice, therefore, without surprise, that the shaver now introduced to me has a dignified charm of manner and grace of attitude, while taking the small hairs out of my nose, and the gray hairs out of my eyebrows, which almost causes me to forget the excruciating anguish arising from so unlooked-for a proceeding. He polishes me up, indeed, to such a powerful and surprising extent, that I do not know my own face in the pretty little tortoiseshell and mosaic-framed looking-glass, which he hands to me to admire in it the perfection of his art. He has shaved me with such a light hand, that I set that individual down as a goose who shaveth himself in Turkey. My chin is as smooth as a very dark species of ivory; my eyebrows have been miraculously arched: I feel in vain for the favourite tuft on my right ear; my visage and all thereto pertaining is as bare as the palm of a lady's hand. I have grown quite juvenile during this strange operation. I came hither as rusty an elderly gentleman as needs may be; I shall depart an adventurous youth on my travels, and hotel-keepers will rejoice to take me in. I vow and declare that my moustaches are twisted into points sharp and dark, and insinuating enough to go straight through the heart of "sweet seventeen." The barber contemplates the improvement in my personal appearance with due gravity and enjoyment; I am the last triumph of his art, and he is proud of me. If it was not for a slight twinge of a most intrusive and unaccountable rheumatism, I should be proud of myself. The barber veils his eyes with his hands, and prostrates himself before the Beys Adé. I notice with a kindred pang that Hamed is distressed at the depth of his reverence, and I prophesy that my store of Turkish small change in the Albanian pouch will sensibly shrink ere that barber departeth.

Let us dress and go our ways. Hamed brings my linen, which has been washed at the bath during my ablutions, and holds a curtain before me as a screen from the vulgar while I put it on. He is always very particular in this respect, and he will not allow me to be seen by profane eyes in my shirt-sleeves on any account. I must be arrayed in the full glory of a gay-coloured plaid shooting-coat (bought of a Maltese Jew), and I must have on my eye-glass, which I hear the Rhodians have mistaken for a British military order of a high class, before he will let me go forth. His fierce rugged face and well-knit figure, the splendour of his Albanian dress, and his glittering arms, contrast, as they often do, oddly enough with the employment he has imposed on himself. And now comes the quarter of an hour so pathetically mentioned by quaint improper old Rabelais;—I must pay for the loss of my skin, and for my renovated youth. Unhappily for my slender purse, which has long been in a galloping consumption, people in Turkey do not pay what things are worth, but what they themselves are supposed to be worth. Now they appear to find it convenient, wherever I owe anything, to call me Beys Adé, which signifies something altogether out of the common way; and therefore I am ruthlessly mulcted of a sum rather greater than that which I should have to pay in Bond Street, viz., about ten shillings, which is a powerful sum for a bath. If my servant had not blown my trumpet with such haughtiness and vivacity while entertaining his little world of admirers in the ante-room, I might have got off for twopence, as other people do. Ah, Hamed! Hamed! I have a fear that thy vanity will surely bring our noble to ninepence.

CHAPTER XXXIX.

MONKS AT HOME.

IT is the best house in Rhodes, and it belongs to some monks of the Franciscan order, who are established here : it is called a convent, and there is a spacious and handsome chapel attached to it, far more than large enough to accommodate the few Catholics who dwell on the island. The house is situated close to the sea, and well exposed to those delightful north winds which here temper the fierce heats of summer. It is built of massy stone, however, and. the warmth may be well closed in when the winter comes. The furniture is of cypress wood, simple but substantial; it has a peculiar smell, not pleasant, till you get accustomed to it; vermin will not harbour near it; and thus, even in July, there is neither fly, nor mosquito, nor other travellers' tormentors in any part of the building. I look out from the window, and the white-crested waves come pouring along like the host of an invading army. Beneath lies the still garden, the convent court, the children learning their primers. Far away stretch the distant battlements of the town ; beyond again the blue mountains of Caramania and the Greek Isles, lonely and lovely. It is a glorious abiding-place.

The convent is permanently inhabited by two monks ; one is a tall burly man, not unlike the abbot in Landseer's famous picture ; he has a loud voice, a pleasant smile, quick human feelings, and a lively interest in all passing occurrences, he is not, perhaps, very learned, or very wise ; but I am sure he is very good.

The other brother is a thin worn man, who does not seem to have been made of stuff stern enough to be anything but a priest. The very hair of his head looks devoid of energy, and hangs limply down his wan cheeks : his small weak eyes are often full of tears : he seems disappointed, but I do not think he could ever have had any vigorous hopes or expectations. He is not fond of water ; I doubt almost if he has strength enough for soap.

The superior has a passion for English clocks and German pictures of the saints ; a portrait of the French emperor decorated the walls of his apartment ; it has, besides, two plain rush-bottomed chairs, a writing-table, and a book-shelf. The brothers are always at home. To say truth, the cells, which are very snug rooms, of these monks are amazingly dirty, in consequence of the strict observance of Salic law in the convent. Housekeepers make homes pleasant enough to the masters of them, but impossible to strangers : women mostly do. Now, as the Franciscan convents are built for all comers, it is as well, perhaps, they are left dirty and free. It must be admitted, however, that the establishment has rather a bachelor air : there is a propensity to be cracked in the crockery-ware, which sometimes takes a traveller by surprise ; there is a sort of waste and disorder about things which would justly grieve a female mind ; and yet the monks assured me that they lived, hospitalities and all, on £70 a year.

And they live well : the convent is open to travellers, without charge. If the rich give, they do so unasked, and the poor on the other hand receive money to carry them on their journey, which more than balances accounts. I learn that a great many German travellers live altogether at free quarters among the monasteries of the Levant, and that they even amass a little sum of money to go home. The Catholic religious institutions are very numerous in the East ; they are even a means, I sometimes think, of gaining considerable political influence. We have few or no religious establishments, save here and there a consular chaplain. At Rhodes alone, there are two Franciscan convents : both are supported by voluntary contributions : both are houses for the hungry and the desolate, hospitals for the sick, pleasant abiding-places for wayfarers. Both have always one or two soldiers of the Church, always living, watching, and well-doing there.

They are not hermits. The rules of their order permit them to do very much as they please in a land where there is surely no necessity for adding to the privations which must be borne. They have none of the incomprehensible gettings up at night, and the bitter asceticism, of the Greeks. They live like other people, only better, that is, more wisely and purely. They live well, very well. The Catholic peasantry contribute liberally to their wants: if the supply falls short, they write to one of the large and wealthier establishments, when money is sent them. They are forbidden to collect wealth, beyond that needed for their immediate wants: they observe the restriction rigidly; they take no fees for the performance of any religious rite, and they live altogether on the charity and piety of their neighbours. Assuredly they richly deserve, by self-denial and sacrifices of many kinds, all that is bestowed upon them, by long exile from their homes and families, and by lives which, I do believe, are a stainless example to all men. They seemed, while I was with them, always ready with wise advice, with ready sympathy, and readier service to the afflicted.

I learned to love the two pious simple men, and to respect their tranquil, useful occupations. I felt surprised when the time came for my departure, since we take but little heed of time, save in sickness or sorrow. I could hardly persuade myself I had been living three weeks at the convent, till Hamed vouched for it with rather a wry face; for it seemed he had been in mortal dread of the ham which formed an unfailing part of the good fathers' meals. I left the convent at last, therefore, with those feelings of friendship and gratitude one can hardly fail to experience on receiving kindness and hospitality from those who are strangers to us alike in faith, country, and manners.

CHAPTER XL.

THE SAINT AND THE SULTAN.

I WENT to see a Moslem saint this morning. He was living far away from most people, on a bleak barren hill-side. His dwelling was a miserable hut, built partly of rough stones, partly of mud. Through a hole in the roof was stuck a little common crooked stick, from which floated a dirty white calico rag. There was something half-ludicrous, half-wild and striking, about the place.

The saint himself was inexpressibly dirty, and there was a strange look in his eyes as we rode up, which seemed to bode us no good. I was at first not unapprehensive of hostilities; but Hamed advancing, prostrated himself before the man of God and spoke some cabalistic words, which had at once the effect of softening his holiness into the utmost good-humour. He now began to smile and bob about in the childish manner peculiar to his class when they desire to be civil. He kissed me and blessed me, and then seated me next to him, and patted my hand. His mind could not understand the fact that I could comprehend what he said, and he therefore insisted on Hamed repeating and translating into abominable Albanian Greek every obliging word to be found in Oriental dictionaries, or out of them. It was odd enough to hear those high-flown phrases between the puffs with which he was coaxing a troublesome little impromptu fire to boil some coffee. I think I see Hamed's honest rugged face now looking up at me swollen and red with blowing, and yet jerking out the saint's compliments with such awe-stricken respect and exactitude. He assured me afterwards, that I should be happy during the whole year, in consequence of the distinguished manner in which this pious man had received me.

And in truth, if the saint's good-will can avail, I daresay I shall be; for we got on amazingly. As the day was cold and damp, I made the coffee into gloria with some very excellent brandy, of which I had a little flask. The saint drank several cups of this mixture with much animation and celerity. I think he liked it, for his respected nose quite glowed afterwards, and he asked for the flask as a keepsake. I shall long recollect that snug damp morning in the saint's hut. We drank gloria and discussed pipes beside the fire, which brightened up at last, till we could hardly see for smoke and inward satisfaction. I remember the saint's dog seemed to look upon my advent as a sort of red-letter day, and leaving the guardianship of the domain to Hamed, laid himself down at full-length before the fire, and looked up at us with friendly drowsiness. I found that the saint's rags concealed a good deal of shrewdness and observation. They concealed also a pleasant wit, for which I was rather less prepared. He was a man who had had some acquaintance with courts and camps, and I dare say there was a curious history attached to him, though I could not get at it. In the course of conversation, upon fifty other matters which I have more or less forgotten, we at last got on the subject of his Highness the Sultan.

"Pooh! Sultan!" said my new acquaintance, in answer to a question I had just put to him. "The Sultans had no money at all till the time of Mahmoud II. The privy purse was entirely the invention of that potentate after he had destroyed the Janissaries and made the priests tremble. The former Sultans were kept in such strict order by the Oulemah, that they had nothing. All those magnificent presents you tell me you have heard of their giving to people who pleased them, were never actually bestowed. The Oulemah even had an objection to their squandering gunpowder. It was only to be used on certain solemn occasions, which were very jealously watched. A certain Sultan having commanded cannon to be fired on the birth of his son, the clergy in a body resisted the innovation. The Sheik-ul-Islam (the Turkish primate), who alone was a friend of the Sultan, hurried to the palace to warn him of his danger, and they were sitting together in council upon it, when a tumult was heard at the gates. 'We shall pass an evil quarter of an hour,' said the Sheik-ul-Islam, 'but I will sacrifice myself to save you.' Then advancing towards the turbulent priests, he offered to resign his post to the ringleader if he would still the tumult. 'I have no objection to take your place,' replied the stern priest, 'but he (the Sultan) must be dethroned nevertheless.'

"The Sultan was a mere puppet even in the hands of the Janissaries; but Sultan and Janissaries were only puppets in the hands of the Oulemah.

"Nobody could ever find out what has become of the amazing fortune which must have been left by Mahmoud II. It must have been something almost incredible, for he declared himself the heir of all public functionaries, and actually seized their estates without bating a fraction of their value. A pasha, a friend of mine, by great favour was allowed to get off on payment of £65,000 (English money) on his father's death. He hurried to Constantinople to appeal: 'Either pay the money,' replied the officer charged to collect such sums, 'or resign the estate entirely into his highness's hands. We have an exact inventory of your late father's property, so that it will be impossible to deceive us.' How the inventory was obtained, the pasha never knew; but he saw that even his household furniture was inserted in it. He paid the money, therefore, and became a poor man, as he has ever since remained. Refusal to confess the value of an inherited estate was punishable with death. There was a sort of uncouth justice in this, for most of the officials were guilty of great abuses, and the Sultan often, therefore, merely laid hands on moneys he should have received long before. Rich men were often forced to accept office as a means of despoiling them. An official had but a gloomy choice of evils; if he was honest, he was required to pay the Porte much more than he received; if dishonest, he was punished for extortion whenever it happened to be convenient to the Government to look after him: yet the practice of absolutely selling public employments is recent—*quite recent.*

"The singular reforms of Sultan Mahmoud II. were received with much disfavour, and a stinging satire soon appeared on the subject. It was attributed to a poet employed in the Finance Department, an odd post for a poet. The Sultan summoned this literary individual before him, and his life was probably saved only by his wit.

"'O, Sultan!' replied the poet, when the terrible charge was brought against him, 'I should never have written so dull and pointless a satire as that; if your sublime highness will only command the reeds and paper to be brought hither, I will immediately give ocular proof of the fact.'

" The Sultan smiled grimly, and was pleased to consider the defence sufficient."

I am sensible that I have not given the conversation of the saint in his own quaint metaphorical language; but I have given the substance of it faithfully. When at last I rose, he presented me a little amulet (a piece of lead and leather); I have reason to think that Hamed piously stole it shortly afterwards, for it disappeared mysteriously.

CHAPTER XLI.

MACRI.

THE village of Macri is not precisely what may be described as an eligible neighbourhood for the residence of a quiet family; indeed, I should say, quite the reverse. What with the inconvenient frequency of earthquakes; a strong propensity on the part of the inhabitants to build little tumble-down houses which are constantly being blown away when they are not burnt down, or burnt down when they are not blown away; taking also into consideration the uncomfortable circumstance that the surrounding population are as truculent a race of banditti as any which exist, even in Turkey, and reflecting that it is in the highest degree imprudent to take an afternoon's walk without being armed to the teeth and attended by four or five friendly bravoes,—perhaps Macri is upon the whole as near an approach to an earthly pandemonium as is needful.

I do not think that the disadvantages which will appear to the unprejudiced reader to attach to Macri as a residence will be much compensated by a few curious remains of antiquity which are to be found there; but if any sceptical person should feel desirous of establishing himself at Macri nevertheless, I may as well say at once that it possesses an ancient theatre in moderately good preservation, and some singular rocky caverns which are said to have been dungeons at a time when people appear to have been peculiarly fond of shutting each other up in disagreeable places. There are also some old and rather interesting tombs, to enliven the mind of a contemplative person; and having said this, and that it is situated in Asia Minor, almost opposite Rhodes, the inducements for an enterprising individual to locate himself at Macri may be considered as summed up.

I spent some days there; I cannot say that those days were agreeable either in a sensual or intellectual point of view, because I should be sorry to mislead any one by the statement of an untruth; but they were instructive—very. I was made acquainted with a little incident of local manners while there, which struck me so forcibly that I cannot refrain from endeavouring to communicate to the reader some of the refreshing surprise and excitement which it occasioned me. It furnished me with the surprise and excitement above mentioned, because it is impossible to entertain the smallest doubt as to the truth of the circumstances; and for my part, I am apt to think that a downright sensational drama in every-day life is almost as good as a play; it may be sometimes even more interesting, especially if you know some of the actors, as I did. Having now played the overture, therefore, let us draw up the curtain, so that a sympathetic public may judge for itself and wonder. I have small hope that the reproduction of this little piece will excite inquiry into the circumstances, still smaller that any good would arise if it did so; but there is no harm in trying; it is a healthy employment for the intellect, like doing exercises at school; nobody pays any attention to them; the world wags just the same, though young Cato has written two hundred and fifty lines of blank (very blank) verse in censure of vice, and Master Brutus has turned that tremendous period in judgment upon folly; still all this does good after a fashion; so may I.

Well, then, he was a baker by trade, and he was betrothed to the prettiest girl in the village. The ceremonial of betrothal is held very sacred among the Greeks, it is thought almost equal to a marriage, sometimes quite so, especially by the parties who are chiefly interested in entertaining that opinion. It is as well to state this, for it forms the only shadow of a cause for what follows.

In the present instance the betrothal remained a ceremony— nothing more: the baker turned out to be a rogue. There is a tradition that all bakers are rogues in the East; and it was such a frequent custom to hang them not long ago, that the profession became as perilous as the army, only not so honourable. The fact of the baker being merely a rogue would not have much mattered; in fact, among a Greek community, he would probably have been rather respected than otherwise in consequence; but his roguery was of that unlucky sort which only serves to get its possessor into discreditable scrapes, and leaves his pockets empty afterwards. This was unpardonable. Both the girl and her friends plotted night and day to break off the match without having to pay for the fracture, according to the Greek ecclesiastical law made and provided in such cases. They succeeded. A doctor appeared upon the scene, wooed and won the maiden, while the local archbishop's consent was easily purchased to annul the former contract and perform a new one.

So there was great joy at Macri among all who took any interest in their neighbours' affairs—a pretty considerable portion of all communities—to think that the pride of the village had escaped from the clutches of the villanous baker, who never had any money, or was likely to have any, and had married a medical man, who was going to settle among them, and whose services were a good deal wanted, from the circumstance of all sanitary measures being looked upon by their masters the Turks with much disfavour, as interfering with the designs of Providence for the time being.

The baker declined to participate in these festivities; he was otherwise engaged. He owed a great many little bills in the neighbourhood; he had intended to pay them with the dower of the doctor's wife; he did not mind losing the lady, but the loss of her means irritated him. The dower, indeed, was some forty or fifty pounds; not only enough to pay the little bills, but to have a few weeks' rational drinking afterwards.

Now an ordinary man would have considered the affair hopeless, have despaired, and gone about his buisness; but the baker was of a far more sanguine temperament. Supposing the doctor could be got rid of, the girl might still be frightened, or excommunicated by a rival bishop, into marrying him, and he would not only regain the lost dower, but might lay his hand upon some of the doctor's savings besides: the strange medical man was said by the gossips of the village to be of prudent habits, and might have put by a good many sly piastres somewhere. At all events, the thing was worth a trial—at Macri.

So the baker mustered a little money, by some disreputable means or other, and he went to the Aga, or chief Turkish magistrate. He informed that potentate he had a small business on hand, and if the police should be by chance about on the following evening, why they need not notice anything particular. Meantime, he trusted his Mohammedan acquaintance would accept a solid token of his extreme regard.

The Aga, dear innocent man, accepted the outstretched palm of the Greek, and pressed it in his own, without the smallest hesitation ; in fact he had never had so high an opinion of the baker as at that moment, and took leave of him with so many marks of friendship, and promises to attend to his wishes, that the wily Greek at once perceived that he had bought the Aga at more than his current price. At all events, come what would, he was safe, for it should be his business to take care he was not outbidden by the enemy, who, for the rest, had not the smallest idea that he could have got any money.

Accordingly, the baker assembled some roving blades of his own way of thinking, and he laid formal siege to the doctor's house, promising them part of the spoil whenever it should capitulate. As he had ten determined Zebecks, or mountain robbers, to back him, this event did not seem likely to be long delayed ; yet the garrison, consisting only of the doctor and his wife, held out with remarkable energy and perseverance ; indeed, they first surprised and then frightened the robbers. These brave men, like all the Zebecks, loved pillage dearly, but they had no stomachs for fighting ; so, finding the fortress would not yield for mere bullying, they ran away with all possible haste and discretion.

The baker, however, was too much of a man of resource to be foiled altogether ; if the doctor's wife was really and truly lost to him, why he could still have her sister. To be sure, she was only ten years old, but she looked quite eleven ; and besides, she was defenceless, for she lived with her father, in as rickety an old house as could be. He would go there and take her away; at all events, her father would buy her back again, if nothing else came of it.

So the eleven bravoes go to the old man's house, and seize his little child; not without a struggle, however, and the father falls, seriously maimed. This is all that is known. The next morning the doors of the rickety house are found burst open, the old man weltering in his blood, and the maiden gone.

Who shall follow? Why the truth is, it is a difficult question. The Aga does not interest himself particularly about it; why should he? Accidents will happen in the best-regulated districts; and such accidents as these happen in his every day; there is nothing unusual, nothing startling about it. At length, however, the father's importunities, his abject despair, or, what is still more probable, a part of the remains of his fortune, which has escaped the robbers, starts a rival band of banditti in pursuit of the baker. There is no difficulty in finding him, everybody knows where he is; and pursuers and pursued entering into a friendly parley, over some roast lamb, the girl is given up. She has passed seven days with the baker, and returns to her friends rather more dead than alive. She has since been subject to fits whenever the door of the rickety house opens suddenly; and she often wakes up starting, with a wild scream, for she dreams of the baker.

That is all. You think the drama ought to have a different ending, O my public! You would like to know that the baker was punished? Pooh! *that* would be mere poetical justice, and folks in authority have nothing to do with that. Indeed, what time have cautious Earls at the head of the governing family to attend to Macri? As for any of the working placemen, it is more than their places are worth to attend to that or anything else, but the art of " booing."

CHAPTER XLII.

A PASHA AT SEA.

I AM not sure it is a pleasant thing to travel with a great man. Aides-de-camp, and secretaries in the suite of an Excellency, do not find it a very agreeable manner of passing their time. Ease and freedom of any kind are of course out of the question: the quick sharp walk on deck of a morning, and a yarn with the captain, becomes impossible. His Excellency has had an indifferent night, and would be excited to a state of nervous indisposition by any person moving about on deck. His Excellency holds mysterious conversation also with somebody in the most convenient part of the ship, when he gets up. It would be in the highest degree improper to come within hearing. His Excellency has an objection to whistling and singing. It would be also irreverent to indulge in these pastimes. Loud laughter disagrees with him, in other people. Smiling might incur the suspicion of treasonable sarcasm; reading of sulkiness; silence of stupidity; watchfulness of prying; inattention of disrespect. It is necessary to be dressed in the presence of an Excellency, and resolutely to keep down your appetite while he is sea-sick. The delightful, lazy, lounging, do-nothing board-of-ship life is converted into a mild species of martyrdom. I would ten thousand times rather let his Excellency go alone; but the wind has been raging for weeks, as I believe it only does in the Ægean. If I do not accept a passage in his Excellency's steamer, it is by no means clear when another occasion of going away from the place at which I am staying may turn up.

I go on board a pretty little steamer, therefore, in the break of daylight, having been warned so to do. His Excellency, however, will not start before ten or eleven, and I may pass the intervening time reading the pages of the very worst of Murray's guide-books, a literary study with which I have been lately rather surfeited. While thus employed, my legs receive rather a vigorous washing by some Turkish sailors employed in cleaning the decks. I cannot say that this process adds particularly to my personal comfort or appearance; but it is well to put a good face on things generally, and I do so with much vigour and animation. I am chiefly assisted in this endeavour by reflecting on the surprising apparition of my nose, as seen in the shadow of the rising sun on the gangway. I think of the agreeable surprise it would cause any jocular small child who might come upon it suddenly. It does me good to think of the innocent glee he would be likely to display on the occasion. Hullo! here comes his Excellency the Pasha; a Pasha of three tails; he must be something powerful. Stay, a twist to my left moustaches, my cap arranged a little more jauntily, my damp boot, fortunately of patent leather, polished hastily off on the back of my right trousers; now I am ready. First comes the pipe-bearer, swaying the long pipe with its jewelled amber mouthpiece; its intoxicating fragrance fills the air. Then appears a valet sedate and important; he carries an orange-coloured dressing-gown lined with ermine, and a telescope; another follows, carrying some immense *maps!* There is a bustle of coffee-boys in the distance. The captain paces the lower deck nervously, and at last a very bright scarlet cap is seen briskly coming up the pretty cabin steps.

It is his Excellency, who is just up. His suite come forward and surround him. He asks a question, and then turns quickly towards me. He is a spare, gentlemanly,—very gentlemanly, looking man, rather above the middle height. He walks altogether on his heels, and with stiff knees, something like the British bucks and bloods of the last century; he is fair and fresh-coloured, so fresh-coloured as to give one rather a suspicion of cosmetics. His beard is so well trimmed and carefully arranged, that in May-fair it would only pass for rather an elaborate pair of whiskers. He wears a short light brown cutaway coat, *very* cut-away coat, of British make, I think; light

T

grey trousers; jean boots, with polished leather tips; a white waistcoat; rather an amazing shirt-front of fine cambric, and a jaunty cravat. He carries a blazing yellow silk pocket-handkerchief in one hand, and an opera-glass, of rather an unusual size, and mounted with diamonds, in the other. His pipe-bearer follows him, still waving the pipe, and a valet is carrying a bottle of eau de Cologne. He looks not unlike a very gay elderly British nobleman of the old school out yachting with a party of ladies. At least that is the idea he gives me as he comes up smiling pleasantly.

I declare Lord Granville himself could not be more easy and débonnaire. In three minutes he has taken me affectionately by the arm, and we are hopping about the deck together; I say hopping, for I have the greatest difficulty to keep step with him. He is five minutes expressing his gratification that I speak Greek; then we sit down side by side on a sofa which has been prepared for him, and smoke out of the same pipe, which he offers me with the utmost frankness and courtesy. I am almost sorry to say we breakfast with our fingers; but my new acquaintance assures me that this is a rule it would be imprudent to break through in public, for, Mahomet *not* having possessed forks, many of his countrymen would think it the height of impiety to use them.

His Excellency is not a sailor; so we run into a charming out-of-the-way little creek towards evening, and cast anchor, that we may dine and pass the night in peace. His Excellency observes that his countrymen have not yet brought the art of navigation to any great perfection, and that, on the whole, it is quite as well to remain quiet after dark. I silently agree with him.

"Won't you go on shore?" says my new friend in a chirruping jolly voice. "I will order my boat to be got ready at once. I do not wish to go on shore, because I should be overwhelmed by presents from the natives; and you know a present in Turkey always costs more than it is worth."

Accepting the offer, I went on shore, and passed the afternoon with some Greek monks who had a very wealthy convent in the neighbourhood. There were some women among them, and some maniacs under medical treatment. The Greek superior inquired anxiously as to the cause of the Pasha's visit. His alarm was not either quite without reason, for I noticed that several Turks of the great man's suite came to the convent empty-handed, and carried away bundles. My friend the Pasha, however, was to the full as badly off as the monks in this respect, for I noticed that, finding he did not come on shore, a whole shoal of small boats put off for the steamer, and he told me afterwards, pointing to a bundle of dirty-looking nosegays, that their visit had cost him something considerable.

"Those dogs," he said, "bring me a few faded flowers or a bunch of grapes, and expect from me the price of a week's labour in return. Ah, we managed things differently before the Tanzimat! I see, however, that even you are beginning to find that the manner in which we used to treat the Greeks is the only way to deal with them. You must return to it some day," he added, with an air of perfect conviction; "there is no doing anything with those fellows without hanging and the bastinado."

Next day, about noon, we came in sight of the island of Cos. The Pasha was dressed in uniform, and buckled on a jewelled-hilted sword of honour which had been given him by the Sultan. He then took his place in an arm-chair at the stern of the vessel; and smaller chairs having been placed all round, he awaited the arrival of the chief Greek and Turkish authorities, who immediately came off in boats to receive him.

First came the governor in full uniform: he prostrated himself at the feet of his superior in command, and kissed his boots; then he retired and made way for others, who all did the same thing; his Excellency standing up with the utmost gravity. I noticed that the Greek primates all kissed their thumbs instead of the Pasha's boots. Every one remained standing till permitted to sit down. When they were seated, one or two were offered pipes and coffee, some only coffee, some nothing at all, each according to his rank. There was a good deal of conversation of rather a lively nature, and I went to the other end of the vessel, not to be in the way; but the Pasha sent for me, and handed me over to the attentions of the governor during my stay on the island. A horse and a suite of servants were immediately placed at my disposal, and the governor provided my meals daily from his own table ; rather an expensive way of living, though convenient enough where there are no hotels. The Pasha sent for me after dinner, in the evening, and we smoked several pipes together. He was very tired and wanted to be amused. I was surprised at finding him quite alone, but he told me that no one dared present themselves till summoned ; he looked very odd indeed as he said this. He was hopping about pipe in hand between the sofa and a small table covered with a travelling silver spirit-case, some water-melons and sweetmeats. I think he had been hopping for some time on the same road.

"I have been very busy all day, very busy," he chirruped. "It is impossible to get the truth about anything from these Greeks. However, I have pretty good information from other sources, so it does not much matter. When I was busiest this morning," he continued, "a man in the Austrian consular uniform called upon me ; he stayed about half an hour, and I did my best to be polite to him : at last he went away, and about a quarter of an hour afterwards, an individual appeared in the French consular uniform (I know all these uniforms, you know, from seeing them so often). He also stopped half an hour ; then came another person, as I thought in another uniform ; but I remarked they all said the same things in the same tone of voice, and at last, putting up my glass to examine my visitor carefully, I found it was the same man who had come back again.

"' But,' said I, hesitating, 'I have seen you before.'

"' Oh yes,' replied the man, 'I always make an official visit of half an hour for each consulate ; and I have seven.' He came back four times afterwards, always in a different uniform ; and, indeed, he has been with me nearly all day. Now this is really—really—(Will you take some rakee ?) too bad." So saying, his Excellency brought me a little silver cup full of that fiery liquid, and popped a small square lump of jelly into my mouth afterwards, with his own fingers. I agreed with him while it was dissolving. Then we had some more rakee, and hopped about the room arm in arm quite jovially.

"Look here," said the Pasha, "how everything is changed; I remember going to one of these islands with a relation of mine when I was a boy; he *was* a Pasha, and then there was no Tanzimat. Well, the primates had offended him, and he sent for them all; when they came into the room, where he was sitting, and prostrated themselves barefooted before him, he ordered them out again in a terrible voice. After having made them wait outside for some time, he called them back : he did this several times. Then he caused empty pipes to be presented to them, with the bowls towards their lips, instead of the mouthpieces. When he had made them tremble like whipped hounds, he addressed them in a furious voice. 'Now you know me, you dogs,' he said ; 'I am Blank Pasha ; begone this once, all of you, and beware how you give me cause of offence again.' There are no such times now," added the worthy gentleman, and his face, which had quite lighted up with pleasure during the recital of this pleasant anecdote, darkened visibly.

It was late when I took leave of my new friend. Placing my hand in his, and pressing it with a good deal of natural kindness, he led me towards the door, but stopped on the way at the little table. "One drop more," he said. "Ah ! you must have one more, you know, and I will drink one with you.

"You think I take too much of this," he continued, presently setting down his glass; and this time there was something strangely pathetic in his tone. "But what am I to do? I cannot amuse myself with books and writing as you Franks do ; I have only my chibouque and this. Ah !" he continued, and I thought there must have been a marvellous jumble of conflicting ideas in his head,—"Ah, I am afraid a Turkish governor is not equal to a European coachman !"

It was one of the first men in Turkey who spoke thus, and there was an air plaintive and touching enough about him as he did so. I am not a tall or a stout man, but I seemed to tower like a Lifeguards-man beside him, and his hand in mine was as weak and frail, from excess, as an infant's.

CHAPTER XLIII.

THE MAN OF COS.

THERE was a man of *Cos*; I think he should be called the man of Cos. He was the most astounding person I ever met. He was not to be spoken to without smelling salts to revive one during the pauses of his conversation. He was big and grand; and, like all Levantines, he was fussy and important to a degree long past belief. His name was Charles, and he had acquired the nickname of Charlemagne, from his great ways. He introduced himself to me in the longest and loudest words to be found in the largest dictionaries and speaking-trumpets. His phrases positively took one's breath away to listen to them: they rose and swelled like the music of some vast organ. His hands swayed about like the sails of a windmill. He called me "Notre Illustre Cosmopolite," without having the smallest idea of who or what I was. He used this strange name so often, and rolled it about in his mouth with such a smack, that I am sure he liked the taste of it.

When he had talked to me about half an hour, he disappeared as suddenly as he came, leaving me in a state of the wildest astonishment. He had never given me an opportunity of saying a word. I had not the least notion of the purport of his visit, and I should probably have left the island under the impression that I had dreamed a strange absurd dream; but while I was gradually settling down to this opinion, there was a heavy step on the stairs, and the bald head of my stout friend appeared coming up again, glowing with perspiration and importance. When he had re-entered the room, he walked to the extreme end of it, and standing bolt upright, appeared to survey me with mute admiration. "Sir," said I, much overcome, "what is the meaning of this singular conduct?"

"Singular conduct! Notre Illustre Cosmopolite!" replied the man of Cos, in a tone of respectful but vivacious dissent; and then and there he made me a speech of congratulation on my "auspicious arrival in the land of Hippocrates, Apelles, and Ariston," who, however, he added with the most ludicrous dogmatism, were not of course to be named the same day as "our Illustre Cosmopolite."

Being at last fairly exhausted—it would be better to say melted—with his own eloquence, the man of *Cos* put his hand in his pocket and drew out a piece of blue cotton, which appeared once to have formed part of a defunct umbrella. With this he gravely wiped his face; then pausing suddenly, he held the blue cotton rag at arm's length, and looked at it with the utmost aversion. "Northumberland!" now shouted the man of Cos in a terrible voice. A pale-faced young man who had been waiting outside the door appeared hastily. He did not look at the man of Cos, but bent his whole attention upon me and smiled blandly.

"Northumberland!" repeated the elder, in accents of offended dignity, "why didst thou put this thing in the pocket of thy father's coat, when thou knewest he was about to pay that homage which is due to our illustrious Cosmopolite? Answer thy sire quickly."

"Because your Excellency had nothing else which would serve for a pocket-handkerchief," answered the son.

"Nothing else!" cried the man of Cos, with a look of displeased astonishment, which was one of the most ludicrous things I had seen for an age. "Nothing else, rogue! Where are the red and yellow silk handkerchiefs from the banks of the Indus, which were given us by the glorious stranger who commanded the *Brick*, after which I have given you your romantic and beautiful name?"

Then, appearing to recollect himself, the man of *Cos* started up frantically, and afterwards sunk down with his head in his hands and groaned out, "Fallen fortunes! fallen fortunes! may our illustrious Cosmopolite never know such!"

I offered him a cigar as a reviver, and he woke up at once with the cheerfullest of smiles, giving his lusty chest a thump till it sounded again. He began then a philosophical essay on contempt of money, and concluded with the verse of a comic song. His son watched him during these strange antics with a pride and belief in him which was quite touching.

"Sire, my lord, excellency, illustrissimo, for I have not the honour of knowing to what order of society you may belong, except that it is the highest, of course the very highest—the humble individual before your highness (which I think is the best and most fitting title for me to give you during the ignorance to which I have before alluded) is not undistinguished in the annals of his age ; the name of *Gasconnade* will be not unknown to posterity. I have received honours of no common nature from the sovereigns of Europe. Africa, Asia, and America have not been unmindful of my humble merits. Your own lovely and gracious queen, I mean her Majesty of Great Britain and Ireland, including the East and West Indies, and the Australias, with the Isle of Man and Gibraltar, has been pleased to remember my existence, and has forwarded me the Order of the Garter, I suppose it is,—at all events it is something very great,—by the captain of a *Brick* which came here for silk last year. I entreat your Highness, our illustrious Cosmopolite, to observe that M. Gasconnade (Excellency they call me here) is no vain talker. What he says he means, and what he means he says. Truth is the guiding star of his existence. Northumberland, get your unworthy sire, get your unworthy progenitor, the Order of the Garter which was brought to him by the captain of the *Blackque-Eyed Suzanne*. Begone !"

The son disappeared, and presently returned with a large official envelope exceedingly dirty, but sealed with an immense seal, and addressed in a most flourishing handwriting. This the man of Cos opened with a mighty parade, and drew out one of those small crowns of gilt thread which naval officers are accustomed to wear in front of their uniform-caps.

"There, illustrious Cosmopolite," said the man of Cos, handing me this treasure very gingerly ; " I believe that is the insignia of the Order of the Garter, which I am told is the most distinguished decoration in your country. Your Highness will, I trust, convey the thanks, the humble thanks, of Jean Marie Louise Gasconnade to your sovereign, and say that he is not ungrateful for the glorious honour she has vouchsafed to him."

A small child now came in and whispered something in the ear of the man of Cos.

"Away," said the Knight of the Garter, majestically; "tell your mother his majesty the Emperor of France has not yet sent me a remittance, and that imperial royalty such as his is not to be disturbed by unseemly importunity.

"I almost forgot to mention to your Highness, that during the short time you have been here, my son, who has a natural gift for poetry and the fine arts, has composed a poem in English—oh yes, in English, to commemorate the epoch of your visit to our fortunate island. Here it is," continued the man of Cos, taking an immense sheet of whity-brown paper from the breast-pocket of a brass-buttoned swallow-tailed coat at least twenty years old; then planting himself upright before me, he extended his right hand, and began to read the first line of the popular composition,—

"Ow doss ye leetel beezee Bee;"

which may be found in another orthography among Dr. Watts's hymns. The effort, however, was rather beyond his powers, and presenting me with the paper unread, he sat down and again made use of the piece of blue umbrella.

"Chevalier," said I, vastly amused, "will you allow me to offer your son a small token of my esteem, in exchange for his most amiable verses; and then, can you recommend me something in the shape of a *laquais de place*, or a guide?"

"It was to offer myself and my son, indeed my whole family, in that capacity, that I ventured to do myself the immense honour of waiting on your Highness," said the man of Cos, swaying himself deferentially about, and pocketing his son's gratuity as if by accident. "Your Highness will of course see the fortress; I will command the troops of the garrison to get under arms and receive you. Northumberland, you will be his Highness's aide-de-camp, servant, slave, while I go and obey his respected commands in another direction."

He was gone, the slamming doors on his passage firing a sort of salute after him. I think he slammed them to have this effect.

" Chevalier ! " said I, putting my head out of the window.

" Your Highness ! " returned the man of Cos, with his hat touching the ground, and facing about like a field-marshal speaking to the Emperor of Russia.

" Never mind getting the garrison under arms."

" Your Highness wishes to go *incognito*, to hide the splendour of your rank and name from the inhabitants of our unworthy island. Never, never shall it be said that the men of Cos knew not how to receive an illustrious Cosmopolite. Never shall such reproach rest upon their name ; unless, unless," added the man of Cos (a majestic wave of the hand), " your Highness wishes it."

" I do wish it."

" Your Highness—Highness, what say I ? perhaps Majesty ? —shall be obeyed ! " So saying, the man of Cos darted off with the utmost speed upon his errand.

CHAPTER XLIV.

COS.

COS is the island whence the lettuces came, which are known as Cos, goss, or gause lettuces, according to the taste and fancy of the market-gardener who may happen to be interested in their sale. Cos is now called Stanchio; it is about twenty-one miles long by five or six broad: on the southern coast is a fine picturesque range of mountains, and the rest of the island is one of the most charming and fruitful plains I have seen in the world. It grows all sorts of things; it would utterly exhaust a weak-chested man to enumerate part of them: corn, cotton, silk, oranges, lemons, grapes, wool, pomegranates, figs, and melons, are but half its treasures. It produces some of the best wine in the East; so good that a traveller will very rarely have a chance of drinking any of it. The climate is delightful; fresh and breezy in summer, dry and mild in winter. It would give a very fair idea of a paradise of a limited extent, if it were only in good hands. I can fancy a piano, a few pleasant ladies for a pic-nic, a double-barrelled-gun, a couple of decent pointers, a few clever hacks, some good story-tellers for dinner, and a cottage *ornée*, uncommonly well for three months of a year at Cos. I should not object to remaining there even four months; under other circumstances, it might be liable to the reproach of dulness. This, however, would not be so much the fault of Cos as its misfortune, and the inaptitude of the people, who might be residing there under difficulties, for a purely rural life.

If you listen to persons who read geographical dictionaries and that kind of thing (a parcel of dusty-fingered old fogies, to say the least of them), I have got a sort of dim idea that they will tell you the place was famous at some impossible time or other—perhaps among the ancient Greeks, I shouldn't wonder —for a temple erected in honour of a fashionable physician, named Æsculapius. I should like to see Belgravia erecting a temple in honour of Dr. Placebo! I remember also meeting with a fusty elderly man, who would tell me that the present tumble-down old town, inhabited mostly by Turks, is merely the site of one of the most beautiful cities of the ancient world —I think that is the cant phrase—and that in this defunct town was an immortal sculpture of Venus rising out of the sea, the masterpiece of a fellow I think he called Apelles. Augustus, going to Cos for change of air, carried this Venus off to Rome, and left the Coans to put up with their loss as best they might. The people of Cos, however, need not have complained of this, for he left so many a living Venus behind, that their little island acquired quite a reputation for their loveliness, and became a favourite resort of enlightened travellers in consequence.

I could not get rid of my communicative friend till he had told me a long story about an event certainly not mentioned in Pinnock's " History of England." I remember he called it the Trojan war, and he would have it that two kings of Cos, Antippus and Phidipus, were there. He brought that weary old man Homer (whoever he may be) headlong into the conversation in support of this assertion. All I can say is, that *I* found no kings at Cos, and the only pair of monarchs I can fancy occupying so small a territory, without coming to loggerheads, are the kings of Schwartzwurst-Schenkenshausen and Brentford. My antiquarian acquaintance assured me, however, that they not only actually lived and reigned at Cos, but were succeeded by a republic, a termination so probable for a monarchy, that I almost inclined to believe he was right. I tried very hard to get away without being told about Hippocrates, who appeared to be almost as much the man of Cos as the magniloquent individual who had called upon me on the morning of my arrival. Hippocrates was born at Cos, and was almost as fashionable a doctor as the above-named Æsculapius. The Coans appear to have the most cheerful feeling on the subject of medical men, and look upon them with much benignity, chiefly from the fact (as I am given to understand) of their never being taken ill. Both Æsculapius and Hippocrates also gave advice and physic gratis, a quality which no doubt endeared them much to a people so reasonably fond of money as the Greeks.

Hippocrates, whisper the Coan gossips, dealt a little in love affairs, and cured one Perdiccas, King of Macedonia (I have not the smallest idea who was Perdiccas, or where is Macedonia, so do not get alarmed, my public), of a wasting sickness, by introducing him to a young lady named Philas, whom, it turned out, he had seen before—a hint for Doctor Febrifuge!

It does not appear that the Coans thought it necessary, however, to erect a statue to Hippocrates. Perhaps they were deterred by the difficulty of representing him. He used to cover up his head,—some say in token of humility, others because he was bald,—some because he was noble, as we put on coronets,—some on account of the weakness of his head,—some on account of its strength,—some as a sign of delight in travelling,—some as a pleasant hint as to the obscurity of his writings, and some, that to leave his hands free he took up the loose part of his gown, and tucked it up over his head. My own opinion however is, that he did so to prevent the Coans taking his likeness; and I hope the future historian, whoever that hard-worked individual may be, will thank me for the suggestion. At all events, I have told him all I learned about this noted character among his townsmen.

Getting rid of my musty acquaintance by a stratagem of which I am proud to this day, I walked on with the son of the man of Cos, past an ancient Greek tomb, with a brass cock in the centre (it was used for a fountain, and looked melancholy enough with its untranslatable inscription), and so on to the famous plane-tree. It is said to be a thousand years old. A critical public will perceive that I do not vouch for this fact; I tell what I was told by the son of the man of Cos. It is said, also, to be thirty feet in circumference. Its enormous branches, fully the size of ordinary trees, are very near the ground, and supported by marble columns—whitewashed, of course!

Here I took my stand to watch a man being shaved in the barber's shop over the way: some black men gambling, some old soldiers, very old soldiers, cheating a raw recruit at the same pastime ; to watch the governor's horse champing at his bit, and making his golden housing quiver with impatience for the gallop he will never have ; to watch the grave smokers seated on a party-coloured mat, and silent as the Fates ; to watch the old grey-bearded Turk who has always a large marigold between his turban and his head ; the two sheep always tied by the legs and tumbling over each other when they try to escape ; the eternal dog and the donkey always wandering nowhere ; the weary woman looking so blankly out of her bundle of clothes, and wondering at the stranger ; the boy always eating a cool juicy water-melon with black pips, and the negro slave with his everlasting grin ; the mysterious twilight archways which lead to more mysterious streets or Turkish houses, or away into the sweet pomegranate and orange gardens beyond the town ; the uncomfortable (always uncomfortable) Greek with his black turban, eating his spare meal of cheese and olives ; till, at last, the scene grows into the Arabian Nights as usual, scene for scene, picture for picture, just as we find it in many pages.

And now away into the breezy country through the laughing vineyards, and up to the hill-top, with its intoxicatingly beautiful view of the blue sea, and the fairy islands far away ; so on to the fountain of Hippocrates. I do not know much about the fountain, except it was reached through a dark passage ; and I knocked my head on the way to it. On a lantern being brought, however, we proceeded onward, and found a small stone chamber with a hole at the top, and some sparkling water running through it.

Thence we adjourned to a shepherd's hut in the neighbourhood, which was a far pleasanter place. We had a kid baked whole : it was dressed in true gipsy fashion. A large fire was lighted in a hole in the wall ; when the fuel was burnt out, the kid was placed in whole. The mouth of the hole was then closed up with a large stone fixed in its place by wet clay ; when this clay dried and turned white, the kid was done to a turn. We spent the afternoon, seated gravely on the mud floor of the shepherd's hut, without speaking a word, and indulging in that sort of dreamy silence which, I think, forms part of a shepherd's life. We did not think of anything particularly, but we were in a kind of reverie, from which it was not easy to rouse ourselves: we did not hear when first spoken to. I think we sucked our tongues and picked little holes in our clothes; we could hear the hum of nothing in the air. When the sun was gone down, we all seemed to wake up and think of supper, without any previous communication whatever. It appeared in the shape of a goat-milk cheese and mountain honey; then we had some uncouth tunes, on a quaint, funny little fiddle, played by the patriarch of the family, a most reverend old gent; and afterwards, somehow or other, we all fell asleep: there were about ten or twelve of us, shepherds' wives and children included. When we woke, it was broad daylight again, and our horses were neighing for their corn.

CHAPTER XLV.

CHIOS.

SHARP race the Chiotes! The island has, perhaps, given birth to some of the sharpest men in Europe. I take it, that neither Yankee nor Yorkshireman, Scot nor Jew, can touch the Chiote, with respect to sharpness. They are so sharp that they have even succeeded in pointing the dull wits of the Turks. There appears, indeed, to be something very sharpening in the very air of Chios, and the Turks who live there are as different from the rest of their race, as the good burgher of Ghent or of Bruges may have been from the sparkling Frenchman of the court of Louis the Fifteenth.

The population of the island is almost entirely Greek, and the Turks do not amount to more than one thousand souls. Our amiable acquaintances have not disdained to learn the doggish language of the infidels at Chios; for the truth is, the Greeks will not learn theirs, and the Moslem lords have found it convenient to hold intercourse with them for the purposes of commerce, which is the chief business of their little island. The state of affairs here, generally, is more satisfactory than usual. There are but fifteen Turks in authority throughout the land, and they are all mortally afraid of the Greeks. Infractions of the law are almost unknown. The local manners and customs are less constrained than in any other part of the Turkish dominions. The intercourse of the sexes is frequent and open; and young ladies go out for an afternoon's ride with their betrothed husbands quite in the European fashion.

One meets with Turkish Greeks, and Greek Turks, jocular-philosophical, wide-awake Turks, who quite take your breath away with surprise at the extent of their mental acquirements

—Turks, who are not jealous of their womankind, but allow them to go about unveiled. In a word, I am very much disposed to think that Chios is a fair century in advance of the rest of the Turkish empire; it is a thousand years in advance of many places in Syria and Asia Minor.

I think I have never seen so many beautiful women in one place as here, though I am bound to confess that a buxom British lass would have been a marvel among them. I certainly never saw so much general comfort and competence among any people whatever. They appear to thrive wonderfully on the wine, almonds, grapes, olives, and mastic in which they deal; and I should think, that to be one of those snug, pursy Chiote merchants was a very good business.

The fine library of Cordy, the most distinguished of modern Greek scholars, is preserved here; but the trustees under his will refuse to deliver it all in the present state of political affairs, and the most valuable books are consequently kept back. The books, however, which have been received are kept in a lofty and convenient room attached to the high school.

The Chiote schools are particularly interesting, and some of the wealthy Greek merchants in Europe contribute about £250 a year to their support. The trustees have thus been able to purchase some valuable philosophical instruments, and the education bestowed on the scholars is altogether of a very superior kind. I have always hope for the Greeks when I think of their schools; but at Chios the Turks also come in for a fair share of the praise, and there is a Turkish naval school established here, which is very ably conducted. The gardens round the town are singularly delightful, and it was pleasant to pass the afternoon there among orange and almond trees; among fountains and creaking wells; among women and children, laughing and prattling over their healthy toil; but I think the fortress or inner town, where the Turks chiefly live, interested me most. It contained so many fearful traces of one of the most terrible events of history; its little narrow streets were so mysterious and suggestive; I found so many relics of the middle ages, so much that was quaint and rare, that I was never tired of wandering about there. I used to sit cross-legged in coffee-houses, smoking dignified pipes, and feeling my beard grow. Sometimes I unbent, and held refreshing converse with many sorts of men; for I wore the red cap, and thus excited little notice—it was thus I made the acquaintance of a tailor: we had looked at each other for several days with a fixed kind of fascination; we were evidently sympathetic souls; at last I made overtures of friendship, which were graciously received. The tailor made way for me, and I sat down beside him; but he was an irate little man (or how could he have been a tailor?), and he said "Chuff!" as he did so. What chuff may mean I am unable to determine with satisfactory accuracy; but I interpreted it as a sign of impatience at my taking so long a time in sitting down, and I have reason to think I was not mistaken in so doing.

The tailor had come to the coffee-house because he had no fixed residence of his own, and he was using the raised platform on which we sat as his shop-board. I found out, after some adroit questioning, that he was a Greek; but, for a wonder, he appeared to wish to pass for an Osmanli, and was got up with great care for that purpose.

It was a quaint scene of out-of-the-way manners, to watch him, as his angry little eyes followed the rapid motions of his needle, and he jerked his work remonstratively from side to side to get the right light on it. He had long nails, not unlike claws, and every time he refilled his needle, he straightened and stretched the thread upon them, with an indignant, cracking sound which was quite startling. It was easy to see that my new friend was poor, as working tailors are apt to be; I think, also, he was drunken, political, and henpecked, though this is but a surmise. I noticed some unquiet glances which he cast at a termagant who came to the neighbouring fountain, and which confirmed me very much in this opinion. I think, indeed, that class qualities are the same in all places.

On the other side of the tailor sat a smart Albanian, fierce, dusty, and travel-stained, as that wild race always seem when not in any regular service. His eye had a quick, restless glare, and his jaws were set with a clasp of iron. I knew that there was murder on his dastard arms: I knew it, and my neighbours knew it! we could even guess whose blood it was, for the wild work done a few days since on the opposite coast was the talk of all men. Yet there sat the life-taker in the midst of us, and who should say him nay?

Near the Albanian, again, were two Turks, dressed in gay summery clothes of red and yellow cotton, which they love. They had knives in their girdles, but peace in every solemn movement: they sat gravely talking of their ailments and the healing art. Within the room was a motley group of Turks and Greeks. The place was very bare and rather dirty; a raised fireplace was in the centre, and around it were placed little brass pots, for making coffee as it was wanted. Draughts, of which the Turks are very fond, coffee, and conversation seemed the only amusements going on. There was no noise, no uncouth music, no drunkenness and revelry, as in the Greek coffee-houses; we could hear the rippling fall of the neighbouring fountain quite plainly.

On the day which I have described, I remember I took my way from the coffee-house to the prison, which is under the house of the Bin-Bashee, or captain of the fortress. I easily obtained admission: a low door turned groaningly on its rusty hinges, and then opened on to another one, at the end of a glum little passage. It was quite dark, so dark that, though it was noonday, we were obliged to light a lamp before we could discover anything.

When I at length could distinguish objects, it was to notice a tall, handsome, faded man, extended on the floor, heavily manacled and shackled. Beneath him was a carpet, worn all in holes—nothing more.

The jailer stirred up his prisoner as I entered, rather roughly, but not unkindly, and the man rose with a groan. Oh, such a groan of pain and weariness!

I walked round the prison, though the stench was stifling. On one side was a fresh tomb: the last prisoner had been buried there; some pieces of unplaned deal, still white and new, covered his remains. Anything more fearfully dreary and filthy than this prison could not be conceived. The floor was of damp earth, the walls were mouldy with foul exhalations, and the solitary prisoner's face was flushed with a hectic fever, as well it might be. His only exercise was a short walk to the *other* prison every twenty days; the other prison being distant about a stone's throw. His diet was, mercifully, low enough. He told me he could see *sometimes*, because there was a little chink in the outer door which admitted the light. He had no occupation; he did nothing; he saw nobody; he never spoke; he had, however, one companion: it was a little dog—a tan-coloured spaniel, very thin and faded, like its master. The dog showed no wish to go when the door was opened; he seemed to have doggish sagacity enough to understand the state of affairs very well; he did not bark when we entered, he only wagged his tail in a very gentle and deprecatory manner, as if he hoped that he was not taking a liberty, or did not intrude, or something of that kind.

The man had been imprisoned thus for a whole year. It is marvellous how human nature could have so long supported a trial so stern.

He had been arrested *on suspicion only* of a murder, which was never brought home to him; there was even strong reason to suppose that suspicion had fastened on the wrong man. He was exculpated by the positive testimony of a Greek, who avowed himself to have been a witness of the murder. But then, the question was, could the Greek witness be believed? In common justice towards the Turks, it is proper to say—he could not. A Greek witness would probably have sworn anything to defeat the ends of Turkish justice. So that not even at Chios can we wonder at the Turks being very cross with that people: nothing can be done with them save through fear and punishment. It is an unpleasant, nay, a revolting assertion,—the pen seems to me to grate on my ears while I write it, yet I have had means enough of being radically convinced that it is a true one. Kindness is useless, for they do not believe in it; rewards they attribute to sinister motives; they scoff at promises, they sneer at clemency; and if you let them alone, they do mischief. The Greeks are, I do firmly believe, in every respect the most hopeless and inconvenient race of men in the world; and yet they have some qualities which are quite provoking in such a people. They are pleasant-spoken to a proverb; hospitable, polite, wonderfully obliging in those small things which make up the everyday affairs of life: they are all this without any sinister motive, for it is their nature to be so. Here is an instance: I am scribbling these lines in my pocket-book, seated on a stone by the seaside; some Greeks have seen me from their windows, and one of them has brought me out a chair, coming some hundred yards to do so. He waits for no reward or thanks; he does not even disturb me as my pencil glides over the paper, but he puts down the chair with polite gravity, and walks away. Nevertheless, perhaps there is no out-of-the-way or unhandsome, yet plausible, thing which that same man would not do by me on a further acquaintance. I confess the Greeks are a puzzle which I cannot put together; they are the despair and astonishment of all who have to do with them. One of the most exasperating things about them is that they are never in the wrong. A Greek may have done something which makes your very flesh creep with indignation; you know he *has* done it, for he has done it to *you;* your eyes saw it, your ears heard it, you are suffering even from the effects of his misconduct: but only give him leave to talk, and he will plainly prove himself to be in the right at once. He will be in the right on every principle of law or equity which you can name to him; and, then, how is it possible to be hard with a man who, having convinced you against your ears, eyesight, and interest, that he is the injured man, and not you, meekly offers his back to the stroke, and bows before you, with the air of a martyr: he is ready for anything your brutal wrath may inflict upon him; strike, for the shame is yours, not his. There is a charming passage in one of Mrs. Norton's books, where she quotes Spenser, I think, to prove that a beautiful form is but the temple of a mind as fair! I have seldom, however, seen finer men or lovelier women than some of the Greeks, and yet—but really the task of condemning them is too easy, even for a volume of sketches.

CHAPTER XLVI.

THE MONASTERY.

THE new monastery at Chios is certainly worth a visit, and the Superior is a very well-fed and amiable man. He escaped from the island at the revolution, and has passed thirty years of his life in Western Europe, twelve in England.

The history of the monastery is somewhat curious. In the eleventh century, two monks, named Joannis and Nicetas, were hermits who dwelt on a mountain, in the odour of sanctity. Now once on a time it chanced, as they lay awake by night, they saw a bright light burning a little way off. They took no notice of the light at first; but as it appeared every night regularly at the same time and in the same place, they went down at last to examine from whence it might proceed. They could not, however, discover anything, and they returned to their hermitage with the conviction that there must have been somebody concealed among the trees, and that he had fled at their approach. Perceiving, however, that the same singular flame always kept burning after the evening had set in, they resolved to set fire to the wood, that it might no longer afford a refuge to people who were doubtless about no good there. One myrrh-tree alone remained unharmed in the general conflagration, and on examining it carefully, they found an image of the virgin on one of its branches. They cut out the image, which was very perfect and beautiful, to take away to their mountain chapel.

The Virgin, however, pointedly expressed her disapprobation of her new residence, and every night, while the monks were asleep, she descended from her niche, and took up exactly the same place where they had first seen the light which had excited their reasonable curiosity. She did the same remarkable thing three times following, and at last the monks, fearful of resisting her determination any longer, built a chapel there, and dedicated it to her especial worship. The Virgin was not ungrateful ; for when some Arabs came to rob the monks, who were understood to be very well off, and were so, she took a very decided means of bringing the Arabs to grief. In trying to detach some very beautiful mosaic-work which belonged to the chapel they make use of a pickaxe ; this instrument, striking sharply against the stones, caused the sparks to fly about, and very soon kindled a flame which burned the Arabs to a cinder. A rope which they had brought to bind their booty, and part of a pickaxe, are preserved in memory of this extraordinary circumstance. The benefits of the Virgin, however, by no means ceased with the roasting of the robbers in their own fire ; she also informed the monks that Constantine Monomachos was about to become emperor of Constantinople. This individual, at the time the monks were favoured by that announcement, was in exile at Mitylene, and expected death every day ; he was much delighted, therefore, when the monks waited upon him with their agreeable prophecy ; being a Greek, however, he of course declined to express the slightest faith in their communication. But the monks had obtained their information from far too authentic a source to admit of the smallest doubt, and they therefore at once resolved to turn the incredulity of their emperor to some account. They asked a boon, in case their news should prove true. Constantine, naturally disposed to be liberal of' those things which he never expected to possess, at once granted their request, and gave them his signet-ring as a pledge of his good faith. When the prophecy was verified, they reclaimed his promise ; and it being a dangerous thing to begin a wrangle with monks, the emperor sent to know what they wanted. They answered, a monastery ; and it is said the emperor was very well satisfied to have been able to redeem his promise so cheaply. In the convent church I think there are some of the finest mosaics I have ever seen, though they were much, and wantonly, injured at the revolution. For the rest, it is a spacious, plain building, with a very large refectory and a very good cook. We had an excellent dinner of hot roast partridges, stewed hare, neapolitan macaroni, boiled beef and fried beef-chops, with nice fresh pepperpods and young almonds, also some water-melons, large enough to break your toes should they fall upon them. Taking a pleasant leave of the worthy abbot and some numbers of the *Penny Magazine* which he had shown us with considerable pride, we rode on to the luxuriant gardens where the mastic grows. I must here express a lively regret that I am not able to say more about the Chios gum-mastic which the Turkish ladies are said to employ in their toilet ; nor could the closest inquiry lead me to ascertain what they do with it. I must add, however, that it is certainly a subject of congratulation that it is not in more general use, for it is very nasty stuff, something like conglomerated turpentine. It grows, I noticed, between the bark and the wood of a little tree : small incisions or notches are made in that tree, and it oozes out in glutinous beads. Mastic is now (1853) worth about twelve shillings a pound ; before the trees were destroyed by the cold in 1850, it was scarcely worth a third of that price. I observed that girls and women of Chios were chiefly employed in mastic gathering : many of those whom I saw in the mastic villages were very lovely. Fancy some ancient statue of rare grace and beauty, dressed in the dingiest of ill-fitting washer-women's cotton dresses ; let her carry a pail of water, or toil in the fields till every muscle is strained and twisted awry ; fancy her dirty, degraded, shrewish, rusty, dusty, and exceedingly uncomfortable,—so shall you see an island maid at Chios. I have but a word more to say of Chios ; and I am sorry to say it is a sad one. After the massacre which followed the revolution, and which has been too often described to need mention here, a certain Greek girl was carried away as a slave into Asia Minor ; she found a home, of course, in the harem of a Turk. A child was born of their union, and then the Turk died, and the girl was left to go with her baby whithersoever she listed. So she returned to her own land, not knowing where else to go, and she married a Greek, who hushed up her story and adopted her child as his own, bringing him up in the Christian faith. They had no other children ; and by-and-by the boy, grown into a fine youth, became the darling and support of their old age. By some means, however, the story became known, as all stories do, however carefully concealed ; inquiries were set on foot, the youth was seized by the Turkish authorities, circumcised, and made an artilleryman. Unable to endure the misery which had befallen him, he fled. When I was at Chios, he had been living in Syria for five years ; he was unable to return, lest he should be re-caught and punished as a deserter. I saw his mother, who asked me to plead for her; she cried passionately, and throwing herself at my feet, kissed them in the abject earnestness of her supplication for the restoration of her son.

I wonder what would have become of me if I had dared to state her case to the authorities ; why, I believe that I should have been promptly annihilated by the Juggernaut of " official regulations."

CHAPTER XLVII.

THE ROAD.

" Spur of steel, upon my heel,
Clanking stunn'st thou me!
With my louder heart-beats
I will silence thee!"

HUNGARIAN SONG.

THE Pasha looks at me wistfully; he is more like a German than a Turk, and I fancy he would rather I did not go. I do not exactly know why, but this is my opinion. It gains strength during every minute of our nervous interview. I see this sentiment on the part of his Excellency in everything he does: I see it even in the awe-stricken deference of the silent servants; in the rapidity with which the pipes of honour follow each other, each succeeding pipe-stick being handsome, and more splendid than the last. I see it in the magical appearance of several sorts of sherbet, and finally in the peculiar uneasiness of the Pasha's seat upon his sofa. Everything, indeed, conspires to convince me that my question was what Lord Chesterfield calls a poser.

Yet the question was simple enough—

"Are the roads safe, Pasha, between Smyrna and Magnesia?" Nothing more, not a word, as I am a scribe and a sinner. This is the momentous question which has disturbed the digestion, and embittered the pipes of my host.

And indeed, all things considered, perhaps the answer may seem easier than it is. If robbers are bold enough to levy black mail on the inhabitants of the most important provincial city in Turkey, and to stop the harmless traveller upon his road, it may be a moot point whether the government is to blame or not. His Excellency's discernment has therefore at once pointed out that it would scarcely be prudent for him even to acknowledge such a fact.

But supposing that the objections to acknowledge it could be got over in an ordinary case, it would inevitably be disastrous to intrust such a confession to a Briton. The Pasha is not unaware that most of that inquisitive and perplexing people have something, somehow, to do with newspapers, another of those pestilent institutions which seem to have been established for the purpose of vexing easy-going governors.

But, upon the other hand, if it would be an inconvenient thing to own with a Pasha's mouth, and to a Briton, that danger could possibly exist anywhere within his, the Pasha's, luminous rule, how much more troublesome still would it be to have that same bothering Briton robbed or slain. Why there would be in the first place a fulminating vizierial letter; there would be one of those awful consular visits, in which nobody would understand anything, except that the consul was a great man, and would not take any pipes or coffee. Finally, Somebody Effendi, who had been looking out open-mouthed for his Excellency's place ever since the day after he was appointed, would step into it without more ado. It was very perplexing. How perplexing, the reader must be a Turkish Pasha to understand,—a Pasha who has just clutched power as the long-deferred reward of a life's intrigues, and half a fortune spent in bribery.

At last his Excellency speaks in rather a confused whisper. I see that he wishes to gain time for reflection. I dare say, few things at this moment would cause my host a more agreeable sense of relief than the circumstance of my being whisked away by magic or witchcraft.

I resume the conversation, and endeavour to make as light of it as possible.

"At all events, Pasha," said I, "I must ask you for such a guard as will place all idea of attack on the road out of the question. Personally, I have no abstract love for a broken head, and I would rather not get into anything like danger, without exceedingly sufficient reason. I am aware that this may appear exacting and eccentric on my part, and that the generality of my countrymen are apt to consider the chance of an adventure with robbers as rather a desirable thing than otherwise. You will do me the greatest favour, therefore, by not overlooking the fact that I am a man of peace."

"I must give you five guards," says the Pasha at last; "I cannot guarantee you with a less number. They shall be all picked men, and I have not a doubt that you will thus arrive safely at your journey's end." The Pasha has not a natural impediment in his speech; but few as these words are, they appear to cost him a violent effort. It has required as much care and patience on my part to obtain them, as if I had been engaged in drawing the cork of a bottle of East-India ale with a penknife. However, they are out at last, and his Excellency looks askant at me with the feeble smile of a party who has been and gone and done it.

Then we have some more sherbet, and the pipes are charged again; the Pasha seeming still as wistful and nervous as ever. At last one of my party good-naturedly holds forth upon the excellence of his rule. Then he plucks up heart, and owns that it is salutary; he seems to have forgotten already that a stranger cannot take a morning's ride in its limits without the protection of a troop of soldiers. It is not worth while, however, to remind him of it; let him drink his sherbet in peace, and presently we shall leave him, with the old, weak, wistful look growing back again into his face, and fixing itself there. Alas! it is a look I have seen very often in Turkey. It is the look of a man who has found himself out, and appears to be wondering if you have found him out also.

At last comes the morning for my start. I have chosen a Thursday—to her who will first read these lines, I need not say why. The day breaks in the same cloudless glory as for months past; and if, as Montesquieu very prettily observes, one never sees the return of daylight without a secret joy, the joy is certainly livelier when we have some animating project for the time before us. Upon the whole, however, the loud neigh of the horses, as they come round, does not call to my spirits so stirringly as usual. I have been passing the last ten days with a great merchant-prince * and a pleasant little tribe of wandering Britons, at the charming village of Bournabat. We have been having laughing rides and moonlight walks; I have been drinking in the words of experience from as noble-hearted and cheery an elderly gentleman as ever did honour to our national name in a far-away land; and who has indeed written his own in indelible characters enough all over the country—now in a road, an hospital, or a college; now in the living and brighter page of poor men's hearts. It does one good sometimes, at least, to meet with those hale, happy, worthy folk who go about doing good, and are a living blessing to their dwelling-place—kind, gentle, warm-hearted people, whom the world has not been able to teach its selfish wisdom, whose minds are as fresh and guileless as at nineteen, and who are all the better for it.

I am fairly sorry to go away; the place and people cling to me with an unwonted charm; and who that has travelled does not know the pain of parting with pleasant people? Sir Walter Scott, however, said very sensibly, that a visit should never exceed the rest-day, the dressed-day, and the pressed-day—an excellent rule; so now for a stirrup-cup, and then boot and saddle. I do not know how it has happened, but partly in those expensive things called bargains, and partly in the still more troublesome and costly form of gifts, my train is magnified to a size which rather astonishes me. Let us review it: there stand the Pasha's guards, tall, powerful men, mostly maimed in some way; they are mounted on fiery wiry little horses, looking very much like business. Then come two baggage horses, one stout and chubby, the other weedy and scrambling—both overloaded, I am ashamed to say, with all sorts of useless things. Then come two beautiful Arabian horses, which I have got by great favour at a high price from Syria; they are swathed up to their eyes, and led by their grooms, girded and caparisoned within an inch of their lives; they pass by, arching their stately necks, and tossing their gay harness disdainfully; the sun makes what little of their coat is to be seen, to shine like the satin of a lady's dress. Then comes a stout Asian cob, short and thick-

* The late Mr. Whittal.

set; he is for the road and can walk six miles an hour. Lastly, ride Hamed and Sadik, my two Albanians, armed to the teeth, and prepared—as they say—to die for me, whenever such a proceeding on their parts should appear in the slightest degree necessary. I am told that all these people and things are barely fitting for a simple gentleman to travel in any degree of comfort or safety between the two greatest cities in Turkey, Smyrna and Constantinople. I might, indeed, say my advisers, dispense with one of the led horses; but without a little of the parade of station, a wayfarer is not unlikely to be exposed to disagreeable things. Besides, it does not much signify, for every one agrees in assuring me that my travelling expenses ought not to exceed five pounds a day. In Turkey, say my wise councillors, there is economy in a certain splendour; for whereas your humble traveller is thought a person of too small consequence to resist or punish imposition, and is therefore cheated by everybody with the utmost diligence and success, a grander wayfarer strikes too much respect, perhaps terror, into the hearts of all men to make such liberties at all likely : he may be a tax-gatherer or the king of the Cannibal Islands in disguise; he may be Somebody Effendi, sent down to have an eye to the proceedings of the local authorities, and will only show his credentials and bastinado when sure of his facts; it is therefore deemed on all hands the wisest plan to conciliate him. He is conciliated, if pipes, pilaff, and free quarters can soften his heart; and the path of that traveller becomes a path of roses.

The last wave of the last white handkerchief has been hidden by the dust of the road, the last kind good-bye has ceased to echo in my ears, and I am fairly on my way in the oldest part of the old, old world.

We wind deeper and deeper into the country; it is a pretty sight enough to watch the little cavalcade pass on through gloomy passes and deep ravines and gentle valleys, where the sunburnt labourers are at work amid their vines. There is a spirit of adventure and newness about it even to me, and I have felt most things of the kind to be nonsense, and laughed at them often enough. It is easy to perceive, however, that there really is danger on the road, and that we may expect an attack at any moment. The country is not only full of the regular klephts or robbers, who abound at all times, but it is now* also infested by captains of free companies going to or returning from the wars.

The guards unsling their guns, and carry them at full cock. We slip the buttons of our holsters, and Hamed loosens his sword in its sheath. There is an expression of great determination and anxiety on the face of the captain of my guard ; and when I offer him a cigar and pass my brandy flask, he thanks me in a whisper, and smiles a very particularly forced smile.

The train halts, and there is a parley in the van. Two of the guards prick forward, one to the right and one to the left : they ascend the nearest heights and look round them : they have dropped their rein on their horses' necks, and their hands are busy with their guns. A third horseman now rides straight on through the defile : he is followed by the led horses, tossing their heads, and then by the baggage. They disappear as if swallowed up in the dark pass ; Hamed and Sadik now close up and hem me in on each side : the captain follows close, quite close, behind. If we are to have a fight, there will be sharp work. I have two revolvers in my belt, and a pair of double-barrelled pistols, in all sixteen shots. There is evidently a stoppage too, and a loud altercation is going on ahead. With the speed of thought Hamed has left my side and dashed on with loose rein. Bold Hamed ! I am glad to see at least that thou art not a humbug, and that thy deeds keep pace with thy brave words. His place at my side is instantly filled by the captain, who glances anxiously at me, and then we all ride on together to join in the fight.

There is a long talk, and a great many questions asked and answered. At last I hear the voice of Hamed in front growing louder and louder : we squeeze ourselves with some difficulty past some mules and oxen which block up the pass, and soon stand eight armed men in company, fronting a band of mounted Zebecks. The dashing light figure on the white horse, talking to the Zebeck chief, with one hand upon his rein and

* 1853.

the other steadying the long Albanian gun, is Hamed, my own brave Hamed. They are joking !

"Have you got any tobacco?" (smoke) says the Zebeck chief.

"Oh yes, plenty," answers Hamed, smiling grimly and making his gun rattle.

"Where are you going?" is the next question of the Zebeck.

"To Stamboul, where they hang deserters," sneers the Albanian.

"Who is the Frank?"

"A great lord — greater than the Pasha of Aidin, great enough to have you hung up, if he raises a finger at you."

There is a loud laugh among my guards at the expense of the Zebeck, and a short scornful snort from Hamed. Then the Albanian seizes the bridle of the Zebeck, and forces him backwards with a savage yell; his followers give way, and the road is free. In all, perhaps, this suspicious band amount to seven armed men, a less number than ourselves: they are of a race, however, not given to fair fighting; and had the two advanced guards not seen them waiting for us, they would have emptied seven of our saddles by long shots before they opened farther proceedings: we should have fallen from the fire of an unseen enemy.

By the way, it is as well to add here, in order to explain my friend Hamed's sneer about deserters, that the Bashi Bauzouks, or captains of free companies, joined the Crimean war in great numbers; but finding subsequent reason to disapprove of the discipline and fighting, which they did not seem to expect, they deserted in whole troops with much baseness and alacrity. Such are, indeed, the men who are helping to make the roads dangerous in Asia Minor.

CHAPTER XLVIII.

THE ROAD-SIDE COFFEE-HOUSE.

IT seemed to me as if I had gone to bed last night in the nineteenth century, and awoke this morning in the tenth. The scene around me is more like a dream of the middle ages than an existing reality of to-day. The rude culture of the fields; the armed peasantry; the chartered freebooters; the lovely and deserted country; the rugged roads, and the mean dwellings of a people who scorn their homes, all seem to recall a state of things which I believed had passed away long ago.

For the rest, I frankly confess that there is a sort of all-alone feeling creeps over me in the midst of my armed companions. I am the sole Christian among these wild horsemen and mountain robbers of Asia Minor—and, bless my heart, there is the cholera about, and no medical man in the neighbourhood ! Let us get rid of these inconvenient thoughts as soon as possible. " He who has not what he likes, must like what he has," says a proverb I love well to remember : so I will go and sit in that little den yonder, with the grumbling old man, and try to like the road-side coffee-house at Iaquique.

The building which I have described as a coffee-house comprises a few scrambling sheds, very like farm stabling in the north of England. A few fowls are walking about, not unsuspiciously, as it seems to me, and my train are grouped in every variety of picturesque attitude. Most of them are hacking huge water-melons into wedges with their daggers at their girdles ; some are smoking, others attending to their horses, or gossiping with mine host and his men, as truculent-looking rogues as ever gave robbers notice of a traveller's errand.

There are also some other fellows who do not belong either

to our party or to the coffee-house. They are a powerful swarthy set of bravoes, in gay but worn dresses; they bristle with arms: they are Zebecks, men whose trade is robbing: there is no doubt about it. They will soon tell you so themselves, if you feel any doubt on the subject, or any curiosity. There they sit, however, side by side with the governor's guards, who have brought me hither, and nobody, either here or elsewhere, ever dreams of making an observation on the subject. That is to say, nobody but Hamed, who was for many years a highwayman himself, and who by no means condemns their profession, but only their mode of practice.

"Those fellows call themselves thieves!" he sneers, with the true disdain of a great artist for a pretender; "why they will eat your bread, and then lie wait to fire at you from behind a stone or a tree! They robbed my brother of fifty piastres the other day in this way; he would have killed a dozen of them in fair fight."

Presently there is a scream, and a frightened flutter among the fowls; then, as the shadow goes lengthening along the opposite wall, I gradually doze off to sleep, and dream of the pilaff, which will be ready in due course by-and-by. I do not dream long, and when I awake there is a peculiar tingling in my left ear, which reminds me that I am in the sunny land where the mosquito makes his home. A yell from Hamed, and a blow on the ground, succeed in rousing me completely. It is fortunate a keen eye and a true heart have been watching over me; he has killed a scorpion, which was making full speed for my waistcoat. Well, if I choose to go wandering about in the country of mosquitoes and scorpions, I must consent, of course, to put up with their society.

I have often thought, by the way, that the world is not sufficiently grateful to the insect tribe for the many benefits they confer upon it. In hot countries, for instance, the lassitude caused by the heat and glare of the sun is so great that life would be passed by most people in a perpetual doze, if dozing were only made easy. But it is not; no sooner does the sluggard close his eyes, than a thousand creatures are sent to warn him; if he pays no attention to this circumstance, they immediately go to dine with him, and buzz and bite with the most amiable perseverance till he wakes up; they keep up a healthy irritation on his skin, and draw the heat outwards; they afford him the inestimable luxury of scratching himself, a pleasure so great, that a Scotch nobleman,—I speak of a Duke of Argyle—earned immortality by the simple invention of an apparatus, which he put up in various parts of a benighted country, for the laudable purpose of encouraging so innocent and agreeable a pastime. I know indeed of few means by which a wealthy individual could purchase an honoured and lasting renown more cheaply than by setting up Argyle posts in Turkey; it would be a much more substantial and welcome benefit for the working classes than most of those thought of nowadays. Indeed, there are perhaps few pleasures more harmless and refreshing, more lively and invigorating, than a good scratch. Who among us has not watched with pardonable envy the touselled head and greedy eye (thirsting for more) of many a little country clown or damsel; and did not Manzonetti, a great Italian doctor of the middle ages, give daily entertainment to himself and a couple of fleas? Few persons have rejected received ideas with more philosophical complacency than that doctor; and but few persons indeed have had so refined and original a conception of a sensual gratification. For my own part, had I been alive when the tyrant announced a reward for a new joy, I think I should have ventured to recommend him—a scratch; that is, a scratch properly understood. All men can scratch, but a man must be born or made a scratcher to scratch judiciously.

Marsh Allah! Let me take my pilaff, and treasure up the amusement to be derived from the bump on my left ear till afterwards. We have some rakee and melons to begin with; also some pungent onion salad; some eggs fried in red butter; and then a violent dispute between Hamed and the coffee-house-keeper. The Albanian, who keeps my purse with a dragon's grip, offers the coffee-house-keeper ten piastres, or about two francs; he asks two hundred piastres. Hence the difference, which can of course only be terminated by frantic yelling on both sides. The affair soon waxes warm enough for cuffs, several of which are soon exchanged with great vivacity. At last, however, the coffee-house-keeper takes bold Hamed on his weak side.

"Is not your master a great man?" he asks contemptuously.

"To be sure he is, dog, beast, swine! May your grandfather's grave be defiled!" is the polite rejoinder.

"Why, then, does he expect to pay less than a poor Hoja who passed by here yesterday, and gave me 150 piastres without a word?"

This settles the question, the 200 piastres change hands, Hamed throws himself into the saddle and leads on, ruffled not a little. So much for the five pounds a day we were to spend on the road, and so much for the tricks upon travellers even in Asia Minor.

Three or four hours' more sharp riding brings us into the rich plains of Magnesia, and the storied old city rises before us beautiful as a vision. There are no traces of human habitation anywhere else; in an eight hours' ride we have passed but one small village: the whole country is one lovely unpeopled waste. The only signs of life are vast flocks and herds wandering about the mountains, with here and there a shepherd or a catirgi (muleteer), and the lawless ruffians hanging about the coffee-houses, which are dotted along the road to every two or three miles' distance. At last the evening closes solemnly and grandly over the beautiful landscape, and the moon rises. Hamed checks the led horses, and causing the finest to be unclothed, holds the stirrup while I mount; so we ride in a stately manner through the quaint Eastern streets, the Turks who meet us forming in line, with their hands veiling their eyes, which is the usual salute. My horse, which has belonged to a Pasha, seems to recognize it, and goes curveting and throwing his beautiful head up and down every time I raise my hand to my hat in reply: he is the politest horse I ever saw, and nearly broke my nose with his unexpected courtesy. At last we stop before the fine palace of Sadik Bey, one of the most powerful and wealthy satraps in the land.

CHAPTER XLIX.

MAGNESIA.

> "Could those days come back again,
> With their thorns and flowers,
> I would give the hopes of years
> For those bygone hours."
>
> MRS. NORTON.

I THINK the next fortnight was among the happiest times of my life; one of those sweet glimpses of another and a better existence which are now and then offered to us in far-away places; one of those little halting-spots which give us heart and hope for our onward journey. I wish I could bring some of the light which shone over my own mind, to cast at least a faint reflection upon this "litel boke;" but it is the order of things that we can very seldom reproduce the faintest image of the happiness we feel, and each of us must joy or sorrow in the times and seasons in which Providence has willed it.

I am the guest of Karasman Oglou Sadik, Bey of Magnesia; he has given me a splendid palace on the outskirts of the town, a guard of honour and thirty servants to do my bidding; he is too great a prince to live in the same house with his guest, but he sends daily to announce his coming, and rides up with a gallant company to ask how we fare.

I have said *we*, and in truth I am no longer alone; a gay company of ladies and cavaliers have joined my ramble, and we are all living together, the guests of the splendid and hospitable Turk. His cooks prepare our breakfast and dinner, each consisting of some twenty dishes; horsemen gallop all day long between our palace and that occupied by the Bey, and they scour the country round, that our table may lack nothing.

The Bey has placed his carriage at our disposal, and the master of the horse asks our pleasure, bowing lower and lower every day.

There is a nameless charm in the very air of the place. The lordly terraces of the palace overlooking the rich plains, which stretch far away in fair luxuriance of vegetation; the perfume of a thousand flowers which loads every breeze; the clear fresh sunny atmosphere by day; the wondrous moonlight nights, are all enchanting as in fairy land. I shall surely never see such golden hours again.

We sit of an evening singing sweet English songs, or stray about the paths stringing garlands; we dance and make merry and tell stories. What a holiday from the toil and struggle of life! what a new youth for a dull, dreary, elderly gentleman! Our day is one perpetual round of harmless amusements; the blithe laughing walk in the morning, with the ladies' ringlets loosely blowing from terrace and balcony; the gay breakfast; the easy sleep at noon; the walk before cakes and coffee, while guards and horses come glittering and neighing to the great gates below; the free gallop over the green sward by the banks of the Hermus; the clear voices of dame and damsel as they gallop on with flushed cheeks and flowing hair; the wild burst against the breeze. "A wager, a wager, my gloves for the winner!" Who would not ride for such a prize, and treasure up those gloves for ever as the record of a pleasant memory?

Then comes the sobered dinner, oh, so dainty and discreet! Where is the hoyden now, and where the boisterous swain of two hours ago? The one rustles with laces and silks: she is too august a majesty to come near: she quite occasions a sort of awe, till some gracious pleasantry comes sparkling from her lips again. Then the swain brightens too; the champagne corks begin to go off like a very agreeable volley of alimentary musketry; the gay wit brightens; the feast becomes a revel, when——"What, going so soon, ladies?"

Then one bumper more; for the music is playing outside, and—and—I suppose tea must be ready, for we all go, a merry company, and the joy moves on bravely by the light of the moon.

Hark to the Albanians firing their guns in your honour, ladies! And now the fluttering robes disappear, one after another, along the terrace; light laughter is heard echoing sweetly here and there, through the open doors and windows of this summer land; and then let us draw closer together and light our cigars, while the camel-drivers go by with their charges of precious merchandize, and the bells on the ships of the desert ring us at last into drowsiness—and so to bed.

I do not quite know how long this life lasted: indeed, I could never bear to count the days, lest I should see the end of them. At last it occurred to somebody to think that we had been idling and happy long enough. How he could have the courage to allow any such idea to enter his mind, I cannot for the life and soul of me understand up to this moment. However, this sentiment seemed to catch fire, I remember: we all woke up, and quitted our little dreamland at once. Not quite at once, either; we left the Turkish palace, paying about forty pounds backsheesh by the way, and then set out on our travels. I do not exactly know where we went: I think it was to the sites of some of the most famous cities of the ancient world. I had a sort of confused idea that I set out especially to take note of these places, and promised myself, indeed, several times to do so; but I did not. I think once or twice I heard names which interested me a little. Somebody once said something about Sardis; and somebody else appeared to have an opinion one evening that we were at Thyatira. I am not quite sure that there was not on another occasion a conversation about Pergamos: if there was, however, I did not pay any attention to it. I remember we had a very good cook, and some of the most agreeable talks I ever had in my life. I recollect eating part of a partridge-pie in the ruined palace of Crœsus, and listening to a jocose anecdote at a place which was said, I fancy, to be Philadelphia. I have a dim recollection of riding over a mile or or two of stones in the same neighbourhood: somebody interrupted my criticism on Milton to say that they were the ruins of that ancient city. I felt annoyed by this circumstance, and set him down as a bore for the rest of the day. I am not, however, without a sort of dreamy reminiscence of beautiful gardens, and Eastern ladies with head-dresses of gold coins. Then, I fancy there was something about a marriage somewhere, and a good deal of wild music, and paint, and processionizing, and liqueurs with strange tastes: perhaps the marriage was got up solely to amuse our leisure, for every one tried to please us. I have now and then loose thoughts about flowery gardens, and Cassabar melons, eaten under shady trees, to the sound of a guitar. It is either true, or I have dreamt, that I had so many bedfellows at Philadelphia, and those of such a pugnacious disposition, that my nose and right eye were the subject of much pleasantry on the following morning. A gentleman attached to the party, I believe, once made a remark that our expenses were about ten pounds each a day; but nobody paid any attention to him; and I have to this instant a grateful remembrance that I was still in dreamland.

I would not have missed such a delightful holiday-time, dear public, much as I respect thee, I would not have missed such a holiday to have been able to repeat all that scholars have ever written about the Seven Churches, for they told me afterwards that it was *there* we had been. Do not frown too sternly: I know very well that I ought to have pored over all sorts of books, and rooted up a whole forest of learning, instead of scampering thus, with loose rein, after pleasure. But if ever you are very sore-hearted and weary, if ever you feel as blank and dull as I did, I cannot wish you a pleasanter refresher, anything which will make your blood run more briskly and healthily again, than such a joyous journey as I made in Asia Minor.

CHAPTER L.

THE HAKEEM.

I AM in a wondrous old Turkish town, far away, deep in the heart of Asia Minor, where many of the peculiar national manners and customs of the Turks still linger, after having passed away, at least in part, from those portions of the empire where the people are brought more frequently in contact with the quick practical minds of modern Europe. I do not believe there is much essential difference between the people among whom I am now living and the followers of Bayazid and Timurlenk. Every man I meet, in the market-place, or by the wayside, is armed to the teeth; and their upright bearing, and fierce, proud look, at once bespeak a population whose hope is in the sword. The women, as they pass, closely veiled, along the narrow shady streets, pause at the corners to look round at the Frank, and go on fearfully, or perhaps muttering a charm. The children raise a shout of mingled terror and derision when they see me; and altogether, perhaps, I create a sensation not very much dissimilar to that which might be caused by a Red Indian in full feather, who should unexpectedly make his appearance on a Sunday afternoon in the polite neighbourhood of Pentonville—I say on a Sunday afternoon, because it is probable that most persons would be then at leisure to look at him, whereas the Turks are always at leisure.

Now it is not good to shut one's self up in solitary contemplation, even in a quaint old-world city of Asia Minor; books, and thoughts, and solitude, are very good things in their way, but we must not allow our love for them to gain on us too fast. We perhaps do not meet in the course of a long life more than six or seven people whose conversation really interests us, nor do we after a certain age see many things which affect us very much; but we must not therefore give up visiting and gadding about; for in most professions, at least, and I include the now unrecognized calling of the philosopher, the study of men is more useful than that of books; and if we always prey on our own thoughts, our minds will soon lose all health and strength.

I was full of these ideas while wandering about the streets one day, and I determined at last to act upon the lesson they seemed to read to me. It is seldom indeed that we turn a reflection to practical account as I did this one; but the illness of my servant had arrested our journey, and I was getting hipped and out of spirits. I stopped, therefore, the first decent-looking Turk I met, and asked him if there were no Franks in the town. He told me there were, and with the lofty courtesy of his countrymen, at once offered to show me to the house of an Italian doctor, whom he said had been established there for some years. So I called upon that doctor, and as he also seemed to have laid the truth of my reasonings to heart, we soon became very good friends, and he told me some particulars of his practice, and of the general state of medicine in Turkey, which appears to me by no means without a queer and peculiar interest.

"On one occasion," said the doctor, in the course of our conversation, "I was called to prescribe for a Turkish lady of some rank, who was stated to be very ill. I went to the house in all haste, though it was night and raining, and I asked to see her. The family were highly offended at this presumption, and they haughtily demanded if I was not aware 'that the Mohammedan women never unveiled themselves before a stranger.' I replied, that such a custom might be worthy of every respect in ordinary cases, but that I positively could do nothing for the patient without seeing her. So at last they consented, and the lady was brought forth. I asked what ailed her? 'Peace, man,' said her husband sternly, 'dost thou call thyself a leech, and yet know'st not what ails the sick? Our Hojas ask no such vain questions as these.'

"'Why triflest thou thus with an Infidel, my son?' now cried an indignant old female, who sat crouched up in a distant corner of the room ; 'give me the shoe from off thy right foot, I will pour water in it and give her to drink, that she may be cured.' She did so ; I reluctantly left the house, and the woman died.

"Not many days since, I was again called to attend another woman ; she was in great pain, evidently dying, and I saw at once that my visit was useless : no wonder ; I found on inquiry that the woman had been delivered of a child by a Turkish midwife, and that subsequently she felt something move in her womb : it was, of course, a twin ; but the midwife was persuaded it was an evil spirit ; so she caused several heavy weights to be placed on the poor woman, and then pressed on her to kill the evil spirit above mentioned. It is not surprising, under these circumstances, that she should have committed a double murder ; and she did so."

My new acquaintance told me also some other Turkish remedies, which are curious enough. For instance, on the seventh day after the birth of a child, it is usual to put it into a large sieve and shake it briskly ; this process is declared good for the stomach. Pounded black beetles are considered beneficial to infants, and are highly esteemed as a tonic for grown-up persons. Any one attacked with ophthalmia is considered certain to cure himself if he carries a piece of dried mud from the left bank of a river to the right bank, and then rubs his eyes with it. Popular belief must have a robust life enough to believe this long, yet the remedy is perhaps centuries old, and merely the echo of a miracle ; a Venetian sequino is also highly esteemed in cases of ophthalmia ; it must be used to rub the eye while the patient is fasting. I think I have heard something about rubbing bad eyes with wedding-rings, even in Britain.

Bat's blood is a notable cosmetic. A verse of the Koran, written on three pieces of paper, will charm away bugs. Sterility may be cured, it is said, by a woman washing her face in the blood of a man who has been beheaded ; stepping seven times over his headless body will have the same effect. A dried finger, taken from the corpse of either Christian or Jew, attached to a piece of ribbon, and hung round the neck, is an infallible remedy for the ague.

Four little boluses of fine wheaten bread, made near to the tomb of the Prophet, are an excellent family medicine, if carried constantly in the pocket; the prime remedy of all, however, is, perhaps, to write a few passages of the Koran on a piece of clean paper, put this paper into an earthen pipkin half full of water, and stir it up respectfully till the writing is washed off; then drink the water in which the sacred words have been dissolved, and they will cure all sickness but the sickness of death.

"I dare not interfere with this last-mentioned belief," said the doctor, "and I allow all to practise the remedy who desire it, for it has a strong effect on their imagination, and aids me materially. Whenever a cure is effected, however, it is always piously attributed to the pipkin. Dust from the Prophet's tomb, especially if mixed with the saliva of pilgrims, and made into small cakes, is likewise a universal remedy. Water from the sacred well of Zemzen cures more ailments than Methuselah's pills, which we see in the advertisements; while pieces of the black silk covering of the Kaaba, like the medicine advertised a century ago as good for earthquakes, actually prevents their possessors having any diseases at all. If toothpicks dipped in the water of Zemzen were once to be sent into the London market, the most expert dentists might rest at once upon their blood-stained laurels; for when teeth have only been touched by those tooth-picks they never ache or decay afterwards."

Should readers still be unsatisfied with the amount of curing power contained in the above list of Turkish domestic medicines, I can still tell of two others, almost equally excellent; I say almost; for although putting some finely powdered alum into any tempting species of food, and then giving it to a black dog, is undoubtedly a valuable aid in sickness, perhaps a respectful application by means of magic to a *ginn*, or spirit, is the most powerful and certain remedy of all.

CHAPTER LI.

"THE SAUCY ARETHUSA."

I WISH I was a naval genius! I have been going about all day trying to sing the "Bay of Biscay, O" (with a particularly long O—o—oh!) and "'Twas in Trafalgar Bay," and that kind of thing; for I passed the morning on board "the Saucy Arethusa."

I am afraid my attempt to sing the songs was a failure; but I do not feel the less *loyal* and *naval* (I am sure they are synonymous terms, if ever words were); I should like to relate the pleasant, cheery, open-hearted sort of conversation I have been having with as fine and gallant a set of English gentlemen as ever trod a plank. I hope the words "trod a plank" are naval; if not, I beg to retract them and apologize; I would change them, if I knew how. It is not the thing, however, to relate private conversation. There is a tacit trust in gentlemen's talk which prevents any portion of it being repeated even to the most private and confidential of publics. I regret this circumstance at the present writing; for the first time in my life I regret that clause in the code of honour. I am sure, if I could but do the smallest justice to the frank, fresh-minded, brave, simple, generous talk of those young men, I should send far over the waters a balm to many a mother's heart,—something to make the bright eyes of many a drooping wife grow brighter,—something to make fathers and brothers, and kind old uncles, walk down Pall Mall with a prouder mien, and to dispose them to pray in their silent homes with calmer and more hopeful hearts for those whose quick light footsteps are no more heard, and whose joyous voices echo there no longer.

Yes! I like to recall the talk of those young men; there was something about it so modest and unassuming, so courteous and gentle, yet laughing and unrestrained, that I could not help thinking what a proud contrast they made to the youth of most other nations. My patriotism seemed to kindle afresh amongst those hearts of oak, and my pride in Old England to grow warmer.

The "Arethusa" was lying at anchor near the arsenal of Constantinople; she was going to Malta in a few hours for repairs, as she had suffered severely on the 17th of October, when the bombardment of Sebastopol commenced. She and the "Albion," I am told, were the vessels which stood closest in against the Russian fortress. The "Arethusa" was in action one hour and forty minutes, during which time she fired fifty-two rounds from each gun, and expended more than ten tons of powder. She did noble service, but she suffered herself severely: the explosion of one shell only, killed two men and wounded ten. The blood and brains of the two sailors who were killed were scattered over their comrades; but no man seemed to lose courage, neither was there one moment of panic or dismay in any part of the ship. The stain of blood is still on the mast near which those two brave fellows fell, and it tinges the deck beside it. Water will not wash it out—will tears?

The men—I mean the men before the mast—showed such true English pluck and spirit, that when a shell exploded and slightly wounded one, striking an officer near him sharply on the leg, though without making a wound, the tar merely hitched up his trousers, and said quaintly to his officer,—"*That* was a near shave, sir!" Even a British canary refused to show the white feather when the cabin, in which its cage was hung, caught fire from the explosion of a shell; and it sang merrily during the whole action. It was touching to hear in such simple language how brave men in the heat of battle had cared for the little bird, and rescued it. I saw afterwards a Russian cat, which an officer had saved from a burning hayrick! Hearts so fearless and gentle, so staunch and steady, yet so tender—where shall we find them?

Not even a battle lacks a funny story, if one looks for it? A lieutenant on board the "Albion" was standing near the place where a shell exploded; he was not wounded, but his trousers appear to have had something strangely attractive about them, for the fragments of the terrible missile were drawn towards them, and tore them to ribands! They may become as honourable an heirloom as a notched sword or a dented and battered shield. A sailor wounded in the leg on board the same ship, looked at the shattered limb with the utmost cheerfulness, and merely said, " Well, I can stump about without ye, if they take the other !" A marine who lost an eye went back to his duty without paying the least attention to the circumstance. Another man refused to be bound for an amputation : " Off with un, sir," said he to the surgeon ; " I shan't hurt, if you don't." Unhappily, owing to the cockpit (I think they call it) having been set apart for the wounded, according to ancient usage, the surgeon of the " Albion " was the first man injured ; there was only one other medical man on board ; and after the action a great many of the sailors were found wounded. "Why do you not go and get your hurts dressed?" asked an officer of some of them. ' Ay, ay, sir, time enough for us," replied the spokesman ; "we ar'n't got nothing particular, let the surgeon attend to them as has." And so it seems that the acts of quiet heroism and unselfishness before the mast were quite equal to those of the officers ; and that Englishmen, whether gentle or simple, are marvellously alike,—alike valiant and merciful,—alike heedful of another's suffering, unfeeling only for their own pain. A thing occurred, also, on board the "Arethusa" which two centuries ago would have been called a miracle : a shell exploded and destroyed the whole of a partition, save a portion about a foot square, where hung a portrait of the queen.

It was pleasant to notice the cordial good feeling among the men and officers on board " the Saucy Arethusa." I thought I observed a general affection towards the captain, which one would be glad to see more often. The ship seemed quite inspiriting, fresh with health and good-humour ; and it is really astonishing to note how much a pleasant chief can do to render any place whatever under his command agreeable ; while a costive, surly fellow will render it as wretched and uncomfortable as Mr. Legree's plantation.

Upon the whole, we have excellent reason to be satisfied with our army and navy in the East. They have done almost as much to render us popular and respected, wherever they have been seen, as our diplomacy and consular service have done, and are doing, to render us hated and feared. There has hardly been a single instance of misconduct of any kind among the thousands of men we have sent to a foreign land, where laws are more lax than enough, and impunity next to certain; wherever our heroes have gone,—to Gallipoli, Scutari, Varna, they have borne away with them golden opinions, trophies by no means to be underrated even in Turkey. As for their military exploits, this is not the place to speak of them; enough that we have ample evidence to show that ten of the enemy have hitherto fallen for one of the allies; a kind of odds that must cause blank dismay enough at St. Petersburg! The Russian soldiers are also deserting to us, whenever they have an opportunity; Russian generals have as much to do to prevent them running away as to make them defend their battlements.

And now let us take leave of the gallant ship; hearkening to the gay, kind voices, and looking up to the fair, open, honest English faces of the officers, as we descend the ladder to our caique. It will be another stirring memory for us—a story for our grandchildren—to have been on board "the Saucy Arethusa."

CHAPTER LII.

DOLMA BAKJAH (THE SULTAN'S NEW PALACE).

DOLMA BAKJAH, signifying literally a garden for those little stuffed vegetable-marrows of which the Turks are so fond, is rather a remarkable name for a Sultanic residence; I indeed felt some curiosity to ascertain who gave it that name, and who were its godfathers, or godmothers, on the interesting occasion; but I have not been so fortunate hitherto as to fall in with any wise man of the East who has been either able or disposed to gratify a thirst for knowledge which I still continue to think was but reasonable in the present instance.

The name, however, is not altogether a misnomer; for the ground, on which the palace is still building, has been certainly a sort of Tommy Tiddler's ground to all who have had anything to do with it. There is no reason why, metaphorically speaking, it should not grow little stuffed vegetable-marrows as well as anything else; and I dare say, in point of fact, it has grown a great many of them—too many of them. It has passed into a sort of a proverb among the ribald and envious, that a man would be rich who might possess for his whole fortune no more than five per cent. on the money which has been stolen during only a fifth part of the time which this palace has taken building. We reject that theory as altogether wild and visionary; we would not consent to become rich on such terms; and as we are by no means likely to have an opportunity of doing so, it is as well to state the fact, and make the most of it. It must, nevertheless, be admitted that the palace has been a long time building; so long that the oldest attaché to the British Embassy cannot remember the laying of the foundation-stone. It is said even that the architects and workmen have got into such a hopeless state of confusion, that the arrival of the Greek Kalends is the only date which can be fixed with certainty for the termination of their labours. To be sure, as the palace is understood not to be wanted at all, the Sultan having already more houseroom than he knows what to do with, there is no particular occasion for hurry; and I have therefore no doubt whatever that a large number of little stuffed vegetable-marrows still remain to be grown, before the picturesque dresses of the workmen will give place to the eunuchs and cavasses, the cooks and harem, of Abdul-Medjid.

Forgetting these troublesome, intrusive scandals, forgetting all one would rather not remember just now, I think I never saw a lovelier sight than this Eastern palace, rising out of the charmed waters of the Bosphorus: it stands close by the shore, with its snowy terraces and towers reflected in the clear, calm element. Beautiful as is the reality, however, I love the shadows in the deep waters best; they put me in mind of the home of the Pearl Queen, whither the prince went in the fairy tale. There is quite a kingdom beneath that tranquil sealet; and if some good fairy would grant me one of those dreamy delightful wishes we all have, I suppose, as children, I think I should like to be the king of it. There is something so soft and luxurious, so strange and far away, about it, that I never saw anything which gave me so vivid a picture of enchanted land. I believe, indeed, that half at least of the beautiful imagery of the Arabian and Persian tales owes its origin to shadows and reflections in the water. Far as the eye can reach stretches the same white line of dazzling palaces, with now and then a tranquil churchyard, overgrown with cypresses, and the harmony of the scene is disturbed only by a coffee-house, crowded with revellers and musicians. The sound of their uncouth strains, however, takes a softer tone as it comes mellowed over this sparkling and gorgeous pathway.

We step on shore to the notes of fiddles, and are nearly blinded by dust. It is one of those sharp contrasts between romance and reality which are constantly hitting one in the face, so to speak, and it is not an inapt simile; in Turkey we soon find our paradise vanish when we enter it. There are, of course, a whole host of people who have nothing to do about all Eastern palaces, and at last a limp individual, who allows his contemptuous disgust at Franks to be subdued by the alluring hope of backsheesh, comes forward to attend us. He has no particular idea of there being serious duties attached to the office of guide, or any other—no Turk has. He likes the backsheesh, but no possible argument would persuade him that it is at all necessary to earn it. His attendance merely consists of dogging us solemnly wherever we go, till he is bought off. Several friends soon arrive to help him in an occupation so congenial; but they will hold no intercourse with us, for we are dogs; and when we desire to bark, or, in other words, to make the smallest inquiry, they perseveringly look another way. Your vulgar Turk is really and truly a sulky bigot, if ever there was one; he is almost as intractable and inconvenient as the Moslem gentleman is courteous and eager to oblige. A common Turk will never be civil, unless he believes you have the power of the bastinado over him. But I must describe the palace.

The grand hall where the state receptions are to be held,—and the court of the Sultan will appear in all its splendour,—is a fine, lofty place enough. There are some beautiful specimens of marble among the many columns; but there is too much gilding, and the decorations will not bear close examination; they are done by inferior artists. The flowers which form the chief ornament everywhere are miserable daubs. Passing up a mean staircase, we come to a gallery, carefully guarded by jealous trellis-work : this is where the ladies of the harem will sit to eat sugar-plums, and watch state ceremonies. We wander from room to room, noticing nothing very remarkable. save a good deal of that make-believe which, I think, forms an essential quality of all Orientals.

For instance, we are in the palace of the Sultan, yet there are no real curtains; they are *painted* above the doors and windows—painted a gorgeous crimson velvet, with gilded embroideries. Nothing real in the East. Read history, and you will understand why. The accounts we have of Oriental splendour were true; but they are no longer so. The East was once the treasury of the civilized world. Read Ducas, and

Phranza, and Anna Comnena, and Chalcocondylas, and you will learn how the treasures it contained were wasted by ignorance, profusion, priestcraft, and conquest. But the taste for gold and glitter remained when the ore and jewels had been scattered. A love of show is part of the Eastern character, and if the Turks cannot any longer cheat themselves, they may at least try to dazzle you and me. The interior of Dolma Bakjah is that of a palace, nothing more ; I have seen fifty better, and as many worse. There is no grand conception in it ; no very imposing beauty. The staircases are all mean : the passages are dark ; the rooms generally low ; the carpenter's and joiner's work is bad. The fireplaces—necessary things enough on the Bosphorus—are too small. There is no freedom of handling or grace of idea about any one apartment, though the evidence of almost reckless expense strikes one at every turn. The very floors, all things considered, might have been laid down in silver at a less cost, yet they are not handsome. The best things I noticed were some magnificent specimens of marble in the dining-room, and a charming effect of the setting sun shining down through lofty stained glass windows. The square formal garden is singularly ugly. Let me own I was shocked at the waste of wealth about this needless place. I am not going to speak of many a deserted home I had seen in a distant province, many a bare hut with the housewife wailing in the midst for her husband imprisoned to wring the stern tax from hands which could no longer pay it ; I will not talk of the awful amount of misery I had witnessed but yesterday in the Greek Islands. It is, I know, the fashionable philosophy to say that public works form one of the best remedies for all this, and that the profusion of the wealthy is the hope of the poor : I do not care to discuss the point, though it never convinced me quite ; and I think that, even in the interests of the poor, money may be spent much more wisely than in tawdry shows.

But I feel almost hopeless for Turkey when I look at this useless building, and remember the beautiful antiquities which are falling to decay and ruin uncared for, and reflect how the precious story of the past is being thus blotted out in many places from the world's scanty archives. When I remember the broken bridges over rapid rivers, in which men are swept away on their journeys in winter-time, and are seen no more; the pathless bogs, infested by bands of robbers, between great cities; the ruined aqueducts, the loathsome prisons, and all that melancholy evidence of decay which strikes you in every Turkish landscape, and, sadder still, plague, pestilence, and famine, sitting, "a weird and fearful three," beside so many a foul and wretched hearth throughout the land—when I remember these things, it seems to me that much gold might have been better spent than on a toy, of which the owner is said to be already wearied. So it chanced that as my riding-whip trailed along the ground, and my cigar went out, I forgot the loitering workmen, and the sleepy hum of laziness around, and drawing my hat over my eyes, I had a vision of a patriot king who was other than Abdul-Medjid.

CHAPTER LIII.

THE DESPOT.

A GREEK archbishop is a single gentleman, with a very imposing beard, and with the rest of his person perfectly swaddled up and immersed in clothing. His idea of good taste in dress appears to consist in putting on as many things as possible : the result is singular to behold. There is nothing particularly grand or venerable about their graces, except their names, for they are called *Despots*. I have looked into the origin of this title, and I find that in the time of the Byzantine emperors, it was given to the princes of the blood. When Mahomet the Second took the city of Constantinople, which was all that remained of their empire, he left very great power in the hands of the Christian prelates, and was inclined to have left more, had they ceased intriguing against him. Even the most useless and astounding of their schemes, however, do not seem to have destroyed his goodwill towards them ; both in ecclesiastical and civil affairs, they soon became, in point of fact, the rulers of their flocks, and shortly after assumed the haughty name of Despots. The Greeks took pride in bowing to their authority ; the humiliation of their recent defeat appears to have been soothed by it ; it also offered them an opportunity of showing a safe sort of contempt for the Turks. It is needless to add, therefore, that they took advantage of that opportunity upon every occasion.

The office of Despot gradually became one of very grave importance; of late years, however, it has been shorn of its grandest attributes. The jurisdiction of the Despots, in civil cases, is entirely abolished by law : the hatred between the two races, however, causes it still to exist in *practice*.

It is painful to state, therefore, that as a class, the primates of the Greek Church are utterly unworthy of any influence whatever. It is a matter of public notoriety that they purchase their places ; and even when they have bought them, they are usually "*ridden*" by the sycophants of the *Phanar*. They arrive at their sees crippled by debts, and are obliged to remit a great portion of the money wrung from their flocks, to satisfy the avarice of some influential toady at Constantinople. The result is natural : the Greek Church is as full of abuses as was the papacy when Luther and Melancthon preached reform. The highest ecclesiastical offices are made a matter of traffic ; indulgencies are openly sold ; persons of bad character are ordained to the priesthood for money ; and holy frauds on popular credulity are practised with the most unblushing effrontery. In a word, no means are left untried to obtain a full twenty per cent. on the money the archbishop is very well known to have paid for his place. There is hardly any legal baseness or extortion from which he will recoil in pursuit of this object : it is therefore but right to say that he usually succeeds in it, and has seldom to regret having been tricked into a bad bargain.

A Greek Despot usually lives in a large rambling house, which belongs to his office ; nine times in ten it is old and wants repairing, for it is his grace's cue to hang out a flag of distress. There is that air of snugness and comfort about the interior, however, which is, I think, the peculiar characteristic of the dwellings of clerical dignitaries all over the world. There are a countless number of priests and deacons, servitors, and buxom ladies, living on the prelate : 'they swarm over the house in all directions, and appear to be cooking constantly, except on fast days. Go farther on, and in a cozy room with cushions, a snuffbox, a chaplet of amber, and a host of most sinister-looking clients, sits the Despot. He is sometimes a man of such curious ignorance, that he cannot trust himself to perform the duties of his post. If this is the case, you will find that he has a secretary who never leaves him : you will inwardly acknowledge, also, that this secretary is one of the sharpest men you ever met in the whole course of your life : you will not be deceived in forming such a judgment. In a very few years you will find that secretary (if unmarried) an archbishop himself, and he might very easily be anything he pleased, if with such bright abilities he were only honest.

Neither the Despot, nor the Secretary, nor the sinister clients, will have a word to say while we are there; so we must put on our wishing-cap, and become invisible. Let us suppose we have done so, and imagination will have no difficulty in enabling us to see and hear what is going on.

A mean, miserable, shamefaced fellow has come to tell the Despot that his sweetheart has married somebody else, after having been solemnly affianced to him: he has spent nearly thirty shillings in presents to her; he wants it back again. He also wants a percentage on the fortune which was promised to him: he is entitled to claim this by immemorial custom, and he has come to ask the Despot to support his demand. A great portion of the archiepiscopal revenues are derived from similar claims, and the prelate listens with all his ears, while the jilted swain relates his misfortune: the claim of the forlorn lover amounts to about fifteen pounds. The Despot, who knows the parties, says that the husband of the jilt is poor, and proposes that the sum should be reduced to twelve pounds, in order that it may be the more easily obtained; after a good deal of whining about his thirty shillings, and some very clever haggling with his grace to "make it thirteen," the plaintiff will agree to this.

If the husband of the jilt should refuse to pay up, he will be first imprisoned, then excommunicated, the Church will not acknowledge his marriage, his children will be declared illegitimate, his wife will lose her rights. These are tolerably strong measures; but the Turks allow them to be adopted in simple good faith, and with a generous desire to let the Greek authorities do as they think fit to their own people.

If the husband cannot be caught, because he is the subject of some foreign power, or for any other reason, some or all of the members of the delinquent's family are imprisoned and excommunicated. No matter for what reason a woman refuses to marry a man who has been affianced to her; no matter why a man may refuse a woman in the same position, or how valid soever their reasons may be, this claim for damages will stand good, and the law is far too profitable to the Despots (who get a fat slice of the money) to be in any danger of repeal or modification. In vain the husband or wife of the delinquent may cry out that a fraud has been practised on them; that they had no idea the partner they have chosen was under any previous engagement, and that the obligation to pay immediately fifteen per cent. on their fortune will plunge them in years of embarrassment. Such is the law of the Despot, and the Greeks voluntarily submit to it.

Let our shadows question the Despot and hearken to his replies.

Q. " Who is the man who has married the jilt?"
A. " A butcher."
Q. "Are you sure they are married?"
A. " No; I shall find that out."
Q. " How?"
A. " By excommunicating the woman, if she does not answer."
Q. "To her own shame?"
A. "Yes."
Q. " But suppose she nevertheless persists in withholding information, how can you make a man justly pay fifteen per cent. on a fortune which you are not even sure belongs to him? Again, if, as you say, her marriage is against the law, how can it be legalized by a fine?"

The archbishop will shut his eyes—he does not like close questions even from a shadow; but for once we will suppose him to answer in a plain way to a plain question. Let us fancy him saying that " the illegality of the marriage in question is simply owing to some political regulation, such as Rayah women being forbidden, in some cases, to marry persons not subjects of the Sultan."

Q. (again). "But in that case can a fine to the Greek Archiepiscopal courts, and an indemnity paid to a private individual, set aside the Turkish laws?"

The answer will be "Yes," and there could hardly be one which settles more completely the question as to the reality of the complaints made by the Greeks in reference to the vexatious persecutions to which they are constantly telling us they are liable from the Turks. But the fact is, if a Turk lifts a finger against them, they raise an outcry which is heard all over Europe, while they will submit to be well nigh crucified by their own people without a groan. Of course, these facts do not one whit alter the justice of their claim for emancipation; but it is quite as well to hear all sides of a question, and that we should know how Greek gentlemen behave when they really are in places of public trust and importance.

I do not know that I have anything more to say about the Greek Despots which is likely to interest the reader; all their affairs are very much of the same cast as that cited above;— none of them will hold water! Their proceedings are seldom right either in law or in equity; they are not always even decent; yet they enjoy great authority and influence, as we have seen. They are destined to take a foremost part in coming history; they are the men with whom Russia has found it her supposed interest to intrigue most perseveringly; there are few of them who have not some tawdry piece of jewellery which was made at St. Petersburg. It should be remembered, too, that they are the men who first raised the standard of revolt in 1821, when Solomon, Archbishop of Patras, unfurled the white flag in the market-place of his archiepiscopal city. As they began, so they continued; and Churchmen appear almost as prominently as soldiers in the historical picture (yet unfinished) of the Greek war of independence.

CHAPTER LIV.

HISTORICAL ANECDOTES OF THE GREEKS AND TURKS.

IN 1770, the Empress Catherine II. sent a Russian fleet to Turkey on pretence of assisting a rising of the Greeks. The Muscovite chiefs were two vain, silly fellows, one of whom had been the leman of his mistress; their names were Theodore and Alexis Orloff. All parties were, of course, deceived. The Greeks expected the Russians would work their deliverance ; the Russians growing frightened at their reception, would have it they only came to look on. At last the Greek chief, Mavro Michali, and Alexis Orloff, came to hard words. "Vile miscreant !" cried the Russian with great contempt. "Miscreant !" shrieked the Greek; "I am the free chief of a free nation,—through my veins runs the red blood of the Medici ; but thou, thou—thou art but the slave of a——" It is needless to say that neither party would have anything to do with the other, after this edifying dispute. The fact was, also, that neither could by any means consent to hear the truth.

The Prince de Ligne tells us that the Empress Catherine and Joseph the Second of Austria were talking with delightful flightiness and vivacity about the partition of Turkey, when a courier arrived announcing the revolt of Brabant.

Potemkin is said to have pushed on a war with Turkey in 1787, in order that he might obtain the decoration of St. Alexander Newski ; the real objects of diplomatists, however, seem to have been nearly always the same : by-and-by, I suppose, sensible folk will begin to look after them better. M. de Pouqueville supposes, that had Catherine carried her plans into execution, "they would have only ended in a Russian paper currency ;" luckily, however, she got angry with the King of Prussia, and gave them up. How little the world alters !

When the first republic was declared in France, the wise men of the East could not, for the lives and souls of them, understand what the word "republic" meant. After mature consideration, however, supposing it to be a species of Sultan on a new plan, the sages agreed to acknowledge the Gallic monarch Réboublika, on condition that he should not marry a princess of the house of Austria !

In 1798, the notorious and cunning savage Ali Pasha, of Janina, wrote a letter to General Buonaparte, in which he declared himself already a faithful disciple of the religion of the Jacobins; but he modestly acknowledged that he would wish to be better instructed in the worship of the Carmagnole, which he believed to be a spirit who occasioned the success of the French arms. I have taken these anecdotes from M. de Pouqueville, a French historian, well informed on some subjects.

The following chips are also historical :—

Turkish Definition of Sagacity.

Employ all means of help against an enemy, even that of an Ant.

Turkish Moral Reflection.

Even water may be kept still, but envy is quiet never.

Another.

He who has the power of inflicting pain, has a right to be obeyed.—A reflection which might almost serve as a motto for a constitutional minister.

Paternal Advice in Turkey and elsewhere.

Pay your troops, and you need not think of the people: *cuncta licet Principi.*

An unanswerable Argument.

"My son," says the Amazon Khamco, "he who does not defend his patrimony, deserves to lose it ! Remember always that other men's goods only belong to them while they are strong enough to keep them; if you are stronger, their goods will belong to you."

A great Fact in 1813.

A large band of Suliote women having fought ferociously in aid of their husbands at Veternitza, refused to survive their defeat. Two hundred of them deliberately drowned themselves and their children, rather than fall into the hands of the Turks. They were wise in this choice; for some of the Suliotes falling prisoners into the hands of the infamous Ali Pasha, he impaled most of them; but one young man was first scalped, and then beaten, till he walked up and down a plank in this condition for the amusement of the conqueror.

The wise men of the East believe that there are happy and unhappy hours in life. If a person meets with an accident, therefore, they are apt to say, "He has accepted his evil." In addressing a great man, it is proper to cry out distinctly, "May your evils happen to me!" At the marriage of one Salik Bey, however, in 1817, a gipsy precipitated himself from the top of that person's house into the yard below, exclaiming, "I take the evil of my master!" and broke both his legs. Whether his doing so was merely a part of the festivities, or whether it was voluntary, I know not; but it seems he received a small pension, which so roused the envy of a Dervish, that he made the same leap and was killed. In like manner the Rayahs were accustomed to seek the favour of great people, by lying down in the ruts of the road to be crushed by their horses' hoofs or the wheels of their carriages.

Conversation between a Turkish Gentleman and his Creditor at the commencement of the present century.

T. G. You are come to ask for thirty purses?
C. Yes, lord. Behold my bill.
T. G. It amounts to ——?
C. Thirty purses: I have said it.

T. G. (*examining the paper*). Wonderful! so it does. Well, then, give me fifteen purses, and we shall be quits!

C. Quits? Mercy! Vizier, deign!

T. G. Peace! (*To his attendants*) Away with him to prison.

Reflection of T. G. to a young acquaintance standing near.—
"Thou seest, my son, what dogs these are! If I were to listen to them, I should be speedily reduced to beggary;—and only think, that very man's father hated me! If it was not for my natural gentleness of character, I should hang him!"

Acute, but one-sided Observation.

"A Rayah," says a wise man of the East, "was made to labour—and *obey*."

Excessive taxation was the immediate cause of the Greek war of independence which broke out at Patras. The people having given everything to the authorities, even their children's clothes, and finding that they were still beaten and imprisoned, went riotously to the palace of their archbishop, and threatened to burn his house if he did not insist on the liberation of a man who had been recently shut up. He did so, and the Turks yielded, but too late: the people had tasted victory, but were not appeased,—they seldom are under such circumstances; and Germanos was soon metamorphosed from a prelate to a soldier. He was a fine fiery man, with a long black beard, and when he raised the Greek flag in the market-place of Patras, he is said to have looked very well in that position,—in short, like "a grand *tableau vivant*" at a suburban theatre. I do not speak of him with more respect; for he was as coarse, quarrelsome, and vulgar a rioter as could be: he accused Colocotroni (one of the bravest of the Greek chiefs) of pilfering the public plunder. "Priest!" screamed Colocotroni—for no Greek will bear to be taxed with his profession—"return to the altar, or dread my anger!" "Soldier, and hunter of men," replied the bishop, who had begun both the immediate row and the general revolution, "tremble thyself! If a drop of the blood of a minister of religion be shed, there will flow plenty of yours." Colocotroni *was* frightened at this: he liked threatening very well when he was the threatener; but there was something disagreeable about being menaced by a priest in the secrets of destiny. Demetrius Ypsilante (with his bald head and spectacles), who was always busy, tried to re-establish peace between the belligerent bishop and the pallid *brave;* but in vain. Germanos saw his advantage and pressed it. Edifying as this scene must have been, however, it was nothing to those which passed subsequently.

A great number of idle persons from all countries set out to join the Greek war, in the expectation of making their fortunes; for their minds were brimful of the splendours of the East; they were, therefore, sufficiently disgusted with the real state of affairs. The Senate was composed of a few dingy-bearded old persons, who gave themselves long-winded titles, and wrangled from morning till night. The army were a few baggy-breeched peasants with rusty guns, who were skulking about the hills without shoes or stockings; they were timid or rash, according as they were urged by the needs of hunger or otherwise; they slept in the dried-up beds of torrents, or on the warm side of a rock; they were worn out with fear, fever, famine, and nakedness; they insisted on making processions in order to take towns, and singing nasal hymns instead of marching to fight; and they saw visions and dreamed dreams, such as would put the most robust belief to the proof. On the other hand, the knights errant from Western Europe were at once eager for their own interests, and excited by verses of the Iliad and Odyssey, which each pronounced after his own fashion: they were astounded, therefore, at the state of the wretches, "eaten up with slavery and leprosy," who called themselves Greeks.

Glorious War.

The Turks, who had a pleasant wit, were wont to call their military operations in Greece "Christian hunting!" The Sultan, however (Mahmoud II.), was still more emphatic; he told the Capitan Pasha to "*calcine* the Island of Hydra, and bring him the dust." The dervishes, and other religious persons of the Mohammedan persuasion, were accustomed to dance about in the camp, in a great state of excitement, and crying out, "Exterminate! Exterminate! It is Allah, the Prophet, and the Sultan who command! Hoo-ooh! O-ooh! Ho-ooh!" The population of the Island of Chios was 94,000 before it roused the wrath of the Turks; it was reduced to 900 afterwards; everybody else had been butchered or sold, with the exception of a very few, who were hopeless fugitives. After this we must not be surprised that one of the Sultan's titles of honour is that of Khoun Kiar; or, The Slayer! The storming of Galaxidi is said to have given a good idea of hell.

Pleasant.

"Soldiers!" writes the Russian minion Ypsilante to the dupes he had basely deserted, "soldiers,—no; I will not sully so fine and honourable a name by applying it to you! Vile herd of slaves! your wiles and treachery compel me to abandon you; henceforth all connection between us is broken; I shall only carry at the bottom of my heart the shame of having commanded you! You have violated your oaths; you have betrayed your God and your country; you have also betrayed me, just *as I was hoping* to die or conquer with you!" I think this fellow Ypsilante was one of the most contemptible mountebanks in history; but so great were the wrongs of the Rayahs, that even he could rouse them to revolt.

A Beau's Stratagem.

Some Albanian Turks at Monembasia, desiring to hang a few Greeks, and not exactly knowing how to catch them, took counsel. One lively and sagacious warrior, who knew the Rayahs well, proposed to take them by their ruling passion, which was that of thieving. Accordingly, a cow was tied among some vines, and the animal's lowing soon brought a band of Greek braves to steal her. As they came creeping along through the underwood, the Turks, who were in ambush, sallied out, and captured thirty of them: some of these they hung; others they *spitted;* and sent to thank their companions for having furnished them with so excellent a *roast.*

There was a plane-tree at Cos, which was the delight of travellers. (The classical Pouqueville supposes it may have served as a pleasant shade to the disciples of Hippocrates—I do not.) During the punishment of a revolt at this place, the plane-tree was transformed into a gibbet, and several priests were hung upon it. This is not the only instance of a tree celebrated in that way during the glorious war we are describing. A tree near Loucouvo is still known as the Martyrs' Olive, from a family of fourteen persons having been all hanged on it at the same time.

The Jews.

The Jews took a violent part against the Greeks: one oppressed people will nearly always be found ready instruments in oppressing another. Six hundred Jews formed themselves voluntarily into a corps of executioners at Naoussa. One Jew boasted that he had personally executed sixty-four Christians in one day upon this occasion. The Jews materially assisted the Turks at the battle of Galatzitta; but the ruling passion of the chosen people seems never to desert them; and after the fight they made themselves conspicuous in collecting Greek heads, for the price set upon them by the Turkish generals. They also dragged the dead body of the intriguing patriarch Gregory, after his execution, along the streets of Constantinople. The great reformer of tailors' bills, Mahmoud the Second, went to a convenient place to see them pass by with their bloody load, amid the shouts and derision of the rabble. The Greeks, however, avenged themselves by a cruel massacre of the Jews at Tripolitza; and Colocotroni seized one, with the bitter jest, "What, armed? and a Jew? Impossible!"

A Turkish Diplomatist.

One Angelo, who had been a long time Turkish ambassador at Paris, was so badly paid, that he subsequently was fain to return to his own trade as a tobacconist at Galata. The example was unlucky; for Theodore Negris, having been appointed to succeed him, threw his letters of credence into the sea, and joined the Greek rebels, who immediately appointed him to a wonderful employment, in a bran new experimental government, got up for the occasion. I do not know, however, that he was of much advantage to them, save that he could speak French, and used a knife in eating.

Amazons.

The Suliote women, some of whom we have before mentioned, played a great part in the Greek war of independence. These ladies were not like the golden-footed dames of William of Tyre, who rode to the Crusades upon snow-white palfreys, and with gilded swords. They were a set of stout tawny-cheeked viragoes, armed with slings, who were rather more than in earnest in what they were about. On one occasion, they took seventy-two prisoners, and massacred every one. A certain Miss Mavroyeni, who also formed one of the party, kicked the severed head of a chief with her own feet, crying "Honour to the brave! Victory to the cross!" with other observations to the like effect. They used to carry about refreshments and ammunition in battle with "*une sollicitude enchanteresse*" (says a French writer). They also carried off the wounded to the mountains. They are said to have had voices like the sound of trumpets, and to have fought like furies. At Samoniva they formed a regiment of four hundred and fought in regular order of battle.

Here are some pleasing thoughts :—

Confession of an Elderly Gentleman.

"Alas, my son, I have spilt so much blood, that the red tide follows me about, and I dare *not look behind me!*"

A Sister's Whim.

"I will give thee neither the title of Vizier nor brother, if thou dost not keep the oath thou sworest by the dead body of our mother. If thou art the son of Khamco, it is thy duty to destroy Cadiki, to exterminate its inhabitants, and to place the women and maidens in my power, to dispose of them as I please. *I will never sleep on any mattresses but such as are filled with their hair!*"

Oriental Etiquette.

The heads of persons shortened by order of the Sultan, were salted and taken to Constantinople, to be exhibited for three days to the view of the people. The head of a Vizier, or Pasha with three tails, was exposed on a silver dish, and placed on a marble column; that of a minister, or Pasha with two tails, on a wooden platter under an archway; those of common people were thrown unceremoniously on the ground. In like manner the bodies of Mussulmen were buried by the executioners, lying on their backs, and with their heads under their arms. Christians were laid dishonourably on their bellies with their heads behind them.

Delicate Food.

Previous to a battle, the Turks gave their soldiers a red pilaff, which was boiled with tomatoes to colour it. This was in commemoration of a saying of one of the wise men of the East: "I will give you the flesh of your enemies to devour, and I will slake your thirst with their blood." This banquet is said to have powerfully exalted the imagination of the eaters, and to have rendered them capable of a great variety of things.

A Mohammedan Discovery.

Bal: iemez top. Cannons do not eat honey.

Thankful Guests.

A band of Turks meeting with a sort of hermit, who entertains them hospitably, ask him who he is. The monk replies by stating his religious convictions. "Why, it is a dog of a friar!" cry the Turks, and pistol him accordingly.

Glorious War again.

Part of the Greek prisoners were the property of the executioner who was put to murder the rest; sometimes he allowed them to ransom themselves, sometimes he sold, sometimes he kept them as slaves, sometimes habit was too strong for him, and he "shortened them," according to the expressive phraseology in use on such occasions.

Great Men.

It used to be the custom of persons appointed to considerable offices in Turkey, to keep a *shroud* always by them, never knowing when they might want it.

Effects of Cannon.

When the Greeks got accustomed to the sound of the Turkish guns, they are said to have taken pleasure in hearing it. They awaited the opening of a cannonade even with impatience, and watched where the balls fell, to pick them up for their own use by-and-by. This does not say much, however, for the Turkish Artilleryman.

Crowning Glory of War.

The harem of Khourchid Pasha, Governor of Epirus, were taken prisoners in one of the glorious events of this glorious war of Greek Independence. When at last they were restored every lady was in the family-way.

Finally, let us say, however, with old Herodotus, οὕτω δὴ οὐκ Ἀργείοισι αἴσχιστα πεποίηται. Ἐγὼ δὲ ὀφείλω λέγειν τὰ λεγόμενα, πείθεσθαί γε μὲν ὦνού παντάπασι ὀφείγω, καί μοι τοῦτο τὸ ἔπος ἐχέτω ἐς πάντα τὸν λόγον. I don't know whether the devil is as black as he is painted, I merely print from somebody else's picture.

This I know also, that whatever war may be, it is quite as well to have a peep behind the scenes beforehand, just for curiosity-sake, and in order that the services of its promoters and the gentlemen of their way of thinking may receive the meed of our enthusiastic and undying gratitude. They have, indeed, rung the prompter's bell, and raised the curtain of a theatre which had been closed for a few years. The least we can do is to clap our hands and huzzah!

Orientals do not want for a certain sententious wit, often pungent enough even in war time. A wise man of the East told Bayazid, that if he would spare a certain town in Asia Minor, where the wise man lived, he, the wise man, would be able to present the conqueror with a talking camel in six months or be prepared to suffer the extremest effects of his anger. On being reproached with so rash an offer, he replied,—

"In six months Bayazid, I, or the camel, will be dead, and we have at all events escaped present disaster. Delay is the friend of the unfortunate."

The Arab general, Heggiage, a famous captain, who served under the Caliphs Abdul-Melek and Valid, once met a poor man by the road-side.

"Who is this fellow Heggiage, about whom you talk so much in this country?" asked the egotistical chief.

"A cruel, savage fellow," answered the man.

"Do you know him?" quoth the general.

"No."

"Do you know me?"

"No."

"Well, then, learn that I am Heggiage," pursued the general with a sinister smile.

"But do you know me?" asked the poor man, now anxious to continue a conversation which had suddenly become so interesting.

"No," answered Heggiage.

"I am of the race of Zobeir," replied the man, "whose descendants are mad three days in every year; *this is one of the three.*"

The soldier smiled.

Few people appear to have paid more homage to poetry than the Caliphs. It is on record that they frequently pardoned the most atrocious criminals who sued to them in verse. An individual presented a poetical complaint to the Caliph Moavias, stating that the Governor of Couffah had carried off his wife.

The charmed Moavias wrote at once to that officer, requesting him to give her up; but the Governor replied, that if the Caliph would only permit him to keep the woman for a year, he would consent to lose his head.

The Caliph, interested by so amazing a reply, sent for the lady, and asked her which she liked best, her husband or her ravisher. Aware of his weakness, she cast down her eyes thoughtfully, and the Caliph politely apologized for having asked her so delicate a question. The beauty, however, was only considering how to string together a verse, which should sufficiently express her lawful love for her husband. The Caliph was enchanted on hearing it, and immediately re-joined the faithful pair, who lived happily ever afterwards.

The Caliph Mahidi appears to have been a sensible man, though somewhat of an oddity. Somebody once brought him a slipper, which was said to have belonged to Mahomet: the Caliph received the precious relic with every token of respect, and rewarded the bearer with much magnificence. He was not deceived, however; and turning to his staff, observed sagaciously,—

"Mahomet probably never saw this slipper; but the people believe it to be his, and it is always wise to avoid scandal."

It is recorded of the same Caliph that one day he entered a peasant's hut and asked for wine. When he had drunk a mighty draught, he told his host that he was a courtier; after having drunk deeper he said he was the Caliph, before whom all the world fell prostrate. Upon this the peasant immediately concealed his pitcher of wine; the Caliph asked him if he had done so from shame at having forbidden liquor in his house.

"Oh no!" said the man dryly, "but I am afraid, if you drink again, you may become the Prophet, or perhaps even Allah himself!"

Mahomet was to the full as singular a personage as any of his successors. After each of his victories he had the remarkable habit of hopping seven times round the square tower of Mecca, which was called the Caaba. He gave out a new chapter of the Koran every time anything turned up which required explanation. Thus one was added to countenance adultery with his slave's wife; another to sanctify the seduction of his captive Mary; and the third concerning the charge of infidelity against Ayesha. A Jew and a Christian monk assisted him in these singular compositions; and it was from them that the saintly smack of the Koran is chiefly derived.

The remote cause of the Prophet's death is curious. After the taking of Kaïbar, he lodged in the house of one Hareth, an inhabitant thereof. This man had a daughter named Zainab, who was of an acute and philosophical disposition: she was induced, therefore, to poison her famous lodger, by a train of reasoning at once forcible, concise, and Oriental.

"If he be really an Apostle of God," argued the damsel, "poison will not harm him; if not, the world is well weeded of a rogue." She poisoned him adroitly in a shoulder of mutton, and he lived but three years afterwards, labouring constantly under the effects of the drug she had administered to him.

Perhaps the best thing we know of Mahomet, a prophet who certainly does not improve on acquaintance, is what he said of Cadijah, the elderly widow whom he married for her money.

"Was she not old?" said Ayesha, with the insolence of a blooming beauty. "Has not Heaven given you a better in her place?"

"No, by God!" said Mahomet, with an effusion of honest gratitude; "there never can be a better! She believed in me when men despised me; she relieved my wants when I was poor and persecuted by the world."

Women have played a considerable part in the fearful drama of Eastern history. Mahomet was wounded and beaten by some Arab Jews near Mecca; their chief was Abu Sofian, a personal enemy of the Prophet. They were a wild and barbarous horde, but the men were angels compared to the women. Thus when Hamsa, the uncle of Mahomet, perished in fight against them, Heudah, the wife of Aba Sofian, tore open his body with her nails and devoured his liver.

Caulah, a young Arab woman, also took a prominent position in some of the early Moslem wars. On one occasion she defended her virtue with a tent-peg, and banding with some other viragoes repulsed and utterly routed a company of mailed Greek knights who were sent against them.

Oriental women were also nearly as busy in politics as in battle. The Caliph Moavias was enabled to succeed Hassan, the grandson of the Prophet, solely by the ingenious device of persuading the Caliph's wife to poison him : the Caliph Moavias carried his object by a promise of marriage, which he did not mean to keep. This event seems to show a more unrestrained intercourse between the sexes in ancient times than that which exists now. The manner also in which Mahomet first saw the wife of his slave, shows considerable intimacy in each other's houses among the lights of the new religion.

The Caliph Mahidi was poisoned by a beautiful slave, who *pricked a pear* for him with a poisoned needle.

Soliman the Second had two wives, who were the plague of his life. One was the famous *Roxalana;* the Roxalana of all sorts of operas, and plays without end. The occupation of this amiable lady appears to have been chiefly that of poisoning her rival's children, and she was very clever at it.

After the taking of Nicosia, the Turks sent a cargo of ladies to the Sultan ; among them was Arnande, a daughter of the Count of Rocas. The choice was unfortunate, for she fired the vessel in which she was placed, and blew herself and her companions to atoms.

It is distressing to find that our old story-book friend, the Caliph Haroun al Raschid, was by no means a respectable man ; he fell in love with his sister Abassah, grew naughtily jealous of her, murdered her husband for doing his duty by her, and reduced her to beggary for having loved her lord. He almost exterminated the harmless Barmecides, whose name had become another word for virtue, and made it death to speak of their goodness. One man who disobeyed this order was summoned for punishment ; but he defended his conduct so well, that Haroun gave him a plate of gold. On receiving it he showed a rare example of consistency, by crying out,—

" O ye Barmecides ! how shall I cease to bless you, when lo ! here is another of your endless benefits !"

The Caliph tried hard to tarnish even their memory; but his worst efforts were in vain. In the flowing language of the East, it was said "that the world was as a bride to them, so they loved it; when they died, the world was widowed."

The origin of the name of Barmecides is curious. In the year 721 an illustrious Persian took refuge at the court of the Caliph Soliman at Damascus. The Oriental legends say that when he was presented to the Caliph, two precious stones, which the Caliph wore in a bracelet, changed colour, thus indicating that the guest carried poison about with him. The Caliph taxed him with it; and he replied that, having long feared an infamous and cruel death, he had concealed within a ring a poison so acute, that he had only to put it to his lips and die. As he expressed the action of sucking by the Persian word "Barmek," he acquired a nickname, and his family were called Barmecides. Haroun al Raschid was by no means the most ferocious of the early Mohammedans. Omar found out a new way to pay old debts by tying insolvent individuals to a tree, where he left them exposed to the fierce heats of the sun, till they found money—or died.

The Caliph Motavakel (A.D. 855) also invented an ingenious punishment: it consisted in thrusting people into an oven filled with spikes, and then heating it gradually. Being a prince also of a philosophical turn of mind, he was accustomed to ask a few friends to dinner, in order that they might be bitten by venomous reptiles, brought into his palace for the purpose. When they were taken very ill, he tried his medical skill to cure them; sometimes he presented them to a new guest in the person of a hungry lion: once he amputated the hands of a whole company. He was fortunately cut in small pieces at last by his son, to whom he had given the agreeable nickname of Mouthader, signifying one who waits for the death of his father.

The Caliph Caher hanged his mother up by the heels, to make her confess where she had hidden her money.

There is a story that Timurlenk shut up his prisoner Bayazid in a cage, only using him occasionally as a footstool to mount on horseback. It is said also that he tied his hands behind him, and made him eat with the dogs under the table, while his naked wife served the conqueror.* Gibbon and others have discredited this story, but it does not appear so improbable, and it is certain that since the time of Bayazid the Sultans have never married, lest their wives should be exposed to captivity and insult.

Mahomet the Second cut off the heads of the Greek citizens who brought him their wealth, after the taking of Constantinople, saying, "That would teach them to hoard their gold during the distresses of their Prince." He also decapitated the beautiful Irene, to appease a tumult of the soldiery, who complained that he spent too much time with her. He murdered Anna, daughter of Paul Erizzo, for declining his addresses.

Mahomet the Third put ten of his father's concubines, who were with child, to death, immediately on his succession. He had nineteen brothers, and murdered them all.

Amurath the Fourth had a pleasant way of entertaining himself, by hooking people up by the side, and leaving them hanging till they died. He made it a crime to avoid his blows, and the gates of Constantinople were closed for two days to catch a gentleman who had been guilty of this enormity. Somebody announced to him that one of his wives had given birth to a son; when the child was found out to be a daughter, that somebody was immediately impaled. He was especially the scourge of doctors; one of that class having talked learnedly respecting the properties of opium, the sage was requested to gratify his Highness's curiosity by taking some; the Sultan then watched him die with much interest and satisfaction. He disposed also in a very effective way of persons who liked tobacco, by breaking their arms, skinning, and then splitting them up.

It is not surprising, after this, to learn that people used to feel if their heads were still on their shoulders, after quitting his presence. All history is bloody and shocking enough; but Eastern history is unspeakably horrible.

* Another story represents Timurlenk as rather a jolly fellow, who was accustomed to dine a good deal with his captive. On one occasion, it is added, the conqueror asked Bayazid, with a burst of laughter, "if he had never been surprised at a freak of fortune which had chosen two such fellows as them to govern the world,"—*utrum horum mavis accipe.*

CHAPTER LV.

A SON OF THE DESERT.

I WILL relate an anecdote, which has the rather unusual advantage of being true, and which sets forth in the most agreeable manner that charming simplicity and good faith which is generally understood by enlightened people to belong, in a peculiar manner, to the children of nature.

I am glad to have it in my power to chronicle so interesting and delightful an occurrence ; indeed, I feel that it quite eases my mind, and in a manner does me good to do so. I do not, therefore, stipulate for the gratitude of an amiable public, having already enjoyed sufficient reward and satisfaction, to compensate for almost any amount of pen-and-ink occupation, on so inspiring a subject. I simply trust, with a perhaps pardonable vanity, that I may some day receive a slight testimonial from the admirers of the late Mr. J. J. Rousseau, for having confirmed their admiration of uncultivated minds, by adding the beam of an uncontested fact to support the gorgeous fabric of his beautiful theories.

A short time ago, therefore, to begin my narrative, his Imperial Royal Apostolic Majesty, the Emperor of Austria, despatched an officer of high rank in his military service, to procure an Arab horse of the true breed ; and the favoured individual, honoured by command from so august a quarter, immediately set off for Egypt, in order to accomplish the negotiation on which he was employed.

He found, of course, that a special embassy on the part of Russia to the Sultan of Dahomey would not have presented a tithe of the difficulty which he had to encounter ; "for," said everybody to whom he applied, "the fact is, there are no longer any Arab horses of the true breed. No man dare possess one, as the spies of the local governors are everywhere, and it would be infallibly taken from him, for, perhaps, a hundredth part of its value."

" Indeed," added the most honest of his informants, "plenty of people will bring you horses, with pretended pedigrees as long as your arm, or longer if you wish it ; but their words are merely a delusion and a snare. Such a thing as a real Arabian horse is not to be obtained for love or money."

However, this Austrian officer, awfully arrayed, was by no means to be discouraged, and at once plunged boldly into the desert, for the purpose of ascertaining if there yet did not linger here and there, in some distant encampment, one of the beautiful animals of which he was in search. In order to travel with greater safety, he shaved his head (that head which had been the delight of the Prater and the Volks Garten) and dressed himself in the clothes of an Oriental, though his friends are free to confess that he looked remarkably odd in them.

Horses enough were brought to him, sometimes as many as three or four daily ; but they all had hind quarters like those of a goose, and low shoulders. The free riders of Austria and Hungary would have laughed him to scorn if he had brought one of these cross-bred brutes home as the result of his journey. He had just begun to despair, therefore, when a howling Dervish, with whom he had recently been on terms of the most affectionate intimacy, gave him news, that at some extremely out-of-the-way place, there actually was an Arabian mare of the rarest breed and beauty. Having conveyed this information to the disguised Austrian, he promptly asked for a consideration, after the custom of his country. The officer agreed to give it, but on condition that he should be taken to see the mare. The Dervish remonstrated, however, about this, and alleged, reasonably enough, that it was not usual in the East to expect any service from a person who desired a reward ; but the Austrian being penetrated with the importance of his mission, which he now believed to be upon the eve of its accomplishment, persisted in a determination which appeared so extraordinary to the Dervish, and absolutely would not buy the mare's nest, which the reverend man had offered to him.

So the Dervish went upon his way; but having in the end bethought him that the money promised by the stranger would be an extremely convenient addition to his means, returned a day or two afterwards, and agreed to conduct his eccentric friend to the Arab who owned the wonderful mare. Upon this, the Austrian gave him a present, and the Dervish, who had not calculated on such imprudent confidence being placed in him, showed the very strongest desire to decamp; but his paymaster held him fast, and he was at last reluctantly induced to perform his promise—an event which had probably never before occurred to him.

After many days' journey, the travellers arrived at the tents which contained the object of their search; but when the Arab chief heard the reason for which they came, he laughed them to scorn, and said at once that he would sooner sell wife, children, and friends, ten times over, than part with his mare.

"Sell my mare to you!" he continued, in a state of the wildest amazement; "why, I would not even let you *see* her!"

"Thy servants have already seen her," quoth the Dervish, who by no means hesitated to exercise a diplomatic economy of the truth. "Lo! my friend, also thy guest, is a Weelee, and if you will not sell the mare to him, yet let him fasten round her neck an amulet or talisman, to guard her from all mischief."

The Arab was not proof against such an inducement, and, finally, admitted them to the honour of an interview with his mare, taking good care to burn alum in the stable, while they were looking at her, as a precaution against the evil eye. When they came out, also, he required them to cry "Mashallah!" and to bless the Prophet for the same purpose.

Finding that the Arab resolutely refused to enter into further negotiations with him, and determined not easily to relinquish the hope of obtaining a prize, in pursuit of which he had absolutely consented to shave his head, the Austrian envoy established himself only a few days' journey from the Arab encampment, and determined to wait upon fortune, and ply the Sheik as vigorously as possible through the Dervish.

This plan succeeded admirably. The wily diplomatist had not been long in his new lodging, when one fine morning the owner of the mare called upon him, and occasioned him equal delight and surprise by offering to sell his horse, without even the seven or eight hours' wrangling which is usually considered indispensable for the transaction of the smallest business in the East.

The Austrian closed with the bargain, paid up like a gentleman, and received his treasure. The Arab wished him good luck as he did so, with a smile that amply testified the mutual nature of their satisfaction.

The Imperial, Royal, Apostolic officer was still enjoying his exultation, when his friend the Dervish approached him, with a mien so mysterious, that it was plain the saintly man's mind was burthened with some matter of importance.

"Attest the unity!" said the Dervish, greeting his friend.

"By all means," replied the Austrian, who was not very well up in his part as an amateur Mohammedan, and therefore did not give the usual reply, made and provided in such cases.

"I extol the absolute glory of him who is all-knowing, with respect to secret things!" continued the Dervish, stroking his beard, and looking more intensely important than ever. "How much did your generosity give for the mare?"

The Austrian replied that he had given a sum equal to nearly £400 sterling of our money.

"And how much will you give to keep her?" pursued the saintly man.

The conversation was growing interesting; but the Austrian was fairly puzzled.

"Know, then," continued the Dervish, with great complacency, "that the ingenuous man who sold you the mare would not really consent to give her up on any terms whatever. He has, indeed, brought her to you, in order to obtain the amount of tribute, which is now being required of him with unusual severity by the government; but he has the firmest intention of retrieving his irreparable loss this very night. He is as a bitter colocynth, a viper, and a calamity throughout the desert!" added the Dervish, his cheek glowing with a generous envy, as he pronounced these laudatory epithets on the Arab; "and you must lose the mare unless I aid you. Will you give me ten pieces of gold if I do so?"

The Austrian having complied with these terms, now learned that his only chance of retaining his prize was in the most immediate flight. Running away was not exactly in accordance with his previous military habits; but he had really no choice upon the subject; so he and the Dervish set off with great alacrity.

It was well they lost no time about going; for they had not ridden far, when they found the whole country was aroused and pursuing them. At last, however, after many hours' riding, in which they owed their escape solely to the speed of their horses, they arrived among a tribe of Arabs who were hostile to their pursuers, and, what was still more fortunate, stronger. The chief with whom they sought refuge agreed to protect them as long as they remained with him, but would not answer for them or the mare when they left. The fame of the mare, he added, was known everywhere, and the chief who had sold her would neither spare blood nor trouble to get her back. So the Austrian, taking counsel with the Dervish, prevailed on him to go forward alone, and ask an escort from the chief authorities sufficiently strong to enable him to convey his prize to Cairo in safety. The Dervish promised to do so; and it is a remarkable thing to relate that he kept his word.

The Austrian, however, had still difficulties enough; his Arab host assured him that, with the most friendly intentions, he would be unable to prevent any of his people yielding to the temptation of horse-stealing, if they could find an opportunity; and the only manner in which he could offer him the least chance of preserving her, was by fastening one part of an iron chain round her neck, and the other part round his own waist, then picketing her carefully, and sleeping beside her; even thus protected, however, he must sleep lightly, or the Arabs would inevitably file away the chain and carry her off in triumph.

One may judge that the imperial and royal envoy did not pass his time in a very amusing manner under such circumstances; but he held on, and at last the escort came and he departed with it. His troubles, however, were not quite over; for while the mare was being led through the streets, somebody fired at her from a window, and the ball passed through her clothing, though without wounding her. Search was made for the delinquent, and he was found out to be our old acquaintance the Dervish! "Why didst thou do this thing?" was asked of him when he was brought before the authorities.

"It is written that thou shalt not make friendship with the Franks, lest thou be considered of them," said the Dervish, sententiously, quoting the Koran. "I discovered this man to be a Frank, after I had given him aid and counsel. Woe is me! I had sinned; but the gates of repentance were open, and I passed through." These amiable and affecting sentiments being really to be found in the sacred volume above mentioned, the Dervish left the court with all the honours, and the Austrian officer returned, let us hope, to receive the thanks of his sovereign, after having merited them so well among the simple and artless children of the desert.

CHAPTER LVI.

CONSULAR FREAKS.

THE Foreign Ambassador has happily a very great deal of power just now in Dahomey; why, or how, or which, or wherefore, nobody seems very clearly to understand. The infallibility of his Excellency has become one of the beliefs of the age: he is a sublime mystery; he is fearfully and wonderfully made; he is the only ambassador now going on the face of the earth; he is his own prophet; he is an effulgent wonder; he is the unknown man; he is the Mrs. Harris of diplomacy; he is the spirit of red tape made perfect: a man cannot look upon him and dine; a woman cannot behold him and speak! Turkey is his—his birthright—the spoil of his pen and inkstand! Sultan, pipe-sticks, pashas, primates, and effendis are the slaves of his will; their business is to bow down before him,—they have nothing else to do in life,—they should leave the rest to him; all they have to do is to come when they are called, and to veil their eyes in the presence. The world, generally, is recommended to conduct itself on the same principle.

With allied armies constantly about to march for Turkey, his Radiance is not only always, and at all times, "the coming man," but he is also the present man, and the man who was. No person has the smallest right to use any of the tenses of the verb to be in the first person; his *genius* has seized upon them; they have become the property of his *greatness* by right of prescription: ministers of foreign affairs, commanders-in-chief, admirals, and other persons who are allowed to gaze on his splendour at a respectful distance, are commanded to bear this in mind. In a word, his Magnificence is king, lords, commons, and clergy at Stamboul. It is a glorious charter—deny it who can—to live in the imposing shadow of his very remark-

A A

able countenance: the land of Turkey enjoys the rapturous bliss of living in this shadow: this is why things generally are in such a marvellous state of perfection there: this is the real reason why Turkey overfloweth with milk and honey, whilst the inhabitants thereof are accustomed to pass the golden hours of their perennial spring in music and dancing, with all manner of rejoicings. They have no care for to-morrow, or for the day after, neither for the day after that; since, wherever the Ambassador may be, there is the true Tom Tiddler's ground: and is not he the perpetual resident, protector, and patron of happy Islam?

Among those blissful and highly-favoured mortals who are stationed here and there throughout this unworthy world, to carry out the diplomatic philosophy, and bear the blessings of this amiable reign of their sovereign to those benighted places to which the light of his august presence is denied, are the foreign consuls and consular agents throughout the Ottoman dominions; it is what is familiarly termed a "good time" for these gentlemen, with foreign fleets in Ottoman seas and foreign armies in Ottoman lands. With Britannia led blindfold by the wise man of Bickerstaffe, and smiling benignly on Turkey—her new acquaintance—your foreign Consul has become a very great and remarkable apparition: I mean, of course, great with a reflected greatness, and remarkable only by a curiosity borrowed from his amazing chief.

The boast of every petty consular official over his cups, when they were deepest; the shadowy rod he has impudently held *in terrorem* over people who offended him, actually appears to have descended; the boast to be verified and backed by the armed force of thousands. Therefore, the consul and consular agent,—yea! even the deputy sub and the deputy sub-assistant, are exalted in the sight of all men.

The consuls and consular agents hold high jubilee over the "good time" which has arrived for them: they widen the borders of their garments; they lift up their voices (and sticks) haughtily in the market-place, against whosoever saith them nay; they may be known to all men by the hymn of triumph and rejoicing which is ever in their mouth: "There is but one

Ambassador now going on the face of the earth, and I am his consular agent!"—or deputy, or deputy assistant sub, as the case may be.

I will, however, proceed from general statements to the detail of a few pleasant and refreshing little facts, which have fallen more particularly under my own gratified observation. I have enjoyed so rich and ennobling a sensation while reflecting on them, that it is perhaps pardonable in me to hope that a grateful and delighted public will decree ME some distinguished honour merely as their historian.

Freak the first : a foreign subject, not very well worthy of faith, complained to his Consul of some wrong he had received, or had not received, from a Turk. He complained through his brother, the Consul's dragoman ; for the Consul, of course, did not understand him, seeing that he complained in Greek. The Consul took the truth of the complaint for granted ; how could he do otherwise ; he was, as are nine-tenths of his brethren, in the hands of his dragoman ; he had no means of inquiring into the truth of anything, save through this functionary, who was, in the present instance, a wily low-bred Greek, and, moreover, brother of the plaintiff. So the Consul honoured the local Pasha with a visit on the subject.

The Pasha was a pasha of three tails, a man of rank about on a par with that of an English duke, if any possible comparison could exist between them. To this Dahomedan dignitary the apt exponent of the consular philosophy addressed himself on his business, stick in hand. A pipe of honour was offered him, according to the custom of Dahomey; he threw it down in dudgeon—it broke—its value was thirty pounds ; and I wonder what was the local value of the Turkish pride and good feeling thrown down with it. The Consul menaced the abashed Pasha in his own house, stick in hand. He said his say—that is, the dragoman, a low, wily Greek, said the say for him. Those who know how a Greek will talk when he knows he may insult a Turk with impunity, can imagine the polite language he was likely to use very much better than I can describe it. The say being said, then the Consul strode away, with his nose very much raised in the air ; he did not wait for an answer; it was not strictly necessary to the object of his mission that he should do so. The Pasha was only too glad to comply with his request on any terms; his Excellency had the same salutary dread of an ambassador or his representative as is implanted in the breast of the Grand Vizier, or even the Sultan; he knew that complaint or remonstrance would be alike useless; they *could* only result in his immediate dismissal from office. As for a quiet half-hour's respectful and explanatory conversation with the Consul, it was of course out of the question, for neither Pasha nor Consul knew three words of the other's language.

Freak the second affords a pleasing commentary on the rights and immunities of foreign travellers in the ambassadorial dominions; and I think I may venture confidently to assume that no Briton can read of it without feeling his cheek flush with grateful pride in the cautious and prudent man who has brought about a state of things so agreeable and satisfactory to our fellow-countrymen. A traveller, in a remote part of Turkey, misconducted himself so grossly as to call for the intervention of the police. Nothing particular was done to him; he was merely brought before the Pasha, and the error of his ways was pointed out to him. Being also a Greek, who was supposed to have illegally purchased British protection, the Pasha ventured to express some doubt about his nationality; so the traveller (a small tradesman) complained to his Consul, and the policemen who were concerned in arresting him were instantly deprived of their employment.

Freak the third displays the importance of the foreign Consul, as well as the general free-and-easy tone of his proceedings, in rather an entertaining point of view.

An elderly Pasha mildly requested a Consul, who had grossly insulted him in the presence of the members of the mixed tribunal over which he was presiding, to remember that he was in the presence of a gentleman. " Pooh!" sneered the shadow of an Ambassador; "you are all rogues together." Now it is by no means improbable that the respected Consul might have been singularly exact in his estimation of the characters assembled before him while delivering this powerful sentence;

still, most of our fellow-countrymen will probably agree with me that it required some strength of mind to utter it; and they will doubtless rejoice sincerely that a foreign functionary can make known his infallible opinions with impunity, whatever may be the amount of estimable foreign bluntness with which he may be disposed to convey them.

If, however, any silly and absurd person should say we are hardly just now in a position to hector the Turks with anything like generosity or good grace, that silly and absurd critic must forget, or can never have known, that any Ambassador who makes a speech or writes a despatch remarkable for licentious intemperance of language will shortly after come to the highest honours. It is therefore but fitting and dutiful that his subordinates should keep this instructive moral ever before their eyes; and if they cannot, even in their cups, hope to imitate it, they can still try, as I am bound to say they do, with the most laudable zeal and perseverance.

I knew of one consular individual who sold passports at a fixed price ; six bankrupt traders, shoals of ignorant and roguish natives, who had obtained their posts solely with a view of bullying the Turkish authorities; several consuls with *delirium tremens*, and of one with periodical fits of insanity.

I have known men plunged in the darkest depths of ignorance holding as many as four or five European consulates, and riding rough-shod over all Turkish things in consequence. One man I met, and of whom I have before spoken, was in the enjoyment of no less than eight consulates. He had been deprived, however, some time before of British employ, for malpractices too glaring even to be tolerated in Turkey.

The local governor told me, drearily enough, that this individual at one time pretended to give official employment to no less than sixty persons, who were thereby entitled to his august protection. Each, of course, paid an annuity to his consular patron, and found it a very good business so to do, because he was thereby entitled to the privileges of a Frank, or foreign subject, and absolved from many of the taxes, duties, and burthens of his countrymen.

The usual staff, however, of each consular agent, I learned

seldom exceeds five or six nondescripts, an equal number of servants, one secretary, one chancellor, one assistant ditto, and one *captain of the port*, for *each* consulate. These officials are of course usually among the richest people in the place.

I could point out, by the dozen or by the score, similar and equally gratifying instances of our consideration and power in Turkey : I refrain from doing so, simply because I believe that there are limits even to national pride. I fear, therefore, that if I multiplied useless examples, after having proved the fact, I should only weaken the charming impression which the circumstances I have already related must have necessarily made upon an attentive public.

To understand the case, however, in all its inspiriting truth, let us for a moment entreat that public to reverse our relative positions. Let the attentive reader above mentioned suppose a Turkey consular agent—a Wapping crimp, for instance— stationed perpetually at Eel-pie Island. Fancy him personally altogether above the law, and marching about Twickenham on a Sunday, with a policeman before him to clear the way. Imagine him licensed to sell perpetual exemptions from the assessed taxes and the jurisdiction of the Central Criminal Court, also freedom from the station-house. Picture to an excited imagination a person similarly situated in every seaport and principal town of Great Britain. Fancy most of them driving rather a brisk business, especially through means of touters and servants.

Then, fancy these persons having a wonderful and cautious man, living somewhere in an extensive palace at Stamboul, venting his ill-humour habitually on the Queen ; having strong opinions in favour of the oppressed Christians in Ireland ; in frequent communication with the managing man of the Fenians, and turning yellow in the face, or writing rude letters, if called upon for the purpose of expostulation or remonstrance.

Fancy this great luminary refusing to hear or see with his own ears and eyes, or anybody's else ; fancy him joining many newspapers in his own absurd Hallelujah—"There is but one man in the world, and I am the man ;" fancy him believing it with his whole cautious heart, shutting himself up in a pride and voluntary ignorance something similar to that of a Great Mogul. Fancy him having been for many years in power, yet disdaining and unable to understand our wishes, or conciliate the sorest of our prejudices; hating us, hating everybody round him; the very type of a "hedgehog rolled up the wrong way and tormenting himself with his prickles." Fancy this luminous man, far above human reason or comprehension in his ideas generally, unapproachable, silent, mysterious, terrible, spoken to by his familiars only with trembling lips and anxious eyes. Fancy him sincerely wondering even that the earth did not open and swallow up every heretic who did not believe in him.

Then fancy all these things a matter of universal notoriety, the table-talk everywhere between Dover and Thule; so shall you have some idea of the glorious and blissful state of Turkey governed by Lord Cacus from Downing Street.

I remember to have heard some vulgar impossible person once say, speaking of British Government appointments, that if the worst men were purposely taken and put into the best places, and the best men into the worst places, the distribution of offices could be hardly more regrettable than it now is. He said that our embassies and consulates, instead of being regular lighthouses of information in foreign countries, are often mere strongholds and lurking-places of some of the worst abuses that have disgraced the worst governments in the worst times. My contemptible informant added, that he could number the exceptions on his fingers where he had not found these officials arrogant, pretentious, and incapable; he said that these were sometimes the most venial of their bad qualities. "I believe (added this absurd person)—and I cannot wonder at it, considering how the appointments have been hitherto bestowed—that the British consular service is even more inefficient than our diplomacy; I believe it is bringing our name daily into shame and abhorrence in many places; I believe, especially in the Levant, that it is hourly undoing much that the wise and temperate conduct of some few real statesmen has been trying so nobly and earnestly to effect." But I have said that this individual was a vulgar and impossible person, so that his opinions can matter little.

CHAPTER LVII.

ARMY INTERPRETERS.

SEVERAL refreshing anecdotes, illustrative of the high standard of capacity attained by our army interpreters in Turkey, are now in brisk circulation, and supply an unfailing fund of entertainment at the dinner-tables of Sebastopol and elsewhere. I have been favoured with a few which have recently made the most agreeable sensation, and I will proceed to transcribe them, in order that the general satisfaction existing among us regarding the progress of Eastern affairs, may be thereby increased to a state of more invigorating delight.

A band of worthy Mohammedans recently fell in with a portion of the British army; it was not a prudent thing for them to do; but being Turks, they relied on the general report about a recent friendship having sprung up between their nation and ours, which may be true; unluckily, however, they interpreted this report according to their own ideas, and believed our friendship for them to be based upon a more intimate acquaintance than it turned out to be. In consequence of this erroneous supposition on their parts, they advanced to meet the portion of the British army above mentioned with the utmost confidence and cordiality. What, then, was their horror at being mistaken for Russians, and promptly made prisoners, in spite of their most energetic remonstrances. It appeared, on subsequent inquiry, that these stupid people actually could not speak English, and therefore the army interpreter present could not make out what they meant, and naturally imagined that their noisy expostulations were intended for a defiance of the banner under which he had the happiness (and emolument) of serving. He stated this conviction upon his part, and the improper spirit reported to exist was promptly put down in the manner we have related. The prisoners thus captured remained some time under confinement before their nationality and amicable intentions were made known by accident to their captors, who, of course, were not a little annoyed at thus losing a subject of glorification, which had already formed the matter of several painfully spelled despatches, forwarded to head-quarters. However, the affair occasioned a good deal of sparkling conversation, and gave birth to a joke of Cornet Lord Martingale's, which has quite made his reputation as a wit in the aristocratic regiment to which be belongs : " We always shut up turkeys towards Christmas," said his lordship ; " it makes them fatter for killing." The point of the young peer's jest, however, was partly broken off by the haggard appearance of the prisoners, who, having had nothing but salt pork served to them, had supported themselves merely on the bread which was given with it, according to a regulation, which the interpreter had a dim idea was somehow or other connected with their religious tenets.

Another anecdote, which has tended a great deal to enliven the monotony of the besieged, has been good-naturedly afforded them by the capture of an English officer's groom, a Turk from Broussa. He had been so silly as to stray from his master, and shortly after falling in with some British soldiers, he was handled rather roughly by them ; being taken to the camp, he was thence sent up to Constantinople, and lodged in the Bagnio, where he now is. The gist of this joke is, that the absurd fellow not only could not speak English, but absolutely did not know a word of French, which might have saved him in the present case at once! The interpreter was, therefore, naturally of opinion that the man was a Russian spy, or some person equally disreputable, and thus occurred the pleasant little accident related. There is an idle story that the man has been induced, by some intriguing and mischievous person, to set up a preposterous claim for indemnity, and also for some arrears of wages, which appear to have been due to him at the time of his capture. I trust, however, that so disagreeable an incident will not turn up to check the cheerful flow of merriment the story has hitherto occasioned, both among besiegers and besieged. It would be hard, indeed, if we had to suffer in purse in consequence of efforts so benevolent and charitable, to beguile the unavoidable tedium we have been obliged to inflict upon the Russians by our warlike attitude.

While gossiping upon subjects so grateful to our national feelings, and creditable to our sympathies with the brave men to whom we are opposed, I cannot refrain from adverting to a lively little story which has also tended much to raise the spirits of our allies, and heighten the warm feelings of affection with which we are naturally regarded by the Turks. During a recent engagement it is pleasantly said that the followers of the Prophet displayed rather unusual agility in running away. On being rallied on this subject the following day, the Turkish commander stated that he had retreated so precipitately in consequence of the orders which had been conveyed to him, by signs, through an officer, who appeared to have been despatched to him in great haste for that purpose. He had at once shown his readiness to act upon the commands he had received, however much they might be in contradiction to his own previous intentions, and he had done so. The reply of the Mussulman has been universally received with a perfect concert of laughter.

No right-minded person can reflect, without a decent enthusiasm, on the exquisite discrimination which has hitherto guided our appointments in the East. The harmless and amiable character of most of the gentlemen (not employed in our diplomatic relations with the Porte) must be a subject of endless and joyful contemplation to our noble and enlightened nation; and when we think how, and by whom, some of the most important offices are discharged, that joy must infallibly be raised into wonder and awe.

One of the chief interpreters of the British army, now arrayed in an imposing position before the most splendid of the Russian possessions in the Black Sea, is a gentleman who for some time carried on the scientific profession of a travelling physician, who roamed from land to land at his own expense, and practised in the proudest defiance of the written rules of the vain art, to which we subscribe in Britain. He was himself his own College of Physicians and Apothecaries' Hall ; though probably originally of humble birth, and speaking his native tongue but imperfectly, this able man soon acquired that vast fund of terms connected with his calling, which at once pointed him out to fill the honourable and responsible post to which he was eventually named. Another of our interpreters was a sage almost equally famous; he was a German renegade, said to have been released from his allegiance to the Austrian Crown in consequence of a brief connection with M. Kossuth and his acquaintances. This ardent student appears to have pursued his studies with such energy after his nomination as army interpreter, that several of his most important manuscripts were found in the carriage of Prince Menschikoff, when that vehicle fell into the hands of the British army. These valuable compositions, however, do not appear to have occasioned that scientific glow in the bosom of our commander-in-chief which they were probably designed to arouse, and it is said that the sage has formed another in the melancholy catalogue of learned martyrs who have fallen victims to their erudition.

Some of the rest of our interpreters are wise scholars, whose qualifications were long the theme of the various distinguished visitors who have from time to time enjoyed their conversation while transacting business at the splendid bazaars of Constantinople, or wandering over the mighty structure of St. Sophia. These remarkable men, long attached to the staff of the various great Perote hotels, appear to have been miraculously inspired with the knowledge necessary to interpret for our armies ; and if they have now and then made some mistakes, the candid inquirer cannot fail to have remarked that many of the most distinguished of the cousinhood of England, who have recently arrived in Turkey with the most startling Oriental reputations, have also as frequently been staggered by the singular difference which exists between the Turkish which astounds Belgravia and May Fair, and that which is unaccountably spoken by the Turks.

Let us cast the enraptured glance of observation over the whole of that vast empire which belongs to Britain, and over which the luminary of day never ceases to cast its beams, and we shall find the same cause for mutual congratulation and patriotic pride. Our public servants, like the poets described by their great Roman colleague, are born, not made; true, we have no college for the study of Oriental languages like the dull Austrians; but lo! a race of prodigies appear to aid us by miraculous interposition in the hour of need. True, we magnanimously give our diplomatic appointments to Tweedledum and Tweedledee, but it is only to be electrified by the magnitude of the results which they achieve, and the splendour and extent of their abilities. True, the most important commands in our army and navy are given to the cousinhood of Britain, but that cousinhood has shown itself worthy of the occasion.

In taking leave, therefore, of any young gentleman who has recently entered her Majesty's service, and who may chance to cast an eye on this little eulogy of our institutions, let me affectionately warn him to avoid endeavouring to qualify himself for promotion by any vulgar arts; long studies, zeal, energy, genius—the fruit only of thoughtful and patient labour —these will inevitably stand in his way. Let him rather seek a connection with Lord Cacus, either by advertisement or adroit flattery, if he wishes really to get on; let him resolutely and perseveringly address himself to gaining the affection of some cautious place-holding family, and all these things will be given to him. Did I wish to offer one example more striking than another, I could point out the emphatic warning afforded by the fate of those silly fellows who have been applying themselves for years to the study of Oriental languages at her Majesty's embassy at Constantinople. They appear to have entertained the ridiculous idea that such a course of application would further their advancement in life; while, not very long ago, a young heaven-gifted gentleman, with a fine cautious connection, has been promoted over the heads of the whole of them.

CHAPTER LVIII.

REFORM IN TURKEY.

I THINK I was the first *—I do not speak boastingly—to point out the serious and ungenerous error of the Turkish Government, in throwing so few honourable careers open in the public service to the better class of their Christian subjects. This fault was the more glaring and mischievous, because the Mohammedan subjects of the Sultan in Europe are in a very great minority, compared with the rest, and the class so excluded necessarily became something worse than lukewarm in their patriotism and general good-feeling towards the state: they had, in fact, no country, properly so to speak; they were indifferent to successes or reverses in which they took no part; and they looked with positive aversion on a government of which they bore most of the burthens, but shared none of the honours.

A race of men was thus excluded from their fair voice in political and military matters, who are almost unexampled in activity of intellect and fertility of resource; who possess minds at once subtle and firm; and who, if they have not taken a leading part in the recent history of the world, have certainly only wanted the opportunity to do so. The military force of Turkey has been shorn of a soldiery which would have rendered foreign support needless; which has produced, even within the memory of the present generation, a Karaiskaki and a Kolokotroni, a Kanaris and a Botzaris.

The exclusion from public service in civil affairs was indeed merely a vaunting and offensive law, which by no means obtained in practice. The foreign affairs and diplomacy of the

* 1853.

Porte have been in the hands of the Greeks almost since the conquest; and the names of the Mavroyenis and Mavrocordatos of a bygone day are almost as well known in Turkish history as those of Mussurus, Trikoupi, or Aristarchi are now. Nevertheless, it is probable that the regulation which nominally excluded Christians from the civil service was not the less galling to the majority, merely from not being carried out in one or two instances. All the great pashaliks, with their subordinate officers, and all the great functionaries of the law, were exclusively Turks or renegades; in the army no Christian ever obtained a considerable command, except on the humiliating condition of renouncing his religion. Thus it happened, that even the few persons really employed in situations of responsibility were far too deeply penetrated with the wrongs of their race, to be very safe servants of a power which despised them; and at last, the injustice wrought on them did not want for a specious colouring enough; indeed, they almost invariably betrayed such trusts as were confided to them, and their relations with the Government long had the uniform end of treason on the one side, and the bowstring on the other. Men will not live quietly under grievous and degrading disabilities; able men will no more submit tamely to wrong, than armed men will to insult: the one class, however kindly, will become soured and angry; the other will strike. It is therefore with no small satisfaction I have the pleasure of recording what I trust is the beginning of the end of this injustice.

During the siege of Silistria, M. Gratzulesco, a young Wallachian gentleman of high respectability, solicited an employment in the Turkish service. After some demur, his request was granted : he was appointed to a colonelcy, and has since done the most notable good service. In the early part of the present month also (November, 1854), Prince John Caradja, son of the well-known Greek diplomatist, was appointed to a majority on the staff. He is the only Greek who has hitherto enjoyed military rank, and who has thus become personally interested in the defence and honour of the country which gave him birth. Let us hope, sincerely, that these will merely be the first names on as long a muster-roll as the necessities of Turkey may in prudence and reason require. It must be allowed, indeed, that when the Porte does do a thing, it does it handsomely! Being once resolved to give commissions to Christians, she made one a colonel and the other a major in a summary manner, which would be the delight of a dramatic writer in search of a climax more than usually brilliant. The appointments are, however, generally said to be most excellent ones; and perhaps it was as well to place them rather high up, that they might be seen the better, and that all the world may know another unwise prejudice has been swept away before the gradual enlightenment of public opinion of the East.

I think it is Swift who tells the story of a man who said the country was going to the dogs when he lost his place. We sneer at that man; yet his complaint does not want a certain gravity and importance. Persons who are not at their right post in the world are apt enough to be mischievous. We may, indeed, put them in the watchhouse, but that certainly will not quiet them, and would be but a clumsy way of mending matters, if it did. The Christians in Turkey had suffered so many wrongs, that they began to have something of the pride of sorrow; they were not averse to displaying their woes as a sort of marketable commodity: they had a very good assortment, and they sold very well. Now, however, their staple stock in this line has been taken away, and even the most persevering grievance-monger will do well to think about retiring from the business. When the Turkish civil service is entirely thrown open to Christians, as I trust it will be, the agitator's trade must be ruined at once.

Such silent reforms will do more to save the throne of the Caliphs than all the fleets and armies of the West: they will more advance the cause of civilization and progress than all the revolutions which have ever come and gone. Let the intelligent Rayah only honestly fulfil the new duties which will devolve on him; let him only show himself able and worthy to act in the enlarged sphere which is opening to him, and he may trust to time for the rest: he may wait upon events, for he is certain to find them his very good friends.

Had the Turkish Government emancipated the Christians before the war, the war might have been prevented almost in the eleventh hour; and this measure would still form the best basis of a lasting and honourable peace: it would avert the otherwise inevitable reaction which will take place against them in Europe, whenever that peace draws near: it would do away with the necessity of that overweening foreign influence under which the country absolutely writhes: it would relieve us from the lurking feeling of shame we have while supporting our new allies: it would extinguish the smouldering flame of those fierce discontents which broke out in Epirus and the Ægean last summer, and which are now only smothered, to blaze out again, perhaps, some day with irresistible fury.* Lastly, it would make the crusade mania in Russia simply ridiculous, and, as far as I can see, go a vastly long way to cut a road through the mountains of diplomatic difficulties which are rising round us every day, higher and higher, to shut out the fruitful plains of tranquillity.

One thing is quite clear: the emancipation must take place, sooner or later; therefore why not now? We can never withdraw our forces from Turkey, after having only incurred the reproach of posterity, for having, indeed, enabled her to resist an unprovoked invasion by the sacrifice of a torrent of the best and bravest blood in Britain, but having also assisted in the perpetuation of intolerable and illiberal wrong towards many millions of Christian men; our children will see but a poor defence in the only plea we could leave on record, that the Turks are bigoted and unmanageable in these respects. It is our duty to convince them of their error. Thus Robinson Crusoe would cheerfully have used his gun to prevent Friday from being eaten up; but he would have by no means allowed Friday to exercise his own appetite on a slice of roasted single gentleman after having done so. He required Friday at once to renounce the habits of his previous life as the price of his salvation: he did not for a moment take into consideration the amount of self-denial this would cost: he did not lend him his gun to go out man-hunting, and then compose a feeling apology for his having

* As they have just done in Bulgaria.

digested his neighbours merely in compliance with the prejudices of his early education. On the contrary, he most emphatically discountenanced those practices from which Friday had hitherto derived a gratification, which appeared to him so reasonable; and pointed out to him that he was under a very grave mistake. Nevertheless, his biographer does not mention that Friday had a worse opinion of Robinson on this account. It is probable that he might not at first have thought so well of a tough old goat as of a tender young lady, and might for some time have expressed a certain sense of disapprobation at seeing an aged goose on the table, when he would have preferred a baby, or a fine-flavoured single man. He appears, however, to have got reconciled to these inconveniences, and even looked upon British Robinson with the most lively affection. Now it occurs to me that there is a moral in all this, which those who run may read; and I shall be very much obliged to them for so doing.

Personally, I have not much respect for the diplomatic difficulties which are always ingeniously found by the interested parties to stand in the way of such measures as this. The best possible means of surmounting those absurd obstructions, is quietly but resolutely to ignore their existence. There are always far too many people to cry out against prudent reforms till it is too late. They court broken heads, with a diligence that reminds one of the Irishman, who dragged his coat through a fair, requesting any gentleman belligerently disposed to tread upon it. Now this is just what Turkey has been doing, and is doing. She is offering a provocation for the world to quarrel with her. Really I think it would be a good plan to insist on her picking up the coat, and going about her business. It will certainly require a greater love of shindies and knocks than most people can afford to indulge, to stand by her through all the scrapes and disgrace she is likely to get into if she does not.*

* Every one, save the wise man of Bickerstaffe, has found out these truths now; nobody in office but Lord Palmerston would learn them when this warning was written; and he had been deprived of all control over our foreign affairs by a cabal.

To conclude, the first step is everything in such matters: the principle has been now conceded, and has been found to work well; it cannot, therefore, be extended on too broad a basis. A reform so necessary and so important can hardly be too complete.

CHAPTER LIX.

HINTS TO TRAVELLERS GOING TO TURKEY.

BY all means take a macintosh, despite of Lady Mary Wortley Montague's dream of perennial sunshine, and all the prattle of travellers who had nothing better to do than to copy the "Arabian Nights' Entertainments." The climate of Constantinople enjoys only really fine weather about four months during the year; four months more may be called extremely variable, and the other four months cold, wet, windy, muddy, and uncomfortable; therefore, take a macintosh, a couple of stout greatcoats, and a large boating cloak:—the latter is an article of notable value in a caique on the bleak waters of the Bosphorus.

It is as well to have a few good horse-cloths, a strong hunting-whip to beat off the legions of dogs which worry one at every step; a tough iron-pointed walking-stick for the sharp slippery hills in Turkish towns, and a useful clasp-knife, with all sorts of conveniences, are both valuable; so is a horseman's vade-mecum. A policeman's small lantern is well worth its place in your baggage, as the Turkish paper lanterns are highly inconvenient in a hurricane, such as blows, three nights out of six, at Constantinople. A man who now[*] invented a nice pocket-lantern, protected by patent, might make his fortune, as no persons are allowed to walk about at night in Turkish towns without a light; and they would run the risk of breaking their noses if they did so, as there are no street-lamps.

English percussion-caps and gun-wads are good things for presents to Turks who have European guns, but in most places the hope of shooting is altogether a delusion; it is especially so at Constantinople: a fowling-piece, therefore, may or may

[*] 1854.

not be taken, for the same reason. Avoid English horses, and certainly bring none with you : they are unsafe on Turkish roads and pavements. The barley food given them plays them sad tricks ; I know a stable in which three valuable English horses died in one week. Besides, there is a glut of horses altogether at Constantinople just now : a friend of mine sent up three thousand, and their sale did not pay their expenses. Good sound horses have been recently selling for ten pounds apiece, or even less. I mention these facts about horses, because most persons going to Turkey will find themselves obliged to ride, whether they are horsemen or not.

Take as much English saddlery, therefore, as you are likely to want. Pistol-holsters also are good, if only to carry cold tea on a long journey in hot weather.

For the rest, take a portable bedstead, an air mattress and pillow (the best things for keeping off vermin), some oil-skins or macintosh, to spread under you when obliged to sit on the ground, as you frequently will be ; some Oxley's essence of ginger ; some good opium, quinine, and Sedlitz powders (in bottles), with plain practical directions for their use (the first of these medicines has often proved of great service to me) ; a gold pen and pencil-case, a portable inkstand, a little match-box and a supply of German tinder (no other light will stand the Turkish winds) ; some patent buttons, a few straps, a cap or wide-awake, some butcher boots, and an umbrella. You will not require many clothes, save a few pairs of tweed trousers and waistcoats, a couple of shooting-coats, one dress suit, and a few plain shirts. A portable bath is useful when you can get water. A little patent coffee machine (those made at Vienna are the best) is a great comfort, for it requires some time to become used to Turkish coffee, and tea is often out of the question. Avoid getting wet with the utmost pertinacity ; keep warm, no matter how,—it is the only way to escape fevers. Above all, wear flannel, to prevent the possibility of a sudden chill. Wear a silk sash round the waist by day, according to the custom of the country ; it is almost an impenetrable armour against dysentery, which is one of the curses of the East. At night wear a flannel belt, as a protection against the cramps in the stomach, which are so general just now, and which seize their victims usually in the dark.

A key-ring, which you can always wear on the finger, is worth having, to lock up valuables, as our new acquaintances are often too clever by half with their fingers. If the key-ring has also a signet, it may be useful, should you require to send a servant to a Turk; for it will gain unlimited credence for anything you may wish him to say. Of course, you must not let it get into the hands of anybody whom you cannot trust.

Have a very serious conversation with your banker as to how you are to carry your money. Circular notes will not do at all; they suffer an unaccountable depreciation of fourpence in the pound; so do bank-notes.* The fact is, it is a harvest-time for money-making gentry here, and they are reaping all day long. Take no ladies with you, but such as absolutely wish to get married, and who can stand the staring of a *table d'hôte* (you must dine at the *tables d'hôte* at Constantinople) with less blushing than I should like to see a connection of mine do. If, however, they are perfectly broken in at *table d'hôte;* if they have not an ounce of objection to smoking; if they like coarse compliments and rudeness by turns; if they are absolutely indifferent to rain, wind, mud, weather, expense, and discomfort, by all means let them come. They are certain to find plenty of beaux, at least one hundred and fifty to each lady, and all with their hair curled, and a powerful smell of bergamot. In short, the Perote is perhaps the most offensive type of the gent or snob extant.

It is impossible, indeed, to convey an idea of our social discomfort; there is no society except in the house of the kind-hearted Austrian Internuncio; it is not at all the custom even to make calls elsewhere. This is all done by pasteboard. A Perote lady is rather proud of her array of visiting-cards; but if anybody actually entertained the wild design of going to see her, he would probably find her in curl-papers and a dressing-gown at four o'clock in the afternoon, or, still more probable, hear a great bustle and scuffling of feet, and be denied admittance by some scared and astonished servant speaking over the

* 1854.

banisters. The Perote gentlemen chiefly spend their time in excessively loud conversation, smoking paper cigars, and in inventing the latest intelligence from the seat of war: they are seldom at home, and their style of life is not inviting when they are. The few people who might be disposed to keep pleasant houses are often too much occupied to do so. Diplomacy also kills most nice things here; it is quite an overgrown monster, which crushes and bullies everybody. Then there are a good many petty jealousies, a good deal of that lively rancour which exists in most small communities. I call us a small community; for, though Constantinople is a capital town with 600,000 inhabitants, the Christians who live together perhaps barely number 200. In a word, therefore, people either know each other very intimately, and enjoy friendships which are superior to circumstances, or they perhaps do not see each other more than two or three times a year, at the loud, staring, cheerless embassy-balls, during the Carnival. There are no carriages, and few people indeed care to wade in the dark through broken boggy streets, ankle deep in mud, to carry a paper lantern in a frantic wind, simply to drink a cup of weak tea at a house where their advent is likely to occasion the utmost astonishment. The dullest book and the loneliest glass of negus are better, to my thinking. The fact is, that, to a man who has not really something to do, who is not doing it all day long, so as to be absolutely indifferent about all other things, Constantinople is intolerable, and most other Turkish towns are worse. There are no theatres or public amusements, nothing but the weariest Italian opera ever dreamed of by a hypochondriac; it is dark and cold and dirty, and filled with noisy young Perotes, who are all in love with the Prima Donna (usually forty-eight), and show it. There are no exhibitions, no field sports; there is nothing at all, in fact, but antiquity-hunters in difficulties, and a few noisy parties of young men: with all that, I suppose Constantinople is at this moment the most expensive place in all Europe to live in; none but the most favoured of the cousinhood of Britain, none but the closest connections of the very finest old families, who have the very warmest berths under Government, at all make head against the expense of it.

Coals are more than eighty shillings per ton : corn has been recently imported from England : houses cost more than in Belgravia or May Fair : the price of clothes is fabulous.

The commonest necessaries of life have risen to a price which is the dismay of every one. My dinner, a slice of fish and a chop, with a pint of beer, costs me five shillings a day, without the waiter: my breakfast, a couple of eggs and two small rolls, costs me exactly one pound twelve shillings a week : tea, butter, and sugar, are extra. Common French wine costs nine or ten shillings a bottle (at hotels) : the Broussa wine costs about three shillings and sixpence; but it is not good the second day after it has been opened. The wages of servants are in the same proportion. I have half a servant, who costs me about three pounds a month, and the gentleman who has the other half of him pays more. Grooms' wages are about five pounds a month : horse-keep dearer than in England : furniture bad, inelegant, and expensive. Nearly everything, however, being imported, and most of the tradesmen only coming here for a few years, to make money enough to set up in Europe, there is little need to continue the catalogue. I paid eight shillings the other day for a pair of gloves, and forty-two francs for a riding-whip that would have cost about five shillings in London or in Paris. One hotel-keeper told me that he had made twenty thousand pounds within the past year: another said this was not true; but they must be really coining money, for they have it all their own way; and at any of the good hotels it is quite a favour to get a place at the dinner-table, though the cost is considerably more than at the hotels in Paris, and would kill a German *Gastwirth* on the Rhine with sheer envy.*

I do not think I have anything more to say, except that it has been raining almost without intermission for these last ten days, and shows no signs of clearing up. The streets are a slough of despond, and the air seems of a dullish yellow. My groom is blowing into his fingers from sheer cold, and tells me he has bad eyes; so have I, and so have many people here, just now. Holding them open in the cold water of a morning

* Constantinople is still one of the dearest capitals in the world.

is the best remedy I know of; it has relieved me many times, and may relieve my groom. It is necessary, however, to see that the water is the true, muddy, drinkable water; for if quite clear and clean at Constantinople, there is, probably, lime in it, which might be dangerous.

I will put on my fur coat, therefore, and communicate these observations to him during our ride; for, of all things in Turkey, perhaps the most essential is to overcome the gradual disinclination to exercise which is so apt to creep over one. I let my fire out, indeed, every day at three o'clock for this purpose.

FINIS.

Woodfall & Kinder, Printers, Milford Lane, Strand, London, W.C.